Smithology

Thoughts, Travels, and Semi-Plausible Car Writings: 2003–2023

Sam Smith

Foreword by
Jason Cammisa

Introduction by
John Krewson

With the exception of quoting brief passages for the purposes of review, no part of this publication may be reproduced in any form or by any means, including information storage and retrieval systems, without written permission from the author.

All stories with the subtitle "Hagerty" are reprinted by permission of the Hagerty Group, LLC. © 2023 by the Hagerty Group, LLC. All rights reserved.

All stories with the subtitle "*Road & Track*" are owned by and the copyright held in the name of Hearst Autos, Inc., and are reprinted with permission. All rights to the *Road & Track* name and logo are owned by Hearst Autos, Inc. All rights reserved.

All stories with the subtitle "Roundel" first appeared in the BMW Car Club of America's *Roundel* magazine and are reprinted with permission.

PHOTOS: Fernando Alonso: Ryosuke Yagi/Flickr via CC BY 2.0. Rick Mears: Penske Racing handout, author collection. Denise McCluggage: Tom Burnside/Revs Institute. BMW 2002 drawings courtesy BMW AG. Ford GT courtesy Ford Motor Company. Aircraft images in "Jet Hunting With Thrasher" © 2023 by Camden Thrasher. Images in "The Little Things" © 2023 by Dave Burnett. Images in "To Believe You're the Best" credited in-line. Goodwood Revival video stills © 2024 by The Goodwood Estate Company Limited. All photography not public domain is reprinted with permission.

All other interior text and images © 2024 by Sam Smith. All rights reserved.

The information in this book is true and complete to the best of our knowledge. All recommendations are made without any guarantee on the part of the author, who also disclaims any liability incurred in connection with use of this data or details. We recognize that some model names, for example, mentioned herein are the property of the trademark holder. We use them for identification purposes only. This is not an official publication.

Library of Congress Control Number: 2023921075

ISBN: 979-8-9894967-0-9 (Paperback)

ISBN: 979-8-9894967-1-6 (eBook)

Front cover: The author in a 1970 BMW Alpina 2002ti race car, Laguna Seca, 2016.

Back-cover inset: Two Smiths and a Citroën, coastal Oregon, 2018.

Cover design by Justin Page

Cover photos by Dave Burnett

Epigraph and "About the Author" photos by Beth Bowman

Published in 2024 by Talahi Press, Knoxville, TN, USA — www.thatsamsmith.com

Smithology

*For Adrienne, who has always been there,
even when she knew better.*

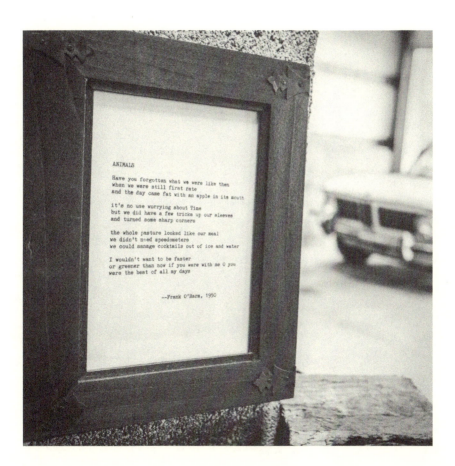

Contents

Foreword   xiii
by Jason Cammisa

Introduction   xvii
by John Krewson

Section One
The Things You Learn
(Whether You Mean to or Not)

THE GIFT   13
When you can't say no.

MY DINNER WITH MAHK   16
Sacrifice, Le Mans, and dessert.

DAJIBAN!   20
In the wilds of Japan, where the Swifties go faster, the big vans are better, and the fun grows on trees.

THE CHAF AND THE FURIOUS   31
Films of substance, consumed appropriately.

FIGURED OUT   36
The numbers don't matter.

INDOOR STORAGE   39
Memories and where we keep them.

WET BEHIND THE EARS   42
In deep at the Pacific Marine Expo, lessons bubbling to the surface.

OVERSHADOWED   45
Reflections on a drive to the light.

TO BELIEVE YOU'RE THE BEST   49
In the Moment with sacrifice, Stirling Moss, and those who try.

THE AIR OF A GNAWING-ON   67
Learning to screw up when you already know how.

LIVE AT BIRDLAND   72
Tracks and roads and Rufs and me.

GONE AWAY   75
Early coda.

Section Two
The Machines

BRAND OF ENCHANTMENT *Italy the unimprovable.*	89
THE DREAM OF CITY LIFE *"Mr. Brauner, is your JDM hootbox trying to seduce me?"*	93
THE ONE *An oral history of the McLaren F1, the supercar that broke us all.*	99
FIFTEEN SIMPLE RULES FOR DATING MY 1930S FRENCH PROPELLER CAR *Which is not mine at all but does go RAWRRR in fancy fashion and almost definitely won't chop your hands off.*	117
RED BLOODLINE *Wherein the author screams like a dead Mantuan from a Nazi-slugging Alfa Romeo while trying not to be a rank-and-file diphead.*	128
URGE OVERKILL *Rennsport Reunion and the Stuttgart machine.*	141
THE BIG LEAGUE *Strapping into Fernando Alonso's old Formula 1 McLaren, a thing that really happened, WTF, yes.*	145
PATERNAL INSTINCT *The familial warmth of the purchasing knee-jerk.*	166
SNOW-BLIND *Every car lives. As for death, that's up to you.*	170
DAY OF THUNDER *The turn-both-ways, thank-your-sponsors, Frequently-Asked-Questions guide to being an apex-jumpin' badass in your very own personal NASCAR stocker.*	173

Section Three
The People

THE DOG DAYS OF ACQUISITION *Vehicular choice with a fuzzbottom in the mix.*	191
YOUR DREAM, NOT MINE *Big hair and small family in a Caterham Seven.*	195
WAITING FOR RÄIKKÖNEN *Drivers, humans, and the gorilla suits in between.*	202
DRIVING WITH ALOIS RUF *An anniversary chat with the man who built a 211-mph yellow and beat the world from his garage.*	205

MEARS AND MY FEET	219
Fables of the Rick-construction.	
JET HUNTING WITH THRASHER	224
"Oh hell yes, is it fun."	
DAN GURNEY, AMERICAN	241
Losing the Big Eagle.	
ALONSO EX MACHINA	246
A titan steps down.	
RULES AND BROOKS	250
Denise, who mattered.	
THE LITTLE THINGS	254
On French cars and daughters and ice cream. And turtles.	

Section Four
The Places They Take You
(And All That Implies)

HOLY WOOD	263
Starstruck at the wheel at the Goodwood Revival, the greatest vintage race on earth.	
ARMS INTO MOTION	278
The eternity in a tick of the clock.	
BACK TO SCHOOL	284
What we forget as we get older, what we don't, what we can't.	
THRONE OF GAMES	294
At America's only permanent F1 track, taking a flag on the big field.	
WALL DRUG	297
In rare air in the heartland, getting high on the fumes.	
INDY!	300
Looking back, on the eve of the 100th running, as America's Race keeps pushing forward.	
SURVIVORS	322
Daydreams and other truths.	
THE LE MANS ALL-NIGHTER	331
Fords, Toyotas, and brain-warping sleep-dep in what will forever be known as the year you had to go.	
COVENTRY WAKE	346
A 400-mile journey from disbelief with the only Jaguar we all remember.	
THE ART OF BRACING FOR THE RAIN	357
Beneath the clouds, learning to look up.	
GREENS OF SUMMER	362
In the Moment with a life, a wife, and a film.	

Section Five
The White Rat
(Our Hero Finds a Smelly Friend)

PART ONE	383
A 2002 for 1800, and Why	
PART TWO	394
Stay of Execution	
PART THREE	400
I've Seen Tired, and I've Seen Pain	
PART FOUR	409
This Thing Cannot Get Any Worse	
PART FIVE	418
Your Trailing Arms Are Too Short to Box With Carl	
PART SIX	429
When You're On the Way to Fix a 2002 and Your 2002 Breaks	
PART SEVEN	438
Until You One Day Wake Up and Have Actually Gone Someplace	
And What Since, Huh, Smith? (A Rat Epilogue)	447
Afterword	449
Acknowledgments	451
A Brief Ask of the Reader	457
About the Author	459
The Last Page	461

Foreword
by Jason Cammisa

A candid conversation between the author and an old friend, held on the internet in the fall of 2023. Mr. Cammisa requested this discussion be printed under the following title—a phrase that the author suggests lacks context and makes him look, well, less than great, but also, uh, he totally kinda maybe did that once? (It was long ago. Nobody died.)

— SAM SMITH DROPPED A CAR ON ME —

JASON CAMMISA: It's true. This was almost 20 years ago. The two of us were on staff at *Automobile* magazine, working for a legendary editor named Jean Jennings, who is amazing.

> SAM SMITH: My first full-time job in journalism. Back when car magazines had huge head counts and massive test fleets. It was heaven. We each started there in 2006, you a few months after me. I remember this tall New Yorker swanning through the office on his first day, talking German cars with big hand gestures.

by Jason Cammisa

JASON: Anyway! We were in my garage, working on one of his old BMWs. He was next to it, holding the jack handle, and I was underneath, doing something important. He slowly lowered the rear off the jack stands. The front stands were still there, thankfully, so I didn't die.

SAM: Never let it be said that I don't care.

JASON: Having the floor of Sam's 3-series compress my chest was useful, actually, as the pressure helped me heave out an "OW, you stupid f***!" at a decibel level I had previously only hoped to attain.

SAM: It's important to have goals, you know?

JASON: The car bent my foot in half, you dork! In a way feet don't bend!

SAM: Oh, hush, you were fine. And in my defense, I was envious of your good looks and talent and wit and boundless engineering knowledge and how deftly you could throw a car sideways for photography, and I was almost definitely positively maybe not trying to "accidentally" kill you and take your job.

JASON: At any rate, Sam said he "forgot" I was under the car when he lowered the jack. I'm inclined to believe him. Back then, Sam had a lot of accidents.

SAM: I'm better now. I grew up.

JASON: In that one exact way, yes.

SAM: Age mellows everybody. I have children now. I'm a grown-up!

JASON: The jury's still out.

SAM: The kids are definitely real. I have proof.

Foreword

JASON: See, Sam often appears to be, but is not, an adult. This is why we love him. He sees the world through the eyes of a child, with the same intrigue for the ordinary that compels a two-year-old to spend an hour thoroughly inspecting an ant. And the mischievousness to giggle while subsequently squishing it.

    SAM: My wife says I squish a lot of things.

JASON: I know! She worked at *Automobile* too, back then, as the copy editor. The two of us used to get stoned in my kitchen and bake cookies while you ruined our good time by talking and being yourself.

    SAM: Hey!

JASON: Kidding, kidding!

    SAM: She likes you. I don't know why.

JASON: ANYWAY! Despite his graying hair, Sam remains occasionally awkward and goofy, and occasionally irrational in the best and worst ways. Like so many of us, he is also occasionally racked with misguided self-doubt. After four successful decades on this planet, Rational Sam knows he's just fine, a hell of a writer and damn good at a few other things, too. But his inner monologue is often a spiraling froth.

    SAM: Mamas, don't let your babies grow up to be word junkies.

JASON: We only worked together at *Automobile* for a few years, but we came back under the same roof in 2012, when Larry Webster hired you as executive editor at *Road & Track*. That office was a dream team of magazine and car people.

    SAM: Larry asked me to help build a new staff—I was his first hire, and then we just went after talent we loved and wanted to work with. It meant everything that you came on board. Everyone in the building just wanted to get better and do great work.

by Jason Cammisa

JASON: And it was magic to watch. You were really good at what you did, but anytime anyone gave you a compliment, you became convinced that accepting it meant you weren't just overconfident but also irrevocably damaged.

Sam just wanted to get better, and he still does. His gift is that he's not only aware of his inner chaos but able to regurgitate it through a keyboard, mixed stoichiometrically with insight and clever turns of phrase. He has among all those voices in his head a little George Carlin—his own personal observational comedian, watching his life through a second lens.

Sam's colorful voice could turn boring into riveting, but his life has been anything but boring. To our benefit, he's collected the best of two decades' worth of incredible writing and experience. Each and every page here came from the mind of a man whose deeply damaged brain runs at 7000 rpm and alternates between thoughtful introspection and youthful innocence.

We're lucky to have him. Please get each of your friends to buy a copy of this book, so that Sam can afford to entertain us all for another 20 years.

SAM: Awfully kind of you to say all that, Jay. Thank you.

JASON: Of course. Happy to. Now if you'll excuse me, I need to go lie down. This was exhausting.

Jason Cammisa is a journalist, a vehicle-dynamics consultant, and a car-magazine veteran whose video work has garnered millions of views on YouTube. He wrote his part of this foreword in kindness and good faith, a choice he now regrets.

Introduction
by John Krewson

First, before we get to the stories, a note on the art of telling them.

They say every good story is a love story in some fashion, at the very least to the reader. And when you start writing seriously, there are plenty of experienced and successful people who will tell you that, try as you might, you can't predict your audience, and so you should therefore imagine your ideal reader and write for them.

In that light, a lot of writing is far from being any kind of love story. In fact, a lot of writing is either heartless or pretty cynical. I don't want to be the imagined reader for that kind of thing, and neither I suspect, do you.

Sam Smith's writing, on the other hand, seems to be for the best version of us. He doesn't, and possibly can't, write for just any old reader, even in a car magazine. He's put together in such a way that he sees the automobile as an indispensable, undeniable part of human culture. His definition of vehicular culture is also broader and deeper than traditionally recognized. Together, these perceptions reflect a genuine and honest attempt to understand how cars fit in with contemporary humanity and our social history. Which makes it a pretty good trick that his stuff can be enjoyed by anyone, not only car people, as long as they are curious and thoughtful and like to think. It helps a lot that he usually remembers to have fun, or at least candy.

by John Krewson

In the world of automotive journalism, there is an influential school of thought that the numbers are the story. I have had editors tell me, in so many words, that when it comes to writing about a machine, people just want to know how fast it goes. This is reductive, shockingly unimaginative, and small-hearted at best, even if we drove our cars around as fast as possible at all times instead of spending a meaningful portion of our lives in them.

Very little of what we do at the wheel involves numbers. This is true even for those of us who like going pretty fast. Almost every healthy person, organization, and pop song agrees that living life by supposedly important metrics is unhealthy. And condensing into pure math everything that the automobile truly represents negates the work of a lot of good people and doesn't begin to address the big question of exactly why people like to move, travel, and drive.

Not to mention that it's suicidally shortsighted on the face of it, coming from an editor. If how fast is all people want to know, what's the rest of the magazine for?

Which brings us to the science, and the science presents us with a choice. The uncertainty principle tells us that we can know the speed of a thing or its position, but not both. Sam makes his preference clear. Life is, in fact, our own big uncertain story, and if he's exploring that story with us, he'd much rather tell the part about where we all are. Or at least where we're trying to go. Of course, this is all more art than science, so the act of close observation doesn't necessarily disturb it, if you've developed a light touch.

Sam seems to have developed his touch organically. Note that the man was raised in a car-obsessed but oddly literary household, with a father who ran a combination British-car restoration shop and bookstore, and so Sam grew up reading, racing, and generally feeling romantic about automobiles. You couldn't come up with a better scenario for growing a car writer if you gave Dan Gurney and Henry Manney co-ownership of a cloning vat. Moreover, writing about cars allowed Sam to fall in among, or actively seek out the company of, a scruffy but lovable band of misfits including but not limited to engineers, race drivers, bloggers, designers, programmers, bons vivant, insurance salesmen, indie musicians, exotic car dealers, and a comedy writer.

Introduction

He seems to have taken no great damage from any and borrowed well from all. Also he eventually married a copy editor, and if you've ever known a good copy editor, you'll know that this balances the rest out.

The stories here encompass, as you'd expect, singular machines, ambling road trips, and fabled racetracks, along with the normal triumphs, epiphanies, surprises, and sadnesses that make up any life. The thread that ties Road America to raising daughters, Jaguar E-types to leaving one's childhood home, and selling a car to getting a puppy? They are each a form of life in motion. When Sam tells you about it all you're left feeling as though you've really traveled, really been somewhere. And then, of course, the next trip starts, because all these trips are part of the big one, the trip where all our destinations are ultimately, implacably the same.

But as it's been tirelessly observed, it truly is the journey and not the destination, how you get there and not where you're going. Sam may be as uncertain as any of us about the latter, but he has a true gift for traveling well. One of my favorite passages of his appears in a column that didn't make this book, about driving a 20-year-old Jaguar most of the way across the United States. "I've never wanted to sit still less," Sam tells us, despite being caught droning somewhere on I-80, the great elastic waistband that runs across the beer gut of America.

If you know him, that's about perfect. If you only know him from his writing, well, same. Sam likes to be in motion. Life may be uncertain, but that has nothing to do with the principles of living.

On to the book itself. As you settle in among these pages, don't worry about how fast you're going; you're going fast enough. Don't worry about where you are; you're where you're supposed to be, or at least on your way there. And don't be surprised if there's more in here than just metal and random meandering.

In some way, every good story is a love story. These are very good stories.

John Krewson is a founding editor of comedy landmark The Onion *and a winner of the James Thurber Prize for American Humor.*

Section One
The Things You Learn
(Whether You Mean to or Not)

Austin, Texas, 2013

Sam Smith

A Word on the Nature of the Author's Career

- or -

An Opening Preamble

I have had, for the last two decades, a strange job. I tell car stories.

The whole thing has been way more interesting than those words might suggest, but I'm getting ahead of myself.

This book was written, edited, designed, and published by me. That process was more work than expected but also heaps of fun. Not least because producing something entirely by yourself lets you pretty much do whatever you want.

On that note, I've always wanted to begin a book with a picture of my car at the office.

More accurately, with a photo of that car *in* an office, parked next to the copy machine.

"Simplify," Colin Chapman famously said, "and add toner."

Done! Life goal crossed off the list. Feels good.

Clearly, you must be thinking, the parking lot was full.

Smithology

That picture was taken in Ann Arbor, Michigan, in the spring of 2014, at the editorial headquarters of *Road & Track* magazine. The diminutive machine between cubicle and copier is a 2003 Caterham Seven. Caterhams are sports cars, small and light, purpose-built in England for speed and feedback. That example in particular was around 1200 pounds of metal and oil leak; it gave induction snort and bugs in your teeth and put your pants about seven inches over ground on a good day.

A Seven is not as bare-bones as cars get, but it's close. You only buy one if you're a glutton for punishment. Which is fitting, really, because you only decide to write for a living if, well, same.

The person in that photo, seated at that desk, is not me. Those legs belong to an *R&T* staffer named David Gluckman, a witty and Michigan-born editor and writer. David had helped dismantle the office furniture to move the Seven into place, and he found the whole idea delightful. It *was* delightful. For one thing, there is always some silly joy in seeing a fish out of water; oil-dripping English bug-teethers do not generally lurk in cube farms. On top of that, the Caterham was just wide enough to block access to both the office restrooms and the supply closet where we kept all the pens. When your staff is built almost entirely of writers and editors on an endless string of deadlines, you drain a lot of coffee and kill a lot of pens.

A few days ago, I was chatting online with an acquaintance from Instagram, a California-based racing driver named Ethan. I had made some throwaway quip about Formula 1, and Ethan had expressed approval. I demurred.

"All I've got is dumb jokes, Ethan. That and dumb questions that lead to more dumb jokes."

"I disagree," he said. "You have incredibly niche dumb jokes. And those are, hands down, the best kind."

Know yourself, Kant said. Or in my case, know the niche you love and the incredible but deeply unstable job you have found within it. Stability being, after all, both overrated and temporary in the grand cosmic scheme, while the joy of landing a childhood dream is basically forever.

That copier photo still makes me laugh.

Sam Smith

I've never made real money or had anything like job security, and I'll probably never be able to retire. I can't believe I've been so lucky.

In the spring of that photo, I was executive editor at *Road & Track*. I was 33 years old and had been working toward that job in one way or another since age 13. I had been writing professionally for 11 years, at *R&T* for 23 months, and buying parts for funky old project cars since what felt like the dawn of time. I couldn't get enough of driving, wrenching, club racing, machines, and history, to say nothing of stories and how we tell them.

"Executive editor" is one of those glamorous but misleading titles of which media organizations are so fond. In this case, it meant that I oversaw *Road & Track's* magazine and website. I was neither an actual executive nor top of the ladder—an editor-in-chief one step up ran the whole thing—and I worked 60-hour weeks while watching our budget and resources shrunk year after year. But creating anything with other people hit me like a drug, especially in that office.

I got paid to write, research, learn, and drive at speed while surrounded by smart people. I tested every new fast car in the country, traveled to interesting places constantly, kept a diary of the breakaway characteristics of various high-performance tires, met and learned from heroes and jerks the world over. I had experiences in and around automobiles and motorsport that money can't buy. A new challenge hit my desk almost every day.

I had worked at other car magazines before, but that one was special. First published in 1947, *Road & Track* was an enthusiast bible, a romance-heavy and history-forward journal of sports cars and motorsport. It was the oldest car magazine in the United States and, with more than 600,000 paying subscribers, one of the largest and most respected in the world. In a business obsessed with performance statistics, *R&T* orbited nuance and emotion. It was the magazine I had read when I was young, it was where I first learned that I wasn't alone in caring about cars and driving for the unmeasurables, and it was where I had always wanted to be.

Smithology

How does a pull like that kick off? As a kid, I couldn't get enough of a machine that solves a problem and makes you happy. I chased a job in that realm because that machine is a catalyst—a fast, slow, artful, inelegant, practical, impractical, and mostly wonderful reason to think about how and why we all behave the way we do.

So much of what I ended up learning made no sense at first. My first magazine job came at the ripe old age of 24. Three weeks in, a senior editor called me to his office after reading one of my drafts. He gestured to my work on his screen as if it were a full toilet. My writing was stilted and try-hard, he told me, the words lifted into place like cinderblocks. Loosen up, he suggested, don't worry so much, think less at the keyboard.

I was convinced he was wrong but kept my mouth shut. Naturally, a few days later, another editor called me to *her* desk, sat me down with the same draft, and told me the exact opposite: I was thinking too little on the page. Take more time, she chided, be more deliberate, have something to say, this is a magazine, not your diary.

I moved my mouth like a fish and assumed I was having a stroke. Then I mumbled some limp summary of what the first editor had said while trying to wrap my head around how two people doing the same job at the same place could each be so wrong.

Here's the funky part: More than a million published words later, I know they were both right.

Sound ridiculous? As it turns out, when you make things for a living, anything at all, from a 300-word car review to the *Mona Lisa*, nothing is set in stone, except when it is.

Disclaimer: I may be wrong about that.

Before that first magazine job, I had been, to precisely zero acclaim, a grindingly slow European-car mechanic in St. Louis and Chicago, a parts clerk at an Illinois Jaguar dealer, and a freelance journalist with enough talent and connections to bring home literal dozens of dollars a month. I had loved reading and writing since grade school, been a hopeless romantic for speed and engineering for as long as I could remember. I had no idea what those things actually meant for a functioning adult, but I knew that I cared massively about them, and that seemed like enough to nail the work.

After a year in that chair—traveling the world, testing every new car on sale, and interviewing everyone from world-famous athletes to local mechanics—I realized it wasn't.

I was confused by that, too. But again, I was young.

When people talk about how cars matter, they often start with how the machine changed the world, the possibilities of a horse's work made smarter. Those answers are real and valid but merely one piece of the puzzle. Like anything worth caring about, automotive culture runs on a simple equation: What you get out is directly related to what you put in. You can view a traffic jam as a source of misery or a chance to breathe.

Every kid who can't explain why they like things loud and fast is really just drawn to the notion of control in an uncontrolled world. How far we can push past known answers; how humanity is at its best wondering what lies beyond a lap record or the next hill.

The machine won't be around forever, but that pull will. And our relationship with it can say more about us than we like to admit.

Again, the job is strange. It is mostly desk time but can become downright absurd in retrospect, when you forget the office dull for the shiny highlights.

Looking back through my bylines can feel like rifling through someone else's life. I drove a Jeep with no doors to an oil-well town on the Arctic Ocean, cupholders catching snow on the tundra. I track-tested a Porsche 962 prototype that won the 24 Hours of Le Mans —230 mph, 700 hp, seven figures of history on the hoof—but I've also strapped into one of the five 700-hp Mazda prototypes built specifically to dethrone that very Porsche in that very race. Work has gifted me first-hand experience with cult collectives in rural Japan, Hitler-fighting Italian armchairs in the Pacific Northwest, and midnight hallucinations amid 30-hour stretches in motorcycle sidecars. To say nothing of countless inspirational lives here and gone.

Who gets to do this stuff? In what world does any of it qualify as employment? Moreover, how is it related to—as this book's stories suggest—buying my daughter ice cream, getting lost at a fishing convention, or watching U.S. Navy jets go full Skywalker in desert canyons?

All I can tell you is that pinch-me moments don't live in memory as you'd think. Several years ago, I traveled to England for a story about competing as an also-ran in one of the world's most cutthroat vintage races. In an odd turn of events, I ended up surprising my backers (and myself, honestly) by qualifying on the front row, at a track I'd never driven, in a 60-year-old Jaguar I had just met.

The whole affair was astonishing and perfect, and yet I remember little of my time at the wheel. What I do recall, with pinpoint clarity, is the night on the same weekend that drank gin in a nearby campground with Jaguar's 95-year-old former development driver, one of my childhood heroes. We talked about risk and heartbreak and what it felt like to nearly die in a race car in midcentury France.

That man is no longer with us; he passed away in 2019. But in those moments, chuckling into his glass in that dark English field, he gave me a small part of what it means to be alive.

I've been fortunate in so many other ways. It's hoary cliché to announce that you grew up around cars, but I did. My father, a longtime *Road & Track* reader, ran a restoration shop when I was young. By the time he semi-retired, years later, the business had condensed into a small store selling automotive books and models. The only constant was the amount of time I spent there after school (i.e., a lot).

In college, a career counselor asked what I wanted to do for a living. "Work for a car magazine" seemed hilariously optimistic, so I told her I had no idea. Think about it for the weekend, she said, and come back with a list of things you like doing. I spent two days reading Douglas Adams, drinking bourbon, and playing *Gran Turismo*. Then I went back on Monday and said that being a writer sounded like fun.

Was I certain, she asked. Then she asked again. When I didn't cave, she offered to help however she could. "You won't make much money, but every day will be different, and you'll be learning all the time."

Being easily distracted and more than a little shy, I didn't stop to ask why she had double-checked. I simply signed up for a raft of journalism and literature classes and read everything I could get my hands on. Then

I graduated a year late, having spent too much time screwing around with cars to wrap my degree on schedule.

That's about when I went stone broke, but not for the reasons you'd think. As I said, I found work as a mechanic, an outgrowth of a college job I had stumbled into at a small Alfa Romeo shop near campus. Somewhere along the line, I discovered amateur road racing. (Summary for the unfamiliar: Imagine driving in circles while feeding your paycheck to a blender and being thrilled about it.) After graduation, possessing both zero financial intelligence and my first regular income, I dipped a toe. Then I dove in, head-first, on a salary that wouldn't have supported a season in competitive ping-pong.

If my story were a movie, this would be the turning point. Where your narrator finds success in some backmarking clunker, gets noticed by Enzo Ferrari's ghost, meets fame and fortune, the end. In reality, I met an almost comical amount of opt-in poverty. I ate ramen for years in exchange for driving the hubs off an uncompetitive old race car, sleeping in borrowed tow rigs and winning only when everyone else broke. I loved it anyway. I loved it so much, in fact, that when I finally ran out of cash and credit limit, I capped the whole thing—funded my last race for years to come—by selling my living-room furniture for one last set of tires.

You can sleep in your car, as the line goes, but you can't race your house. Or sofa, as it were. (I didn't date much.)

I was busted but content, going nowhere happily. And then, in December 2005, I landed an assistant-editor job at a Michigan car magazine called *Automobile*.

The tone shift was surreal. I knew nothing about editing, but that was fine; the "assistant" part was the whole job. On my first day, in the small back room of a rabbit-warren office near Detroit, I was assigned to fact-check a 3500-word story on midcentury Formula 1. I would have paid to do that work, did work like it on weekends for fun, but now there was a 15-person staff and an in-house library to help, and everyone got health insurance and free coffee, and when all that truly set in, I nearly fell off my chair from shock.

At lunch, while slurping up noodles in the office kitchen, I listened, rapt, as the staff's two resident club racers discussed Corvette handling.

At 5:00 that evening, I clicked off my desk light and walked to my car on air. The next day, I stayed until midnight, reading out-of-print racing books from the archive. One week later, in a fit of extravagance, I bought a $12 hamburger and four cheap tires for my daily driver on the same day. I felt like Croesus.

Twenty years ago, the world's big car magazines had money and influence and sat smack in the middle of the culture they covered. They had been in that position for roughly nine decades. A handful of American titles—*Automobile*, *Car and Driver*, *Motor Trend*, and *Road & Track*—were the world's largest and most trusted sources for automotive news and entertainment and their editors knew it. Imagine *The Devil Wears Prada* minus devil and Prada. One week, you were flying to Spain with coworkers to group-test new supercars that wouldn't see dealers for months. The next, you were sitting down with family-sedan engineers who had jetted across the country to give your office an hour-long presentation on the tech tricks that let their new V-6 make more power from 10 percent less fuel. Or maybe that week's guest would be the winner of the last Indy 500 or the president of Lamborghini.

In quiet moments, we were renting racetracks or private roads for tests or listening to the art director tell stories about booking the back lot at Universal Studios for a splashy photo shoot. Being a staff writer meant pitching your own adventures, unpacking technology and history, meeting the world's most interesting people, mainlining dopamine through mechanical novelty and education. Breaking down the behavior and engineering of new cars was the least compelling part, and even that felt like feeding an addiction.

Automobile brought me things more personal as well. I met Adrienne on my first day there. She was one of the magazine's three copy editors, responsible for detail and clarity. I liked her wit and the way she wore a dress, and she liked me enough to laugh at the dumb jokes. By late 2006, we were dating. I proposed two years later, right before the two of us left Michigan and *Automobile* so I could take another magazine job on the West Coast.

Motion has been a constant in our lives since. We moved around the country every few years, chasing the promise of stability and work. From 2006 on, I traveled for a byline at least once a month and usually more.

From 2015 to 2020, as the industry began to seriously contract, I was gone every other week. I couldn't at the time put a finger on why that grind felt so necessary, but deep down, I think I just knew the salad days wouldn't last.

I developed a reputation as a dependable writer with a lot of ideas but little care for credit, which means I got work. I helped build magazines and websites and books and apps, got asked to reimagine video channels and co-host TV shows on major networks. I was hired to help rethink *Road & Track* in one of the magazine's rare ground-up reboots. That last challenge led to a National Magazine Award nomination, the first time in history a car magazine had made that cut.

I couldn't get enough of the storytelling and the people. Exploring why something happened a certain way or finding out I was wrong and throwing some long-held belief out the window. The tradeoff, naturally, was time at home. When our young daughters began talking and I missed their first words while off on assignment, I was upset, to put it mildly. Five years ago, when I came home from the airport after three weeks gone only to head back out, a day later, for another two weeks, I saw the exhaustion in Adrienne's eyes.

She knew I loved the job and had sacrificed to help me keep it. But as I watched her try to hide the stress of solo-parenting two toddlers for nearly a month while working from home—journalist salaries and daycare don't really mix—I realized it was time.

It had been a hell of a run, and the most satisfying period in my life, but something had to change. And the work was changing itself.

For better or worse, the job I came up doing is no longer possible. The last 20 years have seen the media business collapse. Countless budgets and salaries and staffs, countless publications, have simply disappeared.

This is sad in myriad ways, but some saw it coming. As the tech journalist Kara Swisher once wrote, most media executives seem to have "a genetic predisposition to oppose change and innovation." That demographic, she noted, spent the 1990s and 2000s refusing to bend to "the coming disaster of their bottom lines."

Swisher was referring mostly to newspapers, where the financial gutting was kicked off by the late-1990s rise of Craigslist and the subsequent death of the paid classified ad. But magazines were no exception. When the balance sheets began to crumble, I sat in meetings as old-guard editors griped bitterly about the internet to younger colleagues. Nothing, they insisted, would ever be as important as print, so why should they spend time on anything else?

A reasonable person would have run screaming from all that, but creative people can be stubborn, especially when doing something they love. More important, while the business is now different, it still holds good work made for and by smart people. Which makes me happy.

I climbed onto this unlikely train in 2003. In the years since, I've been fortunate enough to share hundreds of stories worth telling across dozens of outlets. In choosing work for this book, I was drawn to certain themes, which ultimately meant three places: *Roundel,* the magazine of the BMW Car Club of America, where I was a contributing writer from 2005 to 2012; *Road & Track,* where I worked from 2012 to 2020, first as executive editor and then as a globetrotting editor-at-large; and the entertainment division of the classic-car insurance giant Hagerty, where I was a creative jack-of-all-trades from 2020 to 2023.

Each of those places has kindly allowed me to republish some of my work for them here. For that I am in their debt.

These pages hold columns and feature stories. Also rants, daydreams, interviews, travel dispatches, track tests where emotion outshouts lap time, even short fiction. Each piece of writing is headed by its original publisher and print year and arranged, nonchronologically, under one of a few themes.

How you approach all of that is up to you. Take this book in printed order, it'll hit one way, hopefully making a point in the process. Personally, though, I'd treat the table of contents like a map on Sunday: Pick some destination that looks interesting, jump around with mood, go where the wind takes you.

That approach fits the material, I think, but then, I would say that. It's basically how I've lived my life.

The Gift
When you can't say no.

We each have our tropes, the subjects we return to in quiet moments. Two of mine: the things we think worth saving, and the people who help (indulge?) our damage.

Roundel, March 2006

I just got off the phone with Ben. Ben runs a shop in Chicago. Fun place, funky, filled with old BMWs.

Ben is my friend. So he claims.

Good guy. An enabler, though. Or maybe he's just smart enough to ask the questions he knows I'm dumb enough to answer. I've never quite figured out which.

Ben, you see, is trying to *give me a car.*

Now, initially, I thought he was trying to sell me the thing, and so I spent a whole two minutes on the phone trying to convince the man what an absolutely horrible idea that was. The first defense was simple: I have no money. Solid reasoning, logical. And yet it completely and totally fell apart when the party of the first part informed the party of the second part that the vehicle under discussion would, in fact, be free.

Back up. Regroup.

Alternative strategies were deployed. The second angle of attack centered on how the car in question had, at last check, no engine or transmission whatsoever. Under the People With No Cash Have No Business Acquiring More Methods With Which To Lose It clause, I am officially exempt from dragging home devices for human transport that don't at least possess the basic ingredients for moving under their own power. No driveline? Done, walk away, lawn sculptures with potential need not apply, voilà.

I felt good about this approach, safe. The feeling lasted whole seconds. Right until Ben offered to give me a used motor and gearbox in exchange for an afternoon or two of trade wrench labor at his shop.

My time is basically free these days.

Running engines are not.

Desperation set in. Counterargument three, such as it was, was a desperate Hail Mary—a short-lived and half-hearted little number geared solely off the fact that I do not need another car. Much less another one of *those*, i.e., a BMW 2002.

No, I told my friend. Less than convincingly.

As the word left my mouth, a voice in my head went on a tear. *No, it said, everyone needs an '02, of course they do, especially you, you love those cars and only have one of them. Plus, that one is a race car, not at all suitable for gooning around on the street, a thing you love to do.*

Be quiet, I told the voice.

What's more, it carried on, *you don't actually* own *that race car, do you? You once owned half of it, but then you traded away that share at some point last season. For a new set of race tires.*

Ah, right. That did happen.

Tires, the voice continued, *that you immediately mounted onto the very race car you no longer owned.*

Where else would they go?

At which point you asked to borrow the car from its current owner. Who then helped you load it onto a trailer and watched, smiling, as you towed the whole blessed mess off to one last race. For, as you told yourself, "old time's sake."

Not untrue.

Still, though. Not ownership. Doesn't count.

Now, Ben is a nice guy, but free cars are always suspicious; automobiles fall somewhere between lunches and sex on the list of Things You Aren't Getting For Nothing Even When You Think You Are. In this case, that suspicion was kept at bay because I knew how and why my friend had acquired the thing.

At some point, some wild-eyed wrenchgoon somewhere had removed the engine from a 1970s BMW 2002ti and junked the shell. A short while later, that lump was bolted into a tired and lightly rusty 1969 BMW 1600. The 2002 was the first truly successful small BMW sport sedan; the 2002ti was a high-performance, twin-carburetor version; the 1600 was the 2002's predecessor. The three models are kissing cousins and look virtually identical.

Except: 2002ti's are kind of rare, and their related clutter is both valuable and hard to come by. When the 1600 came up for sale in Chicago, Ben saw a chance to get his hands on some uncommon parts and bought it. The only problem was the car itself. Minus that engine, 1600s just aren't that special. This one in particular was simply a semi-rusty old BMW, clad in about 10 different colors of paint and wearing an interior that appeared to have lived through five or six ice ages.

For reasons I have never been able to fathom, a multi-colored, semi-corroded, wholly unattractive 2002 shell is not an easy thing to get rid of.

Compounding matters, if you run a business . . . and if you already have a couple of solid 2002s lying around . . .

Well, as Ben pointed out when pressed, he hated to admit it, but the 1600 was probably going to have to be thrown out.

Stop the presses.

We decide the fate of material objects all the time. Toss out the toaster or end the vacuum's misery? They're appliances, they wear out, it's expected. With cars, though, things are always a little different. Personality and character grab footholds, often whether you want them to or not. In some cases, you even start to feel a little . . . pity.

A free car not total junk. A chance to save one more example of a machine I've always loved from an unnecessary grave.

Okay, so maybe he isn't so much trying to *give* it to me.

Maybe I kinda . . . sorta . . . *asked*.

My Dinner with Mahk
Sacrifice, Le Mans, and dessert.

"Good living" means something different for everyone. The common thread: You know it when you see it.

ROAD & TRACK, JULY 2018

You meet people in this job. I first met Mark Webber in college, though, watching F1 on TV. Maybe not so much met as shouted at, across airwaves and distance. His car would come on screen, and my friends and I would yell *"Mahk Webbah!"* in this terrible fake Australian accent, every lap.

Possibly because Webber is Australian. Also—lest I paint an incomplete picture—because we were idiots.

Then I met him for real. Several months ago, in the Algarve, a region of Portugal that looks a lot like Southern California. Portuguese water dogs hail from the Algarve. So does Bonnie Tyler, who sang "Total Eclipse of the Heart." She lives there part of the year and thus bears a resemblance, on paper, to the average German car executive. Every Teutonic car suit I've met has loved Portugal in the winter and seemed ported in from the video for a 1980s power ballad. German car companies launch cars in Portugal for the same reason that American car companies launch cars in California: It's convenient, and the heart of the machine is unlikely to be eclipsed. Good roads, good weather, close to home.

Webber, now retired from driving, has become a Porsche brand ambassador. Like me, he was in the Algarve for the launch of the 2018 911 GT2 RS. The event dinner—these things always have dinners—was preceded by a cocktail hour. I didn't recognize him at first, with his back to the crowd, talking to a few engineers. He looked like any other unreasonably healthy person, with nice clothes and shoulders of cut glass.

Being a person of class and taste, I daydreamed about throwing a pie at his head on principle. Then he turned around. A voice in my head apologized to no one in particular, then hollered like a dingus. (*Mahk!*)

He sat down at my table. We fell into conversation. The man gamely answered questions about Le Mans—he drove a Porsche 919 there from 2014–2016—plus supercars and the off-record oddities of F1. He told several bougie and charming stories that alluded to the kind of life you'd expect to be lived by one of the planet's premier professional athletes. He was about to hop a plane to Asia, he said, for a WEC race. He was saving to buy a piece of land in New Zealand, large and green, where he could build a dirt-bike track and keep a pile of KTMs. He talked about his various 911s—a 2.7 RS, a 997 GT2 RS.

It was the kind of discussion where you find yourself reveling in someone else's success, but also feeling increasingly silly about any life choices that kept you from, say, getting paid to see the world astride a multimillion-dollar piece of carbon fiber.

Halfway through the meal, I asked some question that prompted a long answer. Webber picked at his salad and began talking. I slowly buttered a piece of bread and considered his words. Plus my vanilla-pudding abs and the physical rigors of being a contractually obligated pro driver. The butter was salty and warm and spread like cake icing. The bread smelled like campfire. The crust crackled in my fingers and left bits of carbonized flour on the plate.

His body is almost surely a temple, I thought. What a pain in the keister that must be. My body is also a temple, but it has graffiti on the walls and a few moldy take-out boxes on the front steps and maybe also a weathered sign out front reading No Trespassing: Hazardous Radiation. I eat things, not always with good intentions. I exercise, but rarely.

The butter did that fresh-butter thing, where the smell reverses through your nose and wafts around your head as you chew.

We discussed the nature of sports cars, old and new. How much testing it took to make the 919's headlights work at 210 mph. A usable pattern that didn't blind traffic. So much frustration, the drivers joked about folding a team engineer into the car's dinky cockpit, just to share how challenging it was, how little they could see.

I conducted a brief mental tally of the endurance races I've been fortunate enough to enter. None produced 200 mph. Certainly not at night. I think I saw 120 mph in a Plymouth Neon at Buttonwillow at 3:00 a.m. once.

"I always liked Le Mans," Webber said, "but I never came to love it."

You do not hear those words without asking why.

"It was too . . . French. But your senses are so heightened. You smell everything from the car. Even trackside barbecues. If someone goes off, you can smell the grass."

"Even on the Mulsanne?"

"Speed didn't matter. It was always there."

My mind vapor-locked, a mash of envy and dreamy France smells.

They brought dessert without asking. A small army of waiters, plates at shoulder height. Two cones of ice cream, hollow centers, in a bowl. Then a tureen of fresh strawberry syrup, thick as lava. It fell over the ice cream in slow motion, layering crimson.

Webber watched as the waiter poured his. A pained look. A third waiter appeared, noticing distress. There was a hushed, huddled discussion. It was made clear that the plate would find another table. Maybe the kitchen. Someone would eat it. The dish disappeared. Webber's shoulders relaxed.

I stared at my cones. I briefly toyed with the idea of not eating them. I flashed back to the fastest thing I have ever driven, a 1990s GTP prototype I tried at Laguna Seca. Downforce like an F1 car. After a few laps, my muscles were so weak, they might as well have been hit by a train. My arms could barely turn the wheel.

Out of shape. Could be skinnier. Then I noticed my spoon was already full of strawberry goo and halfway into my mouth.

It was delicious.

Dajiban!

In the wilds of Japan, where the Swifties go faster, the big vans are better, and the fun grows on trees.

Who doesn't love it when the Japanese indulge cartoonish whim? I pitched this story as a lark. The trip ended up being one of the most uplifting and renewing experiences of my life.

ROAD & TRACK, OCTOBER 2018

The steering said nothing. Not a whisper, a suggestion as to what might be happening at the front tires. The wheel was mostly a knob for making your chair point a different direction—and it was most definitely not a seat but a chair, bolt-upright and miles from the floor.

That perch lived at the front of a huge metal box, the space hollow and empty. Every few seconds, the steering column would burp up little shudders of cowl shake, almost apologetically, as if it were connected to something far away and unimportant and really just sorry to have bothered you, go back to what you were doing, everything down here is cool.

But none of this was the focus. More the bellowing side pipe under the right front door and the way you had to elbow the whole thing into a corner in a sort of broad-shoulders jostle. After which this four-wheeled office building would just kind of slither-whomp onto the next straight and hump off toward the next corner and continue to casually punch large, van-shaped holes in the airspace.

Because it was, in fact, a van. On a racetrack. In Japan.

For some reason.

My chest hurt from laughter. Vans with 160-mph speedometers, jinking over curbs in nose-to-tail trains. They slung through corners in little yaw-slipped arcs, like Trans-Am cars that had grown fat in old age. A gray one with passenger windows, drifting. A faded yellow one with anodized Nitron shocks—British dampers that cost as much as a good used Honda—and a rear wing clamped to the rain gutters with Vise-Grips. They were all 1971–2003 Dodge Rams, originally sold in the U.S. but imported to Asia after the end of a much different life, mostly short-wheelbase, most with a 318 V-8. The Japanese call such things "Dajiban"—*Dodg-e-van, dah-jee-bahn*. A phonetic mash-up, like how the Japanese name for a hot dog is simply *hottodoggu*, or the French version of "the rugby player" is *le rugbyman*.

A guy in the tower was handing out colorful stickers. Each held a drawing of a Ram 150 on 16-inch Watanabes and a plug for Dodgevanracing.com. That site had prompted me to visit Ebisu Circuit, an afternoon's drive north of Tokyo, and the annual track day of an informal club for owners of track-prepped Dodge vans. I found 37 of the things there, in a tiny paddock, marshaled like Hannibal's elephants.

Our photographer was a man named Dino Dalle Carbonare. A 42-year-old Italian expat, fluent in both English and Japanese. Dino has lived in Japan since childhood and is now employed by internet giant *Speedhunters,* where he is the resident expert on Japanese car culture. He helped us parse Dajiban culture, because I speak just enough Japanese to get myself in trouble, or maybe order a hot dog.

We drove from Tokyo to Ebisu in his car, four hours on the freeway. Somewhere outside Kita, he broached the subject of vans and this publication.

"*Road & Track?* People I told about this job were like, 'How does that work? Since when does *R&T* care about Dodge vans?'"

Reasonable questions. This is ostensibly a sports-car magazine. But how often do you see a mutant übervan running balls-out at a track day? Or 37 of them piling into a corner at full honk? For that matter, every van at Ebisu paired a grunty V-8 with yards of sheetmetal and an inarguable hot-rod funk. Those words could describe every likable American car built from 1932 to last week.

For one reason or another, car culture has long been factionized by taste—you like X; I like Y; you don't follow my rules, so we side-eye each other from across the street. If you think about that for more than a few seconds, it seems like bunk. If you like Porsches or Corvettes or street rods or whatever but aren't curious about track-day Ram vans because the notion violates some established sense of propriety, hey, that's your prerogative. After all, cars are mostly a reason to sit at home and avoid new forms of cackle.

Abe Takuro's shop is large by Tokyo standards—roughly the size of an American two-car garage. It lives deep in one of the city's quieter districts, in a residential neighborhood with sardine-can houses and a street layout like a crossword puzzle. A 1990s Ram van sat outside in a metered parking spot, 1200 yen per hour, dark green and lowered over chunky BFGs. Every few minutes, a bicyclist would roll down the narrow front road, swerving past pedestrians. Boxes of Watanabes were stacked on a high wooden shelf in the back of the shop. Several feet below, a metal cabinet held a handful of brightly colored Ferrari 360 brake calipers. They were arranged face-out, one per shelf, like fine china.

"They fit perfectly," Abe said, waving a hand.

Seek Dajiban and you will eventually find Abe. He is 50, with dark, spiky hair and eyebrows that arch when he talks. He named his shop Abe Chuko Kamotsu—Abe Secondhand Cargo Van. When I walked in the door, he was sitting in the back wearing a blue Mopar racing shirt embroidered with the name Diane. He rose to say hello, shuffling between stacked parts before reaching the door.

A cup of coffee was pressed into my hand. ("Sort of tradition in Japanese shops," Dino said. "Often undrinkably strong. It is also sort of tradition to quietly leave it after one sip.")

A dirty Dodge 318 sat on a stand nearby. The U-shaped downpipes of its stainless-steel headers arced up and forward after the primary collectors, because Ram vans carry their engines just aft of the dash, under a large, humped cover. The stock manifolds flow like a clogged sink drain, Abe told me, but header routing is always a great compromise, bits of the van's frame in the way.

I leaned down, admiring the pretty, delicate welds. Abe looked sheepish. A friend of his, Takahiro Okawa, visiting the shop, chimed in, in English. "There is nothing specific for Dodge vans, performance-oriented, so he has to build it."

Takahiro runs Dodgevanracing.com. He's owned and sold three Rams, most recently a lime-green example with a carbon hood, and he confirmed the Dajiban origin myth circulating on the internet: Years ago, Japanese motorcycle racers began hauling their bikes in American vans. Live-axle, V-8 Dodges found favor because the shortest versions were relatively wieldy—at 187.2 inches long, the 1994 van is just 2 inches longer than a 2019 Jetta. One thing led to another, and during a lunch break at some track, somebody railed a Ram through a lap. Laughs followed, so they went full rabbit hole: more brake, extra coolers, rear dampers adjustable through the floor, relocated suspension pickup points, fuel cells, built engines. Half for speed, half to keep the vans from going to powder under the abuse.

No one I met at Ebisu could remember when the track-van trend caught on, though Abe is generally agreed to be one of the first involved. He organized this year's Ebisu Dajiban gathering—the 11th—and the 10 before that. He's also responsible for the Watanabes, a group hallmark: The company, one of the most storied wheelmakers in Japan, did not make a Dodge-van fitment until Abe commissioned one. He remains a primary source for the wheels and claims to have sold around 100 sets.

Mr. Abe.

Abe's gray 1994 Ram 150 serves as development mule for customer modifications; he says that he has "the price of a new Ferrari" in it, and that it hasn't been washed in 20 years. It came into his life more than two decades ago, when he worked at an American-car importer called I-5 Corporation, in Yokohama. The 150 sat on I-5's lot, unsold, for months, so he cheerily drove it home. He likes Dodges partly because he once owned a Viper.

"People make fun of him," Takahiro said. "They don't really get it. But the cars he owned before were modified. Cages, harnesses, track use. He has to do this to feel comfortable. With carpets and airbags . . . it's not his."

People laughed, Abe said, and then the vans found him, owners requesting work. Abe Chuko Kamotsu opened last year, servicing only track-prepped Rams. By summer 2018, the shop had around 100 customers and a steady stream of work.

"Chevy Astro vans," Takahiro said, "are really popular here. But it's a V-6. Ford Econolines and some other U.S. vans have a V-8, but the body and wheelbase are too big for Japan—the short Dodge is just small enough."

In America, I offered, these things are known for being terrible to drive. Like, *terrible*.

Abe rattled off a few sentences, deadpan. Takahiro wrinkled his brow before translating.

"If he gets it where he wants it . . . more than 300 hp, weight about a ton and a half . . . the performance will be almost the same as . . ."—he paused, glancing at Abe to confirm—"a cheap rental car."

The two men collapsed into laughter, arms crossed, shaking their heads at the joke.

So much of this seems to hang on how Japanese car culture works. It is space-dependent, bubbling out of dense cities that appear only grudgingly adapted to vehicles. The tighter parts of Tokyo make Manhattan seem like Texas, and in some areas of the country, you cannot register a car unless you can prove that you have room to park it. So car buyers, Dino said, have long consultations with the police, who hold the reins on vehicle registration. Residents draw maps of their garage or street, making a case. Even the support structure differs; many repair shops are smaller than a Midwest hotel room. They pepper the city in alleys or at the bases of buildings, little caves of wonder beneath apartments or shoved in next to convenience stores, stuffed with parts.

For an American, the country can feel quite foreign, but it's difficult to tell how much of that feeling is reality and how much came with you on the plane, preloaded caricature from books and film. On the drive to Ebisu, Dino told stories of how Japanese culture can nurture protocol and conformity, its structure often inscrutable for foreigners. He married a Japanese national, he said, but even with her help, the country's habits still leave him baffled on occasion.

None of this was laid out with malice—more like how an American might broad-stroke the difference between people in California and New York. I wondered aloud how much truth lay in the stereotypical Japanese approach to hobbies—remarkable commitment and knowledge, plus a dust of obsession.

Dino nodded. "A lot of people, it's just doing whatever they can to stand out on the weekend. So car culture reflects that, and they have zero compulsion about modifying stuff, to the limit, no matter how valuable. Ferrari F40s with modern engine management, R34 GT-Rs with modern everything underneath, God knows what."

"A lot of ideas that other cultures latch on to are rejected here," he said, shrugging. "And a lot of strange pieces of outside life are embraced."

Ebisu Circuit lives on a mountain in a quiet corner of Fukushima Prefecture, 50 miles west of the region's infamous nuclear reactor. The name is misleading; Ebisu isn't so much a track as a collection of them, 10 in total, shotgunned under a lush canopy of trees.

Around that corner, a few practice pads for drifting; atop that rise, two condensed, back-to-back road courses. The old-school optics have drawn TV crews from *Best Motoring* and *Top Gear*. Ebisu's tracks have no significant runoff, just the occasional dirt hill. Rusty pit buildings could have been swiped from a Sixties-era Watkins Glen. Some of the perimeter roads are one lane and too steep to be comfortably walked. If all this weren't enough, the top of the mountain holds an animal safari park, basically a small zoo. Next to the rows of drift-spec Nissan Silvias and GT-Rs are some confused-looking elephants and flamingos and a 20-foot-tall rooftop statue of a cranky cartoon monkey.

The drivers' meeting was held in one of the track's dollhouse-sized safety towers. More than 40 people in a room that would have felt crowded at half that. The presentation was led by a wiry, gray-haired man who talked with his hands: Arakaki Toshi of Tokyo, 53 years old, retired MotoGP rider, friend of Abe Takuro, owner of the yellow van with the Vise-Gripped wing.

His Dodge had more than 300,000 miles on the clock. And he found all of this extremely funny.

"Ebisu is quite lax with the rules," he said, shaking his head. "Tsukuba or Fuji . . . would never accept these races." Most everyone gets parts from Taiwan, he added, because many Dodge parts are made there, and it's cheaper than importing from the United States. They order from America for "name" speed equipment, like Hurst shifters and Edelbrock heads. Then he spit out a string of rapid-fire Japanese that made Dino laugh.

"The special thing about this van," Dino translated, "is that it's quite easy to get Japanese road certification, the Shaken inspection, every two years. Because it's an import, inspectors don't have a lot of regulations to compare it to stock. They just assume that's how it came. So you can modify it, and they'll just pass it!"

The paddock was a diaspora. Exquisite restorations, purposeful beaters. Obviously curated English-language sticker collections. No two were alike, and many of the vans had brought families—the Rams served as both support vehicle and track car, disgorging first picnic tables and folding chairs, then the usual track-day paraphernalia like tools and spare wheels. The only common thread was a perfect stance, usually on jewel-like Watanabes. The most desirable body, Arakaki said, comes from after the Ram's 1994 face-lift, but he noted that backdates are common, late vans wearing early dashes and door-vent windows because it looks cool. And so there were a lot of those, but also early vans with perfectly fitted late grilles and bumpers, a happy mishmash of rampant parts-swapping and meticulous assembly.

They said I could drive one. A few laps. I met 43-year-old Ishii Naoki, from Osaka. He was wearing bright-orange coveralls, and his hair was dyed a similar color. His van, matte gray, had a diffuser and a rain light, and its exhaust was let into the passenger rocker panel under a riveted heat shield.

Ishii offered a ride, first. Acceptance seemed prudent. When I grabbed my helmet bag, his face scrunched up.

"No helmet!"

I looked around. The driver of the next van over was checking tire pressures in a black motorcycle half-helmet. Most of the grid was lidless. I dropped my bag. Ishii cocked his head.

"Safe drive? Or . . . aggressive drive?"

I looked at Dino, unsure what he meant.

"He means, how fast do you want him to go?"

"Oh!" I said. "Aggressive drive! Much."

Ishii nodded again. Then he spent a session flinging his van around like he hated it and one-handing the wheel through traffic. His Dodge had a separate starter button and a B&M ratcheting shifter—great whanging thumps through the frame with each downshift—but also countless aftermarket switches of indeterminate purpose, stickers peppering the ceiling, and a screen that played music videos—first K-pop, then Taylor Swift's "Shake It Off." The exhaust spit out under the right door, guttural basso, five feet below my ears. It out-blatted everything but the video's *ticky-ticky* beat.

A couple of laps, then back to the paddock. Ishii pointed at the van's air dam and said something to Dino about legendary Japanese tuning house Rocket Bunny. He walked me through the cockpit and controls but didn't want to ride, so Dino hopped in the passenger seat.

The hilarity was almost too much to handle. After the ride with Ishii, I climbed behind the wheel expecting to like the whole mess. I was instead gifted with a cross between irrational love affair and half the bad-good car traits in history. Midrange grunt, killer brakes, comically drawn-out motions, and the feeling of riding a bar stool of the edge of a cliff. Fast enough to make me wish I had worn a helmet, slow enough that leaving it behind seemed genius. The left front tire, inches under my feet, made the van seem to spin on my heel. The B&M made hooty-holler clacky noises on each shift, or maybe that was me. I passed another van on the exit of a corner and decided that my kids would probably understand if I never went home.

In the passenger seat, Dino was attempting to stabilize himself enough to take a picture and having only moderate success. Mild surprise crossed his face.

"Is it fun?"

"Blarggh!" I said. We launched over a curb, two wheels in the air.

"Oh," he said. Then he braced against the dash and resumed shooting. Always good to work with a pro.

At lunch, Arakaki, beaming, found us in the paddock. "Three-lap race," he said, in English. His accent drew it out: *reyssss*. Six vans gridded, spectators on the fence.

There were no corner workers or safety officials, just a white Ford Expedition with a light bar serving as pace car. Arakaki removed his windows for weight but left a small pile of dirty clothes behind the passenger seat. The vans drafted, inches apart. Smoke wisped off the inside rear wheel of one on the exit of each corner. Arakaki notched a commanding lead, then won. The whole spectacle lasted maybe eight minutes and reminded me of a dream I once had about ayahuasca and the circus.

Late in the day, we buckled into Dino's car and pointed toward Tokyo. As we drove out of the track's main gate, under a giant carved lion head, past hand-painted signs full of zebra stripes and kanji, I could hear drifting just over the hill—howling tires and what sounded like a Nissan RB six flirting with its rev limiter. A few Dajiban followed us through the gate, blatting into the muggy air. They dwarfed the road in the rearview, stout little car-houses that filled the lane.

I smiled. The sight made all the sense in the world—goofy and encouraging and ruleless and honest. For the first time in my life, I wanted a van. Also a 20-foot monkey statue. I wondered what a van would look like with a monkey statue on top. It was all joyous and funky and real. It felt like an antidote to a problem I didn't know I had, a cure for everything stuffy and self-important in car culture. It was Japan. It couldn't have been anywhere else.

The Chaf and the Furious
Films of substance, consumed appropriately.

> *The events in this column took place in Seattle, where pot is legal and mezcal is cheap. Everyone has a few old friends who are forever there for bad ideas. Chaffee is one of my favorites.*

ROAD & TRACK, JUNE 2019

They have announced a new *Fast and Furious* movie. Ninth in the series, arriving next year. The franchise launched in 2001 with *The Fast and the Furious,* a 106-minute crime opus starring Vin Diesel and Paul Walker and focused on California's import-tuner culture. Equal parts generational touchstone and B-movie goofery.

I had somehow managed to avoid seeing any of these films. Then iTunes offered them as a package, $49.99 for all eight. Being a sucker for loud noises, I bought the package. Then I decided to watch all eight movies in one night, in order, with a bottle of mezcal, because it's important to be up on your cultural references. Also, I had a fifth of Del Maguey Vida sitting idle in the pantry. Smoky, fruity, hint of vanilla. Letting that stuff sit is waste up there with using Sunoco 110 as weed killer.

My friend Michael Chaffee found out about this plan and decided to help. Michael—Chaf to friends—is a software engineer, a motorcycle person, a lapsed track-day junkie. We met in Chicago 15 years ago, when I was working as a mechanic and spending too many weekends at Road America. We bonded over shared love of the BMW E30 M3 and the way air-cooled Porsches look when filthy.

Chaf hadn't seen the films either, but he tends to whirl through life elbows out, maximum attack. It was thus little surprise when he wheeled into my kitchen in Seattle on a Saturday afternoon and plopped a grocery bag of marijuana edibles on the counter. Then he gave me a big hug and announced that he had been trying to empty the bag since breakfast.

It seemed fitting. When the first *F&F* hit theaters, I was in college. Watching B movies less than sober is half of what you do in college. Chaf is 45, one of those people who view body chemistry as negotiable concept. And if you don't think Vin Diesel is best experienced in frontal-lobe Technicolor, well, you haven't experienced Vin Diesel.

By the time I cued up the movies, my friend was installed on the couch, funneling gummy pot candies into his mouth. "Wait," I said, puzzled. "Did you just eat four of those things?"

Generally speaking, two pot candies contain enough marijuana to make a grown man talk to trees.

"Look," he said. "Sooner or later, a *Fast and Furious* movie is going to come on, and I intend to be ready. We should also eat some chips. Chips sound great. I don't want to miss the beginning. Because I want to understand the whole plot."

"Plot" is a loose term here. The opening lines in the first movie are a bellwether. "We just packed up the real money load, and it's comin' your way," a dockworker says. Then three black Hondas attack a semi with grappling hooks, and that's all she wrote: A plane crashing into your living room wouldn't stop you from watching the whole thing.

The Vida looked at me in accusatory fashion, so I broke the seal and whispered sweet nothings into the bottle.

F&F films are not *Casablanca*. Or even quality cinema per se. They might live in the same county as quality cinema. They maybe knew quality cinema in high school, once made out with her sister.

Walker appears in the first act, smiling like a puppy. There is a big drag-racing scene. Diesel enters the competition, glowering, in a Mazda RX-7.

Chaf raised an eyebrow. "That's the first rear-drive car I've seen. They're drag-racing these front-drive things?"

I boggled. "Where have you been for the last 25 years? The Nineties import world was almost entirely front-drivers. Ever hear of Hot Import Nights?"

He shrugged, as if discovering an entire subculture relevant to your interests was just what happened on Saturday nights. Then he pulled some kind of single-serving chocolate pot brownie from his pocket and swallowed it without chewing. On-screen, Diesel aimed his feelings at a small group of people, in the same way that the 16-inch guns on the USS *Iowa* once aimed their feelings at coastal artillery.

But then, explosions are key to these films. Uncontrolled demolition of dialogue, emotion, machinery.

"Amateurs don't use nitrous oxide," a shop owner tells Walker. "You'll blow yourself to pieces!" Another character, observing Walker: "He's got enough NOS in there to blow himself up!" (Shortly after, in a masterful release of tension, the car in question blows up.)

The whole thing reminds you of those 1950s movies about the ills of rock and roll, where the kids are all hopped up on soda pop and everyone is having consequential sex while angry at The Rules. Only with more Toyota Supra. Realism is irrelevant. No one drives without looking extremely constipated. People fire guns from motorcycles. There is a tragic death. Characters have names— Johnny Tran, Dominic Toretto—like 1930s movie mobsters.

The Vida bottle pouted on the coffee table, so I took a moment to apply its contents directly to my face.

Walker, driving through Los Angeles at more than 100 mph, stared at a laptop on his passenger seat, concerned.

"Danger to manifold!" Chaf yelled, reading the laptop screen. His eyes went wide and his arms shot into the air like a football referee's. The camera showed random nuts and washers falling onto the floor of Walker's car, presumably because it was overstressed or furious or whatever.

"This is exactly like an old Saab commercial," Chaf said, pointing at the television.

We finished the first film and moved on to the second. My friend paced, concerned.

"I love this. Legitimately. But how are there eight of these movies? How do they not run out of things to say?"

I frowned, confused. "There were . . . things to say?"

"I mean, on the other hand," he said, building up steam, "if we're on this subject, we should definitely talk about porn. Because at first you're like, 'Oh, it's just a movie with naked people.' And then you watch another one, and it's also a movie with naked people. But you're forgetting the key ingredient here, which is that *you went to the trouble to find more.*"

Kids: Stay off drugs.

Watching these movies, I had several deep thoughts about how important it can be to see your particular brand of culture represented on film. I'd share those thoughts here, but I can't remember them. I can't remember because I didn't write them down, because writing sounded boring and also something something half-empty Vida bottle.

What did not sound boring: cracking open my laptop to log *F&F* dialogue:

"There is something about engines that calms me down."

"I never narc'd on nobody!"

"You're a smart fence, Ted—maybe too smart."

So much camp, you have to watch it in a tent.

"Ask any racer," Diesel's character famously says. "It don't matter if you win by an inch or a mile. Winning's winning."

"Oh yes, I agree," Chaf said. "But this doesn't make driving look fun at all! Say something witty, shift gears, crash!"

I allowed as how that image is pretty much the international stereotype for automotive journalism. Chaf fell back into the couch, giggling. Later, I passed out in the middle of the fourth sequel, *Fast Five*. We didn't make it to eight. I woke after midnight, computer in my lap, browser open to an unfinished delivery order for the local pizza place. (Four large pies, three two-liters of Cherry Coke, two paper plates.)

Chaf was asleep sitting up, mouth open and head tilted back, one hand in a bag of chips.

As I write this, the ninth *F&F* is in the works. It feels like that first scene in *Jaws,* where you know the shark is coming, just not when. Will the ninth one be terrible? Great? More or less furious than installments previous and sundry? The mind melts at the possibilities. But even if I knew, I wouldn't tell. I never narc'd on nobody.

Figured Out
The numbers don't matter.

An old song still worth singing. Originally published as part of the package for R&T's *2019 Performance Car of the Year award.*
Fun game: Try to guess which company that engineer worked for.

ROAD & TRACK, DECEMBER 2019

Some time ago, at a road course few people visit, far from prying ears, I stood in a paddock garage as an engineer from a major carmaker laid out a truth.

"We only care about numbers," he said, "because you guys care about numbers."

"Us guys?"

"Car magazines."

"Performance numbers, you mean?"

"Yep."

My brain did a brief little dance of glee. "Come on. Are you telling me that your employer, [global manufacturer of fine repute and engineering might], would consciously make a new sports car slower than its predecessor, on purpose?"

"Yes. Maybe. But first we'd have to know that the press wouldn't crucify us for it."

And thus, to borrow a line from Monty Python, we witness the violence in the system.

Cars have always sold on improvement. You know the ad line: "Today's model is better/faster/stronger, so ditch your 2015 Toyolet 2000 SUX and get the 2020 Toyolet 4000 SUX!" How could you not want more of what you wanted before? And partly as a result, new cars have long grown more powerful every year. People like fast.

This makes sense. Along with the fact that, for a time, this process also gave rise to an ever-increasing sense of driver control—engineering advancement, in the interest of helping ordinary, non-racing-driver people handle more potent machinery.

Prior to the advent of the computer-monitored chassis, that control generally came in the form of added steering feel, suspension refinement, grip, and braking. And so a 1980s Honda was faster and quieter than a 1970s Honda but just as lively and talkative, and a C5 Corvette similarly topped a C4, and so on. Car magazines came to verify those qualities through performance testing, quantifying talents such as acceleration and skidpad handling. In addition to providing an objective barometer, the process helped us call "rat" when manufacturer ad copy inflated reality.

So we cared, perhaps too much at times, about numbers. And carmakers cared back, and the gyre widened. Possibly into oblivion.

Somewhere along the line, the limits of most new cars exceeded those of public pavement. Regulatory needs made vehicles fatter and more distant. Tire technology hit remarkable heights. And then we arrived at the present, where the vehicular landscape is so defined by extreme performance that some of our favorite new cars—not just the fancy ones—don't have a pulse until double the posted speed limit. If the average 1990s sport sedan or exotic gives a bubbly stream of backroad feedback at speed X, its 2019 twin needs 2X or maybe even 3X to wake the same way.

Restraint can be entertaining—keeping a Plymouth Hemi Cuda from killing you is a hoot, for example. The problem is one of execution. Too many modern cars are dead fish at the wheel, long-legged and asleep at normal velocity, ill-suited to how people actually drive. They're the product of engineers aiming at closed-course laps or a percentage gain on some spreadsheet, à la race cars. But fast road cars aren't race cars, where tenths of a second matter. On real roads, fun is second only to safety and emissions.

We occasionally meet engineers who argue. Fun is speed, they insist, full stop. And in some cases, it is, but that equation only takes you so far. If performance perpetually trumped involvement, the world would beg for 5000-hp automated cars that perform like roller coasters: strap in, hold on, and give up control. And what is a love of driving if not control in the exercise of freedom?

A McLaren F1 rips and snorts over landscape in a way a Bugatti Chiron never will, and the Chiron is an order of magnitude quicker. A Honda Civic Type R will dust a Jaguar E-type, but only one of them pours a cocktail of grace and tactility that can change your life.

Do you want a 1200-hp exotic, stability-tamed and distant below 1 g, or a live wire that needs you present and caffeinated on a 40-mph back road? How often does the average person visit a track, really? Do you want to ride to 60 mph in three seconds or drive there in five?

Progress is human. Give us machines that are safer, more durable, lighter, more approachable at their limits, cleaner, and more efficient. Build them every day for the next hundred years and no one will complain. The numbers are a piece of the puzzle, not the whole. It's time to walk away from letting them dictate the fast-car business. To exit the stage where a quicker Nürburgring time or another 50 hp automatically deems a machine better in some misguided crowdthink fashion. To remember that *how* always tops *how much*.

Except, of course, with the unmeasurables—sound, steering feedback, styling genius, the joy you get when a great chassis cracks into a corner on a winding road. The intangibles that make you walk away from a car in the parking lot, looking back every five feet, glad to be alive. With those, there is no ceiling.

Hallelujah.

Indoor Storage
Memories and where we keep them.

You don't really know what home means until you have to let go.

ROAD & TRACK, NOVEMBER 2016

The house went to a nice woman from down the street. My parents sold it to her, which meant they also sold her the garage, because that's how house sales work.

They lived at that address for 24 years. A single-floor colonial ranch in Louisville, Kentucky, sheltered by an enormous and arcing elm. The tree covered most of the roof, a trunk so large that I couldn't wrap my arms around it, even as an adult. It was there when we moved in, the fall that I started sixth grade, from a smaller house across town. I moved out at 18, on my way to college. Mom and Dad left this summer, moving to Seattle. Where I live, with my wife and two small girls.

They wanted to be near us, but they also wanted a change. So in July, I flew east, to help them drive west. The movers came, and then we loaded another van and a small trailer for us. The day we left, there were pictures in front of everything. Happy faces on the lawn, smiles over tightened throats.

The tree came down years ago, felled by blight, but the house didn't change much. I didn't want to go inside, so I didn't. Correction: I strolled through empty hallways once, on the way to use the bathroom, walking a little too fast. I kept my eyes low, as if I had business somewhere else or the floor was really important.

I left through the garage, mostly because I couldn't avoid it. Old habit: walk in the door, throw keys on the table, head out back.

Dad was almost always there—bent over the bench grinder or an engine stand, or with his head buried under a hood. The cabinet over the main bench was covered with framed photos of airplanes he loved and projects we'd chased—the two of us in the empty engine bay of a 3-series, or the Stearman biplane he bought as parts in the 1970s and later sold, having never found the funds or time to build it. The wall held Alfa posters, BMW ephemera, MG whatnot. All hanging over my late grandmother's Mercedes, a 1972 W108 that she bought new and later restored. Or over the BMW 2002 that we raced in SCCA Improved Touring. Or the '34 MG PA and 2012 Mustang Boss 302, both of which are now gone. A zillion other machines that came and went, residents and tourists.

Over the 10 years we've been together, my wife and I have moved around a lot, following work. A new address every 12 months on average. I didn't get to Kentucky more than a few times a year, but the infrastructure was always there. A cache of parts and reference material. The flatbed trailer parked behind the house. The old Suburban that pulled the trailer, with its collapsed front seats and dead odometer, a spare water pump perpetually stashed behind the third row. All of it sold now, gone to friends or others to help fund a move to a smaller place, closer to family.

In that emptied garage, memories came in a flood. As they do, not always in a way you want or can handle. Bitter arguments and long nights but also deadlines met, sunny Sunday afternoons, happy engine start-ups. Hours and hours of moments, so many that I couldn't process or even acknowledge them as they flew by, each tied to a single room. The rush felt debilitating at first, an overwhelming weight, as if I was supposed to pull everything down, catalog each piece and identify it, to acknowledge its value. There wasn't time, it felt unfair, the task seemed too big.

I eventually had to shut the door and walk outside for air. It wasn't until days later, on I-90 in South Dakota, that the moment began to feel like a gift. An eyeblink fanning out into hundreds of scenes, a piece of space and time owned by nobody else. A strange instance of Brownian motion where, on a planet of seven billion people, I was being drowned in something unique.

The more I think about it, the more it seems like you're supposed to let that kind of thing in. Revel in it. Know when to move on but acknowledge how rare and bright the light is. Which is funny, because in the moment, you feel nothing but irons. You want glow to last forever and end five minutes ago.

Dad hadn't coated or painted the concrete garage floor when he poured it, just left the surface bare. At the time, I thought this was dumb, because who wouldn't want a perfect surface, if you're bothering to build from scratch? And that's what he had done, for the first time in his life: design and lay out a garage, pad to roof, exactly as he liked. Three cars of space, a chain lift and heater, countless other perks always wanted. Modest, but his.

Tears welled, until I stopped trying to push them back. His hands were shaking as he gave me the keys to the van. I'm not sure he noticed.

Years of use had stained the concrete. Black and brown blotches, oil or solvent or ground-in dirt. I couldn't parse them all out or remember their history, but for a moment, I looked down and pretended—pretended I knew which project had made each one. Wishing I could remember and feeling like I had cheated the memories by forgetting. Until I realized that it didn't matter if I knew what caused them. It only mattered that they were there.

Wet Behind the Ears

In deep at the Pacific Marine Expo, lessons bubbling to the surface.

> *When you accept a senior staff position at a large international publication, the gravity of the situation makes your main objective immediately clear: get as many dad jokes into print as possible.*

Road & Track, May 2016

People were selling. Boats and nets and reels and titanium coolers, taglines like THE BUSINESS MAGAZINE FOR FISHERMEN and LISTEN TO THE SOUND OF A BROKEN FIBER-OPTIC CABLE. There was a man hawking something called an ice flaker, which sprays water on the inside of a refrigerated cylinder. The water flash-freezes, and then a rotary blade comes by to scrape it off: Boom, flaked ice to fill your cooler and keep a dead fish cold.

My dad was with me. As we walked past the flaker, he detoured for a look. My father is not an easily distracted man. Also, he does not eat fish. Or have a fishing boat.

"That is very cool," he said, looking at the ice flaker, totally serious.

Do not ruin the moment with a stupid pun, I told myself. *Even though it would be hilarious.*

I took a second to survey my surroundings. I felt equal parts fascinated and out of place. Also as if there were a clock counting down to the instant when my interest would wane and I'd begin doing silly things, like making fish faces into my phone camera and texting the result to the staff of this magazine.

"This," I said to no one in particular, "must be what it's like for normal people at an auto show."

We were at the 2015 Pacific Marine Expo, at a convention center in Seattle. This once-a-year event is the West Coast's largest commercial marine trade show. I moved to Seattle last spring, after a life of bouncing around the country, to be near family and mountains. I came to the expo because it was a Friday, and Fridays are a magnet for spurious reasons to leave the office. It sounded like a car show for people who aren't into cars. Which is, let's be honest, most of the planet.

I wondered what that was like, being normal.

This year's expo slogan was "Right in Your Wheelhouse." Walking the floor, I began wishing for a wheelhouse. If I had one, it would likely be filled with EPIRBs—emergency position-indicating radio beacons, those transmitters that help the coast guard find you when your ice flaker melts down (zing!) or your captain falls overboard while tying his shoes. The ocean is fantastic, but you could write everything I know about it on the back of a life jacket and still have room for a full-depth chart of the Mariana Trench.

Our guide for this outing was my friend Martin Meissner. Martin works for ZF Marine, the seafaring division of the German automotive supplier. He's a big man, Canadian, with a deep voice, what a first grader would scribble if you asked them to draw a redheaded lumberjack who loves fun. When we met at the expo, Martin had recently imported a 1990 BMW 525i that began life with a Bavarian fire department; the car is still in that trim, complete with siren. ("I took it to the German car show in Fort Lauderdale one weekend," he said, "blew the horn, scared the crap out of people." Booming laughter.)

Martin spends a lot of time at marine expos. People buy things there, he said. Unlike at car shows. "Actual orders. Some of these dudes might not have showered today, and they may be a little grizzled, but they've got $70,000 in their pocket, and they need a new engine."

And oh, those engines. Diesels everywhere. Recognizable brands like Mitsubishi, Volvo, Scania. The small ones were the size of a large desk; the big ones would have dwarfed a Volkswagen. At one point, I stood next to an MTU 16V 4000, a 16-cylinder wide enough to have its own zip code. MTU was founded by Wilhelm Maybach—yes, that one—and his son Karl in 1909. The 16V 4000 makes 2680 hp at 1800 rpm, goes 30,000 hours between overhauls, carries 66 gallons of lubricating fluid, and resembles something belched up by a U-boat. I wanted to hang a saddle on it and ride to Hawaii.

May we never reach a day where machinery, in any form, grows dull.

Culture dripped from the gunwales. Captain Keith Colburn of TV's *Deadliest Catch* was the keynote speaker. The featured band was a group called the FisherPoets. No one wore a suit, because even a professional boat person doesn't wear a suit at sea. The fanciest piece of clothing I saw was a pair of khakis, and that guy was carrying an open beer. He was in the beer garden, because of course there was a beer garden. With organized giveaways of Seahawks tickets, because Seattle.

Chiefly, I realized exactly how my friends and family must have felt when I dragged them to car shows past: that hour at the end of the day when you've seen everything on the floor, you don't know what half of it is, the novelty is long gone, and you just need air.

I could imagine someone tugging my sleeve and going, *Hey wait really no look new exhaust routing on the Porsches this year!* After which there would be much eye-rolling and excitement, with no one person displaying both.

"One year," Martin said, as we walked toward the exit, "a guy from Scania brought a cow. It was in a pen and everything, laying patties, stinking up the whole place. He had Monopoly money taped to it. If you asked, he'd say it was his cash cow. Because he was making deals!"

I stifled the urge to do a joyous, punny little dance.

"Cool," my dad said, chuckling.

"I know," I said quietly, glancing toward the ice flaker. "Got chills just thinking about it."

Overshadowed

Reflections on a drive to the light.

This was the first-gen Subaru BRZ, built from 2012 to 2020. People said the worst thing about that BRZ was the low-grip stock tire—it slid all the time. Nah. The best thing about that BRZ was the low-grip stock tire—it slid all the time!

ROAD & TRACK, DECEMBER 2017

We have reached the end of 2017. Not, it must be said, without difficulty. Forest fires. Hurricanes. This country squabbling with itself almost nonstop. If you were conscious at any point in the past 12 months, you have probably come to the conclusion that this was a long, exhausting, and occasionally stupid year.

Allow me to reflect on something little to do with any of that.

We were gifted a solar eclipse in August. The first total eclipse over the continental U.S. in 38 years, visible only in select parts of the country. At the ripe old age of 36, I had never seen a total eclipse, so I hit the road to find it. Partly because celestial wonders are neat. Partly because it was an excuse to leave the house at high speed on what could legitimately be dubbed a space odyssey, thus fulfilling at least half of the dreams I had in middle school, when I spent most of my time in my parents' basement rewatching *The Right Stuff* on VHS and reading *Sport Compact Car* until my eyes bled.

Side note: I did not date much in middle school. In retrospect, it was probably because I was too busy being rad.

And not leaving the house.

To chase this eclipse, I borrowed a 2017 Subaru BRZ test car. The opportunity was a pairing of rare birds, as a total solar eclipse is about as common as a new sports car with a flat-four under the hood. The Subaru was launched in 2012; its engine configuration is currently found in just one other American-market coupe. (Porsche 718. The Subaru is also sold as the Toyota 86, née Scion FR-S, but the 86 and BRZ are identical twins and could share a passport.)

Five years old is young for a person, middle-aged for the design of a new car, and an eyeblink for the solar system, on whose clock eclipses run. In a total eclipse, the moon passes so perfectly in front of the sun that parts of the Earth lose direct sunlight. In those places, you can briefly see the sun's corona, a ring of fire that recalls the Northern Lights, if the Northern Lights looked like the cover of a Yes album.

People travel to witness this miracle, evangelize it. As we once did for the Subaru. In 2012, early press reports pitched the car as the greatest thing since Carl Benz quit horses—a light and affordable rear-driver, slide-happy, drifty and alive. After the new dimmed, everyone focused on the flaws: a loud and cavelike interior, an odd clutch, a recalcitrant shifter. That neat little engine was frustrating and clunky around town, really only happy on a track or a back road.

Those are niggles. In the history of fast cars, people have put up with more to gain less. I've never warmed to the thing myself, mostly because the Subaru shares a reality with the current Mazda Miata, a car built for the same task and to similar metrics, one of the world's most perfectly realized machines. Maybe not as raw and edgy at the limit, but friendlier, less of a rough cob.

If this job has a flaw, if there's a downside to driving hundreds of new cars each year, it's the encouragement to take sides. To pick one thing over another, chase some hypothetical best answer. Which is not how the world works. We hang choice on the space between the lines.

You like this girl's laugh, even if she doesn't share your interests. That apartment feels right, the cheaper one down the street doesn't. The less reliable fridge goes better with your cabinets. The knee-jerk answer isn't always the smartest, and the smartest isn't always what you want.

I took the BRZ to Baker City, Oregon, 370 miles from my house. The internet told me Baker City would see more than 90 seconds of eclipse totality—a completely blocked sun—and it was not wrong. The corona was mesmerizing. The world dimmed and relit as if on some universal rheostat. The light after felt so disarmingly bright by comparison, so punchy and yellow, it seemed to pack under my cheeks when I blinked. The sum experience contained almost everything wonderful and humbling about existence and nothing else.

It was only after, buckling into the Subaru, that I realized the rarity of the feeling: How often do we get a piece of time like that, free of want? How often do we come close but spoil it through focus on the off notes?

Setting aside the oddities of working for a car magazine, I sometimes wonder if human beings are hardwired to find fault. Maybe it's evolutionary, the long tail of some genetic trait built to make sure everyone eats. Which is probably why we have stuff like the internet and the International Space Station, immense pieces of wonder iterated from unrealistic dream to reality. But also maybe a species-wide reluctance to enjoy anything for too long without dwelling on what comes next.

Oregon was expecting up to a million tourists for this year's eclipse. My route home thus meant nine hours of driving on a traffic-clogged route that would have normally consumed six. Two hours in, while creeping at walking speed near the Washington border, my clutch leg cramped up, and I accidentally stalled the car.

Frustration mounted. I counted clouds and exhaled slowly, attempting to decompress. And then, flashing back to the rest of the day, I decided to try.

To work, against a surprising amount of desire and instinct, to enjoy the situation.

I took the next exit off the highway. Then several deeply unnecessary detours. That long and tiring trip grew longer, but after a while, the Subaru's cockpit seemed to grow brighter, and its engine got less cranky.

At one point, down some winding strip of nowhere pavement, I found myself wondering if most of my days had secretly been this entertaining, and if I maybe just hadn't been paying enough attention.

The run home took far more time than planned. By the time I pulled into my driveway, late that night, I wanted to keep the car forever. It was harsh, loud, unpolished. And perfect.

To Believe You're the Best
In the Moment with sacrifice, Stirling Moss, and those who try.

About a year into my time at Hagerty, I began spending my lunch hours in the online archive of Getty Images. Getty is one of the world's largest photo agencies, home to more than a century of photographs from newsworthy events. Naturally, I gravitated toward images from motorsport. I was eventually so jazzed by what I found that I began sharing Getty photos with coworkers, dropping them into the company's chat software each morning.

After a while, someone suggested we turn the practice into a column series. The format began as me pulling detail and meaning from a single image but soon morphed into something else—off-the-cuff essays on human motivation, packed with photos. I named this series In the Moment.

The installment that follows was a house favorite. I've known the Moss story since childhood—the beats and reactions were so familiar, they found the page as fast as my fingers could type. Due to the high cost of photo licensing, I unfortunately can't include every image that originally ran in this story, but the important ones remain. Over a lifetime of bylines, I haven't enjoyed writing anything more.

Hagerty, March 2023

Sooner or later, everyone meets trauma. For some, the strain is mental. For others, it's physical. For a third, less fortunate group, it is both.

Consider the racing crash just below these words. Incredibly, a man lived through it. When he was pulled from the wreckage of that small and fragile car, on a spring day in the south of England, he was famous, one of the best in the world at what he did for a living, a household name in the land of his birth.

Goodwood, England, April 23, 1962. The remains of a Lotus 18/21 Formula 1 car. A human survived this.

The crash caused significant injury. He recovered, though he was, by his own admission, never quite the same. When he died in bed a few years ago, he remained widely beloved, but he had never regained—or at least, could no longer access—the ability that brought him fame. No one was ever quite sure why.

Smithology

We spend so much time discussing the importance of our differences. That we do this is not as remarkable as the fact that we know those differences don't really matter. Most people have a pretty good idea of just how much ties humans together. We have a staggering amount in common; the deltas between us are mostly window dressings of tribe and culture.

Still, we pretend they carry weight: Beware the people from Shelbyville/Foreigntonia/that religious building across town! They'll drive you from your home and take your things! *They hate all you hold dear!*

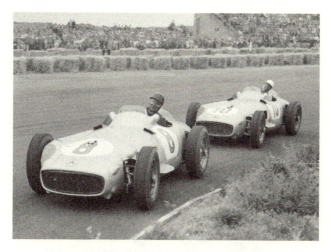

The man who lived through that crash, seven years prior, in an F1 car behind his mentor, a man named Juan. In an era when polo helmets were thought enough.

Not that this doesn't happen. Genghis was a particularly cruel Khan; Ivan was indeed terrible; Vlad impaled people. But most people simply want to keep what they earn and be left in peace. They aren't really interested in going all Mongol on the masses.

Which doesn't mean we don't worry about disasters. Only that the odds are against them.

Is it human nature to think too much on unlikely loss? Or have we simply trained ourselves to, the bad moments from thousands of years steeped in genetic memory?

Do you ever see the aftermath of a car crash and reflexively wonder how the impact felt?

Think about the impact itself. So many parts moved around. This is —was—a 1962 Lotus 18/21 Formula 1 car. Two years prior, it began life as a 1960 Lotus 18 Formula 1 car. By the morning of the race that killed it, it wore several updates, including an English V-8 and the sleeker bodywork of Lotus's 1961 Formula 1 car, the Type 21.

Look at the seat. The radiator, that rectangular mass at right. The dashboard hangs outside the car, limp; the black cylinders are gauges.

The dash location would suggest that impact force caused the steering wheel—removed by the time of this photo—to end up near the driver's right elbow. An assumption we can unfortunately prove.

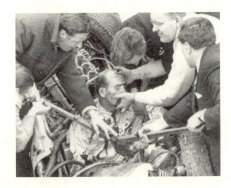

This image is lightly graphic. It is worth sharing, however, for what it illustrates. As we noted earlier, the driver survived and recovered. This image was printed in English newspapers during a relatively conservative time in a relatively conservative country. On top of that, the subject did not find it disturbing.

"The photographs that were taken after the accident," he wrote in his book, *My Racing Life*, "with me trapped in the car, look rather lurid, but in fact I find myself able to look at them quite dispassionately. After all, I knew nothing about it. I was trapped in the car for about 45 minutes, I gather, because the chassis had completely folded up over me."

It has to be normal, to look at that picture and think about the hit.

By extension, it must be normal to imagine falling from the top of the world, right?

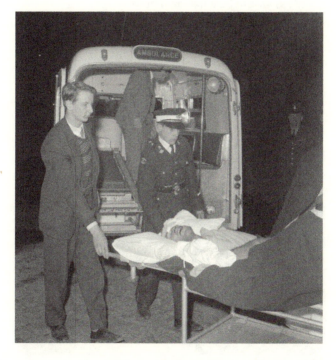

When this picture was taken, on the night of April 23, 1962, Stirling Moss was 32 years old and unconscious. The ambulance in the background had just carried him 60 miles, from a track called Goodwood, in West Sussex, to London's Atkinson Morely Hospital. That morning, he had been an international star at the height of his powers, one of the sharpest and most naturally talented drivers alive.

His crash made international news, even the papers in America, where no one cared about such things. And though he recovered fully, his life would never be the same.

MOSS FIRST RACED A CAR IN 1947. He was 17 then, a former show-jumper of horses. His dentist father, Alfred, had once driven in an Indy 500. At first, he tried to discourage his son. He had hoped the boy would be a dentist. Then the talent became clear. Just a few years later, the younger Moss would be a national hero.

From 1948 to 1962, Stirling Moss started 529 races. He finished first in 212 of them.

Two hundred and twelve.

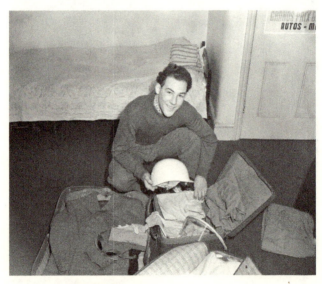

As a young man, 21 years old and already famous, packing for a tour of Europe. He would enter 48 races over the next six months.

The tally is staggering. The man won 16 Formula 1 grands prix but also sports-car landmarks like the 12 Hours of Sebring, the 24 Hours of Le Mans, and the annual 1000-kilometer race at the old Nürburgring. Perhaps the brightest spot on his résumé is an overall win in the "old"

Mille Miglia. A cross-country and thousand-mile open-road race that ran from 1927 to 1957 and ended only when the Italian government grew weary from the body count and outlawed the whole thing. (Fifty-six drivers and spectators dead in 30 years.)

Imagine: A flat-out, nonstop competition, basically a lap of midcentury Italy, with factory teams and the best drivers on earth, over narrow two-lanes, through farmland and the Appenine Mountains, down cobblestone village streets. The Mille was said to draw more than five million spectators across the country. In 1955, they lined roads in throngs, no real barriers or crowd control, watching as Moss repeatedly cranked a Mercedes-Benz 300 SLR—a tube-frame prototype with a Formula 1 engine—to more than 170 mph. He finished in record time: 10 hours, 7 minutes, and 48 seconds, for an average speed of 98.5 mph.

That last figure is impressive at a glance. Think on it even a smidge more and you maybe lose your mind a little.

May 1, 1955, in the Mille Miglia. Moss and his navigator, the journalist Denis Jenkinson, at full steam, inches from crowds.

Success in racing has always hung on both car and driver; Moss himself always said that the Mercedes made the win possible. Even the likes of Ayrton Senna could not land an F1 championship at the wheel of a Toleman. (What's a Toleman, you ask? Exactly.) Today, top-flight racing cars can be separated by as little as hundredths or thousandths of a second, and they do not make huge speed gains from year to year. At the risk of gross understatement, the 1950s were different. Technology evolved far quicker; motorsport was still more art than science, but the balance was shifting. Cars grew noticeably faster every season. No country or designer held an advantage for long.

Moss was staunchly patriotic; he preferred to drive for marques from his homeland. ("It is better to lose honorably in a British car than to win in a foreign one," he once said.) Exceptions were made—he was at one point a Mercedes-Benz factory driver; he loved the Maserati 300S; and so on—but that preference bit him more often than not.

Imagine saying no to a Ferrari, then driving the wheels off a slower alternative while some lesser talent warms the seat you turned down and leaves you behind. Imagine, too, racking up those 212 wins without always having the fastest car.

It's also worth noting that Moss ran at the front, in some of the fastest and most dangerous machines then built, in an age when scores of drivers around the world died at the wheel every year. They competed in cars virtually absent driver protection, in an era where safety gear was so laughable that a cork-lined polo helmet was often mocked as overkill. That Moss survived is remarkable; that he was so good is impressive. That he survived while being that good, while racing that often, life so regularly in the odds? Astonishing.

As with any gathering of stats, there are caveats. This is not Pete Rose, however, and the asterisk only improves the man. Take those 212 wins and 529 starts. Two hundred and twelve divided by 529 is 0.400. Forty percent.

Where else do we see a single member of a team put on the spot to deliver results?

In major-league baseball, Wikipedia says, a season batting average of 30 percent or higher is "considered to be excellent." The site calls an average greater than 40 percent "a nearly unachievable goal."

Ah, you say! That's not a level comparison! Baseball isn't midcentury road racing.

True. There is a difference.

A hitter at the plate is not asked to maintain hours of peak performance in the sustained, 120-degree heat of an uninsulated metal cockpit, or in driving rain. They are not required to endure those conditions without water or food. Nor must they perform in close and often deafening proximity to other hitters, reacting to the boxer-like feints and defenses of those individuals while knowing an error from anyone involved could unavoidably maim or kill.

There is no mental strain from concentrating on car placement to the nearest inch at, say, 130 mph. While engaged in an activity that has recently killed several of your friends. While often mere feet from trees and fences and other landscape furniture. While thinking (but not too much) about the close proximity of spectators and how any one of a hundred small mistakes on your part could at any point end you or them or both.

Phil Hill, America's first Formula 1 World Champion and a Ferrari factory driver, after winning the 1961 Italian Grand Prix at Monza and locking the title. His teammate, Wolfgang von Trips, had crashed during the race, killing himself and 14 spectators. Ferrari did not pay Hill a salary, and the American did not learn of von Trips's death until shortly before this moment. Grieving and racked with survivor's guilt, he wept.

Baseball bats do not often suffer unpredictable and game-ending mechanical failures, and even when they do, those failures do not take a hitter's life. Nor does each season ask that the hitter choose a new bat from a fresh round of unproven designs. Choosing the wrong bat for even a single game does not alter the hitter's chance of success, or fame, or survival, nor does it change the odds on that player's continued presence in the sport.

On top of that, major-league players make a good living. Some F1 drivers of the 1950s and 1960s, even the champions, held day jobs to pay the rent. Moss did well, but he was an exception, a star whose fame and success brought sponsor deals and eventual knighthood.

Fine, you say: What about the current era?

Lewis Hamilton, one of the greatest drivers of his generation, being interviewed before the 2012 United States Grand Prix, Circuit of the Americas, Austin, Texas.

We once used this space to discuss modern Formula 1 star Lewis Hamilton. At time of writing, HAM has started 310 F1 races and won 103 of them. Thirty-three percent. Moss's 16 grand-prix wins came over 66 starts—24 percent.

Numbers are the least interesting part of any sport. Still, a quick internet search will give you a list of all-time Formula 1 win ratios. Those lists are inherently misleading, hung as they are on many variables —politics, engineering, funding, the perpetually changing number of races per season, whether a driver was lucky enough to sign with the right team at the right time, whether F1 was their sole focus, and so on. The closer you get to today, the more those variables weigh the odds.

It's fun to look, though. While writing these words, I dug up one of those lists. Hamilton's current win ratio puts him fourth best among the sport's all-time heavy hitters. Moss is ninth. Jim Clark, a personal hero, is third. Senna is eighth. Michael Schumacher is fifth. The Argentinian Juan Manuel Fangio, a Moss contemporary and mentor, takes top honors. From 1952 to 1958, he notched 24 wins in 52 starts. Forty-seven percent.

So many differences between eras. With Moss, Fangio is probably the most useful comparison. He was just as versatile, yet he did not carry loyalties when choosing a car. For the most part, he simply drove the fastest thing on offer. He was also lucky enough to end his career when he wished, quitting in his prime, neither too early nor too late.

Moss, 22 years old, and Fangio, then 40, before a race in England in 1952. A fierce talent at his peak and another almost there.

Such a long run. The two men were friends. Moss saw Fangio as his superior, a talent he could not match, even on his best day. The older man, however, thought the younger one his equal, a concept Moss never quite agreed with.

59

Fangio began racing in his home country in the 1930s. By 1950, when the F1 world championship kicked off, he was a seasoned veteran. He won five Formula 1 titles, then retired in 1958, at 46.

How Fangio arrived at that decision is telling. He would later confess that he had known without doubt when it was time, could point to the exact moment that he had made the choice.

"You must always strive to be the best, but you must never believe that you are."

— J. M. Fangio

The 1957 German Grand Prix was held at the old Nürburgring Nordschleife—the track's infamous "North Loop," which still exists today. Then as now, it was basically just a long, one-way road in the mountains. Fangio qualified on pole, starting first. By lap 13, he was more than 30 seconds ahead of the car in second. He came into the pits for tires and fuel. Mechanics botched the stop, taking far too long. By the time Fangio left the pits, he had fallen to third, now more than a minute behind second place. A breaker tripped in his head. He drove as he never had, a man possessed.

"I had to risk," he said. "Something I never before did in my life."

Chew on that for a second.

The Nürburgring, 1960.

The old Ring was and remains one of the world's fastest tracks. Fangio's pole lap of 9 minutes and 25 seconds translated to an average speed of 89 mph. This on a 14-mile circuit with more than 170 corners, that was mostly bordered by hedges and trees, in a 1500-pound car with more power than brakes and wire wheels wearing treaded tires roughly as wide as your palm.

After that botched stop, Fangio went even faster, resetting the lap record again and again. By the checker, he had found 7 seconds under his pole time. An eternity.

Fangio's Maserati at the 1957 German Grand Prix, tearing out of the pits after that disastrous stop. His hands are reaching to pull down his goggles.

"If in one turn I was using second gear," he said, "then I went into third. When it was third, I used fourth . . . there is much more risk, this is much less safe, but you go faster . . . I've never been a spectacular racer, but I did things I had never done in my life . . . ."

He won, of course. Some stories simply end as we want them to. And yet, in the process, he forced himself into a different place. Whatever he felt and thought there was too much. He retired the following year.

I LIKE TO IMAGINE WHAT MIGHT HAVE HAPPENED had either man kept going. If Fangio hadn't stepped down, and if Moss hadn't crashed. Or perhaps what either man might have done when younger, for better or worse, had they known what life would bring.

When Moss crashed at Goodwood in 1962, his life turned. He and a raft of other F1 regulars were competing in a non-points race for Formula 1 cars, in front of packed stands. They were likely thinking about little more than the task at hand.

I raced at Goodwood once, several years ago; like many British circuits, the track began life as the perimeter roads of an old RAF airfield. A quick lap there is heartbreakingly fluid—fast corner after fast corner, equal parts risk and drug.

Moss's Lotus flung into the grass at St. Mary's, a quick and narrow left-hander on the circuit's west side. Reliable eyewitness accounts are rare, and Moss himself never remembered the moment. Contemporary reports suggested a host of causes, including mechanical failure and the actions of other drivers, but he never assigned blame.

What we know for sure: He was going around 120 mph, in a cigar-shaped, 700-pound assembly of thin steel tube and fiberglass, when he hit a grassy bank head-on.

> *I had pretty serious brain injuries, and my face was badly crushed, particularly the left eye socket and cheekbone. My left arm and leg were broken, the leg in two places. I was paralyzed down one side for [six months], and when I started to wake up, I didn't know how to speak.*
>
> — S. Moss

When the marshals reached him, he was alive but unconscious, choking on a piece of chewing gum. As they worked to cut him free of the car, photographers swarmed. An X-ray later showed that the impact had physically detached the right side of the Englishman's brain from his skull. The resulting coma would last a month.

England fell into a state of national worry. The press prepared obituaries. In America, *Time* magazine assembled a Moss cover feature, to be run in the event of his death.

Smithology

When I had my accident I was 32 years old, and I had been racing for 14 years. I was driving as well as I had ever done, maybe better. Had the accident not happened, I firmly believe I would have continued for at least another 14 years, and probably much more.

— S. Moss

Slightly more than one year later, in May 1963, after months of rehab, after learning to talk and walk again, Moss returned to Goodwood. He drove down from his London flat early in the morning, then climbed into a Lotus 19 sports racer and set off, on a wet and empty track, to test. He had not been in a race car since the accident.

May of 1964. Testing at Goodwood, a year after the crash, to see if he still had it. He didn't.

I would describe that test, but my efforts wouldn't be a patch on what Robert Edwards wrote in his wonderful *Stirling Moss: The Authorized Biography*:

He drove the damp circuit at lap speeds that were acceptable . . . but without being particularly startling by his own measure, which mattered more to him than any absolute—he was not racing, after all. Passing St. Mary's, he felt absolutely nothing.

63

He realized, with a dawning sense of horror, that . . . all the flowing instincts, the unthinking balancing, unbalancing, and rebalancing of the car . . . were absent. To the uninformed observer, the performance was probably impressive; to Stirling himself, it lacked everything which he had come to love about the sport and his own place in it.

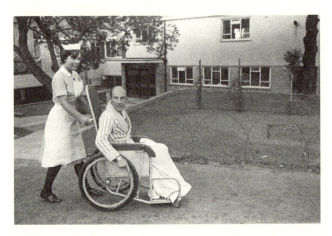

Rehab, June 1962.

Gone too was the schoolboyish enthusiasm for the sheer, fierce joy of it. If his relationship with a racing car had once been a sensuous dance, it was now more like a vaguely recalled hop with a mere acquaintance . . . a disconnecting experience . . . he even spun the car at the chicane.

This was a devastating revelation for him. But perhaps more objectively, Stirling finally realized that this was life in the real world; this was what it was like for everyone else. That the massive advantages he had unconsciously enjoyed for so long were now a thing of the past, alien to him and probably impossible to recover.

He was now as other men. It was a terrifying prospect.

We should not feel sorry for him; for all he lost, he still felt hugely fortunate and did not truck in self-pity. The rest of the man's life was apparently full and happy. He kept busy with various business commitments and enjoyed the continuing evolution of racing and technology, all the way to his late-life presence on social media. He even returned to the track eventually, dabbling in modern historic racing. Which is, if you are not familiar, best described as old cars on modern tracks, something like the old days but also nothing like them at all.

Years after the accident, when Moss retired from driving at speed, it was for good, he said, a firm stop to green-flag activity. He made the announcement on Radio Le Mans, on June 9, 2011. He had been competing in a Le Mans Legends race, he said, a vintage event held on that modern track, and he had scared himself that afternoon. He was 81. He is still widely regarded as the greatest F1 driver to have never won a championship.

I have known people occasionally moved to inaction by the likelihood of a worst-case end. That quality does not make them lesser. If I understand that feeling, it is only because I have fought the instinct my whole life. We all lose things, and we never know when that will happen. The only practical path forward, I think, is to be clear-eyed about the potential outcomes of the risks you are willing to take, embracing reality without letting fear slow things down too much.

The first person to fly faster than the speed of sound was an American test pilot named Chuck Yeager. His life was steeped in risk. You do what you can for as long as you can, he once said, and when you finally can't, you do the next best thing—you back up, but you don't give up.

After that horrible accident, Moss got back in the car, to try. Because of course he did. It is, in the end, all we can ever do.

Sam Smith

Photo Credits

Goodwood crash, Moss recovery: Trinity Mirror/Mirrorpix/Alamy

Goodwood crash with Moss in car: DPA Picture Alliance/Alamy

Hill laurels: Keystone/Hulton/Getty Images

Moss ambulance, Moss packing, Moss and Fangio England, Moss Goodwood test: PA Images/Alamy

Hamilton: Sam Smith

Nürburgring 1960: See Things Differently/Flickr via CC BY 3.0

Fangio Nürgburgring: Willy Pragher/Landesarchiv Baden-Württemberg via CC BY 3.0

All others public domain.

The Air of a Gnawing-On
Learning to screw up when you already know how.

It never changes—the process is the process is the process.

HAGERTY, JANUARY 2022

Today, gathered friends, we shall discuss the eternal light and shade of the no-good, terrible, awful, only lightly bad day.

Fair warning: We shall also touch upon the joys and pains of lacquer, the clumsiness of my father, my own inheritance of that last quality, an exquisitely loud and extremely cheap Italian motorcycle, and, tangentially, a Fender Stratocaster.

But first, my bungling.

I make mistakes. Not every day, but they happen. Trust nobody who can't say the same. There is a place in hell for people who have never failed, and that place is almost certainly dull as roped soap, because people who have not screwed up are not very interesting, and, more to the point, they are mostly no fun. Along similar lines, each of us is gifted natural strengths. These strengths are also curses, in a sense, as they nudge us toward easy answers.

Like water, people tend to follow the path of least resistance. Do the same thing in the same way long enough, you dig yourself a rut.

As a form of quiet pushback there, I paint. Not with brushes. Often car parts. Occasionally model kits. Once, a guitar. I do this mostly because I'm bad at it. This week, I painted one particular motorcycle part several times, painstakingly wet-sanding to primer over the kitchen sink each time I screwed up.

This motorcycle arrived in my life in the same way that nice things don't—i.e., a friend called and insisted I take it. But no, I said! I have no money for extravagant purchases, however cheap! The kids need dental work! The pantry needs Cheez-Its! And so on, adult noises, yes!

But no, the person on the phone insisted: You are a person who rides and fixes motorcycles! (I am.) Don't you love this exact model of Ducati? (I long have.) Don't you enjoy projects? (I do.) Wouldn't you pay my incredibly low asking price, not much more than a sack of cheeseburgers, if the funds magically appeared in your account? (I would have, actually.)

Pay me years from now, he said. Just get it out of my house.

Not being totally dense except when presented with fast-food menus and the occasional Tuesday, I did.

Old Ducatis are like old Ferraris: all grappa-grope and drama, but buy-in is rarely tied to long-term spend. Also, nobody wants the scruffy ones. When the bike showed up, the bike was rattle-can black. It was originally red, of course, because all Ducatis are red, or at least, the Ducatis everyone remembers are red, in the way that every day in Paris is beautiful and Philly cheesesteaks never give anyone the industrial toots. An idea doesn't have to mirror reality to reflect why we show up.

The bike, a 1996 900 Super Sport, was straight and mechanically healthy but an obvious crash victim. Certain bits had the air of a gnawing-on by wolves. That black paint held more sags and orange peel than Florida. Bug fossils elbowed for space with sanding marks and dry spots. The right-hand fairing in particular looked to have played tonsil hockey with a belt sander.

Grime was ever-present. I tested the paint with a rag and lacquer thinner; the rag came away black.

Ah, I thought, I like lacquer.

Smithology

This deal, as it were, went down in early November. When the bike came home, weeks later, it met the ancient and sacred tally of new-arrival rituals: the Ceremonial Crevice Scrubbing, Ye Olde and Thorough Leak Inspection, Professor Smith's Medicinal Letting of Humours and Fluids. Evenings were lost to readings of history and factory service procedures. A to-do list was assembled; parts were ordered. Then, caught up in the bliss of a spare Sunday afternoon, I took a flyer on wet-sanding that trashface paint.

The tank was first. The finish there was deep enough that the embedded bugs and dirt rolled out easy. Buffing produced a solid, level gloss. Embiggened, I got carried away and sanded the rest of the bike, hours on end. Imagine attempting to polish dirt, only the process actually goes quite well, and then, magically, the dirt is a Renoir. Or maybe just a Velvet Elvis. Which is much like dirt but also a hunk of love.

Did the paint come up? It came *up*.

Painting the belt-sanded fairing seemed a sensible next step. (Reality: Not a belt sander. Probably a piece of road, grinding grinding grinding, as some excitable Ducati Boi slid along behind, yelling four-letter words into a helmet.) There was a gluing and filling, then a scuffing and leveling, a blowing-on of primer. Followed by a filling, more sanding, something like a guide coat, fill again, wait, poke at a bit, one last coat of primer, then color, then clear. Many evenings after work, laying paint outside or sanding over that kitchen sink.

With paint, the more you spray, the better you get. I don't paint near enough, so the whole process took more time than I would like to admit. Finally, et voilà, it was nearly done, one more coat to go.

Which is when I porked it.

Later, after a patient and calm repair of the problem, I porked it again. Same piece of bodywork, different mistake. The details of either screwup are irrelevant; suffice it to say that there was each time a sanding, and a return to primer, and a string of four-letter words.

As paint goes, lacquer is particularly forgiving. Problems in a finished work are often easily repaired and blended without starting over, and most flaws can be traced to errors in technique or prep. Spray often, the necessary process and care become second nature. Do it as a hobby, maybe once a year at most, that nature never locks in.

In the beginning, it's just color and work. Then the errors stack into mental noise, one atop another. The din prompts hurry, which prompts mistakes. Sometimes, the simple act of fighting the urge to be impatient . . . makes you impatient.

That fairing is now hung in my office, repaired one final time and curing. Because I am not always the brightest of bulbs, I did not immediately consider the panel's proximity to an old and finished project, a guitar I resprayed in 2018. That instrument was once black polyurethane and is now Sonic Blue, a 1950s General Motors color favored by Ike Turner and George Harrison. More of the old story: countless nights sanding to bare wood, then filling and priming interspersed by more sanding, then repeatedly attempting to spray, outdoors and under cover, a slice of dead tree I had unjustly come to see as fickle.

The guitar project took place at my parents' house in Seattle, a mile from my driveway. Seattle sees a lot of rain, and my house had no place to spray outdoors; Mom and Dad had a near-empty covered garage. More to the point, doing the job there gave casual reason to be around my mother. She had just been diagnosed with the aggressive brain tumor that would eventually kill her, but at that point in the curve, she was just Mom, Alice, funny and full of life, not wanting to make a deal of the obvious future.

Rain brings humidity. Expose drying lacquer to excessive moisture, the finish will blush, growing cloudy. I could probably tally just how many days and hours this process took—to say nothing of cans of paint—but it's more satisfying to pretend I don't remember.

Smithology

Lacquers cure through time and evaporation. Volatile organics creep from wet liquid to atmosphere, leaving pigment behind. Lacquer won't accept a final sand or buff until it has cured to a certain hardness, and that curing can take weeks, tied as it is to weather and composition. When the guitar finally looked half-decent, I hung it in a quiet corner of Mom and Dad's garage and left it to breathe.

Sometime after, Dad was rearranging a few things in there and managed to accidentally knock the head off a ceiling sprinkler. In the ensuing indoor deluge, the Strat fell to the floor, landing on concrete. (This is my father in a nutshell: a lifelong woodworker and a skilled craftsman, but also occasionally a pair of shoelaces tied together.)

The impact produced a few long cracks in the paint, plus two sizable gouges on the guitar's flank. Picture what a toddler could do with a chisel. Years later, those marks remain. I haven't fixed them and probably won't, but that doesn't mean I don't think about it. In the way that paint fumes and losing a parent can bring to mind a lot of things.

Totems are funny like that. That whole period in my life was me learning to deal with a stream of unpredictable events that I wanted to wish from existence, and now, well, those events mean something else.

Twenty-five years ago, I was 15, holding some birthday cash and money saved from odd jobs. Mom drove me to a local music shop, where we bought a mass-produced slab of wood covered in poly. That slab sits in my office now, blue like an old Cadillac, in reach of my desk.

That Ducati will go back together and get ridden. The paint will be done, one way or another, like the tired forks and leaky carbs. In the meantime, that black fairing hangs on a wall, quietly curing. Maybe the last step, though who can say for sure?

Lacquer, thankfully, is particularly forgiving.

Live at Birdland
Tracks and roads and Rufs and me.

Written for R&T's *70th anniversary. Obsessions always gain focus in the rearview. For eight years, from day one to the end, walking into that office left me geeked.*

Road & Track, July 2017

This magazine has taught me a lot, but the first thing I remember *R&T* telling me was that Ayrton Senna was dead. Those quicksilver hands and that bright yellow helmet, the last fiery icon in Formula 1, snuffed from existence, just 34 years old.

It was 1994. I was 13 and had never bought a car magazine. That first one I paid for had a $2.95 cover price and an August date. I still have that issue, though I don't know why. All I know is, whenever I try to throw it out, my arms freeze up.

Senna died in a race in Italy in May of that year. By August, when his obituary met these pages, I still had no clue he was gone. I had barely known he was alive to begin with. Our city paper didn't cover motorsport, and at 13, I wasn't reading it anyway. I didn't watch F1, and the nightly news put me to sleep. A name I didn't know had left a largely foreign pastime I little understood, but my $2.95 stack of paper was upset, so I read.

I had been reading for years, voraciously. Mostly history and fiction, from my father's bookshelf, because that's what was in the house and free. This is probably why, as the world's dorkiest middle schooler, I wanted little in life beyond a Jaguar D-type, a Ruf CTR, a North American X-15 rocket plane, a motorcycle, a brown-haired girlfriend to talk to me while I fixed said motorcycle and brooded, and a fine-art print of a 1962 Jesse Alexander photograph of Lotus F1 driver Jim Clark at Spa. (Goggles on his neck, eyes boring a hole in the camera, a whole era wrapped up in smoky black-and-white.)

Clark died in a Formula 2 car 13 years before I was born. The most graceful driver of a generation, but just one hero in a litany from those books: Colin Chapman, the virtuoso founder of Lotus. Dan Gurney. Phil Hill and Paul Frère, who each had cockpit careers before going on to write for *R&T*. Hundreds of other artists, from prewar Indy to NASA, who had either died or wrapped their glory before my time.

That's what happens when you meet an obsession through its history—you gravitate to emotion, and that usually means years ago, because nobody writes an epic poem about yesterday afternoon. I became convinced I had been born too late.

Until Senna. A polarizing risk of a man in a sport that had long seemed safe and level. I read our tribute in that August issue again and again, feeling emptier each time. One of history's brightest sparks, missed, because I had been too busy pining for the past.

Memories have a habit of going accordion, making old turning points feel like yesterday. But if *Road & Track* is 70, then Ayrton Senna has been gone for 23 years. Jim Clark was once one of the most famous men on wheels, but it'd be long odds for the average 2017 F1 reporter to pick him out of a lineup. Time dims the stage on everybody.

And then there's the Ruf CTR. Or rather, *the* CTR, CTR-001, the prototype. Thirty years ago, in a tiny German garage, a man named Alois Ruf disassembled a late-model Porsche 911. When he put the car back together, it had two turbochargers and a body so pared down, the radio antenna was a wire taped to the windshield. A week later, in an *R&T* test with Frère, Hill, and a mess of big-name supercars, that minimalist bullet went 211 mph, faster than any road car this magazine had ever seen. We nicknamed it "Yellow Bird," after its color and how it moved. Ruf tooled up for production, the world beat a path to his dyno room, and the Bird became widely beloved, a Cinderella legend.

I didn't discover that test until 10 years after it happened. Not a too-late jaw drop, though. Clark and Senna are gone, but you can find a 1980s 911 on half the street corners in America. Those cars are attainable commodities, which is why whipping one to 211 mph seems touchable voodoo, even now. Which, in turn, may have been why I went to find Alois himself, for a story in this issue. Last winter, in southern Germany, when the Alps were tipped with clouds. I figured the man would know something about perspective.

He still owns the car, essentially as it was. Blinding yellow paint, a mad howler of an engine, value like a lottery jackpot. But there was more there than mere old 911. Ruf's car was real and unprecious in a way I almost couldn't grasp, the magazine's golden age writ loud. Countless wins and losses, millions of words, Paul and Phil but also John Bond's manners, Henry Manney's raised eyebrow, Peter Egan's quiet optimism. In everything from the antenna tape to the hand-formed NACA ducts in the rear fenders.

Old cars often ooze story, but this was different. Possibly because the owner was different. Possibly because he fed me an espresso when I walked in the door, then insisted we rip the Bird's tach needle clean off the peg. We talked for hours. In a business defined by numbers and predictability, the man bubbles with happy surprises. Ruf's reputation could float his business for years, but he keeps chasing new projects, machines made better and more involving and smarter. Like most of my heroes, he seems incapable of discussing his life without laughing.

As with Senna and Clark, no one saw him coming. Ruf's appearance reaffirmed everything we care about around here. That surprises are constant if you know where to look. That while you can often guess the arc of the world, you can't predict the points that plot the curve. Or the power of a reset that shows up just when you need it.

Maybe that's why I kept the issue. I didn't know much at 13, but what little I did, I don't want to forget.

Gone Away
Early coda.

We are never so dismantled as when we lose the person who taught us to care about others—and never so comforted as when we realize how many others they taught.

HAGERTY, AUGUST 2020

Years ago, my mother drove a Volvo. An automatic wagon, navy blue, a 240 DL bought new in 1985. A model once seen everywhere, dotting freeways and side streets, until it wasn't, that day when they all disappeared into junkyards. Gone, at least from daily sight.

Mom is gone as well, now. She died earlier this year, at 65, after a 21-month battle with a brain tumor that seemed hell-bent on killing her and finally did. She was a contradiction, a private and often shy woman but also a goofy and vibrant firecracker, the kind of person who found a friend in every new room.

My mother played the piano but long refused to do so in front of family. As an adult, during visits home, I would often pause on the front porch for a second after climbing out of the car, listening with a hope of hearing her at the keys. She was, just once, and the music stopped when

I opened the front door, but the moment left a dent. As did the soft, resigned laugh that followed, before she rose to give me a hug.

The Volvo was special. My parents bought the 240 new, at her urging, when I was four. "I didn't think I was a Volvo person?" she told me, years later, her voice still tinted with surprise. But they signed the papers because of her; she had seen the wagon on a dealer's lot one day and fallen head over heels. The deal happened quick. My dad, a sports-car nut since high school, had never owned anything so intentionally stolid, yet he, too, saw something in the car. Possibly just extreme fitness for purpose, a man with a family admiring a resolved, durable solution.

Volvos sneak up on you like that, especially if parts of your personality defy easy classification. (Dad later quit his job to open a restoration shop that doubled as a bookstore, partly because my father and I are similarly bent, but that's a story for another time.) The blue car, brick-shaped and simple, was capable of sneaking up on precisely nothing else. Not even speed traps. That 240 racked up a stack of tickets over the years, usually in my mother's hands, despite offering a 0-to-60 time measurable by sundial. As far as I could tell, my father found the tickets both funny and irritating but mostly funny, which should tell you something about my family.

Mom and Dad lived on the West Coast when she was diagnosed. Less than a year later, the finances of modern healthcare nudged them back to a more affordable life in Louisville, Kentucky, where they had met as children. They put their lives in storage and moved in temporarily with my aunt, planning to look for a house. When Mom's condition deteriorated, the house search was put on hold. This spring, she simply went to sleep for a week and never woke up.

My dad is like me but a generally better person—quieter, kinder, more thoughtful. I can't fathom what his shoes now feel like, but I can certainly imagine being so suddenly adrift. Probably because it doesn't take much imagination.

Dad needed a place of his own, he said, so he chewed on his finances a while and considered possibilities. The resulting purchase had a roof and walls but no fixed address. A used Mercedes-Benz Sprinter Sportsmobile RV, two years old, with a kitchenette, a shower, a toilet, a diesel, and a dinette that morphed into two beds. The Volvo parallel made me chuckle: He had made interested noises about RVs before but never seemed the type. On family road trips when I was little, he would grumble at motorhomes, their heft and size, scowl as they slouched into the left lane on freeways.

Over the phone this spring, I heard a shift in tone. "I am not an RV person," he insisted. "But I like this." Many calls followed, discussing health, possibility, anything but brain tumors. The classified ad he sent showed an unassuming, slab-sided van, a visual cross between Spacelab and a hormonal Jeep.

Sportsmobile was founded in 1961. The company converts commercial vans into RVs for on- and off-road travel. Its products are unaligned with stereotype—not a motor coach or bus, not an 8000-pound road barn with fiberboard cabinets and a name like Freedom Wolf Rambler. Sportsmobiles are famously expensive for a van but also famously durable, not to mention cheap for a house. Resale value errs high, a byproduct of limited production and quality, which means you can own one for a bit and move on without losing your shirt.

In the months since Mom's death, Dad has generally kept to himself. He tries to be smart about pandemic safety, but he's retired, so there's no mandatory human interaction. Solitude and traveling seem to suit him, and neither is perpetual. Every so often, my wife and I will quarantine ourselves and our kids in the house, verifying our health and lack of virus, then Dad will sling down a highway and come live in our driveway for a bit. Those moments are nice for a hundred reasons.

I hadn't actually driven the Mercedes until last week. A work assignment popped up in Jacksonville, Florida, around nine hours from the house. Too far to drive and work without a pause for sleep. Dad, nearby, offered to come with. We drove down, shot a feature story at a museum, then walked out to the Mercedes and went to bed in the parking lot. The independence was refreshing, business done privately. It probably helped that the emotional wallop of a lost parent can run tidal, strong one day and quieter the next.

When we left for Jacksonville, I had wanted out of the house. I had also wanted to ask my father about my mother, who she was when I wasn't around. In the Sprinter, barreling down I-75, the answers seemed echo-free and better for it.

Dad doesn't seem to know where he'll go when the world drifts back to normal. He seems happy with the RV, despite not being an RV person. Or perhaps that kind of broad labeling is silly, and we all are far more similar than we like to admit, and people aren't ever really gone, they're just no longer present in the manner to which we're accustomed, and we simply don't know or fully acknowledge any of this stuff in the moment, because we can't or won't or don't know how.

The answers grow fuzzier every day. I'm 39. Mom was almost certainly older than that the last time she got pulled over. My last speeding ticket was years ago, though I can't remember when. Funny how few things can make you feel as restless as an inability to recall the last time you got caught.

The Sprinter seemed to lose interest over 80 mph, and thus it never earned any interest from the law and the consequent chance to reset the counter on that forgotten time between transgressions. Mom would have liked it, I think. My daughters like it, our two little girls in elementary school, and they remind me of her in countless ways.

A lot of singing in the house, for one thing. Another parallel, but a funny one, because I can't recall ever hearing her sing. Only the music of a person I miss more than I can say, heard and hinted at over decades, almost but never quite enough.

Section Two
The Machines

Nashville, Tennessee, 1984

WE CANNOT TALK ABOUT MACHINES and my life without addressing the time I did something galactically dumb in what was then one of the hottest cars on the planet.

When it was over, when I was back at the office—when I knew for certain I was about to lose the job I had chased for most of my life—my phone rang. I picked it up, wincing.

Wrong number. Tension bled from my shoulders. Then one of the magazine's senior editors stuck his head in the door.

"Jean's back. At her desk."

My heart tried to climb out my ears.

Seconds later, I was standing in front of my boss, a tall and imposing woman who had worked in our industry since before I was born. She looked up from her computer, unblinking, and pointed at a chair. As one might when a 26-year-old individual in your employ has, on an otherwise quiet weekday afternoon, thrown a hand-built, 500-horse vehicle in your care ass-backward into a ditch.

"What the fuck happened," she said. Not a question.

I took a breath, sat down, and began to talk. I said too much; she listened and said nothing. When I finished, the silence held for a minute.

I was getting fired; I knew that. I had never been fired. I hadn't even had another desk job. I had been in that office less than 12 months and arrived there directly from slinging oil filters and floor mats at the parts counter of a Chicago Jaguar dealer. I briefly wondered if that dealer would take me back, tried to recall the part number for an XJ8 filter, realized I couldn't, broke out in cold sweat.

Jean glared across the desk. I was, she said, a tremendous pain in the ass. My choices that day had locked her into a string of phone calls, insurance discussions, hard looks at budgets. And that, she added, didn't even count the reputation hit once word got out.

I sank into my chair. She aimed a finger at my chest—what was I thinking? Who could be so stupid? You think you can drive, that doesn't matter, the industry has puked out thousands better.

A deliberate sigh. "You have potential. But don't think I'm doing this because I want to."

I blinked.

Smithology

"Let me be perfectly clear: The only reason you still have a *job*"—the word hung in the air for a second—"is because you can write."

I still had a job.

I still had a *job?*

I looked up from my lap. "Uh, thank y—"

"Don't thank me. Don't even apologize. This is fucking unacceptable."

Like an idiot, I repeated myself.

"I told you," she spat back, "*do not fucking thank me*. Or forget."

In that exact moment, I wanted nothing more than a stout whack of amnesia.

"Now get out."

Day's events aside, I was not a complete fool, so I did.

For reasons that seemed entirely sensible at the time and now strike as anything but, I had, that morning, asked to borrow a brand-new, $150,000 Ford GT from the magazine's test fleet.

Resistance was met. I was one of just a few staffers with a competition license, but I was also young. Be careful, they said. Of course, I said.

And yet.

At that point in history, the test fleet of a large American car magazine was essentially a rotating library of sheetmetal. At *Automobile*, where I worked, that library was catalogued at the front of the office, on a wide dry-erase board divided into a grid of models and dates, which cars were set to arrive or depart and when. That board turned over constantly, new vehicles coming and going nearly every day, generally on loan from their manufacturers in hope of coverage.

This system applied to everything on the market, literally every make and model on sale. Moreover, every car that hit that board was factory-fresh, mileage in the low four figures at most. Keys were released to the staff through an opaque calculus that prioritized editorial need, i.e., who had been assigned to test, write about, or photograph what. Once those concerns had been addressed, a car was essentially up for grabs, circulating among editors by seniority for the remainder of its one- or two-week loan. The only exceptions to the process were limited-production exotics like Ferraris and Lamborghinis. The loan agreements for those rarities were generally more restrictive—mileage caps to preserve resale value, insurance mandates for driver age, and so on.

The product in question, model year 2006.

If the whole arrangement sounds like a dream, that's because it was. And in some cases, that's how it remains. Large test fleets, or rather, publications large enough to need them, are now rare, but a few outlets still work that way today.

The industry has changed in other ways, of course. A case tangential to this story: Since 2012, the National Highway Traffic Safety Administration has mandated that every new passenger vehicle sold in America feature, as standard, a complex software-hardware suite designed to keep the tires on the road after a loss of driver control. Those systems are generally referred to as electronic stability control, or ESC for short.

Which brings us back to that ditch.

ESC first appeared on a production car, a Mercedes-Benz, in 1995. Ten years later, the technology had saved countless lives but remained far from ubiquitous. The 2005–2006 Ford GT, for example, did not feature stability control. That fact is relevant only because I would have turned that system off, had it been present. Which is relevant only because a person does not do that sort of thing in a mid-engine supercar they have just met unless they are halfway decent at the wheel, monumentally stupid, or, in my case, both.

The Ford was not a thing to suffer fools. What it was, was a 44-inch-tall, supercharged-V-8 tribute to the time in the 1960s when Henry Ford II spent half the money in creation to land his company a series of overall wins at the 24 Hours of Le Mans. That story is a totem of midcentury car culture; the '05–'06 GT was and remains evocative, massively fast and involving. Nice examples now bring more than double the factory sticker.

A coworker was with me. We left the office like adults and drove sedately to the far side of town, where we drove like dickheads. Maybe 30 minutes later, wanting to be responsible, we reversed course and headed back. The freeway was quickest. I was convinced of much. On the left-turn entry to a long and straight on-ramp, I hucked the Ford into a tidy drift. A stab of throttle and a flick of the wheel as the rear tires spit loose, then more throttle for balance.

The V-8 hosed out noise; the coworker howled. "You're an animal!"

Growing up, I did not make friends easily. I was a quiet kid, racked with insecurity. By 26, however, I had spent a few years in sanctioned road racing, liked sliding cars and was comfortable doing it. And at that wheel, for a heartbeat, I was smug.

The catch, with being smug: If you don't think about the consequences, it feels *great*.

A millisecond later, a voice upstairs reminded me I had always been good at this. I grew greedy, indulged the voice, flicked the steering opposite. My right foot added volume, turned that first bursting drift into a longer, paint-laying slither up the ramp.

The young human brain can be so eager to reveal its roots as a pile of monkey parts. Time slowed to a crawl. *One more,* I thought—a snap decision, the Ford still greasing up the ramp sideways, what could it hurt?

An encore, another flick, Sam is the Greatest. There was now more inertia to deal with, however, more speed and suspension compression after that slither, energy awaiting release. I'd been too preoccupied congratulating myself to think about that, though, and my inputs were too sloppy to keep up. The Ford jinked back opposite, changing direction quicker than before. The monkey wetware bricked. My right foot went full BIOS reset and snapped to the floor, muscle memory from slow slides in the underpowered cars I had learned to drive in.

It was the king of wrong answers. The GT flung around, we were backward, we were bad backward, we were reverse-flying backward and mowing down grass.

Ages later, probably whole seconds, we came to a stop.

My passenger shook his head and cursed. "Jesus. Are you alright?"

Yes, I said. Both true and a lie.

I hyperventilated for a bit. Out the driver's-side window, a car drove by, hubcaps level with my head. We were in a ditch in tall grass, against a line of bushes. Twenty minutes prior, that part of town had been empty. By the time I collected myself and climbed from the car, it was rush hour, the ramp filled with rubberneckers.

A few slowed to ask if we needed help. The rest were cell phone cameras and heckling. An older man in a pickup idled by. "Learn to drive, asshole!"

No shit, I thought. No. Shit.

Years passed. I spent too much time at work, writing, editing, and driving for the place from which I had not been fired, constantly trying to improve at all of it. I moved to California for a different job and to New York for another after that. Then, visiting Detroit one winter, I met the Ford GT's designer one night, entirely by accident.

It was snowing. My wife was with me; we were meeting an industry friend at a jazz club downtown. Walking in, I glanced at the bar and caught an unmistakable face.

Spotting notable car people in Detroit is like spotting actors on the street in Manhattan: If you don't know them personally, you leave them alone. Camilo Pardo, then in his forties, was a local celebrity; he had styled the GT, a design beloved by the industry, then left Ford to consult and paint car-adjacent art, which everyone also loved. He wore a thin goatee and a ponytail in a fashion that reminded me of 1960s F1 driver Jo Bonnier, except Bonnier was Swedish and Pardo's family is from Latin America.

We found a table and I went to the bar to order drinks. The club was busy, and a stool by the designer was the only spot open. He was facing the other direction and talking to a tall blonde. I gave the bartender our order and poked at my phone as I waited.

My drink came quickly, but the others took a bit longer. Pardo's chat ended. He turned to the bartender for a refill. There was a tap on my arm.

"You look familiar."

I shrugged, smiling. "Maybe work? I'm a journalist."

A polite nod. "Yeah, maybe? You have a mysterious look."

Not knowing what to do with that, I tried my best to look . . . unmysterious. "I do?"

"Yes! It's a good look." He pointed at my head. "I like the hat."

Detroit gets cold in winter. I was in a phase where I had convinced myself that I did not look ridiculous in an English-style flat cap.

"Thanks."

"I think I should draw you."

I was, at this point, a few gulps into my cocktail. The bartender had apparently gone heavy on the jet fuel. "Uh. Okay?"

Pardo fished a Sharpie from his jacket and grabbed a napkin from the bar. There was a quick sketch, head down, long and slashing strokes. He looked up. "What's your name?"

He wrote it on the napkin, signing the drawing with a flourish. As I thanked him, the rest of our drinks arrived. I picked them up and nodded, he nodded back, and then I did that thing where you use two hands to carry three glasses across a dark and crowded room and surprise yourself by spilling nothing.

At the table, my industry friend snatched the napkin off the table. "Camilo!" he barked, grinning. "I was telling Adrienne about him. Did he draw you like one of his French girls?"

Adrienne, mid-sip, doubled over and tried to keep whiskey from coming out her nose. The friend laughed, pleased with himself, then went serious.

"No, really, though, I'm sorry. That's very cool."

"Thanks. Weird, right?"

"Did you tell him you crashed one of his cars?" He collapsed into laughter again.

A live band had begun to play on the other side of the room. I held up the napkin in mock offense.

"I have a good art of me now," I yelled over the music, "and you're both just *jealous*."

The two fell to giggles. We spent the rest of the night bar-hopping around Detroit, and I didn't once think about the crash in that GT.

When I got home from that trip, I left the napkin on my desk for a bit, then stashed it in the back of a drawer. It sat there, mostly forgotten, until a few years ago, when Adrienne and I were packing for one of our many cross-country moves.

All moves are the same in a way, the same game of cardboard *Tetris*. I was sitting on the floor in my home office, slowly nesting my life into boxes, the floor stacked with files and books. We had a dog then, a spaniel named Elly. Elly was not a particularly bright bulb, as spaniels go, but she was charming, which is to say, she had a habit of bounding loudly around the house and banging off walls at random hours that I found charming, because I am a dupe for living cartoons that love me.

Elly bounded into my office. It was the kind of surprise HELLO HI HELLO interpretive superball dance that dogs do so well, a train of arbitrary leaps over various items not at all in her way capped by a quick falling-down and some distracted scratching. When she finished, I stood up and turned around, reaching for a glass of water I'd been drinking, to keep it from spilling. Except the dog chose that moment to jump up again and run through my legs and out the door, and then I lost my balance, and then I somehow managed to trip backward over three boxes at once and land in a heap on the floor.

I stood up, sighing, and surveyed the room. The whole episode had lasted around five seconds and tossed half my stacks to hell. More important, somewhere in that whole slow-motion Looney Tunes waltz, the glass had gone horizontal, shotgunning water across the rug. The damage seemed minor at first—a book about Ducatis I hadn't read in years, some papers for a motorcycle I no longer owned. Then I found the napkin. It had somehow ended up with the Duc book and was now soaked and crumbling.

I laid the soggy little thing on my desk, flattening it out as best I could, then recognized the futility and tossed it in the trash. The Ford crash replayed in my head for the first time in maybe a decade.

When I was younger, I would berate myself endlessly for screwups. I thought it was a necessary part of getting better. I can't tell you what changed or when, only that I'm glad it did.

Few things are as interesting as what we don't at first see. Cliché paints the automobile as speed and possibility. It is also, lest we forget, a fiendishly effective device for the production of air and noise pollution, for choking the growth of cities, for separating us from much of what makes life worthwhile—nature, exercise, human connection. We knew none of those downsides when we birthed the thing, and yet the machine itself remains much more than those grumbles. It can be a snapshot of where and who we were in a given moment, from society in general to a person in specific. It can serve as a lodestone for memories and decisions, a snow globe of feelings long gone. A lens through which to view the world or a catalyst for falling in love. A log of mistakes and their lessons.

None of this is unique; we hang similar meaning on many of the objects we make. But it's perhaps hint as to why so many books and films about cars are so boring: They chase the obvious over the animate. Over the inevitable byproducts of life and compromise, how our decisions are always compassed by who we are and where we've been.

We can go places in a piece of that. Use it to bring home more groceries than we can carry, cross a country on a whim, skate through corners on a Sunday feeling more alive than we have all week. How cool is that?

Brand of Enchantment
Italy the unimprovable.

In 2014, Alfa Romeo returned to America after 19 years away. For a while there, virtually every new Alfa we tested was broken. I adored the marque anyway, always have. What's the line from Pulp Fiction? *Personality goes a long way?*

ROAD & TRACK, AUGUST 2018

There is never anything wrong with an Alfa Romeo. Maybe you find parts you don't like, or maybe a piece of the seat falls off in your hand and the sunroof refuses to shut because of some software quirk. That's just the universe poking you with a test light, to see if you're any good. A true dyed-in-the-wool wheel-and-pedal man (or lady, or child) will find everything ostensibly wrong with an Alfa Romeo and then label it not so much wrong as accident.

Too much grappa at lunch on the assembly line. A few typos in the code. The best of intentions, ruined by gremlins.

Because there is never anything wrong with an Alfa.

I worked on Alfas once. After college, in Missouri, for a living. My boss was a man named Carter Hendricks. Carter was an Alfa Person.

His shop was perpetually full of old Italian things. Also a lot of stuff that was not Italian but interesting anyway. We listened to a lot of Billie Holiday, on a small, single-ended tube amplifier that Carter had designed and built. It filled rooms on something like half a watt of output and made instruments seem to be playing inside your bones.

I told Carter that I wanted to be a writer, and so we talked about writing, but also Alfas and Lancias and the 1930s French Grand Prix driver René Dreyfus. Usually with my head buried in an old Duetto or Giulia Super or some other piece of genius. But that action was always unnecessary, because those cars never needed repair, because there was never anything wrong with them.

We argued occasionally. Possibly because I was, in the years immediately following college, an occasionally argumentative and tone-deaf doofus. But there was never anything wrong with Carter. Or me, come to think of it.

I was reminded of those days shortly after the launch of the current Alfa Giulia. Pretty car. Perhaps afflicted by the line-grappa. Last summer, I wrote a piece for *R&T*'s website about the problems encountered with Giulia test vehicles by various journalists. A *Motor Trend* writer had a car refuse to ascend his driveway. A friend at *Jalopnik* was stranded by the side of an interstate. *Car and Driver*'s technical director grew so gun-shy, after watching various Giulias misbehave in testing, that he brought an OBD-II trouble-code reader on the press launch of Alfa's Stelvio SUV.

Not isolated incidents. Obviously the result of mass hallucination. But still.

That web story got a decent amount of traffic. Maybe because I wrote passionately, with staggering skill and impeccable rhetoric. I referenced my history with and love for the marque. (High point: testing Nuvolari's Nürburgring-winning Tipo B grand-prix car. Low point: Michigan's GingerMan Raceway with a 505-hp Giulia Quadrifoglio that collapsed into limp mode at the first sign of yaw.) I have to believe my disappointment registered with the world, because everyone on earth reads my writing, the best thing anyone has ever done with words.

I later referenced Alfa history while filming a YouTube video. Responses appeared on Alfa-enthusiast sites. "Really starting to get annoyed," one read, by "this talk about Alfa not being reliable." Another suggested that I go write for *Kittens and Cuddles* magazine. (Good journalism there, if a bit fluffy.) "Meh," said a third—my thoughts were "nonsense."

I nodded as I read those words; they were right. Flaws do not exist on an Alfa, because no flawed thing is ever worth loving, and the Quadrifoglio was one of the few modern cars I had ever loved. Shame washed over me like cold rain.

A few days after that web story ran, I received a call from Reid Bigland. Bigland was then global head of Alfa Romeo and Maserati, at Fiat Chrysler. He had on the line with him Roberto Fedeli, Alfa's chief technical officer. A 26-year veteran of Ferrari before coming to the marque from Milan. They wanted to talk Giulia.

Here it comes, I thought. There are no problems, on an Alfa.

"I want to apologize," Bigland said, on the phone. "We have had some software issues with the car."

Fedeli spoke English with an Italian accent. They had delayed the start of Giulia production, he said, to make sure the cars were right. Mine and others were not. This was embarrassing, but they would like to make it right. Would I like a loan of another test Quad, for another track day?

It seemed a generous offer. Time passed, and then there was a hole in my travel schedule. I made a few calls and ended up at Buttonwillow Raceway Park, outside Los Angeles, with a blue Quadrifoglio. The car was dialed, fast, dreamy, impeccable. A BMW M3 with better steering. A Mercedes C63 without a box of anvils welded to the front bumper. It chewed Buttonwillow to bits, no hiccups. The best Quad I had driven, in terms of brake modulation, damper goodness, the indescribable variation that can separate identical items built on the same production line.

Which was nice, but also somewhat expected. Grain of salt, right? You do not often get a misbehaving car sent to you by the chief of the dang company.

I was sitting in the paddock thinking about this, windows down and stereo on, when a track worker walked up. White pants and shirt, carrying a flag, the whole deal. She laughed and smiled. Stuck her head in the passenger window.

"This thing's great. How is it?"

I reached over to turn off the music. The second I touched the volume knob, the center-console screen went dead, controls neutered. The music kept going.

I did a double take. Then a smile back, out the window, unable to keep from laughing.

"You know," I said, "it's flawless."

The Dream of City Life
"Mr. Brauner, is your JDM hootbox trying to seduce me?"

> *Griff Shelley read a Hagerty column I wrote about wanting more funky old iron. Then he emailed and offered me his 260,000-mile Volvo for free. One thing led to another, I dreamed up and ran an essay contest where we gave the car to a lucky reader, and now I want a Honda City and to maybe live in Spokane.*

HAGERTY, NOVEMBER 2022

The interior was mostly gone. The engine burped out blats and toots. One lane over, in another car, the owner beamed.
I drove! A Honda City!
A track-prepped 1992 Honda City!
A small car that bops down the road like an exclamation point and thus virtually requires said punctuation upon reference!
Sean Brauner's Honda was not the reason I left my house in Tennessee before dawn on a Monday and flew to Spokane, Washington for just under 24 hours. What it was was icing on the cake.
For this we blame Griff Shelley, another Spokanite. Griff introduced me to Sean. The two have known each other since grade school. Griff

recently helped Hagerty give away a scruffy old Volvo 240 in a contest I dreamed up. I was in Washington for that contest's finale, to hand the 240 to the winner. Griff allowed as how we should stop by his friend Sean's place, maybe take a few of the man's tiny foreign cars to dinner.

Opt-outs were evaluated. A migraine had checked into my skull on the flight. Insomnia the night before had allowed just two hours of sleep. One of my shoelaces was fraying. Trivial stuff.

"Do not," I told Griff, "threaten me with a good time."

This all took place in a Pacific Northwest autumn. It was thus persistently raining, or just about to rain, or perhaps slowly drying up before the sky tried something different for a change, such as having the clouds whiz out a few quintillion bits of water from very high up. I stood in Sean's driveway and recalled, through the miracle of sensory flashback, why I once lived in Seattle. Also why I developed there a coffee intake stout enough to wake Caesar. I looked at Sean's garage, unsure.

"You really don't care if we drive these in the wet?"

"Nah," he said, chipper. "Gives me a reason to clean them again!"

Thirty-two years old, Brauner appears to have solved one of life's key equations. He seems happy. One piece of that happiness is the improbably large four-car garage behind his modest suburban home, built by a previous owner. Inside, on that Monday, sat a track-prepped 1991 Honda Beat (660-cc four, rear-drive and mid-engine, a roadster), a virtually stock 1989 Mazda Familia (1.8-liter turbo four, all-wheel-drive, a two-door hatch). And, in the corner, that modded City.

As the doors rolled up, I stood there, blinking.

"Please tell me," I said, "that you basically woke up one day, like, I have a real job, I have some money . . . screw it, we're buying tiny s*** from Japan."

He laughed. "Basically, yeah."

Later, over drinks, Sean outlined the process. The development of a relationship with a Japanese broker. Hours spent poring through listings on a Japanese wholesale-auction site. Then, finally, a purchase, sight unseen and dusted with faith. Some fun little right-hand-driver common enough to be frighteningly affordable and small enough to be shipped across the Pacific for pennies. Crucially, at no point in all this did Sean pay markup to a stateside importer or hop a plane to Tokyo.

The conversation was eye-opening. People privately import old Japanese cars all the time; because most Americans err toward rare models, however, the process usually means big spend. Having pondered importing an R32 Nissan GT-R for years, I had never considered anything like Sean's approach. I had simply assumed all paths were costly, no matter the car.

When the Hondas fired up, my headache vanished. A stock '92 City weighs 1700 pounds. The 1.3-liter, 6500-rpm four at the front wheels of Sean's car made 100 hp when new. His engine had been modified in Japan before he bought it, however, and might have been stronger. Curb weight was also likely lighter than stock.

I was so geeked, I forgot to ask specifics on either, which is fine, because specifics are irrelevant. We are dealing here with a vehicle larger than a Japanese *kei* car, that class of famously tiny, 660-cc commuter boxes, e.g., Honda Beat. A City is, however, still a Nipponese subcompact, which makes it smaller than any sane automobile sold in America in decades. You could park one in a household bathroom and still have room to flush.

Not a half-bath, though. Only the big ones, with the double sinks.

Dinner was at a brewery about 40 minutes away. I drove the Mazda there and climbed out buzzing. After we ate, I drove the City back to Sean's house, following Griff in the Mazda.

Griff did not appear to be slouching at the wheel. Or maybe the Honda was simply so puny-spicy-loud-vibrate-punk that every lane change at

From a 1989 Mazda Familia, which is not a Stephen King novel but probably should be.

the speed limit required full *touge* aggro. When the door latched shut, my mental age dropped by about three decades. Impromptu stoplight drags were held constantly and lost to anything on wheels. The car resembled every not-sold-here foreign-market supermini I have ever tried, just with more, as the vulgar say, f***.

There may have been a racing seat. The shifter was a footlong chrome stick under a white cue ball. (Pep *Boysozuku*?) The Alcantara steering wheel was dished, but only enough to feed a dog. Somewhere in that four-cylinder fuel compactor lived, on an exercise wheel with a squeaky bearing, a rodent of unusual size. Meanwhile, a large baseball card under the taillights flapped against the spokes of a bent wire wheel stolen from what I can only assume was some poor Tokyo kid's bicycle.

Cliché? Is the rhetorical question a lazy writing device? When the legend turns fact, who doesn't print the legend?

Oh no, he accidentally left flash on and a pothole kept the lens from focusing WHAT IF IT LOOKS UNPROFESSIONAL. Once, I went to Japan and bought two giant bags of squid jerky from a 7-11 near Ebisu Circuit. It tasted like this picture looks.

Every modified car is an assemblage of choices. One of the fun parts of this business is how the sum of those choices can be outside your personal taste but so cohesive as to be unassailable. Turning the City's steering wheel moved relevant items in the car's undergarments, where some enterprising individual had, as the British say, offered up extra spring rate, then installed aftermarket shocks with bags of rebound. A comically excessive yet somehow cheery amount of caster afflicted the front axle. Mere inches away was a large and invisible speaker that kept distracting me in traffic by playing a loop of some middle-aged Tennessee dude spitting peals of laughter.

The City's roll cage was one of those odd setups where the front downtubes bend in such a way as to suggest immediate fold-over in a crash. After some consideration, I simply resolved to not crash. The execution of this plan did not lack entertainment, except when the Honda entered a corner in such a way as to basically scream for full commitment, which was always, which is probably why someone gave it a roll cage to begin with.

On a rain-slicked road whose name I can't recall, that baseball card flapping away, the City and I went hooping into a roundabout at max throttle.

In Japan, in the early 1980s, an earlier model of Honda City offered, as an accessory, a gasoline-powered scooter that had been engineered to fold up and stow in the trunk. That scooter was called the Honda Motocompo.

Years ago, in a friend's shop, I sat on a Motocompo and made a face.

In the roundabout, my face made the face again.

The author, 2017, containing himself.

Tuesday morning, Sean and Griff and I met the Volvo winner, a lovely Maine man named Matt, at a diner for breakfast. I asked how everyone got into cars.

"When I was 16," Sean said, almost apologetically, "a lady in my neighborhood let me drive her Z06."

I blinked loudly. "The Corvette?!?"

"She offered! My mom said it was okay, so I did."

The remainder of that story was cute and not at all salacious. Because of course, why not, people put 16-year-old neighborhood boys in their 405-horse Vettes... all the time?

I drowned my French toast in syrup and pondered moving to Spokane.

In 1989, when I was eight, Disney released an animated film called *The Little Mermaid*. In one scene, a seagull voiced by the comedian Buddy Hackett explains, to the mermaid, various objects retrieved from shipwrecks. One of those items is a tobacco pipe.

97

The mermaid has not lived in the environment for which the pipe was made. She lacks context. The pipe's original owner likely saw it as dull tool; to the mermaid, it is rare and confusing delight.

"It's a snarfblatt," the bird announces, confident, after a short inspection. "To make fine music." Then he puts the pipe in his mouth and blows through it like a trumpet. A glop of sand spurts out.

"I wanted to live deep and suck all the marrow out of a D13C that doesn't know what country it's in." —Honda David Thoreau

At eight years old, I found this hilarious. It is still funny.

Sean told me what he paid for the City, shipping included. My jaw dropped. I would share the figure, but then you might grow obsessed, try to call the guy and buy the car. That, I have come to realize, is my job.

Twenty-four hours in eastern Washington, a dinky Honda, a cured headache. A good day, as Cube said. On the plane home, over this country's vast middle, I alternated between catching up on sleep and daydreaming construction projects for my house.

Somewhere above Nebraska, it occurred to me that each of those projects was entirely unaffordable. Each was something I desperately wanted to add to my life but don't really need, or storage for objects of that type. Occasionally both.

None of those projects was a bathroom. Even though each looked, for all the world, exactly like one.

The One

An oral history of the McLaren F1, the supercar that broke us all.

An icon that defined an age and means so much to so many. And another story for R&T's *70th anniversary. The photos here are my phone snaps—I've been fortunate enough to test two of these cars, including an ex-Le Mans GTR on the track. Both examples were every bit as good as the hype, and that's saying a lot.*

ROAD & TRACK, JULY 2017

The last great analog car was built, in just 107 examples, from 1992 to 1998. The roadgoing version had a world-first carbon-fiber frame; a 627-hp, 7500-rpm BMW V-12; a six-speed manual gearbox; and a driver's seat mounted in the middle, aping an open-wheel race car.

You did not get anti-lock or power brakes, traction control, power steering, or anything even remotely like an electronic safety net, despite the fact that this vehicle cost nearly $1 million at launch. (Or that most of those features were standard on machines costing far less.)

What you did get was the fastest road car in history—231 mph. Even today, it remains one of the least compromised road machines ever built.

None of that was by accident. From general layout to minor design touches, the McLaren F1 was dictated by the will of one remarkable engineer. And it came from a small, eminently focused company at the height of its powers. By 1993, McLaren had won seven Formula 1 constructors' championships and three Indianapolis 500s. Gordon Murray, the F1's chief designer, had come to the marque after a stint at Brabham, where he had penned two title-winning Formula 1 cars. Once in Woking, he codesigned the McLaren that gave Ayrton Senna his first F1 championship.

Neither Murray nor McLaren had ever built a road car, but the company gave him carte blanche. He got whatever he wanted, from an engine cover lined with real gold foil to that landmark V-12. The latter was the work of BMW Motorsport's Paul Rosche, the genius behind the German firm's title-winning Formula 1 four-cylinder. Working with a small team of engineers, Rosche built the F1's engine in just nine months, after McLaren partner Honda got cold feet.

The car weighed 2425 pounds dry. In an age when most of America lacked internet access, the F1 came with a built-in 14.4k modem for sending diagnostic information to the factory. McLaren famously flew mechanics around the world to service it, often at customer homes. Murray had never wanted to take the car racing, but customer demand prompted the creation of a variant specifically for that purpose, the F1 GTR, initially little more than a production F1 with a roll cage. FIA rules left the model 27 hp down on its roadgoing sister, but it won Le Mans anyway. And pretty much everything else they threw at it.

The F1 was unveiled to the public 25 years ago, in May 1992. Astonishingly, every supercar since has been something of a dilution. The Bugatti Veyron is faster but more complicated and distant. Porsche's landmark Carrera GT is a decade newer but slower to 60 mph and more difficult to drive at any speed. Even McLaren's own 903-hp P1 hybrid hypercar, which just left production, is 14 mph slower and a third of a ton heavier.

The F1's origins have been covered to death, but we wanted to illuminate the thing's life past the factory gates. To lift the veil and take a look at the living, breathing car underneath. Because above all, that's what Murray wanted to create—not the museum piece or investment that his work has become.

We spoke with owners, racing drivers, and various lights in the car's orbit, and we found a story that still holds lessons. And a reminder that, while the world may now be faster and smarter, a quarter century later, there is still only one F1.

Living With It

Jay Leno (*Owner*): Well, I've had mine almost 20 years. When the car came out, there were so many other supercars just coming out—Vector [W8], [Jaguar] XJ220, Bugatti EB 110. The Jaguar was the most expensive. Six-hundred-thousand-dollar range. And all of a sudden, you had this car that was close to a million dollars.

How much better could the million-dollar one be? Is it really three or four times better than a Lamborghini or Ferrari? And of course it was, but nobody knew it at the time.

Charles Nearburg (*Owner*): If you blindfolded somebody and put them in it, they'd be hard-pressed to say it wasn't made yesterday.

Roger Chatfield (*Composites technician, McLaren*): When the company was that much smaller, they arranged for the whole factory . . . every person could have a run at one. For me, [McLaren director] Creighton Brown was driving. He said, "We're going to start by demonstrating its torque ability." Basically, he just put it in gear, didn't touch the throttle. The car started moving away. Next gear, car moving away, still no throttle. We're just going up through the gears with no throttle. It's like, This is bogus. This shouldn't be working.

NEARBURG: It's actually sprung quite softly. Much more body roll than a "modern" supercar. You realize Gordon knew what he was doing. He built a package that generates extraordinarily high *g*'s, but it's very comfy. He didn't have to rely on superstiff springs and superbig roll bars to get it to work.

MARK GRAIN (*Motorsport technician, McLaren*): There was a German customer, a businessman. He lived in Cologne, commuted in the car every day. He said, "Oh, I've got a problem, this warning light. I've looked in the manual, can't find anything. Can you send somebody out, see what it is?"

So one of the guys went. It turns out it was the engine cover lifting slightly. The warning light [on the dash] for the engine cover. But the only time the car ever did it was 185, 190 mph. "It does it on the way to work, and it does it on the way back." Every day.

LENO: It makes the greatest noise ever. And there's no flywheel—you turn the key off, it stops right now. You don't get that half-second of *rrr*. The only analogy I can make: One time I did a concert with Paul Simon and Paul McCartney. There wasn't a guitar strum, a string—the song ended *right now*.

NEARBURG: You can tell by the way it responds. You just feel the lightness immediately. It's a joy to drive, a very honest car. Sitting in the middle isn't disorienting, and the only thing that's complicated is paying tolls in a foreign country. When you have half of Italy behind you, standing on their horn, when you're trying to figure out how to get the toll in the damn booth.

LENO: That's the real key to the car: It's incredibly light. The nose does get a little light at extremely high speed. It's not as planted as, like, a P1, but then, it's 20 years earlier. Being carbon fiber, you have the occasional clunk—you hit a road marker, you feel it ripple through the chassis. You drive a new NSX, and that's like a solid billet. You realize the car weighs the same as a Miata?

Ray Bellm (*Racing driver*): I have a contract to [run the McLaren F1 Owners Club], because I went to Ron [Dennis, McLaren's then chairman] in 2011. I said, "Ron, these cars, they're all sitting there doing nothing. No one uses them." Anyone who has a car is a member, just by the fact that they've got a car, and we run tours and do probably 700 or 800 kilometers over three days.

But the result has been that, in 2011, the cars were worth about $3 million, and they're now $15 million. Rich people always want to do something no one else can. So the entry ticket is a McLaren F1.

Henry Winkworth-Smith (*McLaren Special Operations Heritage Manager*): There are more cars being used now than when I started 10 years ago. People have suddenly gone, "Actually, I can't get this experience in anything else." And because the values have climbed, people haven't been quite so worried about increasing mileage.

Leno: It's funny, because everybody talks about no ABS, no stability control, no traction control. Yeah, like an MG! Or a Triumph from the Sixties. And it will get away from you—you go 70 and downshift into third and nail it, that rear end's gonna break loose, unless there's heat in those tires. It's a bit like a loaded gun—you have to know how to handle it, all the time. Not like cars now.

Chatfield: [Passenger seats on] either side of the airbox, driver in front. It's just like a wild dog barking at you, every time he's going through the gears.

Leno: The needle moves so quickly your eye can't follow it. Because if you're looking at it, you're already in jail.

Fixing It

John Meyer (*Senior technician, BMW of North America*): It's like any good sports car: If you don't drive it hard, it's not gonna like it. There were a lot of guys who really thrashed their cars and didn't really have problems.

Winkworth-Smith: Paul Rosche, rest his soul, said, "This engine should be designed, developed, like any other BMW series engine. It should not need an opening for 250,000 kilometers."

Leno: Talk about getting something right the first time! There are a number of them that have [huge] miles. I've never known anybody to have any trouble with it.

Bill Auberlen (*Factory racing driver, BMW*): The GTR had sequential shifting, right? Every sequential I've ever been in is pull to shift up. Gordon's idea was that you're stronger when seated, so the GTR was push to shift up. Three in the morning at Le Mans, you're almost asleep in the car, and all of a sudden—you shift the wrong way.

Luckily, the engine is bulletproof. There are stories about where a water hose fell off and they drove it all the way [back to the pits]. It's melting everything around it, and it makes it.

Winkworth-Smith: The race engines were designed to do 9000 kilometers between big servicing. We had one road engine that the customer decided to send his car to a nontrained servicing place. They used the wrong oil—we found a lot of wear. It'd been foaming up and not pumping around the engine properly. And they tightened up what they thought was a chain tensioner. That put too much tension on the timing-chain assembly—one of the bolts loosened and started smashing up and down underneath the pistons.

So we had that engine back. It went back to BMW Motorsport, got stripped and rebuilt, even re-Nikasil'd. And it's a good story, but that's the only time I've heard of it happening.

MATT FARAH (*Journalist*): My favorite McLaren F1 story is from Ralph [Lauren]. About the year 2000. One of his three F1s. The car wasn't running right, so he plugs it into the wall. The car dials McLaren. Two guys in tweed jackets come over from England, they show up at his house. They go, "Okay, give us the keys."

They come back and go, "You're not shifting high enough," and fly back to England. That was it, the whole problem. That's what owning a McLaren F1 is like.

LENO: You forget—there weren't even [smartphones] when this came out. It just seemed so improbable.

WINKWORTH-SMITH: Until very recently, we were using [original 1990s] laptops [for diagnostics]. Our technicians were being stopped in airports and asked to prove it was a real laptop, because [security] thought it was a bomb. They were like, "No one uses those anymore."

MEYER: It runs on a DOS program!

WINKWORTH-SMITH: There was a *Jalopnik* post, someone took a picture of a laptop here. First off, our workshop manager was furious, because there was a car up in the background and it didn't look all smart and neat. But that article was hilarious, because I probably got 45 or 50 emails offering me laptops. Ranged from, "I have one of these laptops. I'm not using it. I would like nothing more than the thought of that laptop looking after a McLaren F1. Please give me your address, and I will ship it," to some guy who was like, "Well, if you haven't got them, I've got one. I want $20,000."

LENO: We do our own servicing on the car—as advanced as it was in the day, it's nothing compared to now. What's funniest is that the car comes with a tool roll. The most beautiful tool set you've ever seen. Titanium wrenches that weigh mere ounces. The idea that, if your McLaren breaks down on the 101, you're going to get out the tool roll and fix it.

MEYER: Because the cars are driven very infrequently, servicing is by time. Every nine months was a basic service. Eighteen months was a major service. Every five years, the fuel cell has to be replaced.

WINKWORTH-SMITH: It's an FIA-spec bag tank, which is brilliant for crash regulations, but . . .

MEYER: The whole back of the car comes off.

WINKWORTH-SMITH: About 25 or 30 hours? It's easy, but it takes a long time. It's not that everything is accessible. So the fuel tank, it's engine-out. Water-temperature sensor, it's engine-out.

But because you've taken the engine out, you need to do a suspension setup. And they're hand-built; they're not all the same. One car might set up really easy, and the other might be really difficult. To get all the ride heights and cross weights and everything dialed in, it could take a day. You just don't know.

LENO: There are no parts. When you break one, they will make you the part. But there's not a lot of off-the-shelf stuff.

WINKWORTH-SMITH: We've got very few windscreens left, for instance. They have this special coating between the two laminates, no wires in them, which gives you a heated windscreen.

To be British, they're *jolly* expensive. And, you know, you could put a cheaper [F1] GTR screen in, but the voltage is different, you haven't got your wiring, it hasn't got the same blue tint. So we said, okay, the only way we could do it is to invest in [manufacturing a complete set of the car's glass]. It's hundreds of thousands of pounds. But it's important to do it, to keep these cars on the road.

Leno: When I first got it to the dealer for service, they said, "Oh, replace the wiper blade." I said, "Well, I don't drive the car in the rain." They said, "It's part of the service." I said, "How much is the wiper blade?" They said, "$1500." I said, "You know what, don't replace the wiper blade! I won't take it out if it rains."

You're at the point now . . . anything on the car . . . it's a house.

Meyer: At one time, we had four in the shop at once. [BMW], back in New Jersey, was having a heart attack.

Winkworth-Smith: I mean, insurance, kill me. We have this limit of two [in the shop at a time]. We had 14 in here at one point. I got a big telling off for insurance. I think the [extra] cost to us was substantial.

Leno: It's still a car. It's still a 20th-century automobile in the sense that you see where everything is. We broke a shifter fork on it; we made a new one. It's just a shifter fork. It's aluminum. It's not that unusual. That's the funny thing about it. All these cars have taken on this mythical status, but they're still cars. More cleverly put together than most, by a long shot, but it's still a car.

Winkworth-Smith: Whenever we service a car, there will be two road tests carried out. So we truck it to a test track, and we'll do a seven-page test procedure, test every single thing on the car. And that goes from pulling the handbrake at 50 mph to see what the retardation's like, to full-throttle accelerations, to really heavy braking to see what the balance is like, to rating the stereo performance at mid and high volume on a scale of one to 10.

Grain: One of the F1 road cars was on display at some event. The engine cover, it's all gold foil. We'd nicked it from aerospace. [A bystander said,] "You're doing it just because it's a shiny color and it's expensive, and it allows you to bill more for the car." And a colleague replied, "It is the lightest heat-effective material we can use in that application." Everything was there for a reason.

Winkworth-Smith: Over time, [the foil] degrades. People touch it, they try and clean it, it rubs off. That's why we replace it. It's not actually that mental. It's a few thousand pounds.

Leno: It's just so beautifully put together, and so simply. It's not meant to be complicated, it's just different.

Maurizio Zagarella (*Technician, McLaren*): We were called flight doctors. Anybody used to fly anywhere if there were any issues.

Nearburg: Pani Tsouris has driven more miles and knows more about these cars than anybody alive, with the exception, I guess, of Gordon.

Pani Tsouris (*Traveling F1 technician, MSO*): I just came back from the United States. A clutch in Minnesota and a fuel-tank replacement in Florida.

Winkworth-Smith: 24-7, both of us. I switch my phone off Christmas Day, my anniversary with my girlfriend, and her birthday. Pani's test-driven cars at midnight.

Tsouris: Nothing [I do] is an emergency, in terms of fly out tomorrow.

WINKWORTH-SMITH: I think the shortest trip—a guy in Europe got a flat tire. Within an hour and a half, there was a technician at Heathrow, with a wheel in his luggage, flying to the nearest city, who then got a taxi to this car on the side of the road. Three and a half hours later, he was there.

TSOURIS: [For jobs requiring] more than two and a half weeks of work, it's in our best interests to bring the car back. Or try to, at least.

WINKWORTH-SMITH: These days, because of the value of the car, it's almost impossible to write one off. A good example is—if you do a bit of googling, you'll find out who I'm talking about. His car came in, and he'd had a fairly substantial shunt.

The car was in two halves. It had split. The car had done brilliantly, because he'd hit it right in the middle. The passenger [cell] was absolutely perfect. We cut all the damage out of the tub, x-rayed it, crack-tested it, and then, using all the original body molds, the tooling, the layup books, and also some of the original staff that built these tubs back in the day, we rebuilt it.

DANNY ENGLAND (*Composites technician, McLaren*): We are, of course, the only company in the world that is physically capable of rebuilding F1s.

WINKWORTH-SMITH: And now that car is driving around, as good as it left the factory, even down to doing torsional-rigidity tests. And to do that, we had to measure it against another F1. So we stripped two other cars down to make sure it was gonna be the same.

PHIL HARDING (*Development technician, McLaren*): It's not like you can go and pick another monocoque out and build a new car. It's cost-effective to repair something worth 5 million pounds, isn't it?

Racing It

Bellm: The project was born as a conversation between myself and Ron Dennis. I ordered a road car, chassis 046, in 1993. I said to Ron—who I've known for many years—"I'm going to race it." He said, "Oh, don't do that, 'cause it will cause me so many problems. If you want to race the car, I'll build you one for a million pounds."

In retrospect, I should have said yes. I said, "Oh, I can't afford a million pounds for a race car." He said, "Find two other customers, and we'll make three." I said, "This car will beat everything out there."

Mark Roberts (*Designer, McLaren*): Gordon mentioned to me once that he almost felt pressured into it. It was never designed as a race car.

Harding: I think the idea was, we'd just do one to see how it goes. All we did, basically, was the minimum to get away with, to meet, FIA regulations. Air jacks on it, roll cage in, bag tanks, and a bit of solder work.

Roberts: If we didn't do it properly, people would go out and do it anyway. It was considered the right thing to do.

Auberlen: 1998, I drove a Longtail [GTR] at Le Mans. When you release that speed-limiter button on hot tires, I swear to God: I was better-looking, I was taller, I felt better about myself. It's a car that has a spirit and a soul. You're going down the Mulsanne at 200 mph. You could see the wheels light up from the carbon brakes, the flames coming out the back.

BELLM: The first year, '95, was just a stripped-out road car. The steering was so heavy, you could barely hold it around corners. So the first thing we did [was ask] for a new steering rack. And to this day, the steering rack of the GTR is infinitely superior to [that] of the road car.

AUBERLEN: When it first came out, it was at the top of the field, so you didn't have to drive 20 percent over the limit all the time to try to keep up. I mean, there were times when we were probably 30 seconds ahead of the field. You're not even racing at that point.

BELLM: When we first tested it, it was quite a handful, because Gordon Murray didn't believe in rear anti-roll bars. It had no rear anti-roll bar—he thought you could control it all from the front. And because you had so much torque, we had to work quite hard on getting decent traction. But basically the engine was so far and away better than everything else [we raced]—Ferrari F40s and Porsches, Venturis, all sorts of rubbish. Only in '97, when Porsche and Mercedes woke up, did we start to have what I would call naked competition.

AUBERLEN: It's always there. It's a very stiff, rigid carbon tub, and [the Longtail] has reasonable downforce, so it's a very stiff car. You notice that right away. It's very consistent on the tires.

BELLM: It's satisfyingly demanding if you know what you're doing. Frighteningly demanding if you don't know what you're doing. Which is why there have been one or two accidents. In the wet—people don't realize this, but at Le Mans in '95, the car ran with zero downforce. It actually had lift at speed.

Auberlen: I know so many people that, once they get comfortable, they're like, [makes crashing noise]. It doesn't give you a lot of feedback. It's great, great, great, right up until biting you. That window of the unknown—it takes a while to get used to that.

Roberts: During '95, '96, and '97, we were producing monthly or fortnightly updates for the cars. It was a typical Formula 1 attitude. We were just trying all the time to improve the car.

Auberlen: You gotta wait a minute for the grip to come up on the tires. It will not give it to you in a lap or two. And once there, you sort of just flow with the thing. There's no sliding. With the GT cars that we race now, you're always moving something around.

Bellm: I don't want to upset Gordon, 'cause he's a friend of mine, but I always say it's the most wonderful engine in a compromised chassis. The engine was sublime. It wasn't designed as a race car, so all the angles were wrong on the suspension. You couldn't get the car low enough, and if it dropped too low, it locked out.

The '96 car—which is why a lot of us bought '96 cars—they changed some of the geometry, so we could get better grip. But I think other than one car, we all fitted rear anti-roll bars. Gordon was absolutely shocked.

Jamie Lewis (*Electrical engineer, McLaren*): It was a very small team. The scale now is such that you have to have business processes and systems, so a lot of the time, you feel a little bit removed from the core. It's a much bigger operation. You just can't work that way anymore.

Grain: I always remember looking at the grand-prix team, and just thinking, They're a bunch of bastards, they are . . . they do it right. There was always an air of confidence tinged with a bit of arrogance: "Even if we're not the best by winning races, in the garage, we were bollocks. Everything will be in place. Everything will be spot-on."

Smithology

Looking Back

Lewis: Normally, you start a company, build a product. McLaren Automotive exists today because of that car. It was designed to build a company.

Roberts: None of us had any idea of how legendary it was going to become.

Andy Wells (*Parts manager, McLaren*): I didn't actually appreciate it until now, to tell you the truth. We won Le Mans with pretty much a road car. It's the biggest thing I've ever achieved in my life.

England: A bunch of people, all from the motor-racing industry, had no idea about road cars. But that's the bit that made it fun and exciting.

Bellm: The P1, you can drive the rocks off it, and you feel completely at home and in control, because the grip levels, and the electronic-traction levels, and the brake-steer help you a lot. But turn it all off, it's a bit like driving an old F1.

Auberlen: I probably drive [BMW of North America's exhibition F1 GTR] three times a year. I take people for rides, and it blows their minds. The downforce on modern-day GT cars is way higher. When you're skating around low-downforce, it's pinkies up, very dainty on the steering wheel. The F1 is still way faster in a straight line. It will just destroy [new race] cars. And listening to that motor. I mean, the restrictor's right above your head.

Leno: Right now, it's kind of like champagne. It's something you have once a month or on special occasions.

Meyer: If you think about when it was designed and built, everything on that thing was Formula 1. They were not saving any money on anything at all. I loved it. I miss them terribly.

Roberts: Gordon said, "Just go and see what everyone else is doing, and make sure you do something significantly better." So I managed to get hold of an F40 owner's manual and a 959 Porsche manual.... The whole ethos was craftsmanship and that human element, so I thought we should hand-draw the manual. Pencil sketches and watercolor. Nobody would ever be crazy enough to do that sort of thing again.

Bellm: I love the car and what it stands for. It was a massive step forward, basically the Ferrari 250 GTO of the Nineties. We just don't realize how far technology has moved. The gearbox, which was not the easiest. The porpoising at speed, which meant it steered itself. The car tracked a bit, because of the lack of camber and caster. Lots of little aspects that just made the car, made you concentrate.

Winkworth-Smith: They're just so ... different to modern cars.

Roberts: We still refer back to them almost on a daily basis. The purity in the design. The package.

Winkworth-Smith: If you look at what other cars in the market are doing—250 GTO at whatever they're worth these days, 50 [million] or whatever, the general thought is that the F1 is the next one of those.

BELLM: In 2004, I bought probably the cheapest-ever F1. I paid £300,000 for chassis 016R. I sold it for £650,000 and thought I had made a complete and utter killing.

WINKWORTH-SMITH: These days, 13 to 15 million [pounds] for a road car. Apart from the car we own—GTR 01R, the Le Mans winner, we've had some very silly offers—a really impeccable-history race car would be 20, 22 million restored.

AMANDA MCLAREN (*McLaren ambassador, daughter of company founder*): They arranged for me to be taken for a drive [in a roadgoing F1]. Down this residential road, all the curtains are twitching. There was a bulbous lorry in front of us . . . bits start falling off . . . this guy starts sweating. He starts telling me how much the insurance is. More than my house was worth at the time.

NEARBURG: I was told by the staff of the Petersen [museum] that of all the cars in their Precious Metal exhibit, the F1 probably attracted the most attention. And without a doubt among anybody less than 40 years old. When you drive it, it's almost unnerving. People either recognizing it, or not immediately seeing the driver and freaking out.

BELLM: It's unbelievable. It's just pure adulation. People recognize it because it's the iconic car of the 1990s, the first of the all-carbon, the real supercars after the F40, which was a space frame covered in bits of plastic.

LEWIS: I started in '91 . . . probably about 120 people in McLaren Cars. And now it's 3500. The scale of the operation has changed so dramatically that it's almost incomparable. But there's still that sort of core DNA that exists, that Ron kind of instilled in all of us. Attention to detail and doing things right.

Roberts: Obsessive-compulsive disorders. We all suffer from that. And if you don't when you join the company—you will. We're lifers. It gets under your skin.

Lewis: That no-compromise thing.

Roberts: Remember, Gordon and the original team were mostly race people. They lived in that world already.

Nearburg: He's incredibly hardworking. Never stops thinking, never stops doodling, never stops pursuing his passion for how to improve automotive manufacturing. His whole new thing that he's got going on now—building trucks in a box for the third world that can be assembled in a few hours with common hand tools. He's still got such a fertile imagination.

Zagarella: We were all looked after by the business. Even our families. I think that's what made this company great. I think it came from Ron and Gordon, who were very much the same.

Nearburg: One of the most hilarious things is watching [Gordon] drive his little Austin-Healey Bugeye Sprite. He throws on this little leather bucket helmet, and he plops in that thing, and he goes ripping around like he's on the Isle of Man or something. But he's still a very intense, focused, driven guy. My sense is that he's doing this stuff because he wants to make a difference.

Grain: At heart, he was a racer, wasn't he? Still is.

Nearburg: How often in this world does one guy—one guy who is supremely qualified and has all the resources that he needs—how often does that guy get to design the ultimate anything?

Fifteen Simple Rules for Dating My 1930s French Propeller Car

Which is not mine at all but does go RAWRRR in fancy fashion and almost definitely won't chop your hands off.

In the summer of 2022, I arrived at Nashville's Lane Motor Museum on assignment for Hagerty. I was there for a story, to drive 800 miles across the country in a 1950s microcar. That trip was great, but this isn't about that. It's about what happened before the trip began.

Jeff Lane loves odd vehicles and believes cars weren't made to sit. The museum he founded thus holds hundreds of rare wheeled weirdos, nearly all of which run and drive. One of his favorite pastimes involves giving unsuspecting visitors a rip around town in some utterly strange vehicle from the museum's collection, often with little warning.

For me, that meant the Lane's 1932 Helicron. This French fever dream that looked like a 1920s boat on wheels and was dragged down the road by the thrust of a twin-blade propeller between the front wheels. Jeff simply pushed the car out of the museum and fired it up, aiming the propeller at traffic. The next thing I knew, he and I were a few blocks away, pushing the Helicron up a hill, because the road's minor incline required more thrust than the prop could generate in the thin air of a humid Nashville summer. Jeff was unfazed—you drive a Helicron, he said, this happens a lot.

It should go without saying, but I love Jeff.

The microcar trip came and went. When I returned home a week later, I couldn't stop thinking about death by French blade. So I sat down, called up my best 1930s-newsreel voice, and wrote up a fake Helicron owner's manual.

That invention begins on the next page. It is fronted by the story's original preface and capped by its original postscript. Read all three as if you have always wanted to die while holding a baguette and ranting about mother sauces. And when you get down to it, really, who hasn't?

Smithology

WHAT FOLLOWS IS AN EXCERPT *from an owner's manual uncovered next to the ruins of the only surviving Helicron propeller automobile. We have translated the text from the original French.*

This information is enshrined here with thanks to the Helicron's current owner, Nashville's Lane Motor Museum, and to commemorate Mr. Smith's recent test of this remarkable vehicle.

HAGERTY, JUNE 2022

Hello and welcome to your brand-new 1932 model HELICRON propeller automobile! The finest of safe aeromotive land traversement awaits you over the safe years and miles to come!

Your 1932 HELICRON propeller car is a miracle of modern engineering! Propeller travel is the next great step in human evolution! In the coming years, expect to encounter such mechanical marvels as the propeller-driven city bus, the propeller-driven dish-washing machine, even propeller-operated trousers!

In the meantime, congratulations on your wise choice to join the growing dozens of propeller-automobilists around the globe! Please consult this printed operations manual and its accompanying 324-page disclaimer-and-liability pamphlet whenever meeting the slightest question as to the safe and perfectly ordinary operation of your safe and perfectly ordinary automobile!

Is this a safe and perfectly ordinary automobile? Why, of course it is!

Fact the First: Your new vehicle is driven forward, with alarming accelerative thrust, by a 48-inch, climb-profile propeller of the finest natural hardwood! This propeller faces forward into all traffic, wildlife, pedestrians, and other obstacles! Does it really? Yes!

Please note that this machine-ship features the patented Helicron Protective Wooden Hoop encircling its specially developed twin-blade drive device! Two blades which, despite appearances, are not designed explicitly to mutilate the walking pedestrian and/or chop your hands off!

Please do not fear that your fine new aeromotive conveyance will, in fact, chop your hands off! In the entire monthslong history of the Helicron manufacturing concern, this has never happened except only once, and only then to Mrs. Eugenia P. O'Halloran of Keokuk, Iowa, 78 years of only lightly feebleminded age if she was a day, and law professionals retained by Helicron Automobiles and Amalgamated Tubemeat Corp. have determined that she was, in fact, asking for it! No one liked her homemade pies anyway! Propeller-aeromotor without fear, kind citizen!

Please note that the phrase *"propeller-aeromotor without fear"* serves as neither guarantee nor promise of the absence of the inhuman bloodthirst which several noted East Coast clairvoyants and licensed doctors of bodily humours have alleged lives and breathes for all eternity in the drive blades of the patented 1932 Helicron model! Helicron automobiles/A.T.C. does not in any way believe its engineering achievements to be the work of any demon or spirit currently known! This we will swear!

Fact the Second: A safe and fully limbed individual should know and cogitate well on the Helicron starting procedure! The vehicle's lacquered wooden body and stout, ladder-steel H-frame may cause it to appear as friendly as a small woodland creature! Perhaps as a toy one might offer a simple child! We assure you it is not!

- ! -

~SETTING OFF~

TO START ENGINE AND PREPARE FOR A SPIRITED JOURNEY
on the cusp of man's ever-multiplying innovation,
one must follow only a few simple steps!

I. For the utmost assurance of safety, and before igniting the vast drive power of your new Helicron automobile, please locate a suitable parcel of land for travel! This century's rapid march of progress means such environments are now common throughout the globe! Helicron engineers and liability advisers suggest planning your journey to encounter a minimum of crowded areas, public squares, intersections, stop signs, traffic signals, draft animals, small children, large children, agitable farm-stock, inclement weather, sanitarium residents, roadside distractions, situations requiring a traditional reverse gear, and/or bystanders in flowing dress!

II. DON APPROPRIATE PROTECTIVE GARB! Your friends at HELICRON suggest browsing our fine catalog of stylish pilotage equipment! If one is willing to discount light staining sourcing from previous wholesale evacuation of sanguine fluid, most HELICRON stockists also offer a fine selection of preowned apparel at reasonable prices!

III. BEFORE EMBARKATION, OBTAIN AND LOG LOCAL METEOROLOGICAL DATA, including such easily parsed basic variables as ambient temperature, ground-level humidity, local atmospheres of pressure, aneroid barometer variance, statistical anemometer deviation, local time of astronomical twilight, precipitation on hills or inclines along any planned routes, and the quantity of anvil-shaped cumulonimbus cloud formations in the near and greater region!

Fear not, should this sound complex! A child of five could do it!

*A defunct and competing predecessor to the mighty HELICRON.
Accept no substitution!*

IV. INSPECT THE PROPELLER BLADES for leading-edge damage! The HELICRON patented drive aerofoil is a strong and well-considered device, recently certified by the Fédération Aéronautique Internationale! And yet, like any creation of mortal man, it can suffer terminal damage in regular use!

Please take care to regularly witness the aerofoil's edge blades for embedded rocks, errant chips in finish, potential delamination, and-or stray fragments of pavé and human gore!

V. CYCLE THE IGNITION, ENGAGE THE STARTING DEVICE, and witness the propeller turn slightly! Marvel as engine's cylinder firing commences! As have dashing sky captains for years, from the Nieuports of the Great War to the *hangart professeurs* of your local aerodrome!

VI. PUSH FORWARD UPON THE HAND THROTTLE mounted outside and to the left of cockpit! Trust your own personal and divine right of eyesight through the cycling path of the immensely powerful HELICRON propeller! Then drive away! No shifting, no clashing of gears, simple as that! A child could do it!

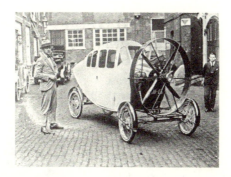

Propeller-automotrication has come quite far since the heady days of engineer M. Marcel Leyat of Paris, pioneer of the form. We salute his flawed and inferior efforts!

A WORD ON STEERING AT HIGH SPEED

The patented HELICRON frame was developed in concert with the French-built and Rosengard-licensed iteration of the British Austin Seven economy car. Its frame is thus a Seven scaffold reengineered and reversed, the once-front steering axle now in service at the rear. In this manner, the HELICRON can turn safely in diminutive radius, while also offering excellent—and safe!—maneuverability.

> **Rear-wheel steering requires caution!** Please do not turn so quickly that the HELICRON lofts a front wheel from the earth, topples distressingly onto a flank, or drifts its propellance blades into the path of vehicular traffic.

(steering at high speed, cont.)

This behavior is entirely normal and in many counties legislated as ordinary and no one should be alarmed at all.

A WORD ON RELIABILITY

The Helicron is a paragon of simplicity! Its unique and safe propeller drive means a complete absence of clutch, differential, or transmission—the Helicron is thus cheaper, lighter, and simpler than the average car! Nor is it stopped by poor traction! Snow, rain, wind—the Helicron will safely carry you to safety across the roads of this great and dangerous world without cause for worry on your safety and especially not for loss of precious bodily fluids!

On an unrelated note, please consider the presence of the powerful Helicron drum brakes: Although these foot-operated items are at the forefront of modern technologic, they cannot overcome the formidable torquing forces of the Helicron engine and propeller, especially when full throttle has been selected!

In case of emergency stoppage—perhaps to avoid imminent collision with public sidewalk or living individual—it is imperative that the hand throttle be immediately closed! Failure to do so can lead to

(The rest of that final sentence was missing from our owner's manual as recovered, the page torn away long ago. The margin carried a hand-inked note, however, in flowing French pen—the following three words, faded but legible. —Ed.)

... *un beau moment!*

A WORD ON THE TRAVERSING OF INCLINES

In rare circumstance, the HELICRON's efficient thrust and staggering abundance of horse-vapeur can meet their match in the power and gravity of an almighty God. Short rises in pavement, inclines of greater than 1.0 percent, elevated parking areas with angled ramps, and-or speed tables of more than 2.0 inches' height can conspire to outmatch the immensely powerful HELICRON propeller!

As the HELICRON's immensely powerful propeller is limited by the physics of the very gases we breathe, this effect may be exacerbated—though never insurmountable!—on days of extreme humidity and air density! Thrust may be reduced despite the engine producing maximum revolutions, and the vehicle may halt, unable to proceed!

The greatest of modern aeronauts have assured the engineers at HELICRON AUTOMOBILES/A.T.C. that no ship of the skies would fare any less!

IN SUCH CASES, IT CAN BE NECESSARY TO EXIT THE VEHICLE AND PROVIDE
A MODICUM OF BODILY ASSISTANCE!

PLEASE OBSERVE CAREFULLY THE FOLLOWING STEPS!

A. Exit with alacrity, taking care to avoid the all-powerful but kind and benevolent thrust blades at fore of the vehicle!

B. Request any and all passengers to exit with alacrity, also while avoiding the all-powerful but kind and benevolent thrust blades at the fore of the vehicle!

C. Stand to the left of the steering wheel! Carefully offer up hand to throttle lever. If that hand is willing, increase throttle to full!

D. ***Pause to secure from propeller blast*** any errant or unfastened headwear or petticoats!

E. ***Commence to pushing the mighty* Helicron *up the hill!*** The propeller, she is a strength, but she occasionally welcomes your help! The Helicron's 1000-pound mass is but a trifle for those stout of mind and body!

If gravity at the top of the incline should cause velocity to exceed a vigorous walking pace, and should the Helicron's innate urge to serve carry it downhill unattended, fear not! Simply run after the vehicle!

Simple as that!

A WORD TO THE ESTEEMED HEIRS OF MRS. EUGENIA P. O'HALLORAN OF KEOKUK, IOWA

While we welcome any and all enthusiasm for the majestic Helicron automobile and embrace opportunities to discuss its foolproof design, we regret to inform that your repeat inquiries have caused our manufacturing office to cease reception of all inbound telegrams and visitors. Please stop calling. —The Mgmt.

Smithology

<u>Original Hagerty Postscript</u>

Yes, the Helicron is real. There is, however, no owner's manual. Smith wrote this entire story after a short drive in the car with Hagerty friend Jeff Lane, likely during hallucinations from ingesting too much Nashville hot chicken.

The Helicron is a relic from an age when aviation dominated public fancy—for a few short decades in the early part of the last century, people were slapping propellers on everything. Even if the result was clearly a bad idea.

The Lane's Helicron was discovered rotting in a barn 20 years ago. Now restored, the car lives in the museum's main Nashville facility, where it is regularly "flown" and demonstrated for visitors. The original engine, origin unknown, is long gone; the prop is now driven by a 40-hp Citroën flat-four of 1980s extraction.

The sum is a terrifying joy to drive and one of the least practical automobiles ever built. We encourage you to visit it and the rest of the Lane museum as soon as you can. —Ed.

Red Bloodline

Wherein the author screams like a dead Mantuan from a Nazi-slugging Alfa Romeo while trying not to be a rank-and-file diphead.

"Epic" is an overused term, but nothing else fits. A prewar Alfa grand-prix car is a timeless piece of genius, an elegant weapon, and a staggeringly evocative relic. When the two of us yawed onto the front straight at Pacific, I heard opera in my helmet.

ROAD & TRACK, MARCH 2016

The craziest thing about one of the greatest drivers in history is that he died in bed. Tazio Nuvolari was born in Italy in 1892. He ran 172 recorded races, many in the forerunner to Formula 1, winning 64 times. He placed second 16 times and third only nine, because, as journalist Ken Purdy wrote, his plan was simple: "Win, or break up the automobile." That he didn't die in the process is remarkable only because most people he drove against did.

Nuvolari's most storied win came 80 years ago, in an Alfa Romeo, when Enzo Ferrari was not yet a carmaker and Alfas were some of the fastest machines on the planet. You have to wonder how the marque fell from such heights. World-conquering grand-prix cars. Excellent, affordable street cars for a few decades after World War II. Then, in the 1990s, microscopic sales, indifferent management, and a chicken exit from North America.

Eight decades is a long time in an industry where attention spans are measured in seconds. But the image is intoxicating: battles at Monaco and the Nürburgring, backed by aristocratic wealth and power. Men who raced and bled in genuinely fast machinery when virtually everything that composes modern motorsport was undiscovered land.

Alfa Romeo returned to the United States in 2014. American dealers will now sell you the 4C, a carbon-framed, mid-engine, $55,495 sports car. They'll soon stock the 505-horse Giulia Quadrifoglio, a sport sedan aimed at the BMW M3.

But these are new products, and for most people, they might as well come from a new company. They don't tell you why you should care, and they don't let you bathe in the moment when a handful of Italian engineers helped run the world. So we did the next best thing. I took a heaping deep breath and climbed behind the wheel.

> "... his hairy arms straight out, and he would sail through the curves in long, flaring slides . . . Sometimes he would throw back his head and scream with exuberance, pounding the side of the car like a manic blacksmith."

That's Purdy again, on Nuvolari, in 1957. To understand old-world Alfas, you have to understand the kind of men—*the* man—who drove them.

Most Nuvolari biographies paint in primary colors. He was five-foot-five and compactly built at a time when raw strength helped drivers go faster. He didn't start driving until 1921, at age 28; over the next 29 years, he was pulled from the wreckage of a car or motorcycle 17 times, walking out of the hospital after each crash. He once won a motorcycle race so encased in plaster that he had to be lifted onto his bike by mechanics. ("His doctor walked away," Purdy wrote. "'You are a dead man if you fall, Nivola,' he said. 'I don't want them even to call me.'") His face bore the scars of accidents.

And oh, how he got those scars. Most people see prewar machinery as primitive—dangerous, if at least slow. But every grand-prix car represents the peak of an era's knowledge. By the 1920s, the average horsepower of a GP field was into the hundreds and escalating annually, but relatively little was known about brakes or handling. Fuels, often based in methanol, were toxic and experimental. Some believed period motorcycle racing to be safer, and it probably was—you were more likely to be thrown clear of anything that could crush or impale you.

Tazio Nuvolari.

Add to this a Wild West approach to engineering, driven by a single goal. Take Alfa factory driver Giuseppe Campari: When he died, gruesomely, at Monza in 1933, it was in a car without front brakes, for weight reduction.

Repeat: They pulled the front brakes off to make it go *faster*.

That Nuvolari triumph of 80 years ago says a lot about the era. The man won the 1935 German Grand Prix, on the Nürburgring's 14-mile north loop. (The track then boasted a 4.8-mile south loop, or Südschleife.) The Ring in 1935 looked much as it does today, save a passing interest in not making people dead. Like most early permanent tracks, it was built to replicate the feel of local roads. There was no catch fencing. A low hedge bordered most of the pavement.

To this we bring our man, 42 and an Alfa factory 'shoe in the afternoon of his career. His team, Scuderia Ferrari, is captained by Enzo, already a legend. The stands hold 250,000 spectators, government officials, and an entire regiment of the Nazi army.

German manufacturers were then dominating European motorsport, largely because Adolf Hitler gave them lots of money to try. That funding produced complex machines at the bleeding edge of progress.

To the Ring, Mercedes-Benz and Auto Union brought technological behemoths making at least 400 hp each. They were collectively dubbed Silver Arrows. The factory Alfas, a model known as the Tipo B, were built by a small group of—fashion has made the term cringeworthy, but it's the only one that applies—artisan engineers.

The Tipo B had been dominant when new, but by 1935, the design was several years old. The four Auto Unions on the grid were good for 180 mph. The five Mercedes were 5 mph behind. Nuvolari's car was lighter and more nimble but 20 mph slower. The German cars were helmed by giants, men like Bernd Rosemeyer and Achille Varzi.

Nuvolari started second, the order determined by draw. He fell to fifth on the second lap, sixth on the fourth. Six laps later, he was somehow leading, apparently through sheer will. At 11, he pitted for fuel. Mechanics botched the stop. Two minutes and 14 seconds after entering the pits—the Mercedes were refueling in under a minute—the Alfa tore out, now in fifth place. Germans in the crowd were said to have relaxed. Nuvolari was visibly irate.

A still from a period newsreel—Nürburgring paddock straight, German Grand Prix, 1935.

He used the anger. Over the next four laps, the Alfa sliced past three cars. Nuvolari found himself second, to the Mercedes of Manfred von Brauchitsch. The Mercedes pit gave the signal to press harder. Von Brauchitsch broke the track record. Nuvolari remained glued to his mirrors. The German overrevved his engine trying to stay ahead. Nuvolari railed on the Alfa. On the final lap, von Brauchitsch blew a tire. Nuvolari passed, then won, more than two minutes ahead of the second-place car.

The Germans were stunned. Their win had seemed so assured, the only national anthem on hand was a record of "Deutschland über Alles." Legend holds that the song played over the PA was Nuvolari's personal copy of "Marcia Reale."

Photos show him sitting on the car, grinning. Nazis scowl nearby.

How can you not love a guy who corked off a bunch of Nazis?

In France, same year, after winning the Grand Prix de Pau.

Even without that win, Nuvolari's car was a tour de force. Tipo Bs were built from 1932 to 1934. Informally known as the P3, the model was the company's third classic-era GP car, after the P1 and P2.

The P1 was a failure, but people remember the P2. A P2 won the first world championship, in 1925, and one killed the great Italian driver Antonio Ascari. A works P2 was also the first car that a young Nuvolari drove at his first Alfa factory test, at Monza, in 1925. (He smirks in photos, brash and confident. The day ended in the hospital.)

The P1 was designed, by an Italian named Giuseppe Merosi, for the 1922–1925 seasons. Its 95-hp, 5000-rpm, 2.0-liter straight-six was uncompetitive, but the car was the first grand-prix machine built under Alfa's golden-age benefactor, Nicola Romeo. When Romeo saw the P1 run against 130-hp Fiats at Monza, he said, "The designer is getting old—is finished. To produce a real racing car, we must have the Fiat men."

So they got them. Specifically, they got a 32-year-old genius named Vittorio Jano. Jano would go on to engineer the P2, but also the postwar Lancia D50 Formula 1 car and Ferrari's Dino V-6, plus a V-8 whose derivations would power the 288 GTO and 360 Modena. In the century-plus history of the automobile, the man is a towering light.

But Jano was Turinese, an outsider. The Alfa men initially regarded him with suspicion. In 1982, Alfa test driver Giovanni Guidotti told a journalist about running one of the man's first designs on the dyno: "We would take maximum power readings by just opening the throttle wide for 30 seconds . . . then *alt!* Because if not . . . she would break. When Jano came in . . . he said, 'No, no, no,' and he took the throttle and opened it wide and hung a weight on it.

Jano with a P2 after Alfa's win at the Italian Grand Prix, 1924.

"It was around 5:00 in the afternoon, and he said, 'Now I'm going home for a bite to eat. Don't touch the throttle, and call me at home about 8:00 to tell me how it's going.' We were flabbergasted. At that time, no engine would last very long at full power. But we quickly learned Jano's engines just weren't like Merosi's or English engines or the French . . . they were perfect, marvelous pieces of design and construction."

For the P3, Jano drew a masterpiece: a twin-cam, twin-supercharged, two-valve, aluminum straight-eight with hemi combustion chambers. It would become one of the most successful racing engines in history, and like every prewar Alfa engine, it defined the car into which it was installed.

Amazingly, this jewel was not new. The P3's eight was essentially a heavy-duty makeover of an Alfa street eight, itself an evolution of a Jano six. It featured monoblock construction—cylinder head and block cast as one piece, with no head gasket. It used two of these blocks, four pistons in each, along with a two-piece crankshaft, literally making the engine two four-cylinders in tandem. A straight-cut gear drive sat between them, sending torque outside the engine and to the left, where it powered the two superchargers, one for each block.

This construction helped torsional stiffness, which helped the engine stay in one piece. Because the result was Italian, it was also achingly beautiful. And strong. In early, 2.7-liter form, Jano's eight made a reliable 80 hp per liter. In 1935, chasing the Germans, it was a 6000-rpm 3.2 with 89 hp per liter.

More than 280 hp, in a 1550-pound car the width of a lawn tractor. V-8 Fords of the day made 85.

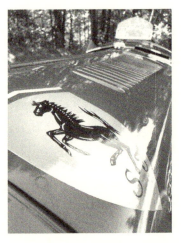

The rest of the P3 was relatively straightforward. Mechanical brakes, later replaced by hydraulic, in a sport where Ettore Bugatti still did refused to trust fluid for stopping. Leaf springs. Friction dampers and a solid rear axle. A rigid front axle, later changed to independent. And coolest of all, a split rear driveline—a small aluminum-cased differential, the size of a handbag, in the cockpit, under the driver's thighs. Two torque tubes angled out of it, one for each wheel. A ring and pinion sat at each hub.

The idea, Guidotti said, "was to prevent wheelspin . . . to make ratio changing . . . relatively easy, and to drop the driver's seat low down, between the shafts. Ha! But when Jano tell our drivers what he plans, Nuvolari snorts through his nose and says, 'No! I don't want to be down in the basement like that, I wanna be up on top of the job! I want to see where I am going in road racing!' And the original idea was changed, narrowed, and we ended up sitting high on top."

Maybe he was wrong, but you can't argue with the results. Thirteen P3s were built. Until the Silver Arrows showed up, they won almost everything in sight.

Smithology

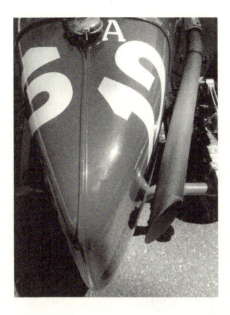

"Nuvolari seemed the most awe-inspiring . . . wheels occasionally lifting slightly in the middle of skids!"
—Motor Sport magazine, 1932

"I didn't have enough strength to horse them around the curves, like the other drivers. So I worked out my own methods. I let the car go."
—Tazio Nuvolari

"If you open up too quickly . . . the tail goes all over the place . . . it'll do about 160 mph with the right gears."
—English racing driver Brian Lewis, 1934

Nuvolari drove many Alfas. The car he climbed into at the Ring was Tipo B No. 50005, a late-run machine updated in period with a widened body and Dubonnet independent front suspension. Its presence at the German Grand Prix is undisputed; shortly after the race, a journalist had the foresight to publish the car's serial number. Nuvolari vouched for it before his death.

Car 50005 is currently owned by collector Jon Shirley. Last July, he met us at the 2.3-mile Pacific Raceways, an old, fast road course near the

Seattle suburb of Kent. The track hosted Trans-Am and Formula 5000 cars in the Sixties, and it hasn't changed much since. There are at least two places where an off can put you into a ravine. In summer, the place looks like Northern California, only greener.

Shirley brought the P3, his adult son Erick, and a thick stack of original Scuderia Ferrari team newspapers. Also the car's current caretakers, local specialists Butch Dennison and Vinay Nelson. The papers read like school yearbooks, just with giant pictures of Nuvolari and full-page, hand-drawn ads for Weber carburetors.

Dennison and Nelson wheeled the car out of its small trailer. "The thing that amazes me," Dennison said, "is how anywhere on this car, just any detail, you can find something beautiful."

Erick Shirley did a few installation laps to warm the engine. Watching him tear by, I was reminded of the week before, when I tried to explain the Tipo B to my wife, over dinner.

"It's a damn Renaissance painting," I said. "It predates the idea that a chassis should be rigid to keep the wheels on the ground. It predates anything you'd call brakes. It predates the idea that racing drivers are ordinary people. And they sold the same basic thing for the street. It matters."

"Sounds really cool," she said. "More pasta?"

I sighed. If only she'd been there to see it. You cannot climb into an Alfa GP car without accepting a kind of filmic ridiculousness: You mount the thing like a horse, a foot on the rear leaf spring, before threading legs down and in, over each side of the differential. Seated, your torso is halfway out of the car. Motorcycles do seem less dangerous. You are intimately aware of where you end.

The methanol feed valve below your leg gets turned on. Someone gives the slender chrome knockoffs a final whack with a lead hammer. Their centers are the car in a nutshell: "Alfa Romeo" in filigreed script, needlessly and wonderfully flamboyant. The slender, arm-length chrome shifter snakes up between your legs in a manner that reminds you of dirty jokes. The three-speed dog gearbox was originally a four-speed, but first gear's gate is blocked off; the gear was removed in period to make room when others were enlarged for durability.

Nelson hands me the car's modern lap belt. I stare at it dumbfounded, surprised. I almost leave it unbuckled. A Tipo B can be hand-cranked or started with an external, plug-in starter, but Dennison suggests a push-start, popping the clutch, for maximum effect. I don't argue. The car bursts alive, a basso, like a dirt bike the size of the moon. ("Most people who hear it from across the shop," Dennison said later, "ask, 'Whose Chevy you running back there?'")

And then I'm on my own.

The wood-rimmed wheel is unavoidable. Pretend you're holding a newspaper open to read it. Now move your hands an inch closer to your chest, replace the paper with a steering wheel but don't change your arms, and think about drifting. Your gut reaction is to call the position tractorish, but that would both elevate every tractor ever built and insult one of the most elegant weapons made by human hands.

There are two clockwork tachometers on the dash. Each one is driven off an engine cam, for redundancy; their short drive cables meet the firewall inches above your knees. In most old cars, a chronometric tach is spastic, a beat behind the engine. The P3's glide like the sweep hand on a Rolex. Your eyes land on them and get stuck.

I would be a tone-deaf heathen if I didn't call the engine astounding. If it had been invented solely to make noise, there would be shrines to it in Rome. The sound is straight-eight incarnate—a six-cylinder's ripping snarl crossed with the crackling blat of a Detroit V-8. You get meaty torque down low, but also a surprising flexibility and eagerness to rev. There is wheelspin in first gear, second, even the top of third if you're sliding, because the tires aren't so much a device for grip as the punch line to a joke about the lack of it.

And above all, more noise. The cockpit serves as an aluminum megaphone, funneling three or four different gear whines and a funk of oil to your face. It combines to help you forget that you just hit 4500 rpm in third (more than 120 mph, based on gearing), that the diff is whirring away near your testicles.

How do you describe a romance? Maybe you start with methanol fumes. I stuck my nose a foot from the pipe when Erick first lit it off, because I knew I might not have another chance. It smelled like bad wine and dying brain cells. Or do you focus on the chassis? Books claim that Nuvolari invented drifting, but the P3 makes a certain technique obvious. Its frame is little more than two steel rails. They're flexible enough to serve as suspension, something I notice leaving the paddock, when the car springs onto the track in an odd little two-phase bop.

Past the pits, flying over a bumpy piece of pavement, I prime to catch a jumping wheel. But nothing happens, just a few skips from the tail. The steering is quick and the wheel close enough that you correct a slide by pulling down and leaning your torso.

The Alfa turns in slow, nose wandy and distant; if modern cars have you thinking about tires, here, you think about the frame. You can feel it twist into a corner, winding up. Once it's set, you don't change much, just accelerate. Which the tires always seem to resent. The brakes don't do a lot, and heat makes them do less. Your foot consumes what feels like feet of distance—it's probably a few inches—before the car slows. Understeer and oversteer are blips, rarely steady-state.

On a smoothish track, it was work. In an open-road race, it must have sapped men to husks.

It is easy to get wrong. Drive ham-fisted, and the frame binds, the car lock-kneed, all compliance gone. The seat buzzes as the inside rear wheel spins. The P3 doesn't have the kind of chassis you can pick apart to analyze, so you just slow down, try again, and keep your foot in it.

Put another way: Think of an old pickup in snow. Now give it bicycle tires and straight pipes and pin the Mona Lisa to the hood. Play deafening opera in the background, with lyrics about top-heavy women of breeding. That equation does not want your modern algebra of pinpoint driving. It only wants your balls.

So you go freehand. This drifty improv between throwing the Alfa like a kart and eggshell-walking into corners, smooth and patient. More pace and forgiveness when the car's up on step. And if you are me, you find yourself merrily yawing up the hill on Pacific Raceways' back straight, purposely ignoring nearby trees, feeling as if you can see deep into the black hearts of those people who say that machines are not emotional things. And you know that they are rank-and-file dipheads without a grain of art in their lives, and you want to take this living red fireball and go penetrate their living rooms at full tilt in top gear and watch them scatter like pigeons and maybe make the family dog leak all over the carpet from abject and unspeakable terror.

Also maybe just use a P3 to get ice cream on weekends, because wouldn't that be a hoot?

No modern car could live up to that. A 2015 Alfa 4C Spider certainly doesn't. We brought one to Kent for symmetry; it felt a lot like the 4C coupe, which is to say, nothing else on the market. Carbon tub, loud everything, unpredictable turbo lag, heavy and distant steering. Lots of sideways, not always when you want. It reminded me of high school: fantasism, with an undercurrent of misery.

But pulling into the pits, I was reminded of every postwar Alfa I've met. Giulia Supers, Spiders and GTVs, Milanos and 164s. Those cars all demanded that you stay ahead of them, but there was a delicacy to their controls, like a good Ferrari. They have little in common with a 4C and a Tipo B save a sense of urgency. Each hints at the notion that fast cars are best when they ask something of you. That machines, like any human creation, are defined by their stories, only so important as what you do with them.

Nuvolari was just 60 when he died. His lungs had given out, poisoned by fumes from the thing he loved. He was still winning races in his final years, though he had grown too weak to climb from a car without help. They buried him in Mantua, his birth village, with a steering wheel in the casket. Alfa Romeo, however, remains alive, and with it, a thread of the man. Also a hundred other men, Ferrari and Jano and the rest. The legend they helped build gives warmth to a thing otherwise cold, makes a flawed little carbon-fiber sports car more than the sum of its parts.

A piece of a slower moment. Not necessarily a better one. But perhaps dappled with a little more beauty.

Urge Overkill
Rennsport Reunion and the
Stuttgart machine.

There's a video online where Werner Herzog passionately outlines his personal disgust for chickens, how offensive and stupid he finds the breed. I've heard similar rants about the Porsche 911. The Herzog clip is funny, but then, I like chickens.

ROAD & TRACK, DECEMBER 2015

We talk a lot about Porsches around here, but there's a reason. Many, actually. Feeling. Also redemption, speed, underdogs, arrogance, comeuppance. And that most human of traits, fallibility. There are spectacular Porsches and stinging disappointments, bits of genius and machines that sully dealer lots like flaming sacks of dog doo. Not all of the former are old, and not all of the latter are new.

Those ideas are mostly undercurrent. Then, every few years, we get a Rennsport Reunion, and it all bubbles to the surface.

There have been five of these events, each factory-backed and held at a track, a gathering of unobtainium cars and star characters billed as both family reunion and the world's largest gathering of Porsche automobiles. I've been to three, including the most recent, held at Laguna

Seca in September. Like its predecessors, Rennsport 2015 was equal parts museum, vintage race, and cult church. Also a remarkably efficient way to make your brain fall down your spine and leak out your shoes.

That three-day event hosted 57,000 people, 320 cars on track, and 1400 spectator Porsches. The best way to describe the sheetmetal is to say that history shows up, all of it, from start to finish. Race winners, unobtainium prototypes, rare birds not seen publicly in decades, from expert-stumping obscurity to predictable crowd-pleaser. (Example of the latter: four Gulf-liveried 917Ks, including the one Steve McQueen drove while filming the 1971 movie *Le Mans*. For reference, four flat-fan flat-twelves sparking up at once will liquefy your knees.)

And the people. I knew what was coming but still marveled. Around 50 "name" drivers walked the paddock, plus a posse of company racing chiefs, from Norbert Singer to the recently retired Hartmut Kristin. With Singer alone, you've got 16 of Porsche's 17 Le Mans wins and enough maniacal rule bending to give a Frenchman palpitations. He look like a high-school math teacher; crowds mobbed him in the paddock.

Smaller glories abounded. What happens when you're two feet away from an idling RS Spyder (Le Mans class winner, 2008–2009)? That V-8, dense and buzzy, oscillates your lungs, the world's fastest drumroll buzzing through your nipples. At one point, three of the things slipped by me in the paddock, bark-droning toward the false grid, their exhaust notes going in and out of phase with each other. If that kind of bodily vibration occurred at home, you'd call an ambulance.

Like a lot of people, I once thought it was all hype. I was almost certainly an idiot. The first 911 I tried, a 930, came while working as a mechanic after college. It was tired, slow, weird. Factory parts were comically priced, and not in the good way. Later, while instructing at a Porsche Club track day, I drove a 996-chassis Carrera 4S. It felt fat and distant. I didn't get it.

That was the wrong foot. Once I started writing for car magazines, redemption came in a flood. The 997 GT3 RS I wanted to bronze and put on a shelf. A 934, a 962C. The utterly transcendent 1980s 911 Clubsport prototype I'll remember until I croak—lift, chuck the wheel, dance to the sound of the Mulsanne. A magic tautness steeped in tradition, everything I'd read about for years.

This is how you build a brand: devotion and stubbornness, maybe a little too much for a little too long.

Rennsport was also a reminder that we don't all process affection in the same way. Take Patrick Long, 34, Porsche's first full-time American factory driver. He owns a few old 911s, and he cofounded an air-cooled-Porsche gathering called Luftgekühlt. He raced three cars at Rennsport. Then there's Australian Mark Webber, 39, the ex-Formula 1 star who drove a 919 prototype to second overall at Le Mans this year. Webber raced nothing at Laguna by choice, said it didn't help him appreciate the cars. Some people want to swim in old drama, have it reach down their trousers and rummage around. Others are content to simply be in the same room.

For better or worse, that room grows larger every year. For decades, Porsche built only sports cars. Judged solely by volume, the company is now an SUV firm that happens to dabble in sedans and two-doors. In spite of this, or perhaps because of it, people still want a piece of the myth. That arm's-length German approach to emotion. (Driving a 911 always reminds me of that YouTube clip where Werner Herzog narrates the children's book *Mike Mulligan and His Steam Shovel*: "His affection for ze masheen vas out of proportion vith social norms.")

At their best, the cars make you feel like you're in on a secret. We know we're not. The ever-rising sales figures of new Porsches are countered only by the ballooning values of the old ones. Don't price 993 Turbos without a strong stomach. Even the black-sheep 914, that Volkswagen-powered 1970s entry offering, is now being chased as an investment. A rising tide floats all Stuttgarters, except tide might not be the right word, because it's hard to imagine this one going down.

Every time a Rennsport ends, someone at Porsche tells a journalist "never again." The logistics are too difficult, they say. The old drivers are getting older; too many of the cars from the company's most important and beloved hours have become too valuable to exercise. But part of the event's glow is its uneven timing, how it always seems like a one-off. Like how you drive a new Cayman GT4 and immediately raid the couch for spare change, because what if it's never this good again?

There will be more Rennsports. The marketing value is too high to ignore, the brand's past too crucial to its current success, the number of people who live and breathe the marque too large. And that inevitability hints at a truth. Yes, the SUVs share parts with VWs. The purists rail because every new 911 is less like the first. But ultimately, the customer base grows because the cars still do something right. How that changes —and why—will fascinate historians for years. Also me.

I shouldn't have to tell you why I want to go back, but I will anyway. I daydream about sitting under a tree above Laguna's Corkscrew for a few more minutes, the Monterey hills in the hazy distance. About watching a family's legacy rip by one more time, one car at a time, like an ear-frying flip book.

Because there's reason for it all. A humanity. A story.

Not that I'd complain if it rummaged through my trousers.

The Big League

Strapping into Fernando Alonso's old Formula 1 McLaren, a thing that really happened, WTF, yes.

> *Months of planning, an eye-popping quantity of insurance, and a 2007 McLaren MP4-22 driven by a writer who had never felt like more of an imposter at the wheel. The car was then 12 years old but still looked sent from the future. Amazing.*

ROAD & TRACK, AUGUST 2019

They left it plumbed overnight. On stands and under blankets, an umbilical running to an external coolant pump. Gauges monitored temperature and flow as liquid gurgled softly. The pump sat in a tall box flown in from England, one node in a network of equipment required to wake the car and keep it from imploding from the simple act of being itself. By morning, the engine was too hot to touch, which meant mechanics could start it without waiting an hour for the pump to warm the car from cold.

Strictly speaking, you don't have to preheat the driveline of a 2007 McLaren MP4-22 Formula 1 car. You could slide an external starter into the gearbox tail and use a laptop to override a few fail-safes, and the thing might fire and idle for an instant. Then it would eat itself. More specifically, it would wipe its bearings, which are fitted to such close tolerance that the engine cannot be turned by hand when cold. And even if the bearings managed to survive that abuse, other engine or gearbox bits would no doubt become deeply unhappy, and the whole assembly would maybe last for a bit or maybe just grow so hot as to seize and then blow the hell up.

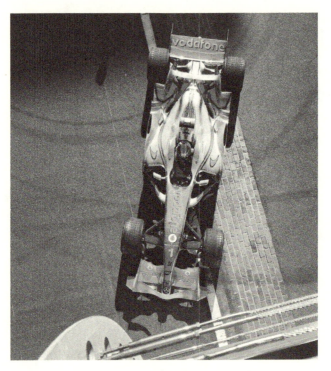

On Indy's famous start-finish "yard of bricks."

Repair estimates on F1 cars are a special breed of gambling, but if you're budgeting a factory rebuild on a 19,000-rpm McLaren Mercedes-Ilmor V-8—and at the moment, no one outside the factory is capable—you should probably set aside at least a quarter of a million dollars. In peak tune, that engine can produce more than 700 hp and a few hundred miles between rebuilds. Pull the redline down by a thousand rpm, that mileage might double.

Therein lies the kicker: F1 cars are designed for abuse, but it's a specific kind of abuse, and so the nicer you treat one, the longer it lasts. Which means they preheat the sucker. And when I walked into the Indianapolis Motor Speedway that morning, in the quiet just after dawn, that preheat was all I heard.

Who knew F1 cars gurgled?

We went to Indy to strap a writer into one of the most complex and expensive racing machines the world has ever seen. Our test car first ran 12 years ago, and 12 years is a lifetime in Formula 1, but the sport's unique blend of hypercompetitive moonshot engineering is unchanged. You can learn a lot by looking at a 12-year-old F1 car and even more by driving it.

Our test car won Monaco, Monza, and the European Grand Prix in the hands of Fernando Alonso. The McLaren is owned by two friends of the magazine and one of the few modern McLaren F1 cars in private hands, because Woking balks at selling them. A small team of factory engineers flew in from the U.K. for the day in order to orchestrate the small ballet of tools and people required to put a car like this on a racetrack.

I got eight laps at the wheel. I also gurgled.

THE GOSSAMER BITS

Formula 1 cars are some of the fastest human-guided devices on the planet, but they are also race cars, which means they are defined by a set of rules. In this case, those rules come from the Fédération Internationale de l'Automobile, or FIA, the world's chief motorsport-governing body. The Formula 1 name dates to 1946, but the FIA has been in charge of European grand-prix racing since the pastime's inception in the early 20th century. For most of that time, the cars have been single-seat, open-wheel, and open-cockpit. Since 1981, teams have been required to own the intellectual rights to their cars (albeit not the engines), which generally means they must design and build those beasts from scratch.

This design process produces a finished car at the beginning of each season, but it also carries on during competition, a constant reinvention. Parts can be designed overnight and flown from the factory to an ongoing race. Aero and chassis bits change with the weather, often literally, and often following a decades-old pattern: a team invents some genius advantage, the FIA finds out about that advantage and bans it, and then the engineers invent more genius. Championships are tilted by grams and hundredths of a second. Somewhere in the middle of all this, a handful of humans strap into cars and run a race.

Win or lose, the process starts early and depends on hundreds of employees per team. Sketching and discussions for McLaren's 2007 car, the MP4-22, first occurred in December of 2005, before the marque's 2006 race car, the MP4-21, had even turned a wheel in testing. The first CAD files were built in March of 2006, under the supervision of design director Neil Oatley. Computational-fluid-dynamics simulations started later that month. Wind-tunnel testing began in May.

At no point in these happenings was there a lack of urgency. The MP4-21 served as starting point, but each of its more than 11,000 parts was obsessively reviewed or redesigned. If there was a way to add speed, efficiency, or reliability, they took it, and cost was generally of little issue. Front-running teams spend hundreds of millions of dollars per season to design and campaign their cars, and the MP4-22 was no exception.

To the untrained observer, the process produced little change. The new McLaren's tub was still a molded composite of carbon fiber and aluminum honeycomb, the engine serving as stressed member. The latter phrase means that the car's central structure essentially stops where the V-8 starts; the engine bolts to the tub, the gearbox hangs off the engine, and virtually everything aft of the crankshaft nose attaches to one of the two parts.

F1 cars have been built like this for decades, but that doesn't make the practice any less elegant. As with most modern open-wheelers, the

McLaren's nose can be removed to change wings or service components like the steering rack. The latter is a power-assisted tube the size of a large cigar, machined from bright alloy and tucked neatly onto the tub's front bulkhead.

But then, everything is done neatly. Suspension is by twin carbon-fiber A-arms front and rear, with inboard torsion bars; F1 cars once used coil springs for that purpose, but coils are heavier, they have more hysteresis, and they're more difficult to package. The primary suspension dampers are carried inboard, atop the gearbox and near the driver's feet. Each damper connects to a suspension upright by a bell crank and a willowy carbon-fiber pushrod with alloy ends.

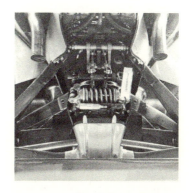

Detail of rear suspension, exhausts, gearbox top.

The pushrods resemble an airfoil in cross section and taper to a razor point. Like many of the car's parts, they are so dainty and finely hewed that you know on sight they could not be any smaller and still do their jobs, because if those reductions were possible, someone would have made them happen.

The theme carries. Formula cars are not large, and at just under 71 inches long and a little more than 37 inches tall, this one is no exception. The assemblage wrapped around Alonso's seat is a carbon sliver 10 inches shorter than a 2019 Mazda Miata and just over 2 inches wider. Every gram is consciously tucked and dense, a ziggurat of gossamer, some panel gaps too tight to pass a piece of paper.

And oh, that mass. F1 design engineers see heft as a cat sees water. Their work is generally designed to come in beneath a rules-mandated minimum weight, then ballasted up to legality. That process is competitively valuable, so teams don't talk about where their ballast goes or even what materials they use. The car is as light as possible, but it has to be the right kind of light, mass in the right place, so the whole gem cracks through a corner and loads its tires correctly. Teams go to great lengths to make that happen, from design to setup to day of use.

Case in point: In 2007, an F1 car had to weigh no less than 1334 pounds with driver and all fluids save fuel. At the first session of that year's United States Grand Prix, in Indianapolis, our test car, MP4-22 chassis six, clocked in at 1340 pounds.

Setup records show that 168.5 of those pounds were Alonso, then 25 years old. By next day, he had lost just over a pound in body weight, so his engineer noted that change in the car's logs and increased its fuel load slightly, regaining the desired balance. At that race, the McLaren carried 48 percent of its mass on the front axle, which means the car had at least one thing in common with a BMW i3S electric runabout.

Little else could be said to have been taken from any road machine. The MP4-22's 10.9-inch carbon front rotors are the color of lava rock and fibrous in appearance, part of a carbon-carbon AP/Hitco/Akebono (pads/rotors/calipers) system that can slow the car at more than 4 g. In max use, the system requires around 350 pounds of force at the pedal. The dampers are made by Koni, though they probably include some McLaren parts, and about half as large as you'd expect.

Those dampers are the crux of a complex suspension that includes front and rear heave springs, to manage ride height under aerodynamic download with millimeter accuracy, because this 1340-pound car makes 3174 pounds of downforce at 160 mph. There's also a rear heave damper, to control the speed of the ride height's change, and an inerter, or separate jounce damper, for the heave damper itself, controlling the acceleration of that part. If all that isn't complex enough, some F1 cars also run two more inerters, one for each pair of "normal" dampers front and rear. (In Indy trim, at least, the MP4-22 does without.)

All of it is connected by gorgeous linkages and castings. These parts are mostly hidden under bodywork, space-program small, and finished in such a manner as to make the average Indy car look like hobo soup. It all makes zero sense the first time you look at it, and your head hurts a little at the work hours and the money, but it's a good pain, so you keep looking, falling into every nook and anodized cranny.

And 12 years ago, against all odds, it worked right out of the gate. The McLaren was a cannon, staggeringly fast even in the heady company of an F1 grid, and reliable as a stone: An MP4-22 led the 2007 F1 drivers' title fight from the second race until the season's final round. Alonso was then a two-time F1 driver's world champion, fresh off a killer run at Renault; his wunderkind rookie teammate, 22-year-old Lewis Hamilton, stacked up nine podiums in the first nine races of the season. The two men tied for second place that year, each one point behind Ferrari's Kimi Raïkkönen, with Hamilton in the chase until the last race.

At the Speedway, a man plugged a small cable into the car's left side. Two more men sat nearby, monitoring laptops that had just lit up. Someone notched a starter into the gearbox. I would have paid more attention, but I barely knew it was happening; I was kneeling near the exhaust and lost, gazing at the welds on a radiator.

This happens around F1 cars. You try to walk by and end up glancing at some tiny and perfect piece of chassis or driveline, and 10 minutes later, you're still there, dreaming down the rabbit hole and imagining what it took to engineer that happy little confection from scratch. And maybe that piece was made on a day's notice, maybe in the middle of the night, to instructions that arrived over email from some distant country, and then it was carried onto a private jet waiting in the dark, winging to a race garage in Asia or Europe, where it was handed to a mechanic who didn't go to bed until the car was back together at 4:00 the next morning, because that's how F1 works.

Someone yelled "Starting!" in an English accent. The engine erupted into blare, thrashy and unpleasant. Blast furnaces are more musical.

I threw earplugs into my ears just in time for the blare to stop. Someone else murmured something about oil pressure. Faces stayed fixed on laptops. The blare began again. One of the laptop men briefly hovered an index finger over his keyboard, then his finger hit the key and the engine burst awake. The blare resolved into a whole note. Maybe 6000 rpm at idle, bright and sunny, the difference between a trumpet and a Chevy caught in a DisposAll.

Nineteen grand! This year's F1 engines turn no more than 15,000 rpm and sound like mutant appliances. This is partly because they wear turbochargers, and turbos are a form of exhaust gaggery. But years ago, I saw the old cars race in person, when they ran the big rpm. At one point, I tried briefly to listen without earplugs; the shriek was musical but also insufferable. A piercing, ice-pick pain, as if a tiny knife was lodged in my ear canal and was attempting to burrow its way out.

Wonderful.

THE 209-POUND WONDER

If current F1 cars sound like blenders, it's by choice. Several years ago, the FIA wrote a rule that saw Formula 1 go low-rpm and hybrid and turbocharged, and the snoozy sound followed. The change was partly intended to improve the sport's relevance without harming its spectacle. Whether that happened is up for discussion, but then, so is the flat-earth theory, if you ignore certain aspects of reality.

Thankfully, relics of the old world exist. The MP4-22's 2.4-liter V-8 is officially known as a Mercedes-Ilmor FO 108T. The design is an updated carryover of Mercedes's 2006 engine, a mill that first barked to life in the labs at Mercedes High Performance Engines in Brixworth, England. In keeping with the past few decades of F1 practice, the 108T's valves are held against their seats pneumatically, no valve springs, their buckets lofted by an onboard bottle of compressed nitrogen. (Reason: stratospheric redlines without valve bounce or excess spring pressure.)

When installed, the engine is barely visible, so low that its valve covers sit roughly even with the centers of the rear wheels. For 2007, F1 rules dictated naturally aspirated engines, meaning, no turbos or superchargers; a displacement cap of 2.4 liters; a 90-degree vee angle; two intake and two exhaust valves per cylinder; and a 95-kilogram (209-pound) minimum weight. The FIA also dictated a freeze on engine development—hence the 2006 carryover—and a 19,000-rpm rev limit. Those choices came on the heels of two great eras: the 2006 rule set, which produced the nuttiest redlines in F1 history (as much as 20,000 rpm), and the 1995–2005 rules, a more open, 3.0-liter formula that gifted the world exotic-alloy V-10s of almost 1000 hp.

Like a lot of F1 rule changes, the 2007 moves were designed to reduce cost and lap speed. And they did, briefly. Then, in a move that surprised absolutely nobody, the teams simply spent that same money elsewhere and clawed the speed back. If this sort of forest-for-the-trees push-pull seems silly, consider that the FIA once banned the use of hyperexpensive beryllium alloys in F1 engines on grounds of the metal's toxicity. At the time, more than one team designer groused publicly about the ban, because . . . well, logic doesn't live here, much.

Power reaches the MP4-22's rear wheels through a McLaren-built, seven-speed, carbon-cased, paddle-shifted, automated-manual transaxle. The clutch, a multiplate carbon unit, is a cylindrical component stack a few inches tall and the diameter of a tea saucer. It is electrohydraulically actuated, controlled by both computer and a small paddle on the steering wheel. The friction surfaces on its plates normally see around 500 degrees Fahrenheit but can stand twice that in moments of slip, as on a race start.

Later in the morning, I met the laptop guy who lit the engine, a Mercedes-AMG engineer named Martin Bourne. Bourne traveled with teams for years, he said, "looking after Lewis Hamilton from 2007 until 2012." He called the McLaren an old car, which made me laugh, and he smiled at it as you might smile at an old pet.

If you do not keep the 108T in its happy place, Bourne told me, grinning, it will shut itself down and tell you to pound sand. That place is essentially a small window of water temp, from a mandatory start-up minimum of 194 degrees Fahrenheit to 266 degrees max. If the V-8 falls below 158 degrees while running, it will decide you are either faffing about or simply not interested in being an assassin that day, self-limiting its grunt from a 295-lb-ft max to a puny 110.

The whole thing is basically doing a tap dance between monitoring its own health and keeping the nut behind the wheel from being a specific kind of too stupid. This is nowhere more famously represented than in the car's anti-stall system: a software trick, common across F1, that automatically snaps the engine to idle if the driver does anything unusual with clutch and throttle. And while all of this can sound finicky, Bourne said, the engine is relatively tolerant of abuse.

"On the dyno," he shrugged, "we'd run them to whatever the failure point is, come back 25 percent, and give them that [mileage] to race in. Because, hopefully, that's a comfortable, reliable margin."

The owner belted into the car first, taking a series of installation laps. I stood by the pit wall, watching heat rise off the Speedway's empty bleachers. *R&T*'s editor-in-chief, Travis Okulski, stood near me, bathing in the Doppler shift: the engine's intoxicating, high-pitched whoop rising and falling and gone again. Echoes made the car seem to be in three places at once. I could literally feel my bones tingle as it passed.

"It's just strange to hear that noise solo," I told Travis. "Like one-twentieth of an F1 grid."

He raised his eyebrows. "Well, it doesn't sound like that. It *is* that."

The moment felt vaguely religious. Travis and I each hold a club-racing license, but that's the bottom of a mountain. How often do you get a private audience with the peak of anything? A 19,000-rpm F1 McLaren, I decided, is a kind of race-car pope: pomp, procedure, rare air. *Habemus whoopem.*

Smithology

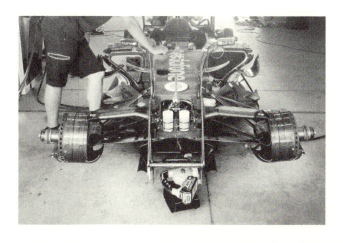

Sidebar: The Rise of Left-Foot

The author's right foot on the McLaren's throttle pedal, as seen through an access port in the car's nose. (The port is visible in the photo atop this page, just left of the N in "Vodafone.")

No one knows exactly when left-foot braking first appeared in Formula 1, but the practice has been common since at least the advent of two-pedal, semiautomatic gearboxes in the sport, i.e., the 1980s. Adrian Newey, the chief technical officer of the Red Bull F1 team, once wrote that modern left-footing dates to the mid-1990s, when he relocated steering components as part of a revolutionary rethink of F1-car nose layouts. According to Newey, the design he implemented meant that the car's structure no longer physically blocked the driver's left foot from reaching the brake pedal.

Left-footing offers inarguable laptime advantage: For one thing, it eliminates the delay inherent in moving one foot back and forth between two pedals. More important, however, it lets a driver use the brakes to adjust a car's attitude without coming off the throttle. The technique is now ubiquitous in top-shelf racing, and many pro cars cannot be driven without it. —SS

SQUEALY-EYED MISSILE MAN

The fit check was deeply surreal. I am five feet, 11 inches and 180 pounds, and my narrow, bony hips would not cram between the edges of Alonso's seat, this insulated, carbon-alloy thing that looks like the rump of a satellite. So the mechanics removed it, visibly disappointed. I was then strapped, with much grunting and yanking of belts, directly to the cockpit's carbon floor.

Seven to 10 laps, they said, over two sessions: get a feel, come in and chat, then back out. No data to parse. "Telemetry isn't cost-effective for a program like this," a mechanic told me. "You need the big mast, a container's worth of stuff, a couple IT guys to run it." Plus, I thought, you need inputs worth looking at, and the last time I leg-pressed 350 pounds was that time three years ago when I kicked an engine block across a friend's shop and nearly threw out my back. I bet Alonso also feels old every day and can't drink a cup of coffee without somehow spilling it in his hair, because we're pretty much the same human.

Speedway personnel set us up with the track's 14-turn road-course layout. That arrangement is slower by average speed than the 13-turn layout used for the 2007 U.S. GP, where the fastest corner was roughly 190 mph. By F1 standards, either track is a stroll: little camber and only a few high-speed corners, so a car's wings and floor don't produce much lateral shove. The McLaren would abuse me, the mechanics confirmed, but less than at somewhere big and fast, like Albert Park or Spa.

Poking at the car before strapping in amounted to dreamy privilege. There were little turning vanes and writhing body foils hidden everywhere, tapering wickers and subtle curves packed into corners where the air tumbled and rolled. The paint was thin enough in places to show the texture of the carbon weave below, mostly where TV cameras wouldn't look. Every so often, a long, flowing surface would be interrupted by a fin or a bigger fin or some other organic shape just hanging out, waiting to nudge air somewhere it needed to go.

Every bit of it mattered. In 2007, Martin Whitmarsh, McLaren's chief operating officer, told reporters that when his team changed from Michelins to Bridgestones, the swap cost them 11 points of downforce, a huge cut. The car had to be retuned to suit, he said; even small details like the shape of a tire can alter the dance and path of air over a wing. (My laps were on specially developed Avon slicks. The Avons are stickier than the 'stones and less picky about treatment, and they can be run safely without the tire warmers long standard in F1.)

The car's owner, a tall man from Ohio, clapped me on the shoulder, cheerful. "This is not a lap-record exercise," he said. "Just enjoy it."

I stood there and wondered how to define "enjoyment" in a world where I was simultaneously geeked and spooked out of my nipples. Then they tightened the belts so much my ribs compressed.

I'm 38 years old. When it comes to age, Formula 1 is like any other professional sport; if an athlete there, a driver, has not achieved something of note by at least their mid-twenties, their body is already on the wrong side of the curve. In 1966, at age 36, the writer George Plimpton famously tried out for the NFL. The experience produced a funny, honest book about achievement and aging called *Paper Lion*. "Good swearing," Plimpton wrote, "is used as a form of punctuation." I looked over the car's high nose and swore.

The seat and high footwell place you low, legs up, toes at chest height. With steering hardware and bodywork in the way, your left foot can only fall on the brake, and your right foot is limited to throttle. The lack of visibility is difficult to overstate. The cockpit somehow manages to be both an oddly comforting suit of armor and a claustrophobic onesie; you see tire tops, shift lights, the little digital gear-indicator display above the tiny and rectangular wheel, little else. If you're close enough to a corner's apex to steer toward it, you probably can't see it, because the nose and tires are in the way. The delicate carbon side mirrors sit on twiggy little stalks barely larger than drinking straws. They also redefine the word useless, which is probably why some of the sharpest drivers on earth can't drive cars like this without regularly crashing into each other.

The steering wheel gives maybe a quarter turn either way before hitting one of your legs, and every control not on the wheel is essentially invisible. A T-shaped knob for brake bias sits on the left side of the cockpit. A fire-system button lives to the right of that, near a spring-loaded toggle that kills the engine. If you sit in front of all this, immobile, for more than 10 minutes or so, absorbing your surroundings, your legs cramp and go numb.

The preflight conversation is Journalist Drives Swank Race Car 101: Don't touch these, a mechanic says, waving at nearly everything. The eight rotary switches on the bottom of the wheel adjust, at one switch each, traction-control gain, traction-control map, differential locking on corner entry, differential preload, differential locking on corner exit, engine braking, engine-mixture map (settings for qualify, race, safety-car rich, safety-car lean, different end-of-straight rev limits, and so on), and engine braking at the apex of a corner. Save the traction knob, each switch has nine settings. I couldn't read their positions in motion. Drivers regularly adjust them at speed.

The engine cranked, that blare again. It sounded different now, vibrating the whole car, nastier and rougher. The vibration quit the instant the engine fired, replaced by a pleasant tingling buzz through the floor. I twitched a toe, pretending I'd been there before, and the thing erupted animal.

They pushed me out of the garage. Butterflies the size of Cleveland. The steering was light with a hint of greasy stiction; the wheel moved in a way that recalled how egg white slips through your fingers.

You have mere moments to get going. The McLaren's engine temperature rises 34 degrees per second at idle, so that temp window Bourne outlined gives you around 40 seconds to use the clutch paddle without waking the anti-stall. Less if you're pushed out of the garage before leaving. Hit the no-go heat peak—engine temp is shown on a stark red display just above the wheel, digital numbers counting up like on the arm of the Predator, not stressful or anything—and you have to shut off the engine, sit there as mechanics plug fans into the sidepods for cooling. Everyone watching.

I got lucky, and the clutch hit the first time out. The mechanics later told me this was incredible chance; the paddle has no feel, and the anti-stall allows almost no slip, but the car rolled from a stop as if I'd been in it all my life. My heart went *pit* and then *pat*, and then the butterflies evaporated.

As did large quantities of reason. A modern F1 car is probably humanity's best insight into the mind of a hummingbird, and that fact became clear after five feet of roll. *Flit* and *flit*, the car goes, batting around masslessly, nuts even by the standards of pro machinery.

Open-wheel cars generally move from your spine, but this was something different; the McLaren seemed at once hung off a house-sized gyro and capable of reclocking itself on a breath. Unsurprisingly, it was staggeringly quick. But road cars have come a long way, and in a straight line, the MP4-22 merely leaps forward in a manner that recalls current Bugattis. The difference, of course, is in lateral grip, transition insanity, and the absurd fashion in which the McLaren warps off an apex. A Bugatti is to this as North America is to a housefly. There's a breathless, plasma-like immediacy baked into everything, iced with a delicacy so refined, you might call it grace, if it didn't feel so ruthless.

The powerband is narrow and blisteringly immediate. Time in gears is often less than a whole Mississippi, as fast as you can say the words: *One-mis, two-mis, three-mis*, and then you've ripped from the bottom of first to the top of third. The rapid gear handoffs mesh into a perpetual crescendo, acceleration tapering noticeably only in sixth and seventh gear. The engine is so crisp and brassy, it doesn't seem real. It would feel more violent if you didn't go in expecting it to feel violent. It was still crushingly violent.

Alonso's setup notes for Indy talk of mild understeer, a sharp or dull nose, slides on exit. All normal racing stuff, and in low-speed corners, the McLaren is deceptive, because it just feels like a car. The nose will wash or the back tires will step, and on the Avons, at least, in the chassis tune I tried, it recovers easily. Input and state changes are reacted to with such resolution as to suggest that the dampers are made of Pegasus feather. They dictate wheel behavior in a language I could listen to all day but do not speak.

I did a few laps, then a cool-down lap where I blinked about 10 times a second. A short debrief followed. (Mechanic: "Everything fine?" Me: "Yes.") Leaving the pits for the second time, I activated anti-stall. Then again after that. It happened so many times I lost count, and then the car had to be shut down to cool, rolled back in the garage, fans plugged in again.

In anti-stall, the cockpit display flashes and the engine rpm self-corrects, like a small intake of breath. Or maybe a patronizing sigh. You sit there feeling impotent. Two mechanics eventually had to help, pushing the car to a rolling start. It was normal, they said; everyone does it. My grandmother used to say that society runs on kind fibs.

The second session revealed slightly more. Mostly that the car's true guano lay in braking and high-speed corners. I do not have enough aero seat time to discuss the downforce save admitting it as present, spooky, and much. But the brakes were otherworldly. Compounded lunacy.

On the second lap out, once the pads and rotors were warm, I rolled up to Turn 1 in the middle of seventh gear. After the "5" brake board—the earliest brake marker in the line—I laid into the left pedal with everything I had. So much pressure that my leg flirted with cramping. The forces at work threw my internal clock for a moment; as the car slowed, I couldn't breathe. A fifth of a heartbeat after getting into the pedal, I began releasing the brakes, to avoid lockup as the car shed downforce. As the "4" marker passed my head, the McLaren fell beneath highway speed. It was at that point both too far from and comically slow for the upcoming corner, the slowest on the track, a second-gear right that 2007 Alonso took at around 56 mph.

Later, in the garage, a McLaren technician said that the middle of seventh gear in that day's trim—he couldn't share specifics on gearing—was "160 to 170 mph." My mind took a moment to reconsider the braking and promptly went to oatmeal.

And then it was over.

It's funny how the brain can trick you into believing the improbable. As I climbed from the cockpit, the McLaren's abilities felt reachable, just around the corner, though they were clearly not.

Wide-eyed, I mentioned that to one of the mechanics. He tilted his head and thought for a moment. With enough test time and data, he said, and a low-*g* track, a competent amateur driver could manage laps near race pace. He had seen people pull it off. The key, he added, is having someone tell you how to push the aerodynamics—advice like, "Take it flat in sixth, you'll be fine." ("Most people see the data," he said, "and just go, 'I had no idea.'")

I don't know what to say about that. I do know that, when I climbed from the car, the world felt smoky and calm. A few minutes later, I sat down and was hit by a rush of nervous energy so strong, my toes twitched.

I know just one other club racer, one other ordinary person, who has driven a post-2000 F1 car. My friend Mark Gillies, a former editor at *Car and Driver*, once tried a 2007 Honda RA107. We talked before Indy. "It's one of the only ways you can realize how good drivers are," he said. "I met Humphrey Corbett once, Alain Prost's engineer. He said that when they put [2009 world champion] Jenson Button in the car for the first time, he was on pace in the first 10 laps."

And then you see the horizon.

Not for nothing are these people widely viewed as some of the best drivers alive. They're definitely athletes: In 2007, F1 cars were capable of more than 4 g in corners; in 2017, when the series went to wider tires, a Mercedes-Benz peaked at 6.5. Picture simply trying to hold your head up in a corner when it weighs six and a half times normal. Much less

Smithology

asking it to play 200-mph chess for 90 minutes. What must it feel like, a life training for that? First, building the skill required to simply play the game—normalizing the car, driving it as you would anything else. Then being so comfortable with the magic of the whole that you can learn to develop and tune it. Finally, weaponizing it, using it tactically.

Now consider how, every so often, a quick F1 driver will reference a legend on the grid, a Senna or a Hamilton, and say something like, "I don't know how he does it."

Operating a machine, in other words, versus using it as a paintbrush.

The whole experience served as a kind of light in the dark—a hint at why people chase a place in the F1 circus from childhood, or settle for driving for a hopelessly uncompetitive team there, or stay in the sport years too long. Because you are then at that peak, a frontier of human striving. We only have so many.

It all sums up into a strange little piece of awe, a feeling that surfaces in the days after you leave the car, hanging there before you go to sleep and popping back to light when you wake up. A phrase that fogs through the slack in your mind, turning over and over and melting into a liquid sweet warmth like so much candy on the tongue:

"I didn't know humans could *do* that."

Sam Smith

SIDEBAR: FIVE STEPS TO FIRE YOUR MP4-22

Starting a Formula 1 car isn't like hitting the key on a Corolla. Mercedes-AMG F1 systems engineer Martin Bourne shared what it takes.

ONE: PREHEAT
"The oil gets warm through temperature soak from the engine. Set the coolant pump on a 60-degree heater. Optimum is 110 degrees Celsius on the water and about 100, 105 on the oil."

TWO: CHARGE THE VALVE SPRINGS
"Next, we've got pneumatic valve springs, so you have to charge the [gas] bottle for that. You must do that before you turn it over; if it's been sitting for any length of time and one of the valves has dropped [due to low pressure], you bend a valve."

THREE: HAND-CRANK IT
"You can't put a starter motor on it, because the starter has so much torque, you won't feel it if there's anything wrong internally. We hand-crank it first [turning the crankshaft by hand], so you can feel if it's catching something. We put bleed bottles on the radiator, do three short

cranks of the engine, then a 10-second crank. When we're happy that the radiators are full, we'll check the oil level."

Four: Check the Oil

"The oil level's quite tricky. The tank can drain into the crankcase—the rear crankshaft seal works when running, but statically, it leaks a little bit. So when we finish running, we drain the engine. It took four fire-ups [for this story] to set the oil level. You sort of creep up on it. The tank's carbon, and an overfill can burst it. The oil has nowhere to go, it splits the carbon, it's a massive scene, engine has to come out."

Five: Light the Mother

"The water pressure has to be set because we're completely full at that point. We get to 80 degrees and we'll do the final bleed, drain the header tank, and put the pressure in. It runs about 1.6 bar. Simple, eh?"

Paternal Instinct
The familial warmth of the purchasing knee-jerk.

> *This car was such a delight. Bowman grabbed it in Virginia, and then my friend Bob Sorokanich and I drove it 2500 miles, Tennessee to Seattle, in winter. Didn't miss a beat.*

ROAD & TRACK, DECEMBER 2018

My dad just bought a Mercedes-Benz. Once, long ago, I watched a person share those words with someone else. It was eighth grade. The guy's name was Timmy or Tommy or Terry or something; memory fails. He sat in the next row up and was leaning across the aisle to talk to a girl.

Timmy-Tommy-Terry yapped a bit about his father's new car. His face wore a look that suggested he desired many things in life, not least the chance to discuss world affairs with that young lady. Preferably while neither of them wore a shirt. The girl listened with obvious disinterest, then returned to her book. Triple-T slumped in his seat. A glorious shoot-down. The lesson stuck: No one cares what your dad just bought, unless they are a rank sucker.

Smithology

In other news, my dad just bought a Mercedes and I care and I am almost certainly a rank sucker.

The Craigslist ad hit my inbox at noon on a Thursday. It was sent by my friend Zach Bowman, who used to work for this magazine. In car-writing circles, Zach is widely heralded for two things: the year he lived in a pickup camper, traveling the country with his wife and one-year-old daughter; and a sense of personal romanticism that would shame an 18th-century Frenchman. We have much in common.

"IT HURTS SO GOOD," read the email header. I clicked the link. My brain found vapor lock.

What do you do when faced with a 30,000-mile 1971 Mercedes-Benz 220 sedan? Does the answer change when the car is priced so reasonably, you wonder if the ad is a scam? If you are me, you find yourself with questions. What would make someone preserve an entry-level Mercedes for decades? Do they still use these things as taxis in Cairo? Will leftover schnitzel keep in the fridge for a night, a week, 47 years?

If you are a certain kind of person, you start scheming to buy the thing. Or you find a friend or family member and convince them to buy it, because you are a man of taste and breeding but, as the saying goes, currently between yachts.

Smith's Craigslist Rule No. 376: If you can't afford the good, find the good a good home.

It was quietly pretty. White, green interior, A/C, a four-speed manual. Capped by that *je ne sais quoi* common to low-mile cars, the details so right and harmonized, you daydream of factories. With old Benzes, I always imagine the plant in Sindelfingen: elves in dirndls, beer spigots in the aisles, stern accountants singing German chanteys about profit margins while signing off on door latches that cost more than a Cadillac. (If 1971 Germany wasn't really like this, don't tell me, I don't want to know.)

Zach knows my father and copied him on that email. The 220 was in Virginia, two hours from Zach's house in Tennessee. Three time zones from my dad, who lives in Seattle. And so three men in three separate locations stared into the middle distance and contemplated how a new German car survives almost five decades without becoming a crappy old German car.

167

I called Dad and made insistent noises into the phone. A few days later, we met for drinks. He had called the guy, proved the car's provenance, bought it sight unseen.

My father buys nothing sight unseen, except maybe lunch. And even then, he squints at the menu for a bit, suspicious.

"Gonna drive it every day," he said, beaming.

Speed is not the appeal here. Your average 1970s Benz wants velocity like cats want a bath. Mercedes rated the 220's 2.2-liter four at 116 hp, then dropped it into a relatively heavy car. Glance under the hood, that horsepower figure seems realistic only if smiled upon by a generous heaven. The engine hulks on its mounts, looking bored with existence.

Still, special company, special time. Mercedes was in the 1970s at the height of its powers, building cars designed to outlast their drivers, and then the generation of drivers after that. Plating thick enough to swim in, indestructible interiors, repairable everything. All designed before the industry labeled such choices wasteful, because who keeps a car for generations? Luxury cars are now immensely more capable but rarely overengineered. The business case for disposability simply makes more sense.

And for my dad, there's another level. In 1972, his mother bought a brand-new Mercedes 280 SE 4.5 from her local dealer. Same chill road manners as the 220, just more grunt. Dad borrowed the thing in high school to take my mom on dates. My grandmother is gone, but every car she owned carried a small dashboard medal depicting St. Christopher, the patron saint of travelers. In a coincidence that prompts warm fuzzies vis-à-vis the clockwork of the universe, the 220's Craigslist ad held a picture of a St. Christopher medal glued to the car's binnacle. That medal is almost certainly not identical to the one that lived in the 280, but pretending as much makes me happy, so why the hell not?

I offered to deliver the car to my dad this winter, Virginia to Seattle. In the way that "offer" can mean "buy a plane ticket before anyone tells you no." Some people get all pearl-clutchy about old cars in snow, but white-weather trips are fun on a bun, and one long jaunt won't turn a floor to rust. He accepted my offer. Then he said he was envious.

I'm reminded of the old line about going home again—how the past is nice to visit but rarely where you want to live. No matter. Old things unused are in some ways not old. My parents still go on dates, because they're cute like that. And 30,000 miles isn't so much the past as a life delayed a little, hanging out in the wings, patiently waiting to get up to speed.

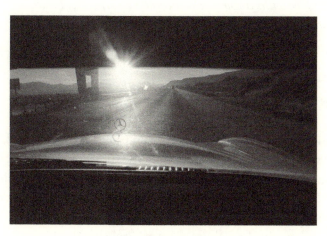

In Wyoming, hustling west.

Snow-Blind

Every car lives. As for death,
that's up to you.

Real life got in the way and I didn't fix this one. The friend who bought it from me did, though. Eight years later, when I was finally able to buy the car back, my eight-year-old daughter asked if we could throw it a homecoming party. Yes, I said. "Good," she replied. "Family is important."

ROAD & TRACK, FEBRUARY 2015

Above all, I remember the drive from California. A blizzard, I-80 in Wyoming, Ted Leo blasting from the speakers. Full throttle at the top of third gear. Snow left the sky in a deathless gust, pinwheeling over the hood like confetti, blotting onto the windshield so quickly the wipers barely kept up.

A friend was in the right seat, quiet. Probably thinking I was going to crash and have us eaten by bears. I remember the steely look on his face as I passed a plow truck in a fit of giddy opposite lock. What I can't recall is the last time I so totally, in-the-moment loved an automobile.

That car is gone now. Last week, two years after the blizzard, it was sitting on an interstate in stopped traffic, my wife Adrienne at the wheel, when a Ford Focus plowed into the trunk at 40 mph. Maybe there was reasonable cause, but I like to think of the Focus guy as a schmuck with a history of feeding paint thinner to puppies, so I picture him on the phone. Adrienne, thankfully, was fine. I wasn't there, which is also good, because there were witnesses, and you should never punch someone in the mouth with witnesses.

The make and model won't matter to anyone but me. The car was old, all-wheel-drive, and rare enough to prompt a trip to San Francisco to buy it. It was in staggeringly nice shape but relatively inexpensive, the kind of doe-eyed survivor that insurance companies love to declare a total loss in a fender-bender. This was not a fender-bender. The body accordioned behind the rear wheels; the trunk floor turned into a Pringle. Because progress is real, the Focus suffered only a cracked bumper cover. My car left on a flatbed, looking like it had been sodomized by a shipping container.

Goodbyes are rarely fun, but this one hurt. Adrienne drove that car every day. She adored it more than I did, had never been so attached to a machine, used the old mountain-goat analogy to describe its winter prowess. (For the record, I have never understood this, because cars take you places, and who rides a goat?) It inhaled long trips and dirt roads, had an interior almost too well-preserved to use. It was the latest in a long line of small and nimble old cars that have seen regular use at my house. But things change. Parts were getting expensive. We have a young daughter, and we had talked for months about wanting more crush space and child-seat room. Modern hardware beckoned. That trigger-pull kept getting put off, but I knew the party was winding down.

And now it's gone, the decision made. People tell me to let it go.

Fine, I fibbed. The blizzard car isn't gone. It's sulking in a corner of *R&T's* parking lot, slowly stewing into oxide. I didn't know what to do after the accident, so I postponed filing an insurance claim, picturing junkyards and circling vultures. (The leak-free transfer case, that uncracked dashboard, a thousand other rare and wonderful things that had escaped the ravages of age, all scattered to the wind.)

That was my car. Those were my parts. I wasn't *done*.

I went out to look at the car today at lunch, walking circles around it, hands in my pockets. If life were a movie, Ted Leo would've swelled, snow would have salt-shakered down, and a Wes Anderson title screen would have appeared. (OUR FRIEND WAKES UP.) Instead, sunshine filled the lot, trucks rumbled down a nearby freeway, and I accidentally stepped into a ziggurat of dog poo behind the rear bumper.

Standing there, decomposition on the breeze, a squinty sort of defiance took over. My spine straightened. I felt like John Belushi in *Animal House*, rambling about the Germans bombing Pearl Harbor.

I spun on a heel and began walking back inside. And as I strode across the lot, I said to myself, *No.*

The problem with thinking like a rational adult is that it gives rational results. Examples: Replacing the blizzard car doesn't make financial sense, not least because values for the model have climbed to absurd heights over the past two years. Even so, repairs would require more cash than the car is worth, and the nice lady who takes my calls at the insurance company already thinks I wear a tinfoil hat. We found Adrienne a new car, a late-model Mazda 3; it does the job, it is fine. Everything has a season, move on, no one leaves the dinner table until you finish your vegetables.

But do you always have to do the mature thing? Moreover, is there such a thing as "the mature thing" if your entire life has been undeniably, almost categorically immature? Is that not simply the inverse of what has gotten you to wherever you are now, and thus foolishly out of character and wrong on a philosophical level? If I close my eyes, can I still see the flying snow and the empty highway and feel the car whip sideways, rat-tat-tat-ing off the rev limiter?

As I opened the office door, I paused, looking back at the parking lot. Dumb on paper isn't the same as dumb in real life. You could pull on the logical threads—it's a classic going up in value, it's rare—but above all, that car was mine, and that's all that matters. And we are coming up on winter, and winter is a good time for projects, and there are blizzards yet to come, and someone has to take a principled stand against the rising tide of mediocrity and . . . and . . .

The final truth blasted forth like a chorus of only moderately intoxicated angels: *I own tools, dammit, and I know how to use them.*

Life is short. Vegetables aren't everything. I want my car back, and I'm going to get it.

Day of Thunder

The turn-both-ways, thank-your-sponsors, Frequently-Asked-Questions guide to being an apex-jumpin' badass in your very own personal NASCAR stocker.

> *If my Powerball ship ever comes in, my first four purchases will be a McLaren F1, a short-wheelbase Dodge van on Watanabes, a 289 Cobra on Halibrands, and one of these. Equal parts atomic sofa and 600-horse joy buzzer.*

ROAD & TRACK, OCTOBER 2017

It's really interesting, he said, how those guys drove the cars, before they learned. When NASCAR was mostly good ol' boys drug up from dirt tracks, not polished kids born in karts. The old guys ran road courses like they ran ovals, he said—using the corners to slow the car, backing it in like a bootlegger, then gathering up the wheel, arms and elbows, before tear-assing to the next turn and doing it all again.

Amazing car control, he noted. And it makes sense: What would you expect from a group of dudes who see a green flag every week? Who catch 200-mph slides as often as some people go to the grocery?

In the paddock at Road America, on that sunny Wisconsin day, Boris Said paused for a moment. He looked at the car and flashed a grin.

"Plus, these things are just *fun*, right?"

So I chuckled and climbed into a 1993 NASCAR Ford Thunderbird at one of the longest, fastest road courses in the country. More than 160 mph and a 753-hp V-8, the engine making an alto yawp not unlike the one in every single *Jurassic Park* movie, that moment when Enormous Bloodthirsty Dinosaur X has broken loose and your TV speakers cavitate and *Oh My God She's Coming Right for Us Start the Jeep START THE JEEP* and then somebody gets eaten.

Fun may have been an understatement.

As a track device, used NASCAR stockers are more laughs than a year of Christmases. They are also relatively cheap. If you buy one, you can take it to track days or go vintage racing, where you will hold the leash of a manual-transmission, live-axle, pushrod, national-treasure throwback that wants to slide and dance like an old truck in mud. All while being something like safe, because every stock car was designed to crash at 150 mph.

We wanted to learn more about this, so we called up Said. In addition to having won the 24 Hours of Nürburgring, the 12 Hours of Sebring, and the 24 Hours of Daytona, Said is what NASCAR calls a "road-course ringer." He jumped into stock-car racing almost 20 years ago and has since coached generations of drivers in road-course finesse, from stars of the last century to Dale Earnhardt, Jr. and Kasey Kahne.

Finally, we sourced our Thunderbird, a Winston Cup car with history. I strapped in to answer a few questions. The kind you will get asked if you are the type of hero to hump a 3250-pound, earthshaking southern mother of an automobile through a track day or a vintage race.

Some people think NASCAR is boring. Left turns and lunkheads.

Those folks are pretty much just incredibly wrong.

NASCAR Turns Right?

Perhaps you were not aware of this. NASCAR's top shelf is known as Cup racing. Of the 36 races on the 2017 NASCAR Monster Energy Cup schedule, 34 take place at an oval track. (Tradition dictates that American ovals run counterclockwise, turning only left.) The remaining two events are road courses: the seven-turn Watkins Glen International, in New York, and the 12-turn Sonoma Raceway, in California.

At a time when big-league road racing is still relatively unknown to most of America, NASCAR's oval preference is partly why the sport continues to draw audiences and sponsor dollars. Oval tracks are more compact than road courses, which makes them easier to understand, broadcast, and spectate. Plus, there's the appeal of sitting in a coliseum while howly-screamy engines pump noise into your face for hours.

These factors are convenient for NASCAR but sad for anyone who likes road racing, because a stock car is one of the funkiest devices in motorsport. On a road course, in professional hands, its DNA invariably produces an old-school show, cars drifting and bellowing while carrying their inside front wheels high in the air and sounding like a herd of mating howitzers.

Nor does the word "stock" mean much. The average Cup car shares as much with a production automobile as this magazine does with a giant redwood. The body is 24-gauge sheet steel. It covers a 5.9-liter pushrod V-8, a heavy ladder frame and tubular roll structure, an A-arm front suspension, and a live rear axle. The latter, a setup found on few if any, production cars sold in America, is located by two trailing arms and a Panhard rod, an arrangement that is itself older than dirt.

As a sanctioning body, NASCAR does not appear to trust progress. For decades, a Cup car's front suspension has resembled that of a 1966 Chevrolet Chevelle. The rear owes so much to an old pickup that the industry calls its trailing beams "truck arms." Until recently, NASCAR required teams to use a Holley 4150-series carburetor, partly because that device was relatively easy to police for cheating. (In a shocking update, the carb was replaced, in 2012, by Holley throttle-body fuel injection. Reactions varied, but the racing didn't really change.)

All of this is by design. NASCAR was born in 1947. The sport's rulebook has evolved since, but the current cars are fundamentally similar to those of decades ago. They are purposely heavy, undertired, and underbraked. Heavy steel wheels are de rigueur, as is a low-grip, 15-inch Goodyear slick. The rules ban driver aids, including anti-lock braking, telemetry during races, and traction control. Compared with an IMSA prototype, a Cup car makes as much downforce as a bag of helium. The goal is to place a premium on setup and driver skill.

Read those last few paragraphs again and tell me that you don't want to watch a herd of pro geniuses drift-fighting cars like that around a hairy old road course like Watkins Glen.

Oddly, road-race people have long made fun of stock cars. When I first started club racing, a driving-instructor friend told me that NASCAR was "a left-turn waste of time." I remember those words often. Usually while watching a Formula 1 race where no one has pulled off any kind of heroic pass or slide, and where the pole sitter won because his aerodynamicist was an unknowable hair smarter or better funded than the other aerodynamicists on the grid.

At this year's Sonoma Cup NASCAR race, the first 21 cars in qualifying were separated by less than a second. The winner, Kevin Harvick, started 12th. The third-place finisher, Brad Keselowski, started 23rd.

It's a bar brawl. The cars are basically longneck bottles broken in half. And they most definitely turn right.

YOU MEAN I CAN AFFORD ONE?

If you have a full-time job, you probably have a shot. The door is opened by sheer volume, because no racing series produces cars like NASCAR. At the start of 2017, the Cup supported 36 full-time drivers. Teams can and do build separate cars for different track types—machines tailored for road courses, but also the various types of oval. Larger teams grind out new cars and bodies almost constantly. (Damage means that cars are regularly rebodied; a well-funded Cup team might produce 50 new bodies per car, per season.)

Teams often sell old cars or those that have aged outside the rulebook's tight tolerances. And because there are generally more used stock cars than buyers, prices are remarkably low. A name-driver car with significant history could cost more than a new Porsche, but a nobody chassis with a mild engine can be had for new-Honda money. A vintage car from one of NASCAR's feeder series is used-Honda territory. For a fast machine from a nationally broadcast pro series, that's almost free.

The 1993 Ford Thunderbird we sourced is not a nobody car. It was built by South Carolina's Bud Moore Engineering, a legend in NASCAR circles and the shop behind Ford's 1970 Trans-Am championship. The Thunderbird is now owned by *R&T* contributor Colin Comer. It was constructed for road-course use in 1993, the same year it won the Sonoma Cup race in the hands of Geoff Bodine.

Comer was kind enough to lend the car for this story. At the track, I asked him why he likes stock cars. He smiled. "They're soft, like a dirt-track car. Fast, safe, forgiving, you can bounce them off curbs. If a Trans-Am car is a scalpel, this is a lead-shot hammer."

Comer's Thunderbird currently wears one of its original Quality Care liveries; an unmuffled, 753-hp, 8800-rpm Ford 358; a four-speed, dog-clutch Jerico manual with a Hurst shifter; and a Ford 9-inch rear axle with a mechanically locking Detroit Locker differential. The front brake calipers are Brembos, and the rears are Wilwoods—real-deal road-racing hardware. They work through tires just 11.5 inches wide. A 2017 Corvette Z06 produces 100 hp less than the Thunderbird and uses rear rubber almost 2 inches wider.

Prior to our test, Comer had the car prepped by Wisconsin race shop Valu Pro. Kyle Bauknecht, Valu Pro's owner and a former NASCAR mechanic and fabricator, came to Road America for support.

"These cars are pretty bulletproof," he said. "If you keep stuff maintained and greased, the consumable bits in the chassis last five or six seasons. They're hard on brakes. You replace pads every event, rotors every two."

"Still," Comer added, "everything is cheap. Control arms and shocks —even the best shocks in the world are $500 apiece, and you don't have to spend anywhere near that for good ones. And with take-off Cup car parts, you can rebuild it all forever, it's just indefinite."

Which brings us to the most important point: To minimize component failure, top Cup teams replace parts long before they wear out. Those used bits are often sold to the public for pennies on the dollar: engines a few ponies short of competitive (yet still likely to make more than 600 hp), pallets full of spares, barely scuffed tires.

"Last year, you could buy a 358 Cup engine from Roush, on eBay, for 10 to 15 grand, ready to roll," Comer said. "That engine probably cost them $75,000 to build." A rebuild on a strong but "not insane" motor, Bauknecht said, is generally around $15,000.

None of which is small money. But consider it in race-car language: The closest sports-car analogue for a NASCAR stocker is probably a used Porsche 911 GT3 Cup. Several years ago, a GT3 Cup engineer I interviewed said that he told customers to prepare for "around $40,000" on an engine rebuild. And that, he said, was if he liked the guy writing the checks.

What Does It Feel Like?

Oh, brother.

It feels like your inner five-year-old has designed a car, and that car is both extremely loud and extremely simple and stuck somewhere in North Carolina in 1974. A pet cartoon. A blessed event. A couch with JATO nozzles up the wazoo.

But we're getting ahead of the story.

The subtlety is surprising. In the 1990s, as now, on television, a NASCAR field looked banal, just flat slabs of sponsor paint. Up close, the cars are an assemblage of compound curves, obviously shaped by

Smithology

hand. One more reason that stock cars aren't stock—mass-produced automobiles haven't had handmade bodies in decades. But every panel on Comer's Thunderbird arcs gently in a few different axes,. The hood and trunk meet the fenders with paper-thin gaps. There are no doors, so you climb through the window, like on *The Dukes of Hazzard*.

With the hood up, you can see the entire front end: suspension, tidy plumbing, tires, frame. The steering drag link, as big around as a soda can. The engine, wider than you expect, and breathing through a composite airbox that feeds off the high-pressure area at the bottom of the windshield. Two giant frame tubes spear forward from the firewall, meeting the radiator and the sparse space frame under the front bumper —a reminder that stock cars, above all, are built to protect driver and driveline. (NASCAR news flash: Drivers crash regularly and often hit each other on purpose.)

In the case of our test car, what you don't see is too much of a showroom '93 T-Bird. Maybe in the roofline, viewed on TV. Or from a hot grandstand, a beer in your hand, the car flinging around some oval at a buck-eighty. It is entirely possible that this is the point.

Nearly six liters of Detroit V-8 and nearly 9000 rpm. Five hundred and twenty-seven pound-feet of torque. It weighed 3250 pounds and felt mad sitting still. It also felt mad while moving.

Predictably, there are sponsor logos. They are shotgunned around the car in places both obvious and not, because stock-car racing has long believed in that sort of thing. Front fenders covered in supplier stickers; switch panels with fat branding; a coffee can of a Wix oil filter, its lettering legible from space. Even the front-suspension ball joints, in a place no TV camera would ever be, have a big "MOOG PROBLEM SOLVER" stamped into their heads, next to the grease nipple.

It's probably because I don't work on enough old American iron, but I can't remember the last time a ball joint shouted anything at me, much less its name. But then, if those letters were small, they'd be out of

179

place. The radiator is an aluminum skyscraper around 3 inches thick. Even the steering box, a power-assisted, recirculating-ball chunk, is large enough to brain an elephant. It would make a small dump truck feel inadequate. And if you stand over it while the engine lights off, a joy filters into your body. You start daydreaming and you just want to thank the crew and the good people at Ford for all their support they gave us a great car the No. 15 Quality Care Motorcraft T-Bird ran real good today thank you God and America and also McDonald's and the good people of the Carolinas don't forget to drink Coke the number-one soft drink in America the Real Thing that name again is Coke WOO BURNOUTS.

In that moment, it almost hurts, loving this country—her capacity for the simultaneously great and ridiculous—so much.

The carburetor needs a throttle pump on start-up, but the V-8 whomps awake instantly, keyed from a toggle on the dash. The lope that results is a wall of cannons. You don't so much hear the cylinders as feel each one, individually, packing air into your ears.

Inside, it takes a minute to adjust to the weirdness. The interior is a bunker of tubing. Visibility anywhere but forward is largely a guess. The steering wheel is inches from your chest and the size of a garbage-can lid. The nose feels a million miles away and hangs over pillow-soft tires and springs. The diff clunks and pops in the paddock, the car hopping and jerking. If you have any experience with old muscle cars, it feels familiar.

Even with gentle hands, the car almost refuses to turn unless you treat the throttle like poison or get grumpy with it, little slips and slides to revector the front bumper.

The former action is nicer to the tires and generally faster, so you do it, despite the fact that the car seems to beg for sideways goofery. The wheel's size and proximity give gobs of leverage, but it makes you move like a gangster mook in a 1950s movie—dancing hands, elbows bent into a tight vee. The steering box communicates in muted tones and really only speaks up if you rail over a huge curb, at which point the wheel sneezes out a blip of kickback. As if to say, *I saw that, now I'm going back to sleep.*

So you drive with eyes and spine, hands numb, like in an old Corvette. The diff unlocks, the car rolls into the corner, the tires crouch into a set, the suspension settles, and then your right foot investigates the carburetor. A beat later, you unwind the wheel, and that foot finds the floor.

The author, up on that wheel.

At which point the universe collapses. There is nowhere that a NASCAR 358 does not pull like stinking bejesus, but it makes linear, madhouse power from 6000 to 8000 rpm. All while pumping out a high-pitched, machine-beast-howl. The transmission has dog clutches instead of synchromesh, so you can rail through an upshift without the clutch, just a hint of throttle lift. Combine that with the engine's body-saturating noise, and the car seems caught in a perpetual, near-breathless bellow, the long shifter moving as fast as you can throw it. The dogs also mean that the lever won't go into gear on a downshift unless you wallop out a big throttle blip. Those downshifts are relatively easy to get right but, like the rest of the car, far from foolproof. Screw up the timing and the rear axle can start hopping, slamming up and down so violently that the car seems to be coming apart.

Even with all that, slowing down is the strangest part. The brakes would possibly work better as anchors if you unbolted the front calipers and threw them out the window on a chain. Stopping distances are almost comically long, and the pads fade into nonexistence—you're laying into the pedal but the car seems to coast—if you brake near their limit for several corners in a row. The pedal is hard as stone and only slightly more possessed of feedback, especially if the pads are baked.

So braking has to be handled with a careful eye and maybe a dust of prayer. After a few laps, I debriefed with Boris.

"These brakes . . . that's normal?"

"They come back if you wait a corner or two. I mean, the newer cars are much better. It's worse in traffic, because they don't cool as well. You just plan for it."

He laughed, so I laughed, because it seemed like the thing to do. Then I drove the car again and laughed in every single corner, the way you do when someone says that your fly is open.

Perhaps all this sounds terrible. Therein lies the central glory of the stock car: It is not. It is a riot, a viceless sweetheart of a race car that eggs you on. When I got a handle on what the Ford wanted, it bounded into corners and did this electric boom-blat out of them, squirming and writhing and generally feeling like a miniature, one-man battleship. You end up living for the stuff the car does poorly, figuring out how to work around it. You grin so hard your face cramps. It's an encyclopedia of cliché, it's hilarious, it's every good-looking ounce of the American South rising up to kiss you on the mouth.

If they made stock cars with 150 hp, you could safely give them to kindergartners.

If I had even a gram less sense, I would sell my kids and kidneys to buy one for each of my friends and maybe even my dog.

Did I mention that used stock cars are cheap? Did I mention that this may be the best-kept secret in the whole blessed track-day-and-vintage-racing world?

Maybe I did. Stock cars break your brain a little.

Ran real good today, she did.

Ford Motorcraft drink Coke God bless America.

Smithology

SIDEBAR: STORIES FROM THE RINGER

Can a sports-car person love this stuff? Boris Said knows better than most.

ON WHAT STOCK CARS WANT FROM A DRIVER:
"It depends on the corner. It pays big dividends to be smooth. You can't force one of these around like a [sports] car—aggressive on the brakes, trailing all the way into the corner with them chattering. You brake in a straight line. When your eyes say turn the wheel, your foot needs to come up, or you'll lock the tire. As soon as it's gripped up in the center, you start going for the power, unwinding the wheel.

"It's not easy, not everybody picks it up. One of my heroes is [Indy winner] Dario Franchitti. When he didn't qualify for the Cup race at Sears Point, I thought, How could he be that bad? He just didn't get the difference. I've seen a lot of guys get in one and look stupid. It's counterintuitive, as different as hitting a golf ball and going to a batting cage.

"A Trans-Am car, you're twice as aggressive, a GT3 car, twice as much as that. The fun here is, you're driving the hell out of it—it's a slow-motion wrestling match. You work your ass off, managing a lot of horsepower, a lot less grip, no aids. It's more of a driver's car."

WHY THAT 1960S-STYLE DIFFERENTIAL RULES EVERYTHING:
"You have to wait for it. Because the car won't turn when the diff is locked, on throttle, both wheels going the same speed. So you roll into

the center of the corner, off the brake, the rear end unlocks. As you feel like it's starting to turn, gradually, you settle the car, feeding in power, to lock the rear end. If you pick up the throttle like you would in a sports car, you'll push off the road, a load of understeer."

BUT THE CARS STILL SLIDE, RIGHT?

"On a [qualifying lap], you can, but it won't take it for long. The tires just go away. When you're fast in these cars, it doesn't feel fast—they're big, and you're never going to get around it."

HIS FIRST TIME IN A NASCAR SHOP:

"I'll never forget. I walked in, and the team owner, Travis Carter, was eating a Quarter Pounder with Cheese, sitting on the bench. He was an old southern dude. They're in the shop, settin' up the car.

"He says, 'Yer' that road-racin' boy?' And I'm like, Yep. Right away, he says, 'So . . . what you like? An 8.5-inch control arm or a 10.5-inch control arm?'

"I'm like, 'So, uh . . . do you know that I've never driven one of these? I don't know?' And he goes, 'Okay.' And then, 'What kinda wedge you like?' I didn't know anything about wedge, either! We go to Watkins Glen the next day. Normally, in Cup, they start doing qualifying runs right away, the car all taped up [to minimize drag]. I said, 'Hey, is it alright if I just go out and run 20 or 30 laps? Just so I can try the car, get used to it?'

"So I'm out there running around, probably 35th or something. And the guy comes on the radio, 'Now Boris, I'll tell you somethin', now definitely you got the most laps of any boy out thar. You ready to try some tires and tape that thing up?'

"So we come in, they tape it up, and I go to second. And that was my career, right there! I remember he took me aside—like, 'These boys are tough. They're gonna eat you up.'

"I didn't know anything about anything. I qualified second. From then on, I got a call every year. Somebody would get hurt or fired or pull a driver out for the road races . . . it was just amazing."

Smithology

COACHING THE SPORT'S GREATS:

"Most of them had the same traits—overdriving. Because the corners were all so different, knowing where they needed to be smoother, and where to horse the car around. Kasey Kahne, for example, he was just always smooth. But in a slow, second-gear corner, you need to muscle it in, work the car, use the curb.

"Other guys, you'd be having to calm them down. And it was really easy once they started building two-seat cars, for testing, because I'd be able to show them, see their feet. I'd be grabbing the wheel, like, turn the wheel! Made a big difference with guys like Carl Edwards, Kasey Kahne, and Kevin Harvick."

ON NASCAR AND PROGRESS:

"All the aids in sports-car racing have made the drivers so equal. Nothing separates them anymore. No finesse, no footwork, no matching revs, no braking technique.... It's all gone.

"I remember when Juan Pablo Montoya came [into NASCAR, after a stint in F1]. I was like, 'Man, that Formula 1 car must have been so badass to drive.' He goes, 'It was f***ing boring! You didn't do anything! Just slam on the gas and shift!'

"I went, 'Yeah, but you shifted a lot?'

"'Yeah, but the car just beeps in your [earpiece], and you shift! You don't think about it.' He goes, 'These cars are *cool*.'"

Section Three
The People

Elkhart Lake, Wisconsin, 2022

IF YOU BELIEVE WHAT THEY TELL YOU, car people are all the same.

This can be confusing, because that "same" varies with who you ask. Reality TV says we're all loners with crossed arms and mustaches. Concours events say that we live and die by period-correct clips on a wiring harness. The old guy behind the counter at the hardware store thinks car culture is dead because EVs are "soulless" and nobody wants a Tri-Five Chevy any more.

Car and Driver was once run by a man named David E. Davis, Jr. Unique individual, good writer, had a thing for tweed. In the mid-1980s, he dove into Manhattan publishing circles and tried to drum up the funding to launch a literary car magazine.

"Those people don't read," someone told him, after a pitch.

Bah and phooey.

We're each pulled here for different reasons; any similarity there is merely evidence of common ground. Our little corner of humanity is not so much a club or a group as a vast and wide-ranging party that sees the machine and its impact as neither low art nor high but both and everything in between. A preference is not a personality, as the line goes; if you and I share the belief that some piece of our existence helps make life worth living, that's an adjective, not a demographic.

Those people don't read. Okay, cool. Explain, then, the fierce eloquence, the vibrant storytelling of F. Scott Fitzgerald, Jack Kerouac, David Halberstam, John Steinbeck, Ernest Hemingway, Kurt Vonnegut, Hayao Miyazaki, George Harrison, Killer Mike, Neil Young, Lawrence of Arabia, Pete Townshend, Frank Ocean, Hunter S. Thompson, Ken Purdy, L.J.K. Setright, Bob Ottum, Denise McCluggage, Jean Lindamood Jennings, David E., and I am going to stop there because that's just the people at the top of my head and this sentence can't go on forever.

If one of those names doesn't ring a bell, take a minute and look it up. Each of those people built a career on language and expression, and each was drawn to the automobile for reasons beyond mere transportation. Did Kerouac know an intake valve from an intercooler? Doesn't matter: The affliction is binary. There's no exam to get in the door, and you either find the subject compelling or you don't. Gatekeeping is for HOAs and colon exits.

Smithology

This book isn't an overview of car culture, merely a slice of the slice that I've met. Nor are the people in this section the only ones on these pages. The stories that follow simply focus on a few who mean more to me than most. If there's a common thread, it's that each of those folks helped give me faith in something. What that thing was, I'll leave up to you.

If the rest of the world thinks we're all just hot-rodders, or concours obsessives, or Yokohama *otaku*—or the ones who live and breathe track days or Jeeps, Le Mans or slabs or 1987 or anything else . . .

Well, hey. Let 'em. They don't know what they're missing.

The Dog Days of Acquisition

Vehicular choice with a fuzzbottom in the mix.

Elly the spaniel is now very old. Still afraid of squirrels, though. A champion.

ROUNDEL, OCTOBER 2011

I acquired a puppy last month. She is the size of a small outboard motor and eats her weight in kibble every three minutes. In a fit of historical reference, I named her Elly, after Elly Beinhorn Rosemeyer, the famous German aviatrix. (Note: Also the wife of 1930s Auto Union racing driver Bernd Rosemeyer. But you cannot name a dog with lady-parts Bernd.)

When I informed my wife of this decision—when I burst triumphantly into our living room and announced that, after weeks of deliberation, our new family member had a name—she did not look up from her book. She did, however, sigh and gently ask me to stop yelling. Then she said that she would, from this point forward, call our dog Eloise, because A) that name was prettier, and B) she had no idea who this Belly Fineborn Roseperson was.

Nice girl. She'll look up one day, realize she has married the village fool, and divorce me on the spot. In the meantime, I will call our dog Elly and teach her to fetch tools, because that is the sort of thing I have always wanted to do. Also because I often find myself stuck under large machinery, critical items just out of reach. ("What's that, Lassie? Timmy's pinned under an M54? Bark twice if it needs a water pump!")

Either way, for the first time in my life, I have a dog. Which is important, because I have spent the last month car shopping, and a certain four-legged fuzzbottom has figured prominently in the process. To wit:

Me, with a laptop, staring into Wikipedia: "I think I need a roadster. Two seats. Lotus Elan, Honda S2000, maybe a BMW Z1."

Wife: "A dog will fit in the passenger seat. Sounds great. You should take long, satisfying road trips in this two-seat car and leave me alone in a quiet house."

Me: "I could, but how would you function? I can only assume you would miss my frequent and triumphant room-burstings."

Wife: "I'll be fine. Promise."

Poppycock. Although I am not at all an egomaniac, my wife cannot function in life minus me. If we find a neat car with a back seat, I reasoned, then everyone can hit the road together. And so I began to look at cars with back seats, and I wondered if I should go a little more practical, perhaps a hatch or neat older wagon, and I asked myself if I should sell the '88 M3 in the garage in order to free up more cash.

After all of that, I proceeded to spend another whole week paralyzed by possibility, not buying or even so much as going to look at anything for sale on wheels. Elly inhaled another 14 pounds of kibble. Time marched on.

There are two schools of thought regarding dogs and cars. Unsurprisingly, those schools also work with babies and cars, or with significant others and any nonessential life accessory. The first approach holds that we should warp want to fit need; this is how fun-loving people end up with minivans. The second approach suggests that you simply ignore need altogether. That path can produce outlandish ends like Ferrari F430s with child seats (don't laugh—seen it) and motorcycle sidecars outfitted to safely carry pet rabbits through traffic (ditto).

Side note: A friend in Milwaukee has a large and horribly valuable collection of vintage Ford products. While visiting his garage one day, I noticed dog hair on the carpet of an immaculate and unrestored 1965 Shelby GT350 Mustang. A healthy six figures of car and museum piece, lightly pooched up.

Surprised, I offered a bon mot. Something like, "Hey bud, some woofbutt sneak in here and prance all over your business?" After which my friend laughed and stuck his hands in his pockets, allowing as how he only drove the family mutts around in his GT350s (plural; he has several) because they disliked the wind blast from riding in his vintage Cobras (again, plural).

This is how to be with cars, I think. Nothing on a pedestal.

I digress again. When I am king of the world, my F430's sidecar will have a child seat for my pet rabbit. For now, however, I find myself constantly returning to the notion of an impractical car, no matter who gets left at home.

Elly, to her credit, does not object to this. (Granted, Elly objects to almost nothing so long as she is allowed to regularly flee squirrels in abject terror and prance down the street carrying dead things found in the yard. But the point remains.) And so I find myself thinking of things like tatty old Lotuses, or ancient sidecar motorcycles, or crusty old Porsches. Anything massively impractical as your only four-seasons vehicle but steeped in romance and feedback and thus very much worth having because this life is short and we're a long time dead.

A certain individual, upon hearing this plan, was not perturbed.

"Please," she said, sticking her head through the doorway of my home office one day, "get something that will run long enough to take you far away. Also, Eloise has eaten part of the rug and yorked it up on the porch. Perhaps you could clean it up."

Me, without looking up from my keyboard: "I do not know any animals named Eloise. Must be your dog."

What happens to the M3 in the garage? Good question. It's a nice, original example with relatively low miles and no apparent problems. I'm not using it that much lately, and letting paws on that perfect leather doesn't feel right. If I sell the M3, I will eventually regret it. If I keep the thing, that just means less money to spend on whatever comes next. Unless the perfect whatever-next comes along, priced perfectly.

I expect you folks will keep me posted on that. Bark twice if you find something, but give me a minute to come out of hiding. Somebody yorked all over the porch, and if I don't make myself scarce, I might actually have to clean it up.

Your Dream, Not Mine

Big hair and small family in a Caterham Seven.

Kids are like kit cars: Deciding to bring one home is the easy part. And until your new bundle of joy shows up, you have no idea how much of the hard work will be improv.

HAGERTY, SEPTEMBER 2021

Every so often, you catch a glimpse of the person you think you want to be. Or maybe it's just the person that another person wants to be, and that person is important to you, and so you take a minute to chew on the person you are, or at least the person you have long tried to become.

Does that make sense? It feels like it should.

This is a story about that glimpse.

A moment for backstory. We are in East Tennessee, near the mountains. Last year, my father bought a Caterham Seven kit, which he finished assembling a few weeks ago. Pop lives about four hours away, in Kentucky, where he's been since early last year, when brain cancer took my mother. The Seven was one of the last things they agreed upon before she closed her eyes and didn't come back. He was thinking of buying one, he told her, but he wasn't sure. Sports car from a kit, maybe too impulsive in an emotional time?

Yes, she said, from her hospital bed, that's a good idea. Do something for yourself. Which is what she always said whenever someone asked if they should take care of themselves.

My parents met as children. There are pictures of them in the same grade-school class, lined up in rows, looking young and hopeful. They began dating in high school and were married shortly after graduation. The divorce papers filed a year later cited irreconcilable differences; a year after that, they found a judge and remarried, unable to stay apart.

Mom and Dad were then joined at the hip for four decades. They had countless shared interests, not the least of which were family and cars and emotional volume controls set to eleven.

So. A Caterham. A kit car, but also a Lotus Seven in blueprint and blood. A Sixties design saved from cancellation by passionate loonballs.

In 1973, an English Lotus dealer named Graham Nearn bought the Seven's production rights from Lotus founder Colin Chapman. Chapman, a famously particular genius known for both breakthrough motorsport engineering and seeing customers as something of a necessary evil, had by then been building the Seven, in one form or another, since 1957. He was ready to move on to more cutting-edge projects and all but annoyed by the model's persistent appeal with customers; Nearn, one of the country's largest Seven dealers, wanted to keep the model alive. The deal made sense for everybody.

Nearn's business lived in the town of Caterham, and for the past 48 years, the company he built has sold hundreds of Sevens every year, both kit and turnkey. A new engine or suspension arrives every third blue moon, but the Seven is mostly as it always was, tube steel and an aluminum skin on wheels with fiberglass fenders and not much else.

Thankfully, with sports cars, less is more. The average Caterham weighs roughly a thousand pounds less than a new Miata. Chapman knew nothing if not minimalist engineering, and Nearn knew what to leave alone, so Cats are a joy to drive, blisteringly resolved and live-wire. You can build cars cheaper and faster, but Sevens tend to end up with people who believe that romance is best when it both takes you somewhere and outshouts the bleatings of real life.

Which brings us back to my father. Born and raised in Louisville and a former flight instructor. Has a soft spot for taildraggers and the writing of Gordon Baxter. He once ran a shop that restored ash-bodied MGs. As for me, I am my father's son, but I also owned a Seven once and miss it.

Because Dad's house was short on space, we decided to assemble his car in the Knoxville shop that I rent with friends. When the work was done, he headed back to Kentucky for a while, pulled by other responsibilities.

"Drive it while I'm gone," he said. "Needs break-in. I was thinking of leaving it in town for a bit. Roads are better here anyway."

I almost said no. Then I remembered that I try to not be stupid on purpose.

The car in question is a 2020 Caterham Super Seven 1600: 135 hp from a 1.6-liter Ford Sigma, plus retro touches like Jenvey "carb" throttles and clamshell fenders. Squinting at it gives 1970s vibes. Sixty miles per hour takes five seconds, slow for a modern Seven, but like all

Caterhams, the 1600 lacks real doors, a radio, or power-assisted anything. As a humanitarian move, I subtly nudged Dad's ordering pen toward the optional limited-slip and rear sway bar. For a crowning touch, I found him a reproduction Lotus Type 47 steering wheel, thin of rim and with a quick-release hub, for old-school Jim Clark hootery. The 1960s Lotus factory driver, sideways often.

Break-in drives are best with company, so I brought a daughter on the first one. Our youngest, Vivien, is six. Her sister, Marion, is eight. Viv is a performative spaz who never shuts up. Marion is the opposite, quieter and addicted to books. I have nothing in common with either girl except absolutely everything, which is partly why my wife occasionally addresses me as if I am a child with a mortgage and a liquor cabinet, and that is all we will say about that.

Marion had homework to do, so I grabbed Viv and hauled her to the shop. My friend Zach Bowman brought his '67 Mustang and his six-year-old daughter Lucy, not least because Lucy and Viv are pals. The pavement wound and coiled through trees. Zach led and pace was carried, the cars flowing with the road, because you do not live in Tennessee and build yourself a grumbly old rat Ford like his unless you believe in hustle.

Most people know that old cars can use you up. Sevens are royalty on this front, more abusive than most. Wind tumbles off that plank of a windshield and smacks your head back and forth; rocks land in elbows while hot dirt hits your face; the whole thing makes you punchy. Not everyone finds it charming. Me, I get five miles in, every time, and ask the same questions: Is this all I need for the rest of my life? Why is every car not an aluminum unitard? Must all other traffic be so stupid and fat?

Miles clipped by. Viv was quiet; she is never quiet. She was also sweating, and my daughters only like sweating when they're running around and skinning knees.

At a stop sign, I leaned over to ask if she was okay. She took a breath, and then this tiny, meek little yes pipped up from under a tangled wreckage of hair.

We carried on.

Maybe an hour later, on a ridge somewhere near the county line, Viv sat up and tried to tell me something. Tiny voice again.

"I should have . . ." she said, and the rest was lost in the wind.

My right foot lifted. The engine's honk ceased, though the wind continued. Bowman pulled further ahead.

"WHAT?" I yelled.

Two hands cupped her mouth, like a megaphone: "DADDY, I SHOULD HAVE BROUGHT SOMETHING TO HOLD MY HAIR."

"OH!" I said. "WE CAN FIX THAT LATER. DON'T WORRY!"

"OKAY!" Then she hunkered back down, quiet again.

Life with a kid hinges on conversations, and you don't always know when they matter. My old friend Seth Teel is the son of a commercial pilot. As a teenager, his dad, Pete, pushed him into flight lessons. Seth didn't mind the training, but he didn't feel any pull to it, either. Late in the process, he got lost during a solo and wandered his rental Cessna into the bee-swarm pattern of a big-city airport. Various forms of brown hit the fan, and the FAA let out a few official grumbles. The experience killed what little interest Seth had in a pilot's license, but his father was philosophical.

"I should have talked to him more," Pete told us once, shaking his head. Seth and I were home from college and drinking beer on his dad's back porch. Seth went palms-up: "Eh, it was your dream, not mine." I watched them laugh about it and tried to imagine all the talking that must have gotten them to that point, and then we opened more beer and rambled on about airplanes and lord knows what into the night.

Pete Teel was a lovely and garrulous guy, basically my second father in high school. Maybe 20 years back, I asked him if he ever grew bored at 30,000 feet. He smiled warmly, then turned the table. "When you're in a car you like, are you ever really bored?" Years later, he was killed by the same form of brain cancer that got my mother. The good ones are always connected, even if we hate the thread.

The Seven drive rambled on. We stopped for snacks at a hamburger stand. Viv and Lucy ate ice cream and yammered, running circles in the grass. As the sun fell lower, the Ford and Seven cranked through foothills and gauzy light. My memory chewed on stuff related and not, in that way that a brain can be completely immersed in one job but also have other stuff idling in the background.

A few months back, Viv told me, apropos of nothing, that she would never learn to tie her shoes. She seemed set on this, so I asked why. Too much work, she said, as if it were obvious—why do we even have laces, when Velcro exists?

Velcro is nice, I told her. But sometimes, you want your shoes to look nicer.

Most kids talk about want as if the world is a stable place. "I like nice," she said. "But your shoes seem very hard to use and not fun. I like my shoes. They are Velcro and simple and smart for me." Then she danced off to the living room, discussion over, to go play kitchen with an imaginary pony.

I stood there for a second, stunned, asking myself if those words held multiple layers, or just one big one with the secret to happiness stuck in the middle.

At a stoplight close to home, I was watching the light bounce off the Caterham's headlights and thinking of airplanes. In the right seat, beneath a whirling hair-bomb so thick as to virtually cover her face, two hands rose up. Strand by strand, she pulled the hair back, revealing a scowl.

Couldn't resist. Knew I shouldn't. "You really liked all this?"

Her face scrunched more, uncertain.

"Did I . . . what?"

The car was not loud, just idling. But it had been a long afternoon. I offered an exit. "You don't have to ride in this again, if you don't want."

A light frown. Confusion. "Yes?"

"Huh?"

"I liked it."

"Oh! Well, good. I'm glad."

"Yes." A nod again. She turned forward, as if things were settled.

"Would you like to do it again?"

A blink. "Yes?"

"Great. We will."

Viv grabbed a fistful of hair with each hand, holding it out of her eyes. Then she sat back in the seat, ready to go.

The light flicked to green. I felt an embarrassing instant of relief, and I thought about my mom and dad. Then the rear tires chirped, and the engine yawped through first gear, and just like that, we were off.

Waiting for Räikkönen
Drivers, humans, and the gorilla suits in between.

"The moral of the story is, we're here on earth to fart around."

— Kurt Vonnegut

ROAD & TRACK, MAY 2015

I rode with Kimi yesterday. I don't know how many people have said those words, but I assume the number is small and that most of those folks own enormous yachts. Oversize boats, like cocaine or your third greatest-hits album, are a way God lets you know that you're making too much money. And most people do not get to ride around a racetrack with a Ferrari F1 driver unless they make too much money.

Kimi Räikkönen. Finnish, 35 years old. A few years ago, at the U.S. Grand Prix, a PR person asked me, "How do you solve a problem like Kimi?" You do not solve Kimi, because he is wonderful.

He is a Formula 1 world champion, for one thing. He is famously icy and forthright, for another. And while we're on the subject of boats, in 2007, our squire entered a Finnish powerboat race with two friends, each man wearing a gorilla costume. Google it: Finns, wave-jumping, enough fake fur to choke a howitzer. You have to assume the idea was cooked up sober. Or not.

Most pro drivers are too polished. The exceptions, the latter-day James Hunts, are outweighed by the brooding Lewis Hamiltons, the perfect Nico Rosbergs. Thankfully, Gorilla Boat is just one star in the Kimi firmament of unpredictable, human, and deeply excellent acts. We must applaud him, fête him, perhaps erect statues to the man in the form of giant apes. I don't know what's appropriate—maybe a gorilla in a crash helmet atop a rearing horse, like in that painting, *Napoleon Crossing the Alps*. Whatever is standard practice for emperors and Kardashians these days.

When I met the man, at Ferrari's Fiorano test track, it followed an afternoon of *Waiting for Godot* tension: *Will he come? Soon. Perhaps. Maybe. He's late. He's off doing Finnish things*, someone said. (Hearing that last line, I immediately pictured pony trekking and snogging in an old Volvo, which tells you how much I know about Finland.)

Unlike Godot, he showed. He stood before a crowd of media in rumpled pants and a Ferrari soft shell, hands in his pockets. He gave a series of awkward half-smiles for photos, trying but obviously uncomfortable. The way he was shepherded around, you got the impression he'd been dragged out of bed against his will, maybe with the promise of ice cream at the end of the day. At one point, I caught him rubbing an eye with a balled-up hand, like my 18-month-old daughter after a nap.

We were at Fiorano for a daylong clinic on the F12berlinetta. Customers had complained that the 730-hp F12 was too fast— gasp!— for the road and homicidal on the track, so Ferrari gave journalists data-logged lapping and instruction from factory test driver Raffaele de Simone in an attempt to prove otherwise. Also, it was raining. (I am no Raffaele de Simone, but the car was a friendly slide-a-roonie. Ferrari customers need to have some grappa and chill out.)

At the end of the day, there were rides with Kimi. It's been said that Ferrari can be too manipulative with its heritage; be that as it may, you stand trackside at Fiorano, next to the farmhouse holding Enzo's old office, and you feel everything they want you to. You hear whispers of Lauda and Gilles and Schumacher, flat-twelves and V-12s and bloodthirst. And then you get in.

Dude woke up.

The car changed him. He was alive, smirking, beating the thing like it owed him money. It wasn't just sideways—it was aggro, a rally driver's commitment and surgical hand movements coupled with a screw-the-car abandon rarely seen outside trailer parks. At one point, after a 110-mph drift that ended with two wheels nipping the grass, I looked ove

"Is that all? Is there more crazy?"

"I guess?" he said, shrugging. And then he went nuttier. The car grew wings, caught fire, flew to the moon. I laughed and clapped, unable to contain myself. He smiled. He isn't known for smiling. I wish we had a hundred more like him.

Driving With Alois Ruf

An anniversary chat with the man who built a 211-mph yellow and beat the world from his garage.

> *"Imagine a dog with no personality." Amazingly, Herr Ruf later set me loose in Bavarian farmland with the original Yellow Bird prototype, the actual 211-mph record car. He's done that for a few folks over the years—no pretense or ceremony, just a machine made for use. Alois is pretty great.*

ROAD & TRACK, JULY 2017

In the spring of 1987, on a 15.5-mile oval in Ehra-Lessien, Germany, a 469-hp, twin-turbo Porsche 911 went 211 mph. Only it wasn't technically a Porsche—the car did not wear a Stuttgart VIN and was known legally as a Ruf CTR. It had been completed just one week before, in a small garage in the village of Pfaffenhausen, by a 37-year-old man born in the house next door. And for a brief, shining moment, it was the most potent production device this magazine had ever seen.

A record we made happen. The July 1987 issue of *R&T* holds a test called "The World's Fastest Cars." That story represented the second running of an experiment we first tried in 1984. The '87 version included nine exotics, from an Isdera Imperator 108i to a Lamborghini

Countach 5000S Quattrovalvole. Porsche sent no less than two examples of its range-topping 959, and a Ferrari Testarossa was clocked at 185 mph. The slowest machine went 176, in an era before computers were used to keep supercars aerodynamically stable. Before the invention of electronic stability control, when an industry discovered how silicon could make a car more stable near its limits. Before the 253-mph Bugatti Veyron made the top-speed question almost irrelevant. In an age when most new sport sedans couldn't crack 150.

The gathered flock for R&T*'s 1987 "World's Fastest Cars" test, Ruf Yellow Bird at middle front. When I visited Pfaffenhausen for the story here, Alois and his wife Estonia had me over for dinner. Before we ate, they showed home movies Alois had shot during the '87 test. With the Rufs' permission, I taped a few on my phone, filming their living-room TV. A handful of stills are included here.*

At 211 mph, the CTR topped everything, a heady achievement. Like all the cars in that test, Ruf's machine was driven by Phil Hill, the magazine's de facto chief tester. Hill was a graceful writer, a three-time Le Mans winner who had driven in Formula 1 for Enzo Ferrari, and the first American to land the F1 driver's world championship. Assisting him was the journalist Paul Frère, *R&T's* European editor but also another Le Mans winner and former Ferrari F1 driver.

The story was penned by Peter Egan, one of *R&T's* most beloved writers. It wore the subheading "Beyond 200 mph. *Mit radio,*"—the last two words being German for "with radio," a reference to the civility of both the test's winner and the remaining flock. In what can only be taken as a measure of the story's four-wheeled stock, Frère dryly called the 959 "not all that exhilarating" at low rpm. (Lest you think the man jaded, at one point, somewhere above 200 mph in the Ruf, he grinned

Bird on the banking, Phil Hill at the wheel, 200-plus.

manically and yelled to his passenger, "This is faster than I've ever gone in my life!")

Egan's story noted that the magazine's staff had nicknamed Ruf's car "Yellow Bird," because that's what the thing looked like, blistering across the land. The moniker stuck, and Ruf proceeded to sell production versions under the name CTR, for Group C Turbo Ruf. Later, he put his friend Stefan Roser in the car, on the Nürburgring, with a video camera. The resulting footage featured a helmetless man in shirt sleeves drifting an entire lap of one of the world's most dangerous tracks. It became one of the first viral car videos, circulated on countless bootleg VHS tapes before enjoying a second life on YouTube.

Same car, 30 years later. When Alois loaned it to me for an afternoon, it came without condition or direction. "Take your time," he said, "and have fun." So I did. On the way back, I laid down in a German farmer's field and took this.

Alois Ruf turned 67 this year. Ruf Automobile GmbH is still in business, still in the same garage it occupied in 1987; the company's 65 employees work for a firm still registered with the German government as a vehicle manufacturer, that still earns its own VINs by reengineering Porsches. But none of Ruf's creations have rung quite as many bells as the Yellow Bird, the original CTR prototype, which Alois still owns. There is no European hot rod more evocative of the freedom of its time, no more epic *Road & Track* test, and no single machine as woven into the lore of this institution.

To mark the CTR's 30th anniversary, Ruf this year released a carbon-bodied, 700-hp successor, turbocharged and water-cooled but again in the shape of a 1980s 911. In late 2016, we spent a day at his shop, discussing Porsches, a changing industry, and the role of sports cars in an unstable world. Plus the undeniable pull of a simple, straightforward machine that looks an awful lot like a 911 but isn't.

SAM SMITH: *Two hundred and eleven miles per hour. Porsche's fastest production model was then 13 mph slower, almost $100,000 more expensive, and twice as complex. I read somewhere that you finished building the Bird less than a month before.*

> ALOIS RUF: About one week. [Laughs.] It was rainy. April, lousy weather—just black sky. And the cars were running at high speed, throwing water. It was crazy. After, we had lunch in Pfaffenhausen, celebrating Phil Hill's 60th birthday. Can you believe it? He said, "It's my birthday today." I said, "Okay, then happy birthday. Let's have a party."

SS: *When your father built a garage, he probably didn't foresee world champions partying in your office.*

> AR: Yeah, the company has been around since 1939. The house [next door] is where I was born. My father said, "This is going to be a big business. The entrance of Pfaffenhausen. This is meant to be a car business." In the difficult years after World War II,

my father was very successful, because he was somebody who could put something together out of nothing.

SS: *Fame is funny. So many folks think the company began with the Bird.*

AR: There was a lot more before. I was born in 1950. When I started to crawl, I was in my dad's workshop. I wanted to know everything. I fell into the waste-oil bucket. [Laughs.] One of the greatest things my father did, that impressed me most as a child, was building his own tour bus. One day, he brings in two big steel beams and says, "My boy"—I was six years old—"in one year, it's going to be ready."

SS: *Something tells me he pulled that off.*

AR: It was ready in one year! He built his own version of a Mercedes 0321H. Used the bus, over 15 years, to take people around. When he was driving it in 1963, a Porsche 356 passed him, lost control, rolled two or three times. My dad stopped and looked after [the driver]. He took him to the hospital, said, "I'll pick up your car, bring it to the garage. Just relax." A week later, he bought the [wrecked] car over the telephone. We fixed it, and that was our first Porsche.

The whole family fell in love with this car. Then one day, we [took it] to Munich, on a Sunday afternoon. I was 13, 14 years old. A young man knocks at the side window. "I want to buy your car. This is exactly the car I was looking for."

SS: *He just wanted a Porsche?*

AR: It was a very rare model. A Karmann Hardtop. He gave us the money [right there]. He was driving another 356, and we drove home in his car. He trusted us. Nobody knew the Rufs at that time. My father said, "I have never seen anything like that. These people with Porsche, they must be special people. Maybe they're crazy, but it's good, you know?"

We built up an image as a specialist. Then in the late 1970s, Stuttgart announced the final call of the 911. [A few] more years, then it's the end. I realized that there is a community of people who want 911s, no matter what. I said, "Even if the community is small, I'll stick with those people, because I like the 911, too. I'm okay with that."

I wanted to continue making special models, because Porsche had shrunk the [non-911 Turbo] lineup down to just the 911 SC. And the answer from Porsche was, "The 911, you cannot do more with this car. This is the end. You should switch to a 928." *(Porsche CEO Peter Schutz saved the 911 from cancellation in 1981 —Ed.)*

SS: *That thinking led to cars like the 1978 Ruf SCR—a 3.2-liter engine in a 3.0-liter 911 Carrera. And, earlier, your own five-speed gearboxes.*

AR: Porsche said, "This car doesn't need a five-speed. Such strong torque. Four is good enough. Most people who can afford that expensive car, they don't want to mess with a fifth gear." Complete reverse of what they do today and did before.

SS: *But it left an opportunity.*

AR: The 911's last call, that was an opportunity. When they decided for a four-speed, we could go to a five. When they went to a five, we went to a six. They always left a gap where we said, "Okay, we can step in and do this."

SS: *So many people found your work in the 1980s, through magazines. The information wasn't available anywhere else.*

AR: Like *Auto Motor und Sport*. You can always play with my name, because it's short, and "Ruf" means "call" in German. It also means "reputation." So the headline was, "*Porsches guter Ruf.*" Which means, "Porsche's good reputation."

SS: *And that you're either saving it or ... trashing it.*

AR: I was not very much liked at Stuttgart for this. Then I made my crusade to California and went to the famous [*Road & Track*] Monrovia Avenue building.

SS: *You just went to the edit office and walked in?*

AR: [Motorsport editor] Joe Rusz said, "Well, show me what you have been doing." I brought those magazines, where [my car] was on the cover, and he started talking to me. [Laughs.]

SS: *And then you were cold-called by Paul Frère, one of history's coolest humans, for our first top-speed test, the one that ran in 1984.*

AR: Frère says, "Mr. Ruf, we want to invite you for a *Road & Track* story." He put that together. I had no clue what this event was. So I took our narrow-body turbo model, with a five-speed gearbox, 369 hp. I asked Dunlop to prepare a set of tires, and I thought, I cannot risk driving them on the autobahn. I may have a puncture or something.

So I put them in the car—two tires on my passenger seat and two in the back. It was totally packed. I drove up to Ehra-Lessien by myself!

SS: *It was this nutty era where manufacturers were actively pushing that barrier. Indy-car speeds with relatively simple engineering.*

AR: Ferrari didn't want to come, so the vice president of the German Ferrari owners club came with an outdated model. He says, "We have to represent Ferrari." The Porsche factory sent a 930 Turbo. Aston Martin, they had bad luck—spark plugs that were too hot, not good enough for a high-speed run. Holed a piston. Nobody expected my car to be so fast. Then we drove home, and Porsche was shocked.

SS: *You were turning their cars into something else. The way that company works—I can't imagine they were thrilled.*

AR: It was always *comme ci, comme ça*. Because there was this jealousy, but at the same time, they could always say a Porsche won. Better than a Lamborghini or a Ferrari.

The car that looks like a frog. A marketing director at Ferrari once told me, "Your car, it works. It's a very good car. But look, next to a Ferrari, it looks like a frog." [Laughs.] It's the Beetle. But then, we knew what "World's Fastest Cars" meant—serious driving, to the bone. If an engine lasts there, it lasts anywhere.

SS: *The second World's Fastest Cars round, in 1987—everything I've read, it sounds more dramatic.*

AR: Much more, because now everybody knew what the event was about.

SS: *There's something with the yellow car that stuck in people's minds. That test and the infamous Stefan Roser video, drifting the Ring in loafers and white socks.*

AR: That project was originally called 945R. That idea came in 1980. I have sketches, design sketches, for what this car was supposed to look like . . . a Ruf supercar. "Nine" because it was based on the 911, and "45" for 450 hp.

That was an exorbitant number at that time. We were thinking how we could achieve that, twin turbocharging, because the [single-turbo] 930 engines, they were already too aged when they came out. But in 1982, I heard through the grapevine that Porsche was going to make a supercar . . . the 959.

That scared me. I thought, Gosh . . . we have no chance. The [Yellow Bird] engine was the leftover from that dream. The five-speed gearbox was our design from 1981, so we put that all into the regular shape of a 911, with the shaved rain gutters, to make the car more distinctive and also better aerodynamically. We kept the car as light and as simple as possible.

It was so great. I mean, Phil Hill was so excited. The guys, they were competing with each other. Paul came in and he had the number written on his palm—336.1 km/h. He was all excited. And then Phil got in the car and came back—339.8 km/h. [Laughs.] It was a milestone.

SS: *The industry has changed so much. So much that was possible for a small company you just can't do now.*

AR: The cars were analog. Cars today are computers from A to Z. But we were introducing, in our car, computer technology for engine management. The system was from Bosch, the so-called 1.2, a racing unit also used in the [Porsche] 962.

Frère after a run in the Bird in '87. He is telling R&T *writer Peter Egan that he has just cleared 337 km/h—209.4 mph.*

SS: *The Bird's engine brain came from a Le Mans prototype?*

AR: To get that kind of performance, you needed a digital management system. And they were not readily available, like today. At the time, Bosch had the perfect match for our needs, and you were walking in and praying they would serve you. Thank God, they had one guy who said, "Okay, I want to help you." Normally, they only talked to the big [manufacturers].

SS: *And yet, even Porsche was a small company until the 1990s. Has your relationship with them evolved as they've grown?*

AR: It has always been curves, up and down, depending on who was running the company and how open-minded they were. With the Yellow Bird, the second high-speed run that we did at Nardó, in 1988, Porsche actually sent an engineer to collect data. They wanted to know cylinder-head temperature and all these things. It was great to work with those men because we spoke the same language. But then you get a new CEO, and everything's over.

SS: *The tuning business, in particular, is so different from what it was.*

AR: Things that used to be possible are just not possible anymore. Everything is reduced to electronics and laptops. But we aren't in that business anymore. We are a manufacturer ... We are concentrating on building our special models. People have come back to the more ... down-to-earth cars. Modern cars have stability control and all kinds of stuff. All of that is perfect, but it takes away some of your personal engagement.

SS: *Does a car have to be imperfect to be interesting?*

AR: It's difficult to say yes or no. But you want to have this machine with its own life and tale. Imagine a dog with no personality.

SS: *Part of the industry is now chasing a kind of simplicity—machines, like the Corvette Z06 or 911 R, that digitally simulate analog feel. Does any of that interest you?*

AR: Yes. But more interesting is—and again, this is a small market—four wheels, a steering wheel, superlight weight, and power. The weight ratio is everything. And what type of horsepower. How do these horses *feel?*

Maybe we run an engine on the dyno and we come up with a beautiful number. I say, "Okay. Great. But I want to feel them first." We call this, in German, the *Popometer. Popo* is the butt.

SS: *It's conflicting, though, if you love technology. Because progress has undeniably made the automobile better, safer, faster, easier.*

AR: It's a great achievement. Anybody can drive anything. With the 911, they used to say, "Widowmaker. This must be a crazy guy that drives that car, a hero." And today, anybody can drive a 911, because it's so tamed. [Cars are] so much alike, it's unbelievable. If you were blindfolded, you sometimes wouldn't know which car you were in.

SS: *A lot of people think Porsche doesn't understand the appeal of simple. That it's more than just numbers—the widespread protest when the last 911 GT3 wasn't available with a clutch pedal, for example.*

AR: When Porsche had only one model, it was a cult. Flashing headlights when you saw another, and sometimes you would stop, talk, make friends. "Let's go for a beer." Exchange information. "Did this also break?" "Oh, yeah. Of course." [Laughs.]

But you never blamed the company, because this was part of the whole charm. And when Porsche was in negative headlines, you would quickly order another one to help them.

SS: *So much of that culture changed because car companies had to change. Government regulations mean that manufacturing a safe, clean, fast automobile has become exponentially more complex.*

AR: It used to be, you went there, at the factory, picked up your car. You had to pay in cash. There was a little vault. There was blonde lady sitting there. Thick glass, like at a bank, and you were counting your money, and she pulled the money in, and she gave you a receipt, and then you could pick up your car.

SS: *How long did that last?*

AR: To the 1980s, even. And then, [they gave you a new car with] an empty gas tank. [Laughs.] But you were given a free lunch. The same lunch that the workers ate. The same ladies that served the workers, but you had white tablecloths and fancier napkins. Harald Wagner, the sales chief, he would maybe give [your wife] a scarf as a present.

That was the charm of that company. When you were picking up a car and loving it, no matter how simple the food, because it was the best in the world on that day.

SS: *What would you change about Porsche, as the company sits now?*

AR: Too corporate. Every way, shape, and form.

SS: *To be fair, though, the market pretty much requires it.*

AR: Back then, when the car was purchased, people had the money made. Today, it's leased. It was a different culture. "Okay, I'm going to lease a Porsche. Ah, I had it a year. I think I will do an Audi now." It's more of a fashion thing. When you had to make every penny to pay for that car first, you had a different relationship with it.

SS: *The new cars you're building…*

AR: We're coming through an evolution, and the evolution is going backward, actually. [Laughs.]

SS: *Judging by how busy the shop is, people like it.*

AR: They like the purity and simplicity. I have a customer in the United States, he's a fashion designer. He says, "This is an honest car."

SS: *The shop echoes that—the place is just so warm and friendly. The building is small enough to see through.*

AR: It's just the way we do things, you know? People say, "This reminds me of what Porsche was in the Fifties and Sixties." Customers knew certain people in the factory. They had this relationship. We want to continue like this. This is the best way, I think.

Mears and My Feet
Fables of the Rick construction.

We were all better once, and young. Some of our youngs were just better than others.

HAGERTY, APRIL 2021

The last time I saw Rick Mears, he was wearing sandals. This is interesting mostly because he was also standing in the pits at Indianapolis next to a running Indy car. If there is one place that America's grand old temple of speed does not want bare toes, it is the hot pits, especially when a snarling, carbon-fiber open-wheeler is about to rip off into a 200-mph lap.

Unless, of course, you are Rick.

In September of 1984, in the prime of a sparkling career known for its almost supernatural lack of mistakes, one of the greatest drivers in history put his March 84C in the fence at an oval in Canada. Mears, then 32, would tell reporters that the crash broke every bone in his right foot and most of the bones in his left, but eight months and four operations later, he was back at it, back in Indianapolis, testing for the 500. Walking was painful, he said, but he couldn't stay away. He said the same thing years later, after notching the third of his four Indy 500 wins but also another high-speed crash, another hospital stay, another broken left foot.

How powerful, the draw of doing what you love, even when it can keep you from... doing what you love.

I saw him at Indy in 2015. Retired from driving, he was working for Roger Penske's team as a coach and spotter. I stood next to the wall, watched a Dallara light its rear tires inches from his feet. Then I asked a photographer friend some silly question about track rules.

"First of all," I was told, "when you're Rick Ravon Mears, Rick the Rocket, one of the coolest cats alive, you get to do a lot of things. But second, when an Indy legend has used his legs as crush space and normal shoes hurt like hell, the Speedway makes exceptions."

I am not Rick Mears. I am an amateur racer, a professional tester of automobiles, a person who finds grins on pavement. I have little in common with the man save a fondness for dark sunglasses and that feeling you get when a car is up on the tire and howling.

And: My feet are broken.

Broken is perhaps misleading. The X-ray says the bones are now healed, but doctors say walking will for the rest of my days occasionally be a shoe full of knives. Blame personal error. Several years ago, I was racing an old BMW in Texas, at the Circuit of the Americas, when the car's gearbox went phooey. Lacking talent with a dismantled Getrag, I stood by that night as friends opened the transmission for a fix. Then I got bored and used a few paddock traffic cones to build a small slalom for our golf cart in an empty corner of the parking lot.

You see where this is going.

Like a lot of race teams, our little outfit had rented a cart for the weekend, to shrink the track's sprawl. Someone—ahem!—had disabled the cart's torque and speed limiters, for giggles. Around midnight, gearbox still in surgery, I may have used my feet as outriggers to keep the cart on more than two wheels, a move best described as a sort of full-body cackle.

A doctor told me that choice was dumb. Fine; true; mistakes were made. Foot tendons were stretched. (Also true: It was fun. What did Edith Piaf sing? No regrets.)

Tendons aren't like bubble gum; a stretch is a one-time thing. The pain lingered, if not loudly. Then, last fall, while filming at Lime Rock, I tripped down a few stairs. A metatarsal in my right foot went *ping!* and cleaved in two. Moments later, the big toe joined in, tearing a shred of cartilage from a place where cartilage normally lives and depositing it somewhere awful else. All that damage formed a gang and went to town. Months of repair later, I can walk and drive again, albeit not as I did. Muscle resolution and fidelity hang on a dice roll. Glassy downshifts under hard braking currently require either no concentration, the old standard, or all the brain I've got. Daily pain is the only variable.

Cool cat, 1980s.

How confidence can sine-wave. I was never Mears in a race car, but I was alright. I now drive worse than I ever have, an obviously blunt instrument. I was 39 years old on those stairs. I have now seen one more birthday.

You're still young, people tell me. Not too damaged just yet.

To which I answer: Cool. I feel young.

Wouldn't it be nice if those three words were the whole story?

Back to Rick. I interviewed him once, at Indy. He wore sunglasses and a hat against the steamy sun. Being a stoic professional, I did not fanboy into telling the man that he seemed a chill nonpareil, this unflappable, white-haired cross between a sober gunfight Lebowski and a philosophy professor with a thing for Cosworths. I wanted to buy him all the drinks.

"You just get back in the car," he said. "You try not to look at it differently—maybe there's a little apprehension that first time, but basically? You just keep going."

That makes sense, I heard myself say, while silently wondering how it somehow also did not.

The mind of the athlete is never not fascinating. A while back, I had a chance to work with Ross Bentley, the renowned racing coach and *Speed Secrets* author. Ross has spent a career studying the soft science of sports—how the brain can traffic-control a body through age and stress, through comebacks and the inevitable fallings-apart. He came back himself, once, in 1993, after a cracked fuel regulator set his car on fire at Indianapolis, the methanol flames gifting first- and second-degree burns to his face, neck, and hands.

I called Ross last week. My feet are not tragedy, I said. If a journalist never again drives smoothly at the limit, nobody cries. But how do pros stick the landing, that mental and physical reassembly, under real stakes? When you're trying to rebuild a livelihood or a life?

The line was briefly silent. "It's a decision," he offered. "You have to make the choice. The voice that says you can't do it—do you want to listen to that, or . . . not?"

Sounds like a starting point, I said.

"Of course. But which comes first—belief that you can do something, or the ability to do it? Will exercising for two months change your belief system? Yes. Because you can tell yourself that you're also doing the physical work. Our brains are amazing. Neuroplasticity, how people can be reprogrammed after an injury or stroke, it's remarkable."

I leaned into honesty. "This thing with my feet seems so petty. I feel silly for being so frustrated by it."

"Part of it is, don't make it easy on yourself. You almost have to go, 'No, I have to make this work.' Visualize it, practice it, work at it. The decision is no small thing, and maintaining it is a conscious effort. The cool thing is, that process is a tool you can use in the rest of your life."

I hung up thinking about change. How we root so many of our actions in fear of loss, which is silly, because we lose something every day, on some level, whether we acknowledge it or not.

One of the unspoken truths of our little corner of society is that cars take as much as they give. From a young age, you simply rely on your body to drive the car, work on the car, race the car, whatever. Then, one day, the equation shifts. The machine doesn't stop asking, but the amount you can give starts dropping by degree, and nobody cares but you. Maybe it means you can't reach over the fender of your '57 Chevy without a disc in your back turning to fire. For some people, past a certain age, simply rolling a creeper around a garage can be so painful that an oil change feels like climbing Everest.

What a ghoulish and private parade, bodily decay. At the age of 20, I probably wouldn't have hurt my feet on those stairs or in Texas; the bits under the skin would have simply rebounded, more elastic. At 30, I'd already be feeling better about it. At 40, it takes a shocking amount of effort and time to regain status quo, and that's assuming the hardware will even let you.

The Sunday-morning takeaway, naturally, is to simply do as much as you can while you have the chance. I find the subtext happier: What's the point of all this breathing and medicine, if not yelling into the abyss? Isn't the best salute to a lost anything the mere act of carrying on, continuing to plug away against impossible odds?

Encouraging stuff, so long as you don't think about it too much.

I leave tomorrow for my first club race in almost a year and a half. That same BMW, and my first time back on the horse since my feet went down. A psychologist would probably label all this rumination inevitable, the death throes of that dream everyone has as a kid, where you quietly believe yourself immune to wearing out and thus the only true immortal in history. Before you get older and realize you're just another happy schmuck aging into dirt.

Dwelling on the process is still possible. People do that in a thousand ways, but only one choice really makes sense: You tie your shoes and walk out the door every morning, even as the process fights back, because you're vertical and breathing. The nature of the deal means that you don't get to name the variables or pick the dates. You simply wake up each day and do it. Because you can. Because you get to.

Unless, of course, you are Rick.

Then you do it in sandals.

Jet Hunting With Thrasher
"Oh hell yes, is it fun."

F-18s in canyons and getting lost in Death Valley. What a trip. I met Camden through cars, but they're never what we talk about. (The Jeep and Land Rover mentioned were reviewed separately.)

HAGERTY, MARCH 2021

There is no sound at first. They bank in silently below the ridgeline, beneath your feet, motions precise and deliberate but slower than you expect. Matte-gray and dirty-looking, too distant to make out and then almost close enough to touch. The noise, deafening and metallic, hits an instant later, gases being shoved aside or torn apart.

At 9:00 that morning, before the sun had driven the chill from the air, we parked the Jeep and the Land Rover at the base of a trail in the high Sierra and began to hike. Forty minutes later, we were 4300 feet above sea level and maybe 1000 feet above the trucks, standing on a rocky outcropping that hung over the valley like an opera balcony.

Camden Thrasher set his backpack down and began fiddling with a hand-held radio scanner. He glanced up at the sky for a moment. "Last time I was here, it was 105 degrees. This is nice."

Camden is a professional motorsport photographer and friend. He lives in Georgia but grew up in Washington State, where airplane culture is as old as Boeing and Navy jets carve low over alpine lakes. In his day job, Camden shoots events like the Sebring 12-hour and the Baja 1000. He has a delightful habit of saying profound things in an unprofound manner and is easily bored.

A few years ago, during a quiet off-season, Camden picked up a welder and turned his BMW 2002 into an off-road mutt with tall knobbies and a six-cylinder swap. Around the same time, apropos of nothing, he decided to start spending his vacations hiking into the backcountry to photograph military aircraft flying balls-out at low altitude.

Once, a while back, I asked him why he did this.

Afterburner jets, a few hundred feet off the ground, close enough to spit at, he said.

I suddenly felt big stupid for asking.

Come along, he said.

Twist my arm, I answered.

And so one day last fall, we drove into nowhere California and watched Air Force and Navy pilots do low-level training runs—500 mph and a few hundred feet off the deck, in all manner of fast airplanes. Because nowhere is usually off the beaten path, we borrowed a Jeep Wrangler and a Land Rover Defender. The connection seemed obvious: Purposeful hardware and speed are powerful drugs, regardless of form; car people are often airplane people, and vice versa. For me, the blame for this form of infatuation can be traced to my father, a former professional pilot who once told me that he got into flying "for the airplanes." One of those subjects that just remains permanently novel and intoxicating, no matter how old you get.

The wind rustled in the trees. I threw a furtive glance east, toward the mouth of the valley. Camden, head down and adjusting something on his camera, waved, dismissive.

"When you're looking for jets, everything out here sounds like a jet."

"Oh." My shoulders fell. "Do you get any warning?"

He gave a who-knows face, smiling. "In theory, they're supposed to make a radio call saying they're entering this route. Whether they actually do or not is a mystery, and whether we can hear it on the scanner is another thing entirely."

Twenty minutes passed. I grew tired of standing and sat down on a large rock. The hunt, Camden had told me, was half the fun, and it began with hours upon hours of research, at home —digging up military training routes online and locating them in the real world, but never knowing when or where the airplanes would actually show, because the American government doesn't make a habit of publishing military flights, because of course it doesn't.

"Lemoore, Fresno, China Lake, Nellis, Edwards," Camden had said, as we hiked, that first day. "Five air bases within 100 miles of here—who knows what they're doing. We could sit on a mountain and see nothing from sunrise to dark, or we could wait an hour and have 40 planes come through. It just depends."

"What do you end up doing if you don't see anything?"

"I dunno? Sit. Think."

To the south, a small gray wedge popped out from behind a mountain. It snapped into a bank, then vanished into a carpet of haze. A blink later, the wedge was below my feet, slicing through a gap in the landscape. The right wing passed my toes almost vertical.

"F-18," Camden said.

The noise came an instant later. That feeling where your inner ear seems to boil.

I stood up, blinking. At the bottom of the mountain, our trucks sat there, as they had moments before. Only this time, they looked very small and very, very slow.

The First Climb

The scanner crackled: "400-plus knots, 500 feet."

My skin tingled. An F-18 passed below, same as the last one, its gray underside canted up like a cat asking for a scratch.

Over the next six hours, that feeling recurred 20 times. Twenty-one, if you count the prop-driven Beechcraft King Air that ran the canyon almost too high to see. A King Air is not nothing, but it is also not a jet. Not the reason these routes exist.

According to the Air Force website, the American military uses "some airspace below 10,000 feet for training operations." In combat, it says, "many aircraft will operate at altitudes as low as 100 feet and at high airspeeds to . . . avoid sophisticated [defenses]."

In order to fly $67 million worth of jet at 100 feet and 600 mph, you need skill, and in a modern military environment, skill means training, which means hours in the cockpit and the kind of intensely manicured pilot proficiency in which the United States government has long specialized. The American military certifies pilots for low-level flight by degree, with an aviator's low-altitude permission based on individual rating, and that rating based on altitude and aircraft—if you fly an F-35, for example, there is one rating for 500 feet, another for 300, and another for 100.

These ratings are qualified for and maintained through frequent bursts of simulator and flight time, and the attendant safety and proficiency protocols are serious as cancer. Many military pilots are rated for 500 feet. Very few are allowed to see 100. Nor do most civilians see these jets this low, period. In the continental U.S., low-level flights take place only in limited, charted airspace, generally where humans aren't.

The FAA and Department of Defense maintain hundreds of Military Training Routes, or MTRs, for this exact purpose. The most famous of these routes live inside an area known as the R-2508 complex, over the southern Sierra Nevada and upper Mojave Desert, but similar training occurs in places like Idaho, the Cascades, and the West Virginia mountains. A YouTube search will show you what those routes look like from the cockpit, but the easiest shorthand is to simply picture the Death Star X-Wing runs in *Star Wars*, then replace the X-Wings with something from McDonnell-Douglas.

During background research for this story, I interviewed a handful of military flyers with low-level flight experience in afterburner aircraft.

"It is fun," an F-18 aviator told me. "Oh hell *yes,* is it fun."

"Fantastic to fly," said another, an F-35 test pilot. "But . . . intense. You can't afford to screw up. At 100 feet, any error is going to be fatal."

This kind of skill can be intoxicating to witness—so much precision in such small space—but the practice is not widely beloved. Conservationists protest the wildlife impact. Rural towns complain about noise. And above all, any time you have an airplane flying near the ground, especially an extremely fast airplane, there is risk. The single most popular jet-chasing location on earth, an overlook in Death Valley National Park, was officially closed to low-level flight in 2019 following an F-18 crash that killed the jet's pilot and injured seven tourists. If you visit that particular overlook, the crash will seem remarkable, but not as remarkable as the fact that events of this nature are exceedingly rare.

The similarities to car racing are not small, but apart from the obvious differences, there is one crucial separation that can make this pastime compelling for a spectator with an automotive bent. I have for the last two decades covered motorsport as a journalist, studying how skilled individuals think and react in extraordinary situations. I have also watched as more than a few international sanctioning bodies squeezed the life and spectacle from an otherwise breathtaking and spectacular practice. Spend enough time watching one of your lifelong loves grow weak under the boot of bureaucracy, you get ideas. One of those notions centers around how getting your nose booped by a 600-mph airplane makes for a far better weekend than, say, trudging off to watch an F1 race where a bunch of oligarch scions compete to find out whose aerodynamicist is smarter and swimming in a larger pile of money.

I Just Want the Airplanes

"I'm not an expert by any means," Camden said. This in spite of having chased jets for several years, living out of a rental Jeep in the mountains for weeks at a time. He makes a habit of driving into the backcountry on short notice, bringing little more than a scanner, a camera, and several days' worth of food. He went to Reno once to shoot next to one of the air-race pylons. ("It's kind of hard to get good stuff there, but it was neat to see what 500 mph looks like from about 50 feet away.") He once kicked off a 10-hour drive on a day's notice because a sympathetic pilot found him online and allowed as how a jet he might have been set to fly might soon be passing through a certain geographic region, perhaps, unofficially, ahem, cough, at high speed, yes.

You meet people like this, you ask why. Even if you know the answer.

"I don't really have a good reason," Camden said. "I just got into it after watching videos online. I like the adventure aspect, hiking and road trips. You have to go find this stuff; it doesn't find you. It takes a lot of work to figure out where the routes are, where they're flying, and how to get to these places people don't normally go. Which is kind of the point. And military airplanes are just impressive to watch."

The government flies jets low all over the country, but the West Coast is uniquely equipped for this sort of hunt. Credit a unique mix of spectacular terrain, millions of acres of public land, and a dense concentration of air bases. America long ago discovered that empty land and abundant sun made for good defense airfield, and so a lot of them got built, in greater density than much of the rest of the country.

Around lunchtime, the mountains grew quiet, air traffic gone. We talked about airplanes, how they can be like any other obsession. What it feels like to sit at a desk, engrossed in working and trying not to think about more exciting things. How my father was once a flight instructor but quit when I was young, after he realized that he couldn't support a family without a much different job.

I mentioned Chuck Yeager's autobiography and the book and film versions of *The Right Stuff*, how Yeager, the first man to fly faster than the speed of sound and the greatest test pilot in U.S. history, nearly died over the Mojave in an F-104 not far from the mountain where we sat. This somehow segued into a discussion of the much-delayed sequel to the Tom Cruise movie *Top Gun*.

Camden laughed. "*Top Gun*. I wish they would just release all the aerial footage. You know, like a ski film. I don't want the plot. I just want the airplanes."

Ski films are basically just hours of lavishly shot downhill footage set to music, no dialogue. The most widely known analogue in the car space is the Steve McQueen movie *Le Mans*, which is basically just a ski film for the Porsche 917K. You don't get goggled athletes dropping into remote runs by helicopter, but you do get 1970s prototypes cranking 200 mph in the rain for hours with gut-punching audio and almost zero dialogue. Years ago, on a rainy Sunday in college, I watched that movie four times in a single afternoon.

"How long do you usually stay out here?" I asked at one point, when things were quiet.

"As long as I can," he said.

Then the scanner again: "500 low-level on Jedi Transition."

"Star Wars Canyon," Camden said, sighing, a little wistful.

Star Wars Canyon is where that 2019 F-18 crash happened. Low-level flight is now prohibited there, military aircraft limited to a minimum of 1500 feet above ground level. The site is also known as both Rainbow Canyon and the Jedi Transition, though that last moniker is lightly misleading; the canyon itself is merely the tail of a larger restricted-airspace route that appears on military charts under that name. As with a lot of jet-chasing sights, YouTube holds tourist footage, and even a few seconds watching that canyon online can give you chills. Nowhere else on earth do supersonic jets essentially burst out of a hole in the ground and fly right through your lap, a few hundred feet from a parking lot.

I once stood trackside at Indianapolis for a story, inches from a corner, during practice for the 500. That kind of access took special dispensation from Speedway officials, but it also produced Dallaras howling five feet away at 200 mph. It was one of those situations where you have to remind yourself to breathe, and that there are live humans in the machine, flinging through the air, pushing themselves, balanced between flight and the exact opposite.

"That was Rainbow Canyon," Camden said. An easy button, he called it. A good week might offer 50 or 60 jets a day. The fireball that bloomed into the parking lot stopped all that.

A few F-16s danced by. They were followed a minute later by two F-18s, which were in turn followed by two T-38s—older, two-place supersonic trainers—banking back and forth in a series of playful feints. Two differing flight styles on the same path: The trailing pilot was abrupt and sudden, while the leader was more gentle, one attitude change bleeding into the next.

I opened our tote of hiking snacks and found a peanut-butter sandwich in a Ziploc bag. An F18 snarled past my knees, close enough to show the pilot's legs through the top of the canopy.

Long ago, you could see people in the cockpits of race cars. Not just helmets but body parts. A reminder of something. The F-18's fuselage wore the letters VFA-22, for a squadron out of Naval Air Station Lemoore. It was only when the air went silent that I realized I had been gnawing on the sandwich mindlessly, mesmerized, so distracted that I had begun chewing on at least part of the plastic bag.

"You can hike to one of those peaks," the scanner squawked. A pilot. "That outcropping. Though I didn't see anybody up there." Then he talked about how he drove down there bird hunting a while back and blew up the radiator in his truck.

I wanted to yell a response. What does every kid yell at pilots? *Hey! I'm down here! Do a barrel roll!*

I looked at Camden. "You ever wonder what it's like to retire from the pinnacle of something? From the peak of a game, as an athlete, in fighter jets, F1 cars, anything? You're young and you think this great part of life goes on forever, no other high even comes close, and then one day, the world decides that you don't get to do this anymore. You've aged out of your prime at the ripe old age of . . . I don't know, 30?"

He raised an eyebrow. Below us, the valley was quiet for a moment.

"You think you'd miss it?" I said. "Or would it be like Michael Jordan and Jackie Stewart, where you leave a pinnacle of human achievement, are just like, I'm done, I lived on that edge, enough?"

Camden chuckled but didn't answer.

"Is that when you start . . . buying superbikes?" I said.

Full laughter. "I never really had much desire to be a pilot," he said, shaking his head.

Because the internet is the internet, talented civilian photographers will occasionally find their contact information posted on some squadron bulletin board. Pilots will fly—unofficially, of course, and entirely unplanned—near a certain location on public land, and they will occasionally, say, bank a certain direction at a highly convenient moment, following the lure of Saint-Exupéry or some unstoppable song in their heart. If that photographer and that pilot are later lucky enough to, say, stumble onto each other's email, as you do on the internet, JPEGs will be exchanged, in the same way that you might attend a track day and feel compelled to buy a picture of your car in a certain corner, even if you've seen that car in that corner and bought the picture a billion times before.

Never underestimate the immense and inexplicable human draw toward any machine that lets us move faster than a run.

The lull quickly passed, and the sheer volume of flights grew overwhelming. By 3:30 that the afternoon, 22 airplanes had buzzed through my lap. F-18s, mostly, plus several National Guard F-15s (menacing and stripped down, but moving more tentatively), that King Air, three evil-looking F-16s. Time began to crawl, but pleasantly so.

"You know, they have other jobs when they're not flying the jets," Camden said.

Makes sense, I thought.

"I've made it a point," he said, "every time I talk to someone in the military, to ask them about their jobs. Because it's a lot more interesting than just pilots, right? They have desk jobs."

"I would have a hard time not sticking a Dymo label on the office microwave that just read REHEAT," I said.

"One guy I know, he's in charge of squadron scheduling. He's only in the jet when he's not at his desk."

"You think that comes across as benefit or bum deal?" I asked.

"Like, 'We're going to let you do all the afterburner knots in this multi-million-dollar hot rod, inches over the desert, basically every kid's wildest dream, it'll be rad, I promise. And also, uh, please collate these TPS forms. You will get paid the same for both jobs, which is enough but also not very much, so if you want money, go work for Facebook.'"

The chuckle. Then the noise again. After a while, you stand, Pavlovian, on hearing it. Late in the day, as the sun trudged toward the west, the landscape went from a gradient of dark pastels to a stark carpet of trees in haze. The contrast annihilated visibility but the airplanes kept coming. Most ended their run through the valley by popping low over a ridge and breaking hard to the left, snapping beneath the land as if batted out of the sky, vaguely primal, under a tapestry of heat shimmer. My legs went weak.

Is this what birdwatching is like?

Don't tell me if it's not.

The Waiting Part, the Hardest

Naturally, the next day, we sat on another mountain for eight hours and saw a grand total of bupkis.

We had slept the night before on a dry lake near Death Valley, a few miles from a small town. I folded the seats in the Land Rover and unrolled sleeping bag in the back. The next morning, the sun rose as it does in the desert, a blue-pink glow that crept lazily over the hills before erupting into a wash of golden light.

Shortly after dawn, Camden and I loaded our gear into a couple of backpacks and climbed a 400-foot pile of boulders at the valley's edge. For the rest of the day, we sat around 200 feet up, waiting, with a 270-degree view of the land below. It felt like fishing, minus the smell and any kind of mucking about with hooks.

I spent the first 20 minutes on that pile getting settled. Organizing gear, poking around the boulders, arranging snacks. When I finished, I sat down on a rock the size of a Volkswagen and watched a lone cloud amble around the peak of Mt. Whitney. Down on the desert floor, on a gravel road, where humans do not regularly report their speed as a Mach number, a minivan trundled past, trailing a long cloud of dust. Nothing else happened for hours.

That did not mean air was silent. Jet noise was audible all day, echoing over the horizon. Two days in, the sound felt something like a call, the heading of a Mecca to face. You could follow a rumble across the land, listen as it circled from west to east, the reverb splashing across valley. All that air rolling and tumbling. I watched heat shimmer across the lakebed and tried to picture the violence met by an air molecule in a turbine: suck-toss-tumble-burn, then shoosh, you're out. For almost no reason, I then found myself thinking on mistakes, how a single poor choice can cascade into other poor choices, one thing leading inexorably to another, until you're spit out the back of your own train of bad decisions, attempting to process what happened.

Around 11:00, two F-18s came rolling across the desert, dark and menacing, so low that they disappeared into the heat distortion rising off the sand. A second later, each airplane flicked into a climbing roll and pitched up directly over my rock.

I had many thoughts about the world right then, and none were suited for a family website.

From a certain perspective, sitting on a pile of rocks for hours, simply for a chance to watch rare airplanes, is ridiculous. What, exactly, are you accomplishing by driving a small truck into rural America, sitting for hours or days, doing little more than collating your thoughts while eyeballing the panorama of creation?

From another perspective, what *aren't* you accomplishing, doing that?

Viper 1, Your Bandits Are Set

Much of Death Valley National Park looks as you'd think, baked and empty. Parts of the western border, however, are lush and rolling, like a lumpy comforter painted with trees. On our third day in the desert, Camden pointed us up a route in those foothills—graded gravel at first, then gnarly two-track. At one point, the Jeep's inclinometer indicated a whopping 14 degrees of slope. The road ended at a small plateau, a shale-covered flat surrounded by trees, with a virtually uninterrupted view. The rocks grabbed at my boots as I walked, clinking against each other like porcelain. Below us, the land tilted and folded, losing elevation rapidly, foliage tapering as the desert rose up to eat it.

Camden set the scanner on the Jeep's hood, then opened the Wrangler's trunk and began rummaging through luggage. A quarter mile away, a branch snapped audibly. The Wrangler itself was covered in silt; when Thrasher shut the rear door, the thunk of its closure dislodged a cloud of dirt that billowed over the hood, coating my face and gear. After three days without a shower, I didn't care.

"I came up here one time before, stayed most of the day," he said. "Saw nothing. There's a road that leads up the hill to an old mine, though—I poked around that a bit. Google Maps says it goes a bit further."

The scanner was a lot more active in that spot, likely because we were facing more broad and open terrain. High above, some sort of flight exercise carried on—the radio merrily burbling things like "Viper 1, your bandits are set," and "hostiles up high, 29,000." A small group of pilots communicated with each other, with one voice, more authoritative than the rest, choreographing and managing the whole thing.

I muttered something about the strange nature of boredom, how a human can sit idle for hours in certain locations without wanting to leave but five minutes in the dentist's chair is occasionally too much. Camden squinted at the horizon. Then he kicked a few rocks down the hill with a sneaker before telling a long and funny story about the time he was out chasing jets and got in a fight with a squirrel.

"He made noises at me the whole day. Just, like, squeaking. Then I threw a rock at him and he left."

I said nothing, chewing on possibility.

"I didn't know what his problem was," he said.

"Well," I allowed, as deadpan as I could manage, "people say you're good at what you do."

An hour passed quietly, then another, and another after that. High above, two condensation plumes swept across the sky. The machines that produced them were so distant as to essentially be invisible. Camden pointed them out, then poked at an app on his phone. "Contrails—not an airliner. They're doing something."

"I wonder what."

"GE has a 747 they do engine tests on. I think it has one giant engine from the triple-7? That was floating around yes—"

A wall of noise sprung from behind us, drowning him out. Two F-22s burst from a seam in the land, a few hundred feet over our heads, then flicked down lower, batting into a shallow set of ridges. Camden, caught off guard, whirled on a toe, yanking his camera into a pan. The shutter's motor drive chattered away, somehow audible over the blare of the jets, until just before they popped out of sight.

A flash of movement on the ground caught my eye. It looked like the shadow of an airplane but turned out to be a bird, a small jay of some kind, biting at a piece of grass. I watched it for a moment, unable to look away.

An Immense Failure

To find the canyon at the end of the Jedi Transition, you leave the tourist burg of Lone Pine, just down the road from Mt. Whitney, and drive southeast down a two-lane highway that seems to end at the horizon. This visual trick repeats a few times, the road's "end" being nothing more than the visible curvature of the earth, and then you are winding down a series of descending S-curves and dropping into the low and ancient graben that is Death Valley National Park.

Death Valley exists because of an immense fault in the earth. A graben is a depressed and sharply defined block of land, rarely small, born where the planet's crust has pressed up against itself with such force as to produce a wide and relatively even change in elevation. Picture a godlike footprint the breadth of a county. In addition to being the lowest place in North America and the home of a spectacular park, the Valley has hosted military flight training since airplanes were built of doped fabric and wood. We went there the morning of the fourth day, to Rainbow Canyon, simply to see the place.

Military aircraft no longer fly through Rainbow Canyon because Rainbow once held a fireball. The idea can be difficult to process in the abstract, and it's even more difficult when you're standing mere feet from literal scorched earth. Humanity has spent much time and effort shaping inherently dangerous practices so as to eliminate or drastically reduce the chance of a tornado of blooming flame. You have to work really hard these days to make fire happen inside a race car, and the phenomenon is now so rare in civil aviation as to make motor racing look positively foolhardy.

The limits of our striving grow safer every year, and for good reason. Which is why the shock of our intense failure, when it comes, can be so . . . shocking, so intense.

The canyon itself is bigger than it looks, a V-shaped gutter in the land whose western maw dumps abruptly into the valley below. The internet is littered with first-person accounts of plane-watching here, blogs and posts from ordinary people who rose before dawn and drove for hours simply to secure a parking space and a seat. Before the crash, an aviation journalist dubbed the place a "Mt. Everest and the Louvre" of plane-spotting, a hotbed of "white-scarf, stick-and-rudder flying." There was, he said, nowhere like it in the world.

I leaned over the railing and looked into the chasm below. It seemed too shallow and narrow to hold anything like a jet. Camden was quieter than usual.

Smithology

"Sometimes they'd run it backward," he said, softly. "You could stand on that ridge"—he pointed to the left—"and watch them come straight at you. There were so many ways and places to shoot it in one place, you were so close..."

Forty feet away, in a nearly empty parking lot, a middle-aged woman in a Chrysler Pacifica sat talking on the phone.

Eight-figure hardware and human accomplishment, in your face and spectacular. Gone now and unlikely to come back, like how we used to run the Indy 500 without catch fencing. The F-18 accident here came toward the end of the route, on the canyon's southern wall, the scorch mark 40 feet below what the National Park Service calls the Father Crowley Scenic Overlook. The parking lot holds a pit toilet and several places where a person without much sense of risk could simply walk along the unguarded canyon edge.

According to a Navy investigation, the pilot, 33-year-old Lieutenant Charles Walker, descended through 4000 feet in full afterburner. Then he simply made a mistake.

"You need to be very cautious of your own biases," the F-35 test pilot had told me. Most of our 20-minute conversation had orbited thought process and risk. "Your own susceptibility. Realizing that you could be disoriented. What kills most pilots [who die in the airplane] is unrecognized spatial disorientation. They just don't realize it."

The art of being aware, without thinking too hard about the act of being aware, because too much of that kind of thinking could pull focus from the task at hand and very much possibly bring an abrupt and permanent end to any kind of awareness whatsoever.

One hundred feet off the deck, I asked—is it uncomfortable?

"Very unnerving," he said. "You need to realize you're literally a tenth of a second away from killing yourself at any moment, right? And you can't just trust your eyes. What looks like a tree at 600 mph could actually be a bush. If you think it's a tree, but it's a bush, you're... way too close, if that makes any sense."

That pilot used the words "wary" and "respect" a lot. After I hung up the phone, it occurred to me that some things are simply a certain baseline of appealing, no matter what we have to do to chase them, and the work to get there is often half the draw. The definitions and

239

justification vary with personality, but an inarguable truth remains: If you have the chance to witness something remarkable, then you know what it was like to be there, in that moment, on that day. Which is more than you knew before.

I turned to Camden. Was it better to come here, I asked, when the canyon was jumping, airplanes every few minutes, or would you rather spend hours sitting in the woods, waiting, as we had for most of the week, with all the detective work and hope?

On the hood of the Jeep, the scanner squawked one more time: "Two F-15s over dry lake, off Jedi Transition, proceeding north."

Camden thought for a moment. He shrugged, eyes hidden behind sunglasses, in a way that did not suggest an answer. One hand went to a pocket as the other reached to pick up the camera. Then he turned once more, looking and listening, back to the sky.

Dan Gurney, American
Losing the Big Eagle.

We don't keep much automobilia in the house. There is a picture of Dan, though. He's grinning.

ROAD & TRACK, MARCH 2018

It means almost too much that Dan Gurney is dead. I was in California when I heard, which is fitting. Dan was born in New York, but he was from the Golden State in every other sense, represented it. The way California represents—or depending on your view, maybe used to represent, or will forever represent—one of the brightest parts of the American dream. That enormous and knee-buckling coast, a collection of astonishing beauties somehow greater than their sum. That raw sense of possibility, chased by virtually everyone who moves there from somewhere else. Like all good places, the state seems to vibrate with a magic outside the rules for the rest of the world.

Like Dan. His company, All American Racers, built race cars called Eagles, in Santa Ana. That house of genius turned out or helped engineer countless other gems, from BMX bicycles to confidential aerospace projects and the revolutionary DeltaWing. But the Eagles, 157 cars from

1965 to 2000, were the soul of the place. They looked like birds on purpose, noses feminine and sharp, because Dan figured race cars should be pretty. "If you have the chance to make something beautiful," he once told me, "and you don't, well, what does that say about you?"

That idea wasn't new, but in a notoriously unromantic industry, it rang like a bell. AAR's products stood out long after the business decided elegance was frivolous. Also like Dan. He was more than six feet tall, for one. Friends called him the Big Eagle, as if he were a head of state with a Secret Service code name. At 33, long before his powers had peaked, in an era when racing was still a cultural force, *Car and Driver* printed bumper stickers putting him up for president. Hindsight paints it perhaps too small an honor.

Fittingly, Gurney's tale reeks of this country. At 19, from modest roots, he built a car that went 130 mph at Bonneville. A few years later, in the 1950s, he found his way to California's burgeoning road-race scene and sparked off like a Roman candle. Europe beckoned. By the late 1960s, he had ascended to rare air on a geyser of talent. There were wins in sports cars, NASCAR, Trans-Am, Indy cars, Can-Am. He drove in Formula 1 for Ferrari, BRM, and Brabham. One of his four wins in the points there—a far greater achievement than it sounds—came for Porsche, in 1962. The feat hasn't been repeated. It was Stuttgart's only year as an F1 constructor, its only win.

With Yankee drivers, only Mario Andretti climbed higher on Europe's peak. But Dan landed a prize that Mario didn't: He won an F1 race for himself, in a car he helped design and build. That was at Spa, in 1967. It was one of the most stirring feats in a sport not lacking in such things, an accomplishment unmatched by any American before or since.

Then as now, European racing was a fortress, accessible mostly to privilege and social power. Eagles weren't built on either. Astonishingly, a week before, Gurney had gone to Le Mans, another continental temple, and won overall, in a Ford. His co-driver was a similar comet, A.J. Foyt. At the time, only a handful of U.S. drivers had landed that podium spot. An American car had done it only once, in 1966.

The rest of his story has filled books. Any of the highlights could consume a Hollywood film: Dan was the first to wear a full-face helmet in Formula 1. AAR built Indy cars that redefined the possible, guttering yesterday's genius by refusing to stop at convention. In the 1990s, the shop designed and raced revolutionary Toyota prototypes that produced more downforce than any current F1 car. The 1978 white paper he wrote on the problems with Indy-car racing, bright and insistent, led to the formation of a new sanctioning body, CART, and one of the greatest eras in Speedway history. Not to mention a rare moment of sanity in a business seemingly bent on shooting itself in the foot. (That paper's central point remains relevant: Motorsport exists for the fans, who want gladiators wrestling beasts. Make any of that less than obvious, people go home.) You can burn days Googling the man but get only a fraction of the picture.

But that's statistics. The runs batted in suggest only a competent businessman, a mind with a knack for engineering, great driver and manager. History has no shortage of those and a massive shortage of Big Eagles. After finishing Le Mans in the Ford, he invented the bit where winning drivers joyously spray the champagne they get handed at the end of a race. You might not know what Le Mans is, but you can imagine Europeans politely sipping the stuff for decades prior. You can also imagine how one American spontaneously decided that joyful sipping wasn't enough.

He made a dent on everyone, including Foyt. Racing's most famous firecracker was and remains a kind of bizarro Gurney, just as much a titan but irascible and prone to unimpressed truth-spitting. (He famously called Le Mans "nothin' but a little old country road," his mouth a pile of grin.) After Dan died, in January, Foyt issued a statement from his Texas office, saying that he never uses the word "legend." Then he called his old friend a legend.

The turnaround hints at the charm. I met Dan only once, a few years ago, but his personality was obvious long before. Photographs of the man rarely show anything other than a hundred-watt smile or studied concentration. Interviews were perpetually thoughtful and bubbly. It all painted a picture so bright and optimistic, the rest of us lit up by proxy, as if his accomplishments were now ours.

And seemingly inevitable. Scotsman Jim Clark, F1 world champion in '63 and '65, once confided to his father that Dan was the only driver he feared. Predictably, the two were friends. It is part of learning the

Gurney legend to imagine that he would be your friend, that he would be friends with everyone you know.

Gurney famously learned that Clark feared him at Clark's funeral. Like a staggering number of his contemporaries, Clark died behind the wheel, because formula cars of the Sixties were both explosively fast—Gurney's '67 Spa win came at an average speed of almost 149 mph—and built with little eye toward safety. The era burned through men like kindling. That Dan survived is a testament to little more than luck, but part of me wants to believe it was because he was Dan. As if fate had favored a sparkler.

Some people would use that gift as a signal to park it, but the man's distaste for stagnation seemed boundless. A 1971 Indy-car invention, the Gurney flap, bled into aviation use. In the early 2000s, he built and sold a motorcycle, called Alligator, that cradled your body like a sling. It was supposedly great to ride, because why wouldn't that work, because who says motorcycles have to be a certain shape anyway?

Questions like that keep humanity from chasing its own tail, but we don't always go there instinctively. We need signposts. My garage wall thus holds a vintage poster commemorating that Spa win; it's an image of the car, but also of the guy's beaming face. I bought it years ago and hung it as a reminder that optimism is oxygen. That we should chase the future reflexively because the past is a known quantity. Dull as doorknobs, next to how much we know about tomorrow.

My friend Jacques Dresang, a Gurney historian, texted me shortly after Dan died. We spoke, briefly, about people. "That's what made AAR successful for so long," he wrote. "Sure, they had gods crafting cars, but the figurehead was the guy next door, who might buy you a bike if you mowed his lawn."

Mark Hoyer, the editor of *Cycle World,* texted in next. As we talked, I was reminded of America's tendency to brew royalty from talent. And how the best of those people lack airs, like the early astronauts.

"He once brought his lunch to our office," Hoyer said. "A sack of In-N-Out. He always wanted to talk what was next. He was gracious and accommodating and wrote me letters. He laughed every time we talked. There was nothing crass about him. I miss that about Americanism."

Such was Dan's appeal—a legend in our circles, but never a household name like Mario or Foyt—that in 2018, you either have zero idea why all of this is stirring for certain people, or it makes you want to find a glass just to raise it.

The day that he died, AAR sent out a press release. The image at the top was a painting of Gurney in the Sixties, broad strokes, a flowered wreath around his neck. He is looking down, with a smile that hints at gratitude. I first saw that picture on my phone, a few hours after his death, riding in a car in California's Central Valley, north of L.A. I had just left a test weekend at Buttonwillow Raceway, where it was cloudy and cold, a sea of hats and jackets.

Typical funeral weather. But as we headed back to the city, rolling through the mountains, the sun broke. The sky filtered into that crystalline California blue, yellow light snapping over the hills. One of those moments that remind you how different the place is from everywhere else. It felt warm and heartbreaking and welcoming and bright, as if anything were possible. Probably because it is.

Alonso ex Machina
A titan steps down.

> *Fernando! Today, 17 years after landing his first Formula 1 championship, the 42-year-old Spaniard is back on the grid. He remains, improbably, a podium contender—dragging subpar cars to the front, nothing left to prove, back in it simply for love of the game. What a stud.*

ROAD & TRACK, NOVEMBER 2018

Some people don't like Alonso. Some of their reasons likely hold water, but I've never been able to make myself agree with them. Or maybe I just don't want to.

Fernando Alonso Diaz, 37. Formerly the youngest Formula 1 driver to qualify on pole, the youngest world champion, the youngest double world champion. A widely acknowledged master of the sport who has spent the last four seasons stuck solidly midpack.

There's something about a person of extreme talent who suffers years of bad luck and bad equipment but keeps hammering when he could retire to some private island instead. But then, motor racing has always been a funky arena for outliers. Serena Williams would dominate with a thrift-store tennis racket, but ability in racing is nothing without tools. Deserving the top rung doesn't mean you'll get the car or team to help you prove it.

The oddities of the landscape can prompt you to examine people in unique ways. You look for familiar archetypes, reasons for allegiance. Phil Hill, America's first world champion, has always reminded me of my own neuroses, the nights I've lain awake before an important tomorrow. James Hunt was basically everyone's party-rat friend in college. Niki Lauda is every brilliant but socially awkward engineer I've ever met.

Alonso is my age, but he always reminded me of how my dad talks about his father. You tend to note the rare occasions when the Spaniard does something obnoxious, because their rarity seems to reinforce years of apparent good-dude-ishness. In 2004, a dumb move by Ralf Schumacher at Monaco saw the two men collide. Alonso's car flew backward out of the track's famous tunnel, toward the harbor, coming to rest near the Armco, front suspension visibly broken. As Schumacher drove past, an arm jutted from Alonso's cockpit, almost politely, holding a single raised finger. I watched that race live, pondering our sad devaluation of sportsmanship and civility while paradoxically finding the man immensely likable. An otherwise genial adult briefly overwhelmed and caught being himself.

It's no secret that pro sports thrive on relatable spectacle—seemingly impossible accomplishments easily measured against a personal barometer, so you understand why those feats are amazing. It's why racing is more fun to watch if you've ever strapped into a race car, and why pro baseball is more impressive if you know just how difficult it is to hit a small pile of cork and leather over an outfield fence.

Some of this might be why racing from the last century—generally possessed of less downforce and more goon-show slides—can seem more interesting. A sliding car is obvious drama, conflict awaiting resolution. This may also be why guys like Alonso are heralded for ordinary mannerisms and imperfections. This year's Formula 1 cars are understandable at a glance only for an aerodynamicist, and they ask every driver to deliver a grindingly specific type of lap, little room for style or self or art. The business of the sport, so balanced on the avoidance of risk, leaves its participants similar. Distant perfection is only interesting with architecture and house cats.

There is, however, always something worth marveling at. Another truism my favorite Spaniard helped illustrate. Almost a decade ago, a video famously appeared on YouTube, Alonso standing in a plaza in Europe. After some egging from a small crowd, he placed a walnut on his shoulder, cracking it with his neck muscles. Modern F1 cars are rumored to see almost 5 *g*'s in braking alone. Friends who have driven them say that ordinary people often go limp around 10 laps in, muscles unable to hold up a helmet.

Consider that the next time a Formula 1 race goes boring: It takes a pretty special ruleset to snoozify a 200-mph chess match where you need Incredible Hulk Neck just to get in the door.

Alonso grinned at the end of that walnut clip, a little sheepish. He was younger then, less often serious in public appearances. Possibly because he had yet to spend years dragging gutter cars up the grid through little more than gusto. But he appears no less human now. When it comes to barely censored personality, F1 really only has Alonso, the Finnish Hunter Thompson that is Kimi Räikkönen, and the grinning ball of light masquerading as Daniel Ricciardo. (Ricciardo perpetually beams in front of cameras, as if the secret to being happy is simply deciding to have a rad time. Maybe it is.)

In his prime, 2006, years before he hit his other prime.

Alonso just announced his retirement from F1. Out, after 17 remarkable but uneven years. IndyCar is a rumored next step. It's where I'd go in his shoes, a likely pay cut but a perfect landing spot if you love uphill battles. Some athletes leave the arena the moment their legacy is locked; some happy loons can't get enough. Nico Rosberg retired from F1 in 2016, confident and done, after landing his first championship there. When Alonso first entered the Indy 500 in 2017, his interviews made it sound as if he had undertaken that notoriously expensive and draining endeavor simply because America's most storied race looked like a good old hoot.

Smithology

Speaking of expensive endeavors: In two weeks, after months of planning, I'm testing one of the man's F1 cars for *R&T*. A 2007 McLaren MP4-22.

Alonso finished third in the championship in 2007 but broke ties with his team in the wake of interpersonal conflicts and an industrial-espionage scandal. Unsavory stuff. Like that Schumacher finger, the scandal served to paint him as less ideal but more relatable, not immune from regrettable instinct. Relatability being what we look for in athletes, and regrettable instinct what we occasionally find in the mirror.

It's always easier to be impressed by someone's work when you learn what the two of you have in common. Good luck with the future, Walnut-Neck. The belts in that McLaren probably won't fit too well, and it won't be because one of us eats too many doughnuts.

Rules and Brooks
Denise, who mattered.

A bright light. The coworker who attended that media event also wrote the foreword to this book. He didn't know her story then, asked if I knew the name: "How was she so f***ing fast?" "Jay," I said, "It was Denise.*"*

ROAD & TRACK, AUGUST 2015

When I heard Denise McCluggage had died, it was 8:45 p.m. on a Wednesday in May. Thanks to the vagaries of magazines, these words, written that night, will not see print for weeks.

You're not supposed to do this now, with the immediacy of the internet. But Denise was a fan of doing things you're not supposed to, so there.

If you Google her, you find endless shots of a petite woman with short hair, laughing. Mostly surrounded by sports cars. A Porsche 550 at Montgomery in 1957. A Lotus Eleven in Nassau in '58. In a single-piece blue driving suit, bright Kodachrome, talking to an impossibly young Stirling Moss. Born in Kansas, her first real job was at the *San Francisco Chronicle* in the 1950s, but she didn't hit her stride until a few years later, covering sports for the *New York Herald Tribune*. She became known for doing what she wrote about, because, as she once put it, why not? That was initially downhill skiing. Then racing. Two magnets for rhythm and grace.

Why wouldn't one lead to the other? Moreover, who has a career like that anymore? In 1958, Denise was nominated to drive at Le Mans for Luigi Chinetti—the man who brought Ferrari to America—only to be turned down because the race was invitational; the race's organizing body said that it didn't "choose to invite women." In 1961, she won the GT category at Sebring in a Ferrari 250. A class win at the Monte Carlo Rally in 1964, in a Ford Falcon. Fifth at the 1960 Watkins Glen Grand Prix, the only woman in the race. This is far from the whole list. Women were shuffled to the side in those years, often in ridiculous "ladies' races," if they were even allowed to compete. And yet she went everywhere, did everything.

One picture stands out in Google. Black and white. Five guys in the early Sixties, around a woman who is grinning in a white turtleneck. She glows like a streetlight on a darkened block.

The men are Fangio, Moss, Pedro Rodríguez, Innes Ireland, Ronnie Bucknum. They may as well be Beethoven, Einstein, Picasso. Golden-age titans and an ordinary person. Only she wasn't ordinary. She was also first-name friends with them, plus Briggs Cunningham, Carroll Shelby, Dan Gurney, Phil Hill, Steve McQueen, and the saxophonist Allen Eager. She lent Dave Brubeck a piano while he formed his quartet. She helped Miles Davis with his first Ferrari, taught his son to ski, dated a prefame McQueen in Fifties New York.

And she wrote about them all—God, how she wrote. Denise's writing is still the best to have ever graced this silly business—beautiful, honest, simultaneously carved from granite and filled with air. She worked for this magazine, for *Car and Driver*, and for *Autoweek*, which she helped found. Plus a hundred other places.

I discovered her at 13, in 1994, when she published her anthology, a 284-page paperback called *By Brooks Too Broad for Leaping*. It took me years to realize, but that book helped steer my life. Its phrasing shimmers, words wrapped up like caramels. Richie Ginther was "built like a short stretch of barbed-wire fencing." McKay Fraser was "as changeable as an April day." The title, from an A. E. Housman poem, hinted at a theme. The author of "To an Athlete Dying Young" spent a life on love and death, but Denise maybe understood those things better. I dare you to read her on Masten Gregory or Harry Schell and stay in one piece. In a business that can spend too much time on idols and machines, she focused mostly on humanity, what pulls us together and drags us apart. And makes us great.

At the 12 Hours of Sebring, 1958, with Phil Hill and the Fiat-Abarth she drove in the race that year.

Rhythm and grace. Jean Jennings, cofounder of *Automobile* magazine, once told me that Denise was the only lady in an industry filled with women. I thought of that line the one time I met Denise, eight years ago, over lunch at the Detroit auto show. We sat in the back of the Audi stand and talked about old San Francisco, Peter Collins, her Land Rover with the license plate DOG. (Get it?) Sparkling wit, kindness, conversation like a plate of warm cookies. I silently wished she would

Smithology

adopt me. A coworker ran into her months later at some media track event, could barely keep up, said she still drove like hell. She was 80.

Denise was not young when she put *Brooks* together, and she knew what she was doing. That book appears to be about dying, but it's really about getting out and being alive. And proof that every rule is fluid. It is peppered with sadness and joy, the loss of great people, and scenes from a world not made smaller for their leaving. When the rest of my heroes passed, she missed them for who they were, not what they represented. Which is also why I miss her.

When the news came, I called my friend John Krewson, a former editor at *R&T*. We traded silences. "She was the ideal," he finally said. "I would want my daughter to be like her. I would want my son to be like her. I wish I were more like her."

Others will write about Denise and share stories. Many people knew her better—easy, really, since I didn't know her at all. I have no stories. I have only what she meant to me. Which, as far as this business goes, is everything.

The Little Things
On French cars and daughters and ice cream. And turtles.

Few things I've written have received greater response—I still get messages about this one. It makes me happy that people remember it, but I take no credit. All I did was go for a drive with a fun little girl and write down everything she said.

ROAD & TRACK, JULY 2018

We went to get ice cream. This was a reasonable act and also slightly ridiculous. She was four years old and my firstborn. I wondered if she would be into cars but didn't have any evidence. So I decided to gauge her in the simplest way possible: taking a quirky, affordable classic on a quick errand. From our home in Seattle to Tillamook, Oregon. Two hundred and thirty miles if you avoid the interstate.

Tillamook is home to Tillamook Creamery, a dairy on the Pacific Ocean. I told her we were going for ice cream. I didn't tell her it was going to take two days, in a car slow as cold mud, along some of the prettiest coast in the country.

The car was a 1972 Citroën 2CV. I borrowed it from my friend

Greg Long. Greg has three grown sons, none into cars. When asked to use his Citroën, he didn't blink.

"You had me at 'convert my kid to a car person.' I've failed three of three and so must support early intervention."

Funny how some things just don't need explanation.

My daughter's name is Marion. Seeing Greg's car in our driveway, she paused.

"Looks like a bug."

"People call these things tin snails," I said.

She jumped up and down. "A snail bug! I love ice cream! It's pretty. Does it go fast?"

"No. It's very slow. Some old cars don't go fast but feel fast, which makes them fun."

She took a moment to process this.

"I'm gonna go tell Mama. She needs to know." She ran into the house and came back 10 seconds later, dragging her sister, Vivien, who is two. Vivien's eyes lit up.

"She should ride in it," Marion said. "I can ride with her, because she might be scared."

"Yeah. I am *scared* of tigers," Vivien said. Raised eyebrows. She then turned on a heel and scampered back to the house, as if to say, I have had enough of that. Marion gave chase, arms in the air.

"It isn't a tiger, sweetie, it's just an old car that goes very slow! Come back!"

I briefly pondered the incomprehensible nature of children.

"Old and slow" is 2CV in a nutshell. You could also call it the French Volkswagen Beetle—an affordable bolide that put thousands of people on wheels after World War II. The name stands for *deux chevaux-vapeur*, or "two steam horses," after the car's original tax category. (2CVs offered 375 cc and 12 hp when production began, in 1948. Greg's had a staggering 602 cc and 29 hp.)

Early 2CVs were so simple, they didn't have shock absorbers. The body is a steel pup tent, all exposed welds and tubing. The engine moans like an industrial generator. The dinky suspension gives sailboat quantities of heel in even a slow lane change. The sum combines the operating cost of a small toaster with the ride of a Fifties Cadillac. Married to that distinctly French notion that driving can be a space between spaces, a breather from daily life.

Some people pooh-pooh 2CVs for being slow and funky. Those people can go sneeze up a rope. Few things are as goofball joyous as driving a 2CV balls-out while being outrun by drivers in the slow lane. Like a Spec Miata, it's a sort of sack race on wheels, where the car's limitations are half the point. And so obvious, even kids pick them up.

She asked about speed a lot. (Reality check: This is a person who once took 40 minutes to eat a sandwich, because she said it was her friend.)

"Why can't we pass that car?"

I thought for a second. "We don't have enough room to get up to speed. And the wind slows us down."

"I would like to go faster than the wind," she said, matter-of-fact. A pause to look out the window, thinking. "This is the funnest day ever in the whole world for me."

"Why?" I got my hopes up.

"Because I get to sleep in a hotel! This car is weird. We've been driving a long time. When do we get ice cream?"

Western Washington: inlets, weaving valleys, stacked firs, mountains poking through the clouds. Logging mills with shorn trees long as a school bus. In the port town of Shelton, Marion sang a song about her toes. She sang it to a small stuffed sea turtle she had brought along. I had that moment where your stomach goes all tingly and you want to hug someone until they pop.

I never pictured myself as a parent. The process sweeps you up in a flush of hormones and universal emotion. Also this looming curiosity as to whether your kids will be into the same stuff you are, so you can share it.

Four-year-olds are an interesting window for that. Old enough to not be a blank slate, but young enough that they don't know how to be anyone but themselves. All base instinct and direct questions.

Large parts of a 2CV's interior are made of cardboard. The door tops suck into the slipstream when you open the dash vents. From the outside, the car looks half Victorian pram, half garden shed. People in traffic either eye you warily, as if you were selling timeshares, or they laugh and nudge a passenger, because *Look, Helen, can you believe that's an actual car? I bet that guy is fun to drink with.*

In retrospect, it makes sense that Marion mistook the Citroën for a Jeep. Somewhere in the Washington woods, when a late-model Wrangler passed us in traffic.

"Daddy! Look! That's the car we're driving!"

"No, that's a Jeep."

"Okay. I know. It's the same car but different." I was reminded how little kids cut the world into broad categories—Good and Bad, Fun and Boring. It also occurred to me that Marion had never talked so much about cars.

The coast in the Pacific Northwest is nuts. There are neon-green sloughs, grass so vibrant it looks painted on the ground. Cows grazing steps from the ocean. Stacks of bundled oyster shells, bleached white by the sun. Roads that loop and burst with the land, mountains to water and back again. Not like California or the East, where the landscape tends to bleed from one mood to another.

She usually gets bored on long road trips. Descends into a nap or gets cranky. I kept waiting for it to happen, but it didn't. Just north of the Washington-Oregon border, we talked for almost 30 minutes about driving, and how little girls grow up to be big girls, and how big girls can drive.

Feeling cheeky, I asked if she liked old cars. Her face melted into a ferocious side-eye. Too obvious.

"I don't know."

"Why?"

"Because. I don't know what to do with . . . the weird stuff."

I allowed as how life is mostly weird. That the key is trying to understand it, without getting too broken up when you don't. Then I let her put a hand on the wheel as I drove.

"It moves!" More giggles.

"That's the steering telling us about road. It's what makes travel fun. A sense of where you are."

"I am in this car! With you!"

"That's not what I meant."

"Daddy, you're silly. Yes it is."

Four-year-old genius. I've spent most of my life struggling to live in the moment, and the kid just knocked it out in a sentence.

We sang songs, creeping up on Oregon. Made-up songs about nothing and everything, from her stuffed turtle to the 2CV's cloth seats. We crossed the truss bridge at the mouth of the Columbia River. The mountains end abruptly at the water there, like an unfinished painting. It seemed to complement the Citroën, this relic from a time when the idea of Car was younger and less resolved. When we were mostly focused on the short view with the environment and mobility, and hadn't yet asked if the final plan for affordable human transport should include exposed welds inches from your eyeballs.

Young kids are incapable of taking the long view on anything. They exist on an emotional roller coaster. Nearing Tillamook, as a joke, I offered to let Marion drive. In that way you can get a four-year-old to believe anything if you're serious enough. Her face collapsed in horror.

"No! That would be unsafe, Daddy! I don't know what this car is, and I *don't* know how it works."

I watched the highway for a moment, thinking.

"Would you like me to teach you?"

"No."

"You sure?"

She thought for a minute, intrigued. "Okay! Yes."

I explained the wheel and pedals. Her brow furrowed. She touched the shifter. "Well, Daddy, the problem is, I don't know how *this* works."

"Hm."

"But we have time, Daddy. Don't worry. Look at my turtle!"

She held the stuffed turtle up in the air, two hands, then fell into giggles. It didn't make any sense, but I wanted to giggle a bit myself. So I did.

Traffic and a few too many stops to stare at the ocean meant that we reached Tillamook after the dairy had closed. We bunked at a small hotel in the nearby village of Garibaldi. The creamery was almost empty when we rolled in the next morning, at 8:00. Astonishingly, it was also open, if deserted. Marion got ice cream. She ate it with two hands. It got on her hair, face, jacket, everything. She asked if we were going home. I told her that we had to. She grinned, face smeared with chocolate.

You may be wondering if this was an excuse to spend time with my daughter. Of course it was. It was also a legitimate attempt to probe a question. As we walked back out to the car, she was silent. I figured we were done—parenting is nothing if not occasionally looking for answers that aren't there.

I was merging into traffic when she touched my arm. I looked over. Her eyes were larger than usual.

"I figured it out, Daddy. My favorite part of the car is . . ."

It occurred to me that I might have made the point of this trip a little too blatant, even if I didn't come out and say it.

"What, sweetheart?"

"It's . . . vroo."

I frowned. Not sure I heard her right, over the engine. Four-year-olds speak a lot of gibberish.

"Um . . . Vroo?"

She made fists with her hands and bounced in the seat. "Yeah! Vroo! Vroom! The fast! The fast the fast the fast!"

The bouncing stopped. Then she went back to talking to her turtle.

I smiled. That's enough, I thought. All you can ask for, as a parent, with anything. Hope.

Section Four
The Places They Take You
(And All That Implies)

Le Mans, France, 2016

THIS SECTION'S TITLE HOLDS the word "places." Predictably, this part of the book contains travel stories. Not always in the traditional sense. Sometimes, the machine can help you see things a certain way, and that process can put your head somewhere else, even if you never leave the driveway.

The media business doesn't really want work like this any more. Editors and clients kind enough to explain why usually do so in the form of an apology. They love your pitch, they say, wish they could take it, but they've been in triage mode for years, barely keeping the lights on, and every published word or frame of video has to pull as much traffic as possible.

I understand; I've been in that chair. Still, I can't help thinking of an old parable: When you're chopping wood, pausing to sharpen your axe can seem like a great way to get behind in the work. Except that sharpening helps you on a longer clock, actually quickens the job in the end, lets the axe cut faster. The gain outweighs the loss.

When you run a website or a magazine or a YouTube channel, there is certain easy work that keeps the lights on. When belts tighten, it can seem logical to focus on that work at the expense of everything else, but that focus has a cost. At least if you want people to care about and invest in what you make, want them to want to come back, to remember your little corner of the world as something more than another half-anonymous dopamine hose.

So much can now be given to us through a screen, but the literal and figurative going still matters. In retrospect, the stories in this section feel like me trying to remind myself of that. Just because choosing to view the world a certain way is difficult doesn't mean you can't.

Holy Wood

Starstruck at the wheel at the Goodwood Revival, the greatest vintage race on earth.

"Getting a race entry at the Revival," an English friend once told me, "is kind of like getting Royal Box tickets at Wimbledon. It's a social accomplishment." He then made a face that said, So why the hell did they let you in?

No idea. Going by time at the wheel, it was the shortest race weekend I've ever had. My car blew its head gasket a few laps in and I had to park it. Doesn't matter. Norman Dewis outdrank me in gin. I camped in a field by the track and used a P-51 as an alarm clock. Magical doesn't begin to describe it.

If you haven't seen Revival footage on YouTube, go look. Watch Indy 500 winner Kenny Bräck flogging a GT40 in the rain, or Le Mans legend Tom Kristensen juggernauting a Ford Galaxie through traffic, or the E-types and Cobras in one of their Hatfield-McCoy dance-fights. Anything from the Goodwood Revival, really. Everyone loves it. My mom even loved it, and she found racing about as appealing as a dirt sandwich.

(A short preface fronted this story when it ran in the magazine. That text follows, edited lightly for space.)

Sam Smith

Every September, some of the greatest names in motorsport descend upon a small track in the south of England. They come for the Goodwood Revival, a race weekend that attempts to reawaken the sport's 1930s-to-1960s golden age.

Polite period dress is required in the paddock. Warbirds take off from the infield. The Revival has been called the world's only real vintage race: seven-figure Cobras and Ferrari GTOs sliding inches apart; modern touring-car stars hammering 1960s Lotus Cortinas; a ferociously unforgiving track with palpable risk. There is no other event like it; tickets sell out annually.

In 2015, editor-at-large Sam Smith raced in the Revival as a guest driver for Jaguar's Heritage division. He qualified on the front row in a 64-year-old car he'd barely driven, at a track he'd never seen, a brilliant result. The details are the stuff of dreams.

ROAD & TRACK, FEBRUARY 2016

Gary Pearson's shop is in a metal barn behind his house. That house is in a field, and that field is nestled outside Coventry, down a farm road lined with hedges. On the day I visited, the area smelled of manure.

Pearson's shop did not. It smelled of old Jaguars, plus a BRM F1 car and a Porsche 917, and that's not half of what was there when I walked in. The Goodwood Revival was days away, and a silver 1951 Jaguar XK-120 sat out front. That car was mine, at least temporarily, for Goodwood. Pearson had prepared it. I had never driven a 120, so we met. I got 15 minutes on public roads. I'd be lying if I said it was enough to feel confident.

Of course, few drivers are confident at the Revival. You don't just sign up; you have to be invited, a process that was described to me as "getting into Hogwarts." The cars are so critical to the show, they're said to occasionally be asked free of driver. (Translation: "Please come. Wouldn't it be great if someone else railed on your stuff?") All of which is to say that any human in one of the event's 14 weekend races is lucky. And attached to a fantastic, history-steeped car.

Which the Jag is. The XK was bought new by England's R. J. "Ronnie" Hoare, the proprietor of famed Ferrari dealer Maranello Concessionaires. It's currently owned by Australian Rory Johnston, who was kind enough to lend it to *R&T*.

A phone snap, on a rural road near Pearson's, after meeting the car.

Like any 120, Johnston's car was a stunning cross between manor house and female birthday suit. The fenders were a sine wave. The interior appeared to have been laid out for laughs: tach in front of the passenger, horn button made large for no apparent reason, except to resemble one of Mae West's . . . horn buttons.

Outside Pearson's, *R&T* photographer Richard Pardon, a Brit, nudged me in the arm. "Quite a thing."

I looked up. "You guys must have a law or something, right?"

"For what?"

"Cars like this. Home soil."

"Huh?"

"It feels like empire. Like I'll be deported if I light it off without a shotgun and a butler."

Pearson, 55, first went to the Revival 13 years ago. When we met, he wore jeans, a shop apron, and faded Vans, calling to mind a Keebler elf raised by Tony Hawk. A quiet demeanor belied years of Goodwood success, often in a Jaguar.

"The weekend hasn't changed much," he said. "That's the magic. The same thing every year; it never gets old. I don't know how they do it."

265

I asked about power, shift points.

"The car goes alright," he said, casually. "Shift at six. Drive to the drum brakes, which don't really work. And it's a proper track." (I love how the Brits use "proper" as the ultimate compliment. Everything from good tea to the Lancaster bomber.) "Not much runoff, fourth-gear corners. But no pressure."

I glanced at the Jag's cockpit. "No roll bar?"

"Doesn't matter, since you're not going to crash it, eh?" A wink.

Outside Pearson's gate, the 120 felt heart-stoppingly wide. It had waterfalls of torque, but also a slow, woolly steering box and a four-speed manual that required the patience of Job. Maybe 250 hp. Plus other period quirks.

"That thing," I said to Pearson, after returning, "where you hit undulating pavement at the right frequency, and the left front wheel's doing one thing, and the right another—it shook like a wheel was coming off. My eyes lost focus. Is that normal?"

"Oh, yes." An impish smile. "And that's a good one."

That night, lying in bed, I thought a lot about fourth-gear corners and roll bars. Then I decided, very clearly, to not.

Here's the thing about that roll bar: It's missing partly because, until the early 1960s, most race cars weren't required to have rollover protection. This is in keeping with the spirit of Goodwood, which aims, with the Revival, to present a polished view of the sport's most innocent era, prior to the arrival of corporate sponsorship.

The approach includes touches like costumed actors, period signage, and restored or reconstructed vintage buildings. The paddock dress code sees most mechanics in white coveralls, most drivers in suits and hats, and most ladies fit for a midcentury garden party. But the Jaguar's roll bar is also absent because—and this is where you have to applaud Europeans for being themselves—it would be ugly. Bolting a fat roll hoop onto a 120's cascading steel qualifies as art defacement, even if it's thoroughly sane and could save someone's life.

The risk is offset, and maybe encouraged, by what makes

Goodwood special. For one thing, the course is the property of 60-year-old Lord Charles March. His family founded the track in 1948; it was mothballed in 1966 on safety concerns, then restored in the 1990s for the first Revival. The pavement is virtually unchanged. There is no catch fencing, plenty to hit, and little more than short berms and bushes to catch uncontrolled cars. Goodwood is where Stirling Moss had his career-ending accident. Bruce McLaren died there, in a Can-Am car. Even in modern iron, it is not a place where you want to go off.

And so the Revival exists with a certain amount of assumed risk, more than most vintage racing. Plus famously close competition. TV coverage shows a cutthroat and drifty street fight that makes contemporary motorsport seem stuffy. Credit European historic racing in general —usually more aggressive than its American counterpart—and the fact that Revival entry lists can include both local champs and moonlighting F1 stars, mostly in cars with big power and low grip.

But the show is unique, and it's helped Goodwood become more than just a Renaissance fair for car people. You get the feeling that the organizers are consciously spurning something. As if the period drag was merely an offshoot of a greater goal.

All of this rolled around my head the day after we visited Pearson. I was standing in Jaguar's Whitley engineering center, in front of three new, aluminum-bodied 1964-spec Jaguar E-type Lightweight race cars. I came to Whitley to meet them, a trip that included Jaguar's heritage garage, in the Browns Lane plant where E-types were first made.

The Lightweights are part of Jaguar's recent effort to "reclaim" its heritage. Six cars are being produced, augmenting the 12 that the factory built in the Sixties. It's a PR exercise, Jaguar trumpeting its past like no other automaker can, but the timing is interesting. The move almost feels like a delayed reaction to the policies espoused when Ford owned the company, from 1990 to 2008. ("The bastards wanted to sell the historic collection outright," an insider told me. "If we hadn't put it in a state trust, they would have hawked everything.") Or maybe it's just Tata, Jaguar's current owner, reminding people what it bought.

The new E-type bodies are built in-house, hand-riveted from digital scans of originals. The finished products cost more than $1 million apiece (still less than an original Lightweight) and sold virtually upon announcement. They are a jaw-dropping embodiment of the Jaguar ethos that emotion can trump anything. Also the idea that good old things are virtuous not because they're old, but because they're inherently good.

Remember that the E-type and XK-120 came from Jaguar's greatest era. From 1951 to 1957, the marque won Le Mans a whopping five times. In 1949, with the XK-120, it built the world's fastest production car when most of Europe was rubble. Amazingly, each of those achievements used the same basic engine: the twin-cam XK straight-six, which powered the 120, the E-type, and the first XJ6, among others.

Amazingly part two, in Jaguar's golden age, most of the firm's accomplishments were engineered by a handful of men. One, Norman Dewis, is still alive. Prior to retirement in 1985, he helped develop everything from the first reliable racing disc brake (a Jaguar achievement) to the chassis of nearly every Jaguar after 1952. He raced at Le Mans. He set a speed record (172.4 mph, in 1953) in an XK-120 on a Belgian highway. He is a certain kind of royalty.

Smithology

Dewis is 95, but he goes to the Revival every year. Jaguar reps suggested I camp with him, in an RV near the track. They also suggested I take an F-type press loaner and go somewhere during the one day in country that I had free, in the week before Goodwood.

The car turned out to be a white, 550-hp, all-wheel-drive V-8 R roadster. It went like bejesus, so I convinced Pardon that we needed to bejesus over to Belgium for a day. We took the Chunnel, the underwater train that runs in a tunnel under the English Channel, driving onto one of its cars in Folkestone. While waiting for the train to leave, I had a short chat with a friendly old British man in an MG sedan:

Man: "Fine car. You're young. What do you do, sell drugs?"

Me: "No."

Pardon: "He's from America."

Man: "So you're over here selling drugs?"

Pardon: "No, the car's just white."

Me, apologetically: "I really have nothing to do with drugs."

Man: "Jaguar's a good car, then."

Inexplicably, a version of this conversation occurred at almost every British gas station I visited. When I asked Pardon about it, he just shrugged, as if this was what happens when you come to England and toot around in the latest version of a national symbol that happens to cost more than a pair of new Camrys.

Nor can I rationally defend the F-type's appeal. The steering is slick but far from talkative. Interior finish could be better. The eight-speed automatic embodies the car: It doesn't always do what you want, but after a few miles, I stopped caring. Maybe because I spent too much time gazing into the front fenders.

Dewis set his record near the Belgian village of Jabbeke, 14 kilometers from the city of Bruges. A commemorative plaque sits on the N377 road at the edge of town, holding a relief of Dewis's face and a description of his accomplishment. We arrived at that plaque after a 50-minute blitz from the French Chunnel port in Calais. Pardon climbed out of the car and knelt to read.

"Hell! One seventy-two! Norman Dewis got balls."

I rattled off a list of the man's accomplishments.

"So, he's far cooler than you, then."

I nodded. "Yes, Richard."

Impish smile. "Not that it'd take much."

"Be quiet, Richard."

I looked at Dewis's face. He wore goggles. The day before, at Browns Lane, I spotted an XK-120 on a lift. Its wheels were off, exposing slender drums, a solid rear axle, and a ladder frame.

It's cliché, but the sight reminded me of blacksmithing. Conveniently, and perhaps predictably, a man was working underneath, hammering on some hidden part with a large mallet. The sound rang through the shop as we left, echoing into the rafters.

He arrived in a suit the day before qualifying. Gray wool, with a string tie and suspenders. Didn't look a day over 70. His white hair was neatly combed. In idle moments, he whistled big-band tunes.

"Yeah," Dewis said later, over drinks, "you should have a roll bar. 'Course, in my day, we didn't. But then, I rolled a C-type, I rolled a D-type, and the only reason I survived is because I'm small. Ducking into the cockpit."

Norman!

I asked if it felt odd, having people romanticize your life.

"Oh, I don't know. I first raced here in 1952. Last one was 1955, in the nine-hour, I finished fifth. I liked big, fast circuits—Reims, Spa. When we were doing this, the crowds weren't such a big deal. Now it's all money."

I was briefly reminded of all the times in my life where I had complained about some minor inconvenience and suddenly felt very small for all of them.

"The track layout," he added, "is identical. The foam chicane wall"—built in the 1950s, to keep spinning cars off pit road—"was brick. But identical."

Dewis was a font of stories. The best are unprintable. The shortest took six sentences: "How fast did we go at Le Mans? In '55, I did 192 down the Mulsanne. A D-type, 6200 rpm. I remember passing another man at night, engines in and out of phase. Enough time side by side for the fella to scowl at me. I waved, because it seemed to wind him up." And then he cackled softly into a glass of gin and said more unprintable things before segueing into a tale about almost getting kicked off the original Mille Miglia because the Italians had never seen disc brakes and thought they were trickery.

It is pretty much impossible to dislike Norman.

Late Thursday, I wandered over to the annual drivers' cricket match, on the lawn of Goodwood House, March's ancestral home. The house is basically a palace, and the lawn is essentially a garden larger than several football fields. The cricket match ends with a driver's meeting in a large tent, where stewards stress propriety. Despite the event's bent-fender reputation—drivers under its flags have damaged everything from $50,000 Minis to Ferrari GTOs worth $50 million—recklessness is clearly abhorred.

The Goodwood pits, remarkably.

As a deterrent, the organizers took a moment during the meeting to show silent footage of crashes. "At Goodwood," March said, "more than any other track, it is absolutely vital to not go for that last-minute pass, the one that puts everyone at risk. I say this every year, but our future is in your hands. We've been very lucky. We have a massive accident, and it's probably all over."

I'd be lying if I said this sort of thing hadn't stuck in my mind for weeks. Along with the rootless possibility that one of the Jag's suspension bits would break, send the XK rolling end-over-end, and leave my children fatherless because of some stupid devotion to Art and Beauty on some English estate they'd never heard of.

I wrote a long, wine-drenched email to my dad that night, rambling. Over years of club racing, my safety was always a constant. How many people would still take a flag if the consequences were . . . closer?

I thought about things and felt worse. Then, illogically, better, as if worrying the problem had solved something. Lying in bed the night before qualifying, I flipped through pictures of the Jaguar on my phone. The car looked heartbreakingly beautiful and risky. For reasons I can't explain, it suddenly seemed unforgivable to go through life without a few beautiful, risky moments.

The first morning came early. It came early because I forced it, shambling out of bed with a wine hangover (English campgrounds are friendlier than you'd expect) at 5:45. Fifteen minutes later, I was bicycling the track on a borrowed 1950s cruiser, watching the sunrise. It felt necessary, as I'd never driven at Goodwood; each Revival race gets a dual-purpose practice/qualifying session of just 15 minutes.

Even at rest, the track is astonishing. Early morning gave the grounds utter silence and the glow of a hundred pastels: pea-green grass and fresh white paint gone cream in the light. A fleet of vintage Land Rovers, olive and dirty, squatted in the infield. The bike's pedals issued an occasional squeak. The noise felt criminal.

Later that morning, the place buzzed. Tweed was everywhere, and the air carried the sweet reek of methanol. Wartime Jeeps shuttled people between parking lots. I saw a small boy eating a bacon sandwich; when I asked, he pointed to a stand selling them, each one wrapped in a reprint of a postwar newspaper. When I paused at a crosswalk for a guy in a suit on a Harley-Davidson, two 1920s Austin Sevens followed, their passenger seats holding bob-haired women in dresses. The dawn light bounced through their curls as if trapped there.

Qualifying was at 11:00. As I walked to the Jaguar, a flash of camouflage darted overhead. In wartime, Goodwood's grass infield served as an RAF landing strip, so the Revival brings out Spitfires. Also P-51s and Hawker Hurricanes, in numbers uncommon since Hitler was vertical. They fly constantly, low enough to spit at, mock-dogfighting every morning as the sun rises. The sound defied description.

Outside the driver's club, I stepped around multi-time Le Mans winners Tom Kristensen and Emanuele Pirro, together in a fedora-topped powwow. Le Mans, Daytona, and Sebring winner Andy Wallace told me where to find coffee. Former Ferrari F1 driver Gerhard Berger ambled around in jeans and sneakers, ignoring the paddock dress code, because that's apparently what you do when you're Gerhard Berger.

Later, in the mess hall—an enormous tent made up to resemble a World War II pilot's club—I ran into my friend Mark Gillies. Gillies, a former editor at *Car and Driver*, races a 1934 ERA, a single-seater with 250 hp, wire wheels, and no seatbelts. He's won at Goodwood six times.

"It's the best race meeting in the world," he said, "if you like fast corners. But you have to slide the car. The ERA averages a 97-mph lap or something—10 mph faster than almost anywhere else it runs. One-thirty at points. The thing about bias-ply tires—they take a bit of yaw."

I boggled. Then I had eggs with Richard Attwood, one of the drivers who gave Porsche its first overall Le Mans win, in 1970, in a 917K. He just came over and sat down. He seemed friendly, so I didn't mention having read about his life since I was 12, when I totally thought we'd be best friends.

"When I was younger," Attwood said, "I would come and watch here, outside Woodcote. See the cars coming off the straight, drifting the whole way." I boggled again, this time directly into a cup of coffee, so as not to make a ruckus.

After a stint where the Jaguar just plain refused to be intimidating, I qualified on the front row. Third place, behind English journalist Chris Harris, in a Porsche 356. Even more surprising, I somehow forgot about the absent roll bar, except when I didn't. Usually in a full-throttle slip inches from the grass, when the idea would pop into my head in a panicky burst.

But the car never gave reason for doubt. On Goodwood's glassy surface, the Jag was creamy. Unsurprisingly, Gillies was right: The tires seemed to thrive when the car was castering. The 120 hiked up its skirt, drifting in dignified dabs.

The track became a string of arcs, one control input at a time—anything more, and the Jag would just bind up and wait for an apology. So I'd head into a corner at full tilt, barely braking, the body shifting on its mounts. The frame seemed to perceptibly twist on entry. The steering column would move a little, after which I'd brace my leg on the transmission tunnel, gripping the wheel to keep from flopping around the cockpit. (There was a four-point harness on the stock seat. It felt superfluous.) All this in an instant, balancing throttle and track and working to go quicker, doing what you do in a normal qualifying session. Because that's what it was, just more ballet.

After the session, I parked in the paddock next to two other 120s. As a group, they looked like Spec Prom Dress, or maybe tea carts prepped for war. A few minutes after climbing out, I ran into Harris, who has driven a host of fast cars around Goodwood. We chatted about the track's ability to make you think. Not always usefully, I offered.

"And yet, I kind of want to try something quick here."

He looked me in the eye. "No," he said. "No, you don't."

Pomp, flags. A jumbo TV screen behind the starter's stand, showing the broadcast feed. Sitting on the grid, engine running, I watched it pan to a silver Jaguar and white helmet.

I tilted my head. The helmet tilted. I waved. Amazingly, the goofus in the car waved back. On the parade lap, as the cars tootled through a lap before returning to the front straight for the start, that goofus watched a U.S.-liveried dive-bomber buzz his head on final approach. He might have yelled into his helmet, just random joy noises, waiting for something to break the mold.

Then, naturally, he botched the start.

Like most European road races, Goodwood uses standing starts. I popped the clutch at four grand, left hand on the shifter. The wallet-sized rearview mirror filled with tire smoke. It's cliché to call engines animal, especially in a car named for a cat. But the cacophony of that start: animal.

At the start, waiting for green.

Crowds filled the periphery. Goodwood sells 50,000 tickets for each of the Revival's three days. Madison Square Garden holds fewer people.

I relaxed my right foot, and the car shot forward. Harris and the pole sitter, a green Jaguar, were a car-length ahead.

Breathe, I thought. Shift into second.

Shift into second?

Shift into second where is second the lever's in the right place the box is balking car coasts an eternity passes don't rush it XK gearboxes are known for slow blip try blip blip try *seriously you old crate what did I ever do to you wait God thank you second gear GREAT SUCCESS*...

And there I was, ripping down the front straight in seventh place, four grid spots gone. The two rows behind were now ahead, having parted around the Jag like a school of fish. The rest of the grid loomed aft.

I ground my teeth, raging at myself. But also at an XK ahead, a black one that started seventh.

Gibberish blew through my skull like confetti: *Who does he think he is? Driving! In ... a car, of all things!*

The pack pounced into Turn 1, feinting and dicing. The Jag no longer felt old. Just a race car, asking very specific questions. So I shifted again and began laughing, because for a moment there, the briefest of moments, I was thinking only of myself, and I was almost unhappy.

How stupid.

I drove. I drove and drove, bit in my teeth, until the tires got hot and the car grew loose. Then looser still, up on step and dancing. Until the brake pedal grew firmer because I was using it less. Until I passed one car, then more. Chopped nearly a second off my fast lap from qualifying. The track felt like an infinite ribbon.

I caught him. Then a blur of laps thinking and jinking behind taillights. The black 120 was visibly more loose, a touch quicker in a straight line but slower in the corners. The driver's shoulders leaned with the car, and on right turns, I could see his elbows dancing. A Lotus Six dove past under braking, so short it was hidden by my car's fenders. I was lapping faster than the other Jag but couldn't pass him, so I went patient. Thinking, dodging, trying options. That silver hood stretched out for weeks. It was like living a movie.

And so I should have been distraught when, one lap later, the head gasket blew. Nine minutes into the race. Spitfires kept flying. Car coughing, I darted into the pits. A camera crew rushed over. Across the front straight, above a grandstand, the Jag filled another screen.

"It's using coolant," Pearson said.

I climbed out and watched the field rip by. As I turned and began walking back to the paddock, something made me pause.

Stay, a voice in my head said, *because you can.*

I turned around, leaned against the pit wall until race end, when I helped push the 120 back to its stall. I gave its flank a gentle pat. Less than half an hour of total seat time, and goodbye still made my throat tight. Funny how that works.

The rest of the weekend was a benevolent fog. A sea of Pimm's Cups. Getting lost in Goodwood's pop-up village, a fully dressed 1960s town with a working grocery. Sideways Cobras three-wheeling through

Woodcote. The stands still packed at 4:30 on Sunday afternoon. I've never been to a race weekend where people stuck around for every last minute of what went on.

Entropy may undo the Revival in our lifetimes; unlike the eras it salutes, the event has a model for its fate. But that throws no shade on the glory, or the fact that progress rarely feeds a romantic. It has nothing to do with nostalgia or primitive cars and everything to do with what we love and why.

So go. Mortgage a kidney, sell your pets, just get there. And I will go back as a spectator, on and on, until the lawyers end it or society collapses and the oil runs out. Because that is what you do, when you find something amazing—you squeeze the juice from it until reality drags you away. Until all you're left with is the fog of memory. That goofus on the grid, waving at himself. And the sound of Spitfires overhead, unmatchable to words, fading, like any other dream.

Arms Into Motion
The eternity in a tick of the clock.

Time, the revelator. (I've always wanted a reason to write that.)

HAGERTY, JANUARY 2022

ENTRY, PLUS (+) ONE-TENTH (0.1) OF A MOMENT: A right. Uphill, heavily cambered, maybe 28 mph if you push it. Sane means 25 or 26 mph, as the hill rises steeply. The sight lines are awful, no visible path out, only a wall of climbing road.

Oaks and maples hug the pavement. This is new asphalt, maybe a season old but already polished in the tire grooves. The sun dapples through the trees, turns the aggregate shiny.

+ 0.2 MOMENT: A foot further in, visibility ticks up. The camber change is obvious, the lane falling off as the road crests. Apropos of nothing, in the way that a person can be immersed in one thing while idly thinking about something else, the driver wonders what to make for dinner.

+ 0.3 MOMENT: *Pasta sounds good?*

+ 0.33 MOMENT: The downshift starts. Left foot lifts from the floor mat. Third to second.

+ 0.36 MOMENT: Left shoe reaches the clutch pedal.

+ 0.365 MOMENT: *Look at that exit! As if the trees had opened to let the road through.*

+ 0.37 MOMENT: Left shoe begins to depress clutch pedal.

+ 0.391 MOMENT: *Why is it always so hard to decide on dinner? Why can't I just be one of those dudes who goes to Smashburger every night?*

+ 0.395 MOMENT: Left shoe produces enough clutch travel that right hand leaves steering wheel, moves in general direction of shift lever.

+ 0.396 MOMENT: A shaft of orange light cuts through the branches and shade, filtering into the cockpit for an instant. A blink later, it's dark again.

+ 0.4 MOMENT: Right foot begins to roll on brake pressure. The nose sinks a tick as the front springs begin the long and relatively slow journey to full compression. Both front shocks lag a hint behind, ever so slightly misvalued for the load and treatment, at least on this particular piece of pavement and in this weather and on this tire.

+ 0.5 MOMENT: *Bolognese sounds alright. Didn't you date a girl who made great Bolognese? Did she leave the recipe? It's probably floating around that old laptop in the bottom of the closet. Next to that big box of CDs from college.*

+ 0.55 MOMENT: *Remember when you used to leave a single CD in the player in the car for weeks on end? Just the same songs, over and over, never getting old? Why was that so satisfying?*

+ 0.559 MOMENT: *In fairness, Van Halen's 1984 was, by itself, pretty satisfying.*

+ 0.56 MOMENT: Right foot bends to the right, angled to briefly blip the throttle, which is inches away. Brake pressure does not change. [*Voice in back of head sings prechorus from "Hot for Teacher."*]

+ 0.6 MOMENT: Bottom three fingers of the right hand pull shift lever rearward, out of the third-gear gate and toward the car's center. The dimensions of the neutral gate force a brief delay as the lever is pushed left, on the way to second gear.

+ 0.62 MOMENT: Clutch is released. The shift is now complete. The tires, having received no upset in engine braking, do not know or care.

+ 0.639 MOMENT: The driver's head turns into the corner. In the movies, this is where the eyebrows drop, because Driving Is Serious Business. In reality, one expressionless human on a mountain back road in flyover country, still thinking about dinner and the rest of his life while also free from those concerns for the briefest of flashes—well, he just looks where he wants the car to go. At which point it goes there, because that is how the body-mind conversation works.

+ 0.7 MOMENT: The steering wheel is turned quickly but smoothly to the right. Maybe 20 degrees. Wheel moves upper steering shaft moves universal joint moves lower steering shaft moves pinion shaft. The meat of a few pinion teeth then find purchase on a linear rack gear, and then that rack gear slides left in its bushings, within the steering-rack housing itself. As the tie rods mounted on each end of that gear are forced to move—left one pushed out, right pulled in—a ball joint pressed into each tie rod transfers force to a steering arm, and the upright bolted to each of those arms is nudged into motion. A steady stream of force is sent to the races and balls of the wheel bearings, to the hubs themselves, to the threaded studs on those hubs, and finally, after a seeming eternity of milliseconds, to the two front wheels.

Those wheels flex ever so slightly—too little to be seen—and then they transfer that torque again, to the bead of each front tire. The lower sidewalls on each carcass twist, contorting. Contact patches are placed in a fluid mix of tension and compression, a conveyor belt of sipes and tread blocks squeezed and stretched as the tire rotates. Slowly but surely, the front bumper points farther and farther to the right. At the rear wheels, a similar dance follows, a beat behind.

At this instant, a chance gust of wind blows a small collection of fallen leaves into the road. Those leaves become caught in the wake of the car's underbody, carried along for a few feet, before being spit out behind the rear bumper and landing on the road again.

The car has officially entered the corner.

+ 0.76 MOMENT: *Bolognese girl had pretty eyes.*

+ 0.83 MOMENT: Another gap in the trees, another shaft of sunlight.

+ 0.87 MOMENT: Peak lat. A release of tire squeal, a sustained sine-wave chirping. The car is now producing around 95 percent of its possible grip in this particular corner.

+ 0.878 MOMENT: *So that's pretty great.*

+ 0.88 MOMENT: Braking has now bled off fully, pressure trailed down to the peak of the corner's arc. Right foot goes to throttle.

+ 0.89 MOMENT: Lots of throttle.

+ 0.891 MOMENT: Further rear-suspension compression, more traction than torque. The driver grins.

+ 0.892 MOMENT: *Gonna have to run by the store, buy some ground beef. Mental note: Rear subframe bushings might be getting weak?*

+ 0.893 MOMENT: In an utterly unregrettable decision, the rightmost pedal becomes trapped between foot and floorboard.

+ 0.92 MOMENT: Hands open the wheel slightly, then more after that, then more still. As the road straightens, the suspension seems to lighten, releasing stored energy, a kind of relief. The outside tires find the edge of the lane, slipping out to the painted markings.

ONE FULL MOMENT AFTER THE START OF ALL THIS SILLY JAZZ AND SWING: The wheel is straight again. The car carries on down the road, and somehow, in a universe where so much of life seems to be constructed of tiresome and expensive hurdles, there is another corner ahead, and another, and another, and the driver gets to do it all again, as long as he wants, and it seems easy, as long as there is time and tire and the hands at the wheel want to keep going.

Which, it must be said, it is another moment on its own, and a nice one indeed.

People say this stuff doesn't matter. That all cars drive the same these days, that EVs aren't that interesting, that modern roads are too crowded, blah blah blah. These complaints are grounded in reality but ultimately irrelevant, which is both convenient and a nice parallel, because in the grand scheme, driving doesn't really matter, itself. Putting a car through a corner at anything like reasonable speed is not curing cancer or creating great art. Most of the trivial and mundane details of human existence add up to more.

But what if...

And forgive the indulgence here...

What if...

Smithology

You love it?

What if you love it so bleeding flipping flapping much you can't get enough? What if it feels like a small and attainable form of grace, or meditation, or simply escaping from everything you don't want to do but have to do anyway? And you know that those who don't understand will never understand, and they will mock or denigrate an entire subculture for enjoying this process, but that's fine, because it just means there's more of the good left for the rest of us?

I suppose it would matter an awful lot, then. To you.

Probably not too much to most people.

But also not too little, to others.

Never met one of those folks myself. Wouldn't have anything to discuss with them if I did. We certainly wouldn't talk about how time seems to stretch out, and there you are, living what feels like a lifetime across a collection of seconds, watching a simple scene coalesce, as you yourself play a not-insignificant role in assembling that scene, no one there to watch or confirm, just a cinema of the real, in a specific location but never entirely of it, built and shown entirely for you.

And then you blink, and you are a few feet farther down the road.

Where it only gets better.

Back to School

What we forget as we get older, what we don't, what we can't.

A flashback to the glory of a new license and having the free time to be stupid. One of many great dumb-idea days I've spent with the marvelous Zach Bowman. On the surface, this is nothing, just screwing around in cheap cars. But the surface is never the point.

ROAD & TRACK, MARCH 2020

I was not cool in high school. Joyously so. And it turned out to be a forecast for life. Too much time between the ages of 14 and 18 being a dork for fun at the wrong moment. Most of that time involved a car.

Take a second to remember the thrill of a fresh driver's license. The new delight of transport freedom. Driving aimlessly and forever because it's not home, because you have nothing but a car and time. Then you get older, and time grows scarce. The release of a pointless day or evening becomes rare all while you end up needing it more and more.

So we dug up two affordable, first-car hatchbacks. We screwed off for a day, tearing into the hills, thinking about age. I'm 38 but my wife says I act 14. *R&T*'s occasionally juvenile senior editor, Zach Bowman, is 35 and from the hills of east Tennessee, where our test took place.

Our photographer, Camden Thrasher, is 30 but seems ageless. He grew up in Washington State, which is like Tennessee with more West Coast. Stars, lined up.

Much like high school, this story goes nowhere and somewhere all at once.

Enter the Corolla, Punching Up
1:00 P.M.

Welcome the 2019 Toyota Corolla SE: $20,910, base and as tested. Between and driving the front wheels, a 2.0-liter I-4, 169 hp at 6600 rpm, 151 lb-ft at 4800 rpm. A six-speed manual or optional continuously variable automatic. A 3000-pound curb weight. Sixteen-inch wheels. A tasteful, lush, and well-assembled interior. Not much else.

For years, the Toyota Corolla has been as basic as cars get. Solid resale, unburstable engines and interiors. Few frills, but a chassis that won't hurt you. Bad Corollas have no sin save dullness. Good ones are simple fun.

This is a good one.

The SE is no hot rod. The brakes will go away if you lean on them too long. You're not going to get any steering feel, ever. But the engine is cammy and lives for a razor-thin area at the top of the tach. The gearbox is clean and direct, the clutch light and easy. Back roads become maniacal games of momentum, trying to use as little brake as possible while reining in soft springs and dampers, flinging through 50-mph corners as tidily as possible. You revel in wringing the car's neck. After all, anyone can master a Corolla; it's a Corolla.

Two decades ago, a generation of kids fell into hand-me-down Asian econoboxes because those cars happened to be in the family and cheap. The industry has changed. The manual gearbox has become an endangered species. Everyone now wants an SUV or CUV, most of which look like cows.

But what fun Toyotas once did, this still does, better than ever.

Enter the Elantra, Eating Corollas for Lunch
2:00 P.M.

2019 Hyundai Elantra GT N-Line. $23,300 base; $24,300 as tested. A 1.6-liter turbo four, 201 hp at 6000 rpm, 195 lb-ft at 1500 rpm. Front-drive. Six-speed manual or optional seven-speed dual-clutch automatic. Another 3000-pound curb weight. Eighteen-inch wheels. A lush and remarkably well-assembled interior. Five seats. Little else.

We chose the Toyota because it's harmless; the Hyundai less so. The Elantra GT N-Line is essentially an ordinary Elantra hatch with stiffer suspension, stiffer driveline mounts, and retuned steering. Spec the manual gearbox and Hyundai will throw in a set of Michelin Pilot Sport 4 summer tires. The car feels huckable and linear, like a Volkswagen GTI from a few years ago, before VW decided that car needed to be wide enough to straddle a lane and laggy with boost pressure. Talkative steering, ropey but precise shifter, enough brake. It bops into corners like a bunny. There's far more grip and composure than in the Toyota, though the Elantra can feel nervous over bumps, as if the suspension only wants perfect roads.

Driving either of these cars is a reminder that adults generally don't buy small hatchbacks unless they have to. A holdover, until you can afford That Really Good Adult Fun Car, which everybody young thinks is better. Turns out it's not always better, just different. And generally more expensive.

Long Live the Airborne Fear of Death
4:00 P.M.

It began with talk of a jump. I never jumped a car in high school. Or maybe that's what I told my parents. Maybe one jump, accidentally. Or more than one. You don't talk about the jumps. Maybe they take away your license after that.

"I know just the place," Bowman said.

The pavement skated through open fields in the hills east of Knoxville. We parked beside the road and eyeballed it. A series of crests, the steepest a long, smooth tabletop.

"I used to run this in the dark," Bowman said.

I put a hand up to shade my eyes from the setting sun and squinted down the road. "Eighty, 90 miles an hour for wheels-up?"

He thought for a second. "More?"

"That," I said, "would be irresponsible."

We almost definitely did not stay and fly both cars at triple digits and full suspension droop, Camden crouched in a field with his good and crackly long lens as the sun began to set over the hills in a golden glow, because that would have been wrong.

"It takes work to get a car up there," Bowman said, as we turned to leave. "More than I remember. Hell of a landing, though."

Some cars just whiff into the air easy. The Hyundai felt like it would fly well, zero drama. Stiff dampers. The Toyota, softer, would have probably taken more speed to launch, longer to settle coming down.

I love that feeling. The skin-tingle you get as a small car decompresses from a landing. How a sort of cohesive settling ripples through the chassis like a dog shaking off after a bath.

But there were definitely no jumps.

"Mom," I Said, "We Were Just Out Driving Around."
5:00 P.M.

It grew dark early, because it was winter. We kept driving. I was reminded of how a country road at night feels like traveling through space alone, as if normal rules don't apply.

It was after five, the end of a workday. Technically, we could have gone home. But that didn't feel right.

Lunch-tray slides felt right.

We bought fiberglass cafeteria trays from a restaurant-supply shop. Two dollars each. Also metal cake pans wide enough to hold the Hyundai's relatively fat Michelins. (PS4s are expensive but fun on a bun. Road glue.)

Lunch-tray slides are simple: Place a piece of metal or plastic under the rear tires of a front-drive car. Set the parking brake. Drive. Experience the blessing of zero rear grip.

We found an empty industrial park. And a problem: For reasons of packaging and cost, most modern cars now feature button-actuated electronic parking brakes. The Corolla and Elantra were not exceptions. Attempting to drive off with the park brake engaged caused either car's computer to disengage the brake. Convenient for normal use, but gets in the way of a parking-lot dirty burn.

We spent several minutes poking at the Hyundai, pulling fuses for traction and stability systems. The brake kept releasing—no slides. I looked at Bowman.

"When I was 16, this wouldn't have stopped me."

"How?"

"I would have slapped a pair of Vise-Grips on the rear brake lines to hold pressure, then done donuts around a parking lot with the wheels locked."

"Man, you have mellowed."

"Maybe?"

I reached into the car and opened a bag of Rap Snacks that Camden had left in the seat. Silent chewing with Migos. Bowman frowned, determined. "You know what we'd do if we were in high school? We'd go to Gatlinburg and Pigeon Forge, and we'd buy throwing stars and fireworks. That is what we'd do if we were in high school."

Gatlinburg is a tourist town. T-shirt shops. Pigeon Forge, nearby, is mostly famous for Dollywood, Dolly Parton's theme park.

I watched the sun bend into a nearby ridge. My wife and kids were at home, about to sit down to dinner.

Bowman looked at me and repeated himself. "I said, *throwing stars and fireworks.*"

You Gonna Turn Down Flaming Balls, Old Man?
6:00 P.M.

Daylight only lets you get away with so much. And my memory says the good parts of high school mostly happened at night.

Tennessee famously treats fireworks like New York treats pizza— sold 24 hours a day, industrial-strength only. The store we hit was a supermarket of boomery. F-I-R-E-W-O-R-K-S in big letters on the roof. Inside, Bowman, the native, became tour guide: This one is brighter; that's a waste of money. This one, they don't weight the base enough, it tips and fires rockets at you.

I responded to everything with, "We need that. Buy it."

Mortars. Smoke bombs. Sparklers long as a five-year-old's leg. And something called the Princess Purse: pink box, unicorns and a castle on the label. Only $12.95. It leaped off the shelf and into my hands.

Be the princess of pyro with this beautiful fountain! the label yelled. *White-purple-gold raindrops of titanium!* Then a disclaimer in bold, stern letters: WARNING: SHOOTS FLAMING BALLS.

Bowman raised an eyebrow. Thrasher shrugged, but then, Thrasher reminds you of Jeffrey Lebowski, if Lebowski spent his career at racetracks, taking trippy photos of cars while eating too many snacks.

"Flaming balls," he said, deadpan.

Bowman went to high school in Virginia, four hours away, where fireworks are illegal. "Fireworks were a big deal. Fridays, your friends would just hand you $20 and you'd bop over the state line. Buy as much as you could, then do a buck-ten back."

"The state-line crossing must have been illegal," I said.

"A trunkful of explosives? Are you kidding? If we'd been caught..."

I surveyed the surroundings. A Dunkin' Donuts sat opposite the fireworks store, same parking lot. My stomach rumbled.

"Do we need donuts for dinner?"

Again, the eyebrow raise.

"I ate a lot of dumb food in high school," I said. "Treated my body like a trash compactor: What can we put in this and watch go away?"

I went in for six donuts and walked out with a discount dozen. They were rock-hard stale but also oddly delicious. When I got back, Bowman was leaning against the Toyota, shrugging at Thrasher.

"I didn't do the traditional dumb stuff in school. Just going real fast, blowing shit up. We had a 150-mile loop, and we'd just rip around all night. If you stopped and saw a movie, great. If you got food, great. If not, you just ripped around for hours."

So we ripped around for hours.

At the River, With Glory
8:00 P.M.

We were standing under the moonlight at the river—some Tennessee river, I don't remember which. A deserted public boat launch. Bowman was eating a donut, gesturing with it for emphasis, thinking out loud.

"The thing about the car? When you're a teenager, it suddenly gives access to all these places that basically disappeared for you when the sun went down. You're let loose for the first time, and you can just, say, come to the river at 9:00."

I knew where he was going but said nothing. Partly because my mouth was full of donut.

"And weirdly, that only happens when you're a teenager. The more freedom you have, getting older, the less you're likely to be here. And the little shitboxes you drive in high school are the first things that give you that."

These cars are not shitboxes, but you get the gist. I pulled another donut from the box. It was the consistency of cardboard but tasted of wet sugar, so I grabbed another and ate two at once. Bowman kept talking, a wistful look on his face, eyeing the river.

"Everybody likes to say cars are the keys to the universe . . . it's easy to forget what that means, when you've been driving so long. Until then, everything is decided for you. The reason I didn't drink or do drugs in high school was because I knew it could prevent me from getting in the car and going at any time. And my home situation was so shitty . . . I in no way wanted to take that from myself."

When I discovered cars, they became the one place I felt half-normal. Because I never felt normal anywhere. Most people eventually learn, long after high school, that this seeming abnormality is the definition of normal for almost everyone. But when you're young and ignorant, you chase what makes you feel better. In this case, a wheeled totem/home that delivers new places when almost everywhere feels like new places.

Bowman: "Even then, you know that there's just such a narrow window. The years where the possibilities are endless, and . . . "

"Doors haven't started to close," I said.

"Right? Any Friday or Saturday night, it was just this." He waved a hand at the road. "My friend Matt would sit in the passenger seat. At each intersection, he'd say left or right. And we'd go on until we ran out of time, arriving where-the-hell-ever."

I threw a stale donut in the river and watched it float. More rockets lit into the air, the report washing through the hills. Mortars, the big guys that go *foomp*.

I lit the Princess Purse maybe too close to the Toyota, walked away, then took a step back toward it, worried about the car.

Bowman put a hand out. "Never move toward a lit firework." (Metaphor alert: Your narrator will chase shiny things to his own detriment.) At that moment, as if on cue, the Purse spasmed out a rainbow—sparks of all colors, 15 feet in the air.

A minute later, Camden attempted to move the Toyota for a picture. He didn't buckle his seatbelt. The car dragged its rear wheels when he hit the throttle. Locked.

Bowman: "Wait. Seatbelt. Did we just figure out how to have the e-brake stick on?"

There in that moonlight, I may have cackled.

I texted a picture of an exploding mortar to my wife. She texted back about 20 minutes later. Not mad, just curious: "It's 10:00 on a Wednesday. Why on earth were you down at the river?"

This Wheel is On Fire. Also That One
10:00 P.M.

Twenty minutes later, we were back at the industrial park.

Turns out the seatbelt trick was the answer: Stay unbuckled, the Toyota and Hyundai would each power drive wheels but leave the parking brake on. High on firework sulfur, I put the metal baking pans under the Hyundai's front tires on the theory that metal plus asphalt always equals mayhem.

Bowman eyed the pans. "We all miss the handbrake," he solemnly announced, "not because it's a better solution to the problem. Because it doesn't prevent us from being assholes." Then he got in the car and dumped the clutch, ripping toward the other side of the lot. A fountain of sparks rooster-tailed up from each locked wheel. I clapped slowly, hands high in the air, walking toward the car.

The Elantra arced around a light pole half-backward at 8 mph. The pans bent, collapsed, blued from heat, then gave up and wore through. The air stunk of roasted metal and cooked enamel. A face popped out of the open driver's window. Eyebrows up.

"Good?"

"Oh, was it good." My face hurt from grinning.

The lunch trays were next. I put them under the Toyota, jumped behind the wheel, and immediately flung the car into a pirouette. When the fiberglass wore down, something told me to stay in the throttle. White smoke poured into the cockpit, blotted out the moon, felled small trees.

"Once the trays burned through," Bowman said after, "I thought, Should we tell him they're gone?"

Thrasher looked down at his camera, reviewing his shots. "He knew, I think."

Trails of white fiberglass dust crossed the parking lot. Near where the burnout had occurred, the dust turned to black, a mirror image of the Toyota's tread. Like a sunrise, it made me quietly happy without reason.

Love for the well-executed ordinary can be hard to explain. On the surface, a 169-horse Corolla is just a quiet little penalty box with no power and a manual gearbox. Some people view that too much like work. But on the right kind of road, a manual Corolla or Elantra GT could probably run down Porsches. Reachable performance, too friendly to bite.

At 16, some part of you knows that. As much as I love a good Porsche, I'd rather be ripping the nuts off some middle-of-nowhere two-lane in a manual Toyota or an old Craigslist find with a cam and a soda in the cupholder and nowhere to be. As I did, then.

This might be what makes me, me. And is probably why, as an old editor once pointed out, no one should listen to me about cars, ever. At least until I grow up.

So good luck, waiting on that.

At Long Last, the Waffle House at Midnight
12:00 A.M.

We ended at a diner in the wee hours. High-school weird nights always ended at a diner in the wee hours. There was something about cheap eggs and staying at a table until someone told you to leave, because you had paid the check an hour ago and the refills were done and the waitress said get out.

I miss it and don't. A time of small problems that seemed big and big ones that seemed small. I vividly remember spending my teenage years confused about almost everything. Wondering if my life was going to be great or struggle or something in between.

As it turns out, for most people, the answer is just yes. Life is good and terrible in equal measure, and better for it. Sometimes you just aren't in a place to appreciate the subtlety. At 38, you wake up the next day exhausted and bleary from the sugar and hours and miles. Your body hurts in a way that it once didn't. But it's offset by the warm glow of remembering what it was like to grab the keys and feel, for the first time and maybe also the last, completely and totally free.

Lord help us if we ever forget.

Throne of Games

At America's only permanent F1 track, taking a flag on the big field.

I had driven at COTA before, testing new cars. I had even stood by myself in that high first corner, gazing out over what seemed like half of Texas, when Road & Track *rented the place for a story in 2013. Starting a race there was another thing entirely.*

ROAD & TRACK, MARCH 2019

When I realized where I was, I knew where I was. Maybe that sounds a little too Yogi Berra. The New York Yankees catcher famous for malaprops. As far as I'm concerned, the man's language changed baseball. (Brief pause for my favorite Yogi quote: "We made too many wrong mistakes." Second favorite: "Why buy good luggage? You only use it when you travel.")

Granted, I know nothing about baseball. Or most sports. I once read Denise McCluggage's *The Centered Skier*, about the Zen side of a controlled fall down a hill, but only because Denise wrote like an angel and won Sebring in a Ferrari. Amazing human. I am a hopeless fool for both her writing and the idea of falling down a hill. The latter is likely rooted in sympathy, a lifelong failure to be athletic paired with a lust for travel faster than running. For whatever reason, I can't so much as jog down the block without getting all these distracting endorphic signals that something has gone very wrong with my body and *is that a street-parked old Jaguar? Whoops, just tripped, almost face-planted on the sidewalk. Exercise is stupid, let's go home and eat a whole cake instead.*

Short version: Sports and I have never gotten along.

Stadiums, on the other hand.

Dogs have a thing for anyone who feeds them, and I have a thing for stadiums. Big, humbling temples of achievement and history where crowds gather to witness stuff that makes your skin tingle. The good arenas are balm regardless of what takes place inside their gates. Where else can you be surrounded by throngs but also feel like you're floating in space? You meet these houses, your blood pressure can plummet, Pavlovian, when the surroundings sink in. From obvious lodestones like Wrigley Field or Fenway Park to the less traditional—the stands at Indianapolis or Le Mans, the grassy hill at Lime Rock, the dust of Laguna's Corkscrew.

And so I knew where I was, at the Circuit of the Americas, when I realized where I was. Home again.

The realization took a while to set. Nine years ago, a group of private investors paid some $400 million to build a Formula 1 track in undeveloped land near Austin, Texas. The 20-turn monster that resulted included an amazing first sector where the pavement swan-dives off an enormous hill. But the negatives were stacked. As with every newish F1 track, COTA's asphalt was designed to serve the holy trinity of TV, safety, and the outlandish speed of a modern F1 car. This meant, among other things, acres of dull, paved runoff and a series of slow and forgettable corners. Endless fencing, treeless sterility.

If only it were different. Racetracks work best when their vibe either apes the natural or feels balls-out synthetic. The parklike feel of a public road or an oval coliseum for 200-mph cage fights. Walking through COTA's gates for the first U.S. Grand Prix there, in 2012, was like entering an unusually sanitary mall. More than a few off-the-record F1 drivers have called the circuit a cookie-cutter hodgepodge of road-course greatest hits. The Austin track's famous esses are an unoriginal take on Silverstone's Maggotts-Becketts complex; Turn 1 is a mirror of the

Druids hairpin at Brands Hatch. The international stars who came to compete in Texas pooh-poohed the place as neither grand and unique nor small and charming, and that, I thought, was that.

Funny thing about tracks, though: Your access isn't limited to the stands. Like almost every other American circuit, COTA is regularly rented for public lapping days and club racing. Events admittedly less approachable than pickup baseball at your local sandlot, but consider the location—the Chicago Cubs won't let you run around Wrigley with your friends for hoots. What kind of jerk complains if somebody cracks the gates and lets the rabble dream on the field?

You can see where this is going. Last fall, for my final club race of the year, I trekked to Austin. After six years of visiting COTA for work and not thinking much about it, I finally took a flag there. A vintage B-sedan weekend at the SVRA's November year-ender.

The car was the same BMW 2002 I've been running with friends for years. The usual drill: Go fast, work on car, beer, sleep, repeat. Plus, here, cresting the rise of that huge first corner, skittering down its back in third and fourth, the car flicking into happy bits of yaw. Who cares if it was something like Druids? Better question: You know what I've never done? Been through something like Druids. Or raced anything, giving it everything I had, on a current F1 track anywhere.

Now I have. A big, splashy world seen through the lens of a multi-billion-dollar game of thrones that I'll never watch from a cockpit. That I've watched on TV since I was little.

What a strange and blissful little spell of time that was. Words fail. The hair on my arms stood up and I felt five again. It's one of the small gifts of being into cars and motorsport—you can walk onto the field in the big leagues, squint, and see things as you wish they were. In a certain light, there are no bad racetracks, just as there are no bad stadiums. They all exist for a remarkable reason, and if you don't race cars for a living, that reason is enough.

Do I wish COTA were nervier and more organic? Sure. But I'd go back tomorrow anyway. I'd go back to all of them. Just so long as no one asks me to pick up some kind of ball.

Wouldn't have the slightest idea what to do with it. To go all Yogi again, I fall down a lot. But only when I'm not standing up.

Wall Drug

In rare air in the heartland,
getting high on the fumes.

I grew up 90 minutes south of Indianapolis but never found the time to see cars at speed there—the TV always seemed a good substitute. Spoiler: It wasn't.

ROAD & TRACK, AUGUST 2015

When a car does 230 mph two feet from your face, you feel it. The sudden thwack of evacuated air. A whole-body muscle spasm. And above all, engine noise, whip-cracking into your core, there and gone in a heartbeat.

Run, it all says. Because there is a surprisingly violent thing nearby, and since the dawn of the human race, surprising objects yowling directly into your colon have meant you're about to get eaten.

Or that you're on the wall at Indianapolis.

I went to the Speedway in May, for Indy 500 qualifying. The 500 is a touchstone, but embarrassingly, I had never ached to see it in person. Or had much love for ovals. I got on a plane thanks to my friend Marshall Pruett, *R&T*'s chief racing correspondent. When I texted him last winter and said we should hang out, he suggested 500 time trials.

"There aren't many fans," he said, "but that's the brilliance. We'll have the place to ourselves as fools crack 230 mph each lap. Standing two feet from cars tracking out in Turn 1 will change your perception of speed and safety forever."

Something shifted in my oblongata.

"YEDGFRAPPA," I typed back, which is what you write when your fingers are so excited, they can't assemble complex words like "yes."

Like much of motorsport these days, IndyCar is in an odd spot. The drivers are fantastic, but the cars—one chassis (Dallara) and two engine manufacturers (Honda and Chevy)—are as compelling as old socks. Outside of the 500, no one's watching, even in historically popular stops. (In June, an estimated 10,000 fans dribbled into California's Auto Club Speedway, a 2.0-mile oval that can hold 68,000.)

Still, the sport's center remains unassailable. Four corners banked at just 9 degrees and 12 minutes, and a 2.5-mile layout unchanged since 1909. Charming, view-blocking grandstand poles, like at Wrigley Field. Deaths and life-changing moments have echoed off those seats. If you aren't humbled on that ground, read more history.

Every big track has "photo holes," nonpublic gaps in the catch fencing for credentialed photographers. The last hole in the Speedway's Turn 1 happens to be inches from the end of the corner, right on the wall, close enough to reach out and touch. Marshall, a former race engineer turned photojournalist, took me there.

Never take eyes off the track, he said. "If things go wrong, you won't have much time to run. Less if you rely on your hearing for warning."

Sure, I said, but isn't there catch fencing?

"The fencing grabs whole cars, but the holes in it are about 9 inches square. Two hundred miles per hour pulverizes things, and pulverized car parts fit through 9 square inches."

I looked at the nearest stands, 20 feet back. Then the first cars came through and pulled my spleen out through my ears.

Indy in person is not Indy on TV. From the front straight, Turn 1 looks like a wall, but drivers enter—235 mph in practice this year—without lifting, tire scrub shaving about 5 mph by mid-corner. It seems impossible, but it happens, lap after lap after lap. And there is still palpable risk. When a driver gets a trimmed-out, low-downforce car visibly sideways in a crosswind and somehow saves it. Qualifying laps attributable only to cojones. Hot days where, if you can't catch a sliding car, you're in the fence.

TV removes the violence. After five minutes on the wall, you hate the cameras. If a driver is fighting understeer, the nose hop-scotching at the apex, they can get eerily close. The air is more violent with every mile per hour and inch; three laps in, you can ID the fast cars solely by sound and pressure. You keep your eyes up even when you don't have to, mesmerized. Trying, all the while, to remember the last time you met a road course and thought, This is the ballsiest thing I've ever seen.

At the end of my time on the wall, I turned to Marshall, dazed. "If you could somehow pipe this experience into people's homes, you'd make billions." He nodded as if it were obvious. Another car tore by and ripped out my lungs through my nose.

By chance, the day after I got home from Indiana, an old club-racing friend called to catch up. As an afterthought, I mentioned visiting the Speedway. "Oval racing is boring," he said, dismissively. "Just a bunch of lefts."

I almost hung up.

Indy!

Looking back, on the eve of the 100th running, as America's Race keeps pushing forward.

"How should we celebrate the 100th Indy 500?" my editor asked. "Explain why people once loved it," I said, "because most don't anymore?" That chat led to an incredible day—the Speedway to ourselves, our pick of cars from the track museum, and the privilege of telling one of the world's most remarkable stories.

ROAD & TRACK, MAY 2016

The Indianapolis Motor Speedway opened to the public on June 5 of 1909. Seventy-five days later, on August 19, the place hosted its first automobile race. It was a Thursday. And then people began to die.

Picture the Speedway as it is now: 2.5 miles, four corners banked at just over 9 degrees, concrete walls, and catch fencing. Now neuter the walls, nix the catch fence, and replace the asphalt with crushed rock and tar. That's Indy, brand-new.

On the 19th, Wilfred "Billy" Bourque was driving in a 250-mile race when he spun in Turn 4. Bourque's car hit a ditch in the infield and rolled, killing both him and his riding mechanic. Two days after that, during a 300-mile race, Charlie Merz blew a tire. He crashed his

National through trackside fencing, killing his mechanic and two spectators. Shortly after, a Marmon hit a pedestrian bridge on the track's north end.

The Speedway is generally seen as the creation of an Indianapolis businessman named Carl Fisher. He and his wife, Jane, were at the track that weekend.

"Every minute," she would later write, "held dramas of tragedy, mutilation, and death. Cars skidded off the buckling macadam and burst into flame. I watched Carl's face grow whiter."

Action was taken. The tar surface was almost immediately replaced by 3.2 million bricks, thought to be safer. In 1911, the track hosted the first Indianapolis 500, a 200-lap event dreamed up as a gimmick to draw crowds. Attendance rose annually. The bricks were eventually replaced by pavement. Speeds climbed, from just above 70 mph in 1911 to over 230 in the mid-Nineties. And as late as 2015, drivers were still crashing, still getting hurt.

Why do we keep going back? Tradition is part of it but not all. The Speedway is a font of bravery and pomp, an irreplaceable piece of our culture. This year marks the hundredth running of the 500, a rare and hallowed pastime in a relatively young country. And if you head to Indianapolis, you can stand on the earth where that race began. Where it happens this year. And where, if we don't screw things up, it will live on.

On a sunny fall day in 2015, we took a photographer and a small crew to Indy. With the help of the Indianapolis Motor Speedway Museum and a few friends, we gathered five Indy 500 cars from various eras. Their differences represent the arc of the race and the automobile, but also a good chunk of what has always made Indy appealing. On a deserted track, I met each machine at respectful speed. In the process, we got an unprecedented look at the soul of America's fastest tradition.

It was a hell of a day.

1911–1950: The Deadly Laboratory Awakens

The cars are rolled over from the museum in the dawn hours. A pickup truck towing a Watson. Two guys pushing a Miller, its spindly wire wheels jittering across the pavement. Then this unbelievable golden light as the sun rises, spilling over the stands on the back straight. It dapples into the garages like melted butter.

The best and most evocative of our grand old racetracks seem to exist in spite of their surroundings. Indianapolis is no different. The Speedway is located in Speedway, Indiana, a suburb of Indianapolis, the last place you'd expect a coliseum. Climb to the nose-bleed seats and look a block west, you see houses. This is likely the only racetrack on earth where the people who live next door do not moan about noise, crowds, or congestion.

The morning we arrive, the trackside catch fencing is missing. The grandstands on the front straight—staggered and steep, like a 1920s baseball park—lack their famous flat roof. The Speedway is in the middle of what track management has dubbed Project 100, a massive construction and remodeling effort aimed at revamping the facility in time for the 2016 500. The project means significant change for a place that prides itself on staying the same.

But this is not a unique moment. The Speedway was built in 1909 as a proving ground for automakers. Buildings have come and gone, stands have grown, safety features have been updated. The only constant has been the geometry and bank of the competition surface. And so you can stand in Turn 1 and squint into the place's early days. You see bricks and space and a zillion other things, a way of life long gone.

And when someone lights off a Miller straight-eight, it all bursts into Technicolor.

Harry Miller was America's Ettore Bugatti. In the 1920s and '30s, his cars rivaled the legends of Europe in sophistication and beauty. The best were 140-mph jewels, graceful and potent, built in a small shop in a still-uncrowded Los Angeles.

1926 MILLER 91

QUALIFYING SPEED: 111.352 MPH (EST.)
1.5-LITER SUPERCHARGED I-8, 150 HP
REAR-DRIVE, 3-SPEED MANUAL

It would be difficult to exaggerate the genius. Miller designed and produced twin-cam, unit-construction (block and head in one casting), supercharged engines when much of America thought a 100-mph airplane was fast. Because he was part artisan and had a fetish for detail, his machines were gorgeous and powerful when most race cars were weak and ugly or strong and uglier. Miller and his chief designer, Leo Goossen, gave us one of the first successful front-drive race cars, one of the first successful four-wheel-drive race cars, and 12 wins in the 500 between 1922 and 1938. Also the bones of the engine—the Offenhauser four—that ruled Indy from the 1950s to the 1970s. (An Offy is basically a Miller eight seen in a fun-house mirror.)

In its early days, the Indy 500 was open to road cars, and they often did well. But Millers took the race from production-based horse-around to thoroughbred war zone. By 1927, a Miller sat in 24 of the 33 slots on the 500's grid. In 1929, a curious Ettore Bugatti bought two Millers in Europe and had them dismantled, so his men could learn something. (One of those cars is now in the Smithsonian, a place not in the business of collecting automobiles, which should tell you something.)

The Indianapolis Motor Speedway Museum has six Millers. As with many ancient race cars, their histories have been muddied by time and entropy. The 1926 Miller 91 that the Speedway lent us for this story wears the livery of Louis Meyer's 1928 500 winner, but it is not that car. The Speedway's car currently sports a post–World War II restoration with an excess of gloss—Miller the man preferred flat finishes and understatement—and the front axle from a later Miller model, the 122. But it is still a Miller. If it were painted polka-dot and riding on four wheels of cheese, I would still cross oceans to drive it.

The museum's 91 is an early Miller, and thus simple, even for the marque. The 90.2-cubic-inch (1.5-liter), 150-hp straight-eight makes power with the help of a centrifugal supercharger; that component, around a foot in diameter and shaped like a snail shell, pokes through the firewall just ahead of your knees. The engine is a jeweler's model of what you expect. The radiator grille is as narrow as a skateboard.

To get into the cockpit, you stand on a rear spring, then thread your legs straight down, through a maze of castings. It doesn't seem like there's room, and then, somehow, you're in, frame and metal bits touching your skin. Your first time in, you tend to just sit there and think about that.

The leather-covered seat feels like a dining chair, upright and short. The brake pedal only affects the rear wheels; a lever outside the cockpit, on the right, operates both front and rear brakes. The updraft carburetor sits over your legs. After a push start, the supercharger kicks out a painful, high-pitched scream. My kitchen mixer sounded identical when I put too much meat in the grinder attachment, right before the drive gears exploded.

I blip the engine with my right foot. It has to be done slowly, as the carburetor isn't designed for low rpm. Most of our support crew winces or plugs their ears. A Speedway employee leans in and watches the tach for a moment.

"That's normal," he says.

I look at the tach, then back at him.

"Really. Rev it to 3500. They spun them to seven in period and went 140 mph on board tracks." The wooden speedways, part of the early Indy ladder, that once dotted the country. These were steeply banked ovals made of nailed two-by-fours. Boards came loose, flung guys to their death. "There was a white line at the top of the track, and if you went over it, you were dead."

The Miller's clutch is obnoxious and heavy. It acts like it wants you gone. The wheel has a gap in the bottom so you can reach the shifter, but it's so close to your chest, you have to swing your legs out to change gear. This is a "crash" gearbox, no synchros or dog rings to help you shift. It's also a bloodsucker. I learned to drive stick in a car with a crash box; they're difficult, but not impossible. This is something different, a telephone game of mystery. I keep expecting a bearing or something to come flying out of the tailshaft and threaten my mother.

The 91 darts into Indy's corners, skittish but stable. The shocks and tires are manic and only settle down north of highway speed, at which point the car ghosts around the track, begging for throttle. The chassis doesn't so much obey steering commands as fall into them. After a lap or so, I put my eyes down the track and think. About speed, how the steering is geared, how you move the car with your hips. (Turn 1, sashay. Turn 2, rumba.) After a moment, it clicks.

"HOLY HELL," I hear myself yell. "THEY SLID THESE THINGS AROUND THIS PLACE."

It bleeds from the Miller's pores, the way the car is constructed: The 91 wants to be drifted, snatched out and caught, at speed. The driver, up in the air, treating the Speedway like a rodeo. Or maybe an ice rink. For 500 miles.

People have written books about Millers. The bible is a text called *The Miller Dynasty*, written by Mark Dees. My father, a fan of the marque for years, kept a copy on the shelf in his office. When I found that book in high school, my mind blew up. American art and science, men feet apart and sliding, leather helmets. Then as now, it felt both distant and heartbreakingly real.

1951–1963: ROADSTER REIGN

The engine lid has to be open when you start it. It has to be open so somebody else can work the throttle, because of course you don't know what a fuel-injected Offenhauser needs to start, because of course you haven't driven one before, because this is 2015 and injected Offys don't fall off trees, even in Indiana, even at the Speedway.

But once, they ruled it.

No car has ever been a Car, capital C, this much. The gas pedal is shaped like the sole of a boot. The sway-bar ends are cast pieces big enough to use in a bar fight. The seat is deep and high-sided, like sitting in a baseball helmet, and upholstered in something that may or may not have been borrowed from Eisenhower's bowling alley. And the whole package dwarfs the Miller. The front tires could be hung on a dump truck.

There is a small, overstuffed pillow sewn into the right side of the cockpit. You're supposed to lean against it. It feels like an old couch.

When the engine fires, the blat punches holes in my skull. The car carries its exhaust over a shoulder, inches from your head, like a soldier with a mortar, which is fitting, because the starter bung in the nose gives it a face like MacArthur chewing a cigar.

Millers were good at Indy, and everyone wanted one. As the Speedway moved toward a one-make grid, entries dropped. Tickets became harder to sell. In 1930, the race instigated what was later called the "junk formula"—changes like larger, production-based engines, intended to make the 500 more affordable.

Craziness followed. The 1931 500 had an entry list of 70 cars, double the previous year's. But the Depression was on. Miller's shop went bankrupt. The track, hurting for cash, began to crumble. World War II put the race on hold. Retired Indy hero Wilbur Shaw did 500 miles of test lapping in 1944 and compared the Speedway to "a dilapidated back house on an abandoned farm."

In late 1945, the track was bought by an Indiana grocer named Anton "Tony" Hulman Jr. Hulman, Shaw said, wasn't from the car industry, and was thus "free to do whatever was necessary for the good of the Speedway and racing in general." (Hulman's descendants still own the facility.)

With Shaw's help, Hulman spent money smartly, and the crowds and purebred machines returned. In 1952, oilman Howard Keck entered a car for young driver Bill Vukovich. It was built by California's Frank Kurtis and powered by a fuel-injected, 4.2-liter Offenhauser. The engine was offset to the left, with the driver next to the driveshaft, not atop it, so the car carried its weight relatively low. The whole thing resembled a 1950s F1 car, flattened.

According to legend, when Vukovich saw his car, he called it a "roadster." The basic design was successful enough that it was soon copied, filling the grid, and the 500 moved back toward being a one-make race.

In 1961, a roadster built by Floyd Trevis won the Indy 500. It did so with a record 139.130-mph average at the hands of the legendary A.J. Foyt. The Foyt who would win Le Mans in 1967 and the 500 three more times, a holy terror in a race car. Who was formidable well into the modern era, retiring in the 1990s. Who still runs a team at Indy. (I saw him there last year, tearing through the paddock on a golf cart, scowling.)

Foyt's Trevis now lives in the Speedway museum. When they rolled it out for our use, the unrestored, cracking paint and hand-lettered logos drew a silent crowd. The design is a copy of a roadster called a Watson, and a Watson's shape makes you think of warm Mays in the Fifties, the 500 broadcast burbling out of a small radio in a garage with an open door. Watsons are the quintessential "old" Indy car, Foyt's car is a heck of a Watson, and A.J. Foyt is one of the brightest human sparks to have ever lived.

1961 Trevis/Offy (Watson) Roadster

Qualifying Speed: 145.903 mph

4.2-liter I-4, 400 hp

Rear-drive, 2-speed manual

I get one lap before most of the above sinks in and my heart tries to claw out of my chest. The car isn't intimidating at low speed. At 80 mph or so, a roadster is ranging, a P-51 before loosing its drop tanks. There's a feeling of space at the wheel—a long nose, lots of air in the cockpit—that makes you think you're safe when you're very clearly not.

It's not as if the packaging doesn't wake you up. My legs rest against the two-speed transmission. They cram in vertically, my feet almost under my knees. The gearbox is noticeably easier than that of the Miller. The Miller's brakes felt stronger. During photography, when I turn around to check distance on our camera car, I get a face full of rear wheel and brake disc. The whole mess is right there, spinning, close enough to touch.

Seventy miles per hour in Foyt's car is about 3000 rpm. Below that speed in top gear, the engine spits and farts. Above, the fuel injection works so well you forget about it. After a few laps, I pop into the pits to talk with Richard Pardon, *R&T*'s photographer.

"How is it?"

"Somewhere under here is a rage-drunk '55 Chevy."

"That bad?"

"It's the best thing."

A few more laps. I find myself wanting to run the hell out of it. I want to hit a road course and learn to drift it. Then go to an oval and try —just once!—to keep balance, loose and moving. Because something about the car says that mortals could handle it.

Maybe not crack off a pole lap, but handle it.

Assuming you didn't die in a minor crash.

Assuming the 75-gallon fuel tank over the rear wheels didn't make the car a sideways nightmare as it emptied.

Assuming you could keep on top of it for 500 miles.

After driving, I sit on the pit wall, watching the car cool. The grandstands are empty, as they have been all day. For the first time, I wonder how it feels when they aren't.

1964–1971: Future in the Middle

"In a fire, pull this."

My fingers find the handle for the car's fuel cutoff.

"Got it."

"No, really."

"I got it."

"No, *really*."

I am sitting in a 1964 Eisert Indy car. The car's owner, leaning over the cockpit, laughs. I protest.

"What do you think I'm going to do? These aren't hot laps. There are construction crews here, for Pete's sake."

"Old race cars aren't supposed to catch fire. But you have to act like they're all looking to do it. Like, 'You in car! Need fire now?'"

He points to the Eisert's swollen belly, which holds almost nothing but fuel. A tank at each of my elbows, rising to my shoulders.

Welcome to the toothy world of the early mid-engine Indy car.

In 1960, an English Formula 1 constructor named John Cooper tested one of his mid-engine F1 cars at the Speedway. Formula 1 was almost entirely front-engine until 1958, when Stirling Moss won the Argentine Grand Prix in a mid-engine Cooper. The layout, which helps both packaging and handling, soon consumed motorsport, and it dominates the space still today.

In 1960, however, Indy was behind. Roadsters were state-of-the-art. At Cooper's Speedway test, world champion Jack Brabham cracked off an average lap speed of just under 145 mph. The winner of the 1960 500, driving a more powerful roadster, averaged 138.767 and went noticeably slower in the corners. Brabham and Cooper came back to the race in 1961 and finished ninth, after which the Speedway soiled its collective pants. Mid-engine cars began filtering into the 500. Two years later, Ford was ramping up its "Total Performance" racing campaign, which meant throwing Dumpsters of money at car racing in almost any form. For the 500, Dearborn called Lotus, which came to the '63 running of the event with Ford-powered, mid-engine cars derived from the Lotus 25 F1 car. American sports-car and F1 star Dan Gurney drove one, Scottish maestro Jim Clark drove a second, and Clark almost won. For one reason or another, Speedway fans and officials still grumbled at the fact that the Lotuses had their engines in the "wrong" place.

1964 EISERT "HARRISON SPECIAL"

TOP SPEED: 180 MPH (EST.)
4.9-LITER V-8, 485 HP
REAR-DRIVE, 4-SPEED MANUAL

Three Lotuses showed up for the '64 500, and one set fastest race lap. In '65, Clark started on the front row and won easily. The 500 was officially dragged up to date.

It was a weird time. By the 1965 500, only a handful of roadsters made the start. Mid-engine Lotuses and Lolas dotted the grid, as did a new influx of international talent. In a mere three years, the race's average speed had gone from just over 140 mph to just over 150.

Now we get to the Eisert. *Road & Track* had originally aimed to use Jim Clark's 500-winning 1965 Lotus for this story, but we discovered at a late hour that the car was unavailable. So we called *R&T* contributor and vintage-race-car specialist Colin Comer. He owns the Eisert, and he was happy to help.

Comer's car never qualified for the 500, though its original owner did try. In many ways, its story says more about the race in that period than does Clark's winner. In grand old Indy tradition, the Eisert was built on trend: The design was a mishmash of two Formula 1 cars, the Lotus 18 and the Lotus 24, engineered and assembled by a well-meaning but small privateer team. The steel-tube space frame was covered by fiberglass and aluminum panels. Power came from a fuel-injected Corvette V-8, destroked to 302 cubic inches and making 485 hp. The sum total resembled nothing so much as a Formula Ford with a gym addiction and a propensity for vaporizing tires.

For a minute, this was how ordinary people aimed for Indy. The 1960s were the last time a nonwealthy driver could show up at the 500 with a relatively simple car and budget and have anything like a hope of qualifying. A short while later, with the advent of aluminum monocoques, turbocharging, and aerodynamic downforce, the money compounded, and the everyman path all but evaporated.

The Eisert's V-8 sounds lumpy, but not exotic. Tentative nips at the throttle produce big, whapping leaps on the tach. Sitting behind that large and flexible wheel, I catch an epoxyish whiff of race gas—the car originally ran on methanol—as it fire-hoses into the engine's open trumpets, just a few feet behind my ears.

The package feels oddly familiar. I used to vintage-race a 1960s Formula Ford, an Alexis Mk 14; it was shaped like a cigar and basically just a squinting copy of a Lotus 51. (Notice a theme?) The Eisert has the same torpedo nose and straight-arm, G.I. Joe driving position. But after climbing out of a roadster, the track is another thing entirely. My tailbone seems buried in the pavement; the walls loom taller. The nose is lighter, darting off center. The steering wheel and frame dance separately. I'm basically lying down, far less exposed than in the Watson.

The stakes seem illogically higher. I wore an open-face helmet for photography and couldn't stop thinking about my chin. How it would feel to grind it down on a concrete wall.

Picturing a fast lap is easier here. If the Watson leads with its jaw, the Eisert pivots around your hips. You steer it with your wrists. It represents obvious and immediate progress, the point where and reason why an entire sport simply woke up one day and went, "Yup, this." And if someone asked me to slide something like this around Indianapolis, I would change the subject.

Comer's Eisert was brought to the track by Don Hoevel, a former IndyCar tech from Illinois. "David Hobbs used to tell a story," he says. "Someone asked him about his favorite corner. Turn 1 at Indy, he said. 'You're out there all bloody month of May, just bangin' around, and you go through 1 over and over. It's just a corner. Race day, they don't tell you . . . the people in the stands, the shadows—it just closes up. It becomes a tunnel.'"

And some people go in, I thought, and don't come out.

1972–1978: Leaps and Bounds and Wings

In 1973, *Road & Track* called the '72 Indy Eagle "the fastest circuit-lapping automobile in history . . . faster than any record ever set by its peers . . . by huge chunks of speed, a completely new standard of car."

I've never driven anything like this, but such is progress that the Eagle feels familiar. It fits the cartoon stereotype of Race Car: fat slicks, tight cockpit, big wing. An odd kind of normal, after the other cars.

Another private owner, a Californian named Philippe de Lespinay. For 27 years, de Lespinay was the informal graphics man for Dan Gurney's All American Racers. He designed the white Olsonite livery on the car you see here. As a thank-you for all his work, in 1986, Gurney gave him a disassembled Indy car. This was it.

The Eagle bursts into a thrummy, complex-sounding idle. At idle, the engine, an Offenhauser, feels sleepy, a beat behind the pedal. From outside, it looks like a government version of the roadster's motor, with the exception of the melon-sized turbo scaffolded off the back. The assembly may as well be a neon sign: Turbo Lag to Eat the Earth.

"Get into and out of the throttle in a straight line," de Lespinay says. "If you get into it in a corner, you will find the wall. If you get out of it in a corner, you will find the wall."

De Lespinay is a French expatriate. His accent turns "wall" into *wohl*. Someone asks if the car will spit fire, for photography. "Yes, but only if you rev it to 7000 at full throttle and dump the boost—off the gas, pop!" (*Pohp!*) "A four-foot flame. I have pictures of this, on the engine dyno."

Indy in the 1970s was a land of gains. Lap speeds exploded upward, thanks to the evolution of grippy slick tires and downforce-producing wings. And the Offenhauser found a second life in turbocharging, partly because it was so durable and took so well to abuse. Amazingly, the engine was still competitive, despite having roots in the 1920s. (In a nice bit of symmetry, Miller genius Leo Goossen designed the '72 Eagle's twin-pump oiling system. The changes he made that year gave a measurable power increase, because Leo Goossen, senior citizen of the early 1970s, was still at heart Leo Goossen, engineering stud.)

If you fall into the wide, comfy Eisert, you install yourself in the Eagle. You aren't getting out unless you have help or time, and reducing one of those variables takes a lot of the other. Similarly, if the Eisert is a bulked-up Formula Ford, the Eagle is a period F1 car gone Incredible Hulk. The rear uprights could anchor an aircraft carrier.

"The gears," de Lespinay says, pointing to the Weismann four-speed, "they are *this big*." His fingers make a circle the size of a coffee can.

But the key was downforce. Wings were prevalent in road racing by the early 1970s, but Indy regulations of the time required a car's aerodynamic devices to be one with the bodywork. In 1971, the McLaren M16 featured a legal "body" rear wing that bent the rules. In the hands of Peter Revson, that car raised the Indy 500 one-lap qualifying record, then three years old, by an incredible 7.4 mph, to just over 179.

In 1972, the rules changed, making separate wings legal. Gurney's shop, driven by designer Roman Slobodynskyj, produced a car of careful details: radiators in the sidepods for improved balance and aerodynamics (now de rigueur, but then uncommon); a wing as high and far back as the rules allowed, seeking clean air; and a wheelbase half a foot longer than the minimum, for stability. The engine was a semistructural member, and Gurney said its output pushed the envelope of Offy possibility. At a time when most F1 cars were still winged cigars, the Eagle appeared single-piece.

It worked. On Pole Day that year, Bobby Unser, driving for Gurney, blew the track record to bits. He qualified at 195.940 mph, an improvement of more than 17 mph. It was a gain not seen before or since.

Unser called the Eagle's advantage "incomprehensible." Slobodynskyj said he hadn't tried to reinvent anything, just make "as good a car as possible." An ignition failure took Unser out of the race he was leading, on lap 31. Gurney's phone rang off the hook, and everything at the Speedway changed again.

At 5500 in a straight line in third gear, the Eagle's Offy is asleep. It's off cam and boost, thrumming along at a trot. The engine makes no particular noise, more a collection of whooshes and stirrings.

1972 AAR/Offy Indy Eagle

Qualifying Speed: 195.940 mph (est.)²

2.6-liter turbocharged I-4, 800–1100 hp (varies with boost)

Rear-drive, 4-speed manual

During photography, I run the car to redline in first and second. Power builds in a surging, almost unsettling wave, the throttle sharpest up top. Redline is 10,500, and the car seems sluggish until 7000. The engine acts as much like the roadster's Offy as the page on which you are reading this acts like an elephant.

De Lespinay exercises his car regularly, and he has driven it at speed on an oval. After I park it, I ask him about throttle lag when the turbo has a full head of steam.

"It's there with small throttle changes, 200 to 300 rpm. You know, I have the balls to get it to 200, 210 mph. Those guys ran them up to 245

—you realize what an achievement it was. All the power you'll ever need, you just have to use it."

One of Hoevel's guys later asks if the Eisert has anything in common with the Eagle. The two cars feel so different, you could fill a book with the answer. The Eisert is a broad-stroke device, the Eagle, a narrow brush. You try one after the other, you start to see how Indy laps became less sliding and more a precise form of flight. And how drivers stopped thinking about navigating the Speedway in terms of feet and started considering the place in terms of inches.

Call it roll stiffness, aero, suspension advancement, whatever, but the Eagle is the first car in this outing that feels like raw science. And if I'm being honest, that's why the thought of a lap at speed gives me the creeping yips.

1979–Present: Rise of the Aero Magic

The last Indy car to change everything was yellow, the color of its sponsor. The paint pigment carried a touch of pearl, which helped it pop on television. Even on YouTube, in footage of the Indy 500 that it won, the car glows.

The official name was Chaparral 2K, but someone nicknamed the car "Yellow Submarine," and it stuck. You can interpret "Submarine" in a lot of ways, but I've always pictured the car doing the impossible, driving beneath air. The Chaparral was the first Indy car designed to take advantage of ground effects: Underfloor tunnels induced low-pressure areas that essentially made the entire body an upside-down wing. Colin Chapman's 1977 Lotus 78 pioneered the science in Formula 1, but when the Chaparral debuted in 1979, the idea was new to Indy cars. That it arrived in the form of a blazing eyeball vacuum was just gravy.

The leap cannot be overstated. The Chaparral was so good, so far above the pack, that it pushed its most famous driver to a mental space he had never seen. Johnny Rutherford used our test car to win the 1980 Indy 500. "At Indy that year," he said, "we had quickest time on every day but one." The cars he'd driven before "only let you go so far. The Chaparral . . . really put you into a nervous situation. The edge of the universe was a lot shallower in the 2K."

Chaparral founder and Texan Jim Hall designed the 2K in concert with Englishman John Barnard; he's admitted that the Sub is almost a copy of the Lotus 79, which built on the 78's foundation. (In a nice parallel, the Chaparral's 2.6-liter Cosworth DFX V-8 is a turbocharged adaptation of the DFV V-8 that both powered the Lotuses and dominated F1 for years.) But the Chaparral lit off a revolution. After, Hall said, practically every Indy car was the same in basic layout and concept.

Al Unser used a 2K to qualify third in the '79 Indy 500. "When they came down to take the green flag," Hall said, "everyone backed off for Turn 1 except Al. It was the most amazing thing you ever saw. He stretched 100 yards in the first turn, 100 yards in the second." The race ended with a gearbox failure, but the next year, Rutherford won. Two years later, the rest of the grid had caught up, and the Chaparral was uncompetitive, but the work was done; the tide had turned.

And then they start the sucker, and my head melts down. *The Yellow Submarine is about to move again and I am going to be in it and what is that noise in the background oh Jesus giggling it's you stop giggling you tremendous dork.*

1980 CHAPARRAL/COSWORTH 2K

QUALIFYING SPEED: 192.526 MPH
2.6-LITER TURBOCHARGED V-8, 800 HP
REAR-DRIVE, 4-SPEED MANUAL

From the cockpit, the Sub feels less important than it is. My hips are too wide for Rutherford's plastic seat, so the Speedway staff removes it, strapping me directly to the riveted-aluminum tub. The underside of the composite bodywork is unfinished; you can see the tiny fibers that hold it together. The manifold-pressure gauge is partially blocked by the thick steering wheel. The Pennzoil logos are hand-painted; you can see the brush strokes from five feet away, feel their ridges when you touch the paint.

As on the Eagle, the pedals sit ahead of the front wheels. Anything you drive into, your feet hit first. The older car's engine bay is less dense, though, and its aero bits are tacked on by comparison. Where the Eagle appears blatantly old, the 2K skirts the question. It isn't of the modern era but seems to flirt with it.

The contrast was sharpened, in part, because we had a modern Indy car on hand. We borrowed a 2015 Dallara from Chip Ganassi's Indianapolis shop for photography; during a spare moment, I climb into its cockpit, threading my feet deep into the carbon tub. You wear a car like that like a suit. It reminded me of 1990s Indy cars I've seen with their engine covers off—MIL-spec connectors, laid out like a NASA clean room. On the Chaparral, the blowoff valve sits atop the engine lid like a sentinel, seemingly bolted there because it had nowhere else to go. Certain parts of the car seem arranged almost accidentally.

"The engine makes nothing below 8000," one of the mechanics tells me. The 2K's tires have age-cracked sidewalls and no one present can remember when that complex Cosworth was last apart—museum cars lead an easy life—so I don't rev it over seven grand. But with a quick shift and the V-8 making just a hint of boost, it does the F1-Cossie noise: WARAAOOOW*crack*BARAAOOW. The first time that sound appears, my hair stands on end.

The Chaparral's gearbox is a giddy mind reader, a Weismann four-speed with a tiny composite shift knob. The lever feels as slick and brainless as the boxes in the other cars were difficult. I circle the track in third gear, low rpm. Even at that speed, there is a sense of precarity, your body like a weight on a string, screwed if the string breaks. Also the innate knowledge that you are an impostor, shuffling through doors that other guys ran through while threading a needle.

Rutherford's fastest lap the year this car won was 190.074 mph. Squinting through the windshield, howling around, tracking out inches from the wall, you can almost imagine that speed. You can also almost imagine the feeling in the instant when it disappears.

The 2K was both the first modern Indy car and the last earthshaking vision in the 500—just as the Lotus 79 was in F1. "Every race car since," *R&T* motorsport correspondent Marshall Pruett once told me, "has been a Yellow Sub, a Lotus." No great leaps, just evolution best explained by an aerodynamicist.

In a way, the evolution here parallels that of motorsport in general. Experimentation has been squashed by restrictive rules and politicizing everywhere from club racing to F1, but it's particularly galling at Indianapolis. In the 36 years since Rutherford first flung the Sub around the Speedway, there have been great drivers and heroic moments, but none have carried the weight of a revolution. If that seems hard to believe, it's because no one in their right mind would say that we're done. That we've reached the end and solved for Race Car, finally out of ideas.

I went back out at dusk to say goodbye. They let me drive one last car, anything from our little group, a few final laps as the sun fell. I have no idea why this chance was offered, but when opportunity presents itself, you do not ask opportunity if it has lost its mind. You just walk to pit road and pretend to not be a few hundred kinds of geeked.

The Miller felt like the only choice. The safety and construction people had gone home, so the track was empty. The smell of fuel danced up from my feet. The skies melted into pink. The car seemed to warm up and canter.

Earlier that afternoon, we had been joined by a young Indy driver, a guy in his 20s, in the prime of his career. We needed an extra hand for a photo at one point, so he hopped into the roadster and drove it, lapping behind a photo vehicle at just off idle. When he was done, a museum staffer casually if he would have raced a Watson in period.

No, the young driver said, incredulous. "I like modern technology!"

I do too. But you know what? I would've come here when the Speedway was just bricks. I would've driven a roadster, a Miller, a turbo Offy. I'm not saying I would've been fast, but I would have strained and put everything out there, a shot at making the show. Not because I have a death wish. Not because I have enough talent to hang a Dallara on the pole. (I don't.) But because there's a deeper idea that's always hovered around the place. Something beyond the history and risk and challenge.

As a people, we don't have a lot of shared totems. Things we know we can come back to, where a collective memory can gild a good moment, or elevate a tame one. And while the Speedway hosts races other than the 500, it truly wakes just once a year, with the jet flyovers and the teeming crowds and a feeling on the ground so special, time in the stands should be mandatory for anyone with a pulse and a U.S. passport. That vibe sits outside the disappointing cars and the rules and the wings, powerful in its own right.

When my laps with the Miller were done, I pulled into the pits, shut the engine off, and watched the sun set from the driver's seat. After a few minutes, the grandstands disappeared. I was left with just a cockpit and a pair of hands. Something in me begged to keep going—to see how far I could press.

That pull is everything. It's us, chasing a better, smarter version of ourselves. Like the Indy 500 itself, it cannot be explained, only witnessed. It's in four corners and a neighborhood in Indiana. It's about to kick off for the hundredth time. Long may it run.

That issue's cover, one of the greats, on home-office wall.

---

1. Meyer, 1928 Indy 500, Miller 91
2. Unser, 1972 Indy 500, AAR/Offy Indy Eagle

Survivors

Daydreams and other truths.

My first-ever attempt at fiction. This ran on Hagerty's website in the guise of a normal column, revealed as invention only in postscript. The bike trek with Chaf was real; the rest was brewed up in my imagination as we outran a storm on Route 50.

Hagerty, July 2021

The road ran to the horizon, as Kansas roads often do. No stoplights, just a blanket of farms, corn and sorghum waving in the wind. The air smelled of manure and wildflowers and the sticky sweetness of a late June evening, that unmistakable combination of season and place, when the gloaming is so long and dense that it settles onto land like syrup, thick enough to eat.

Chaffee had called a month before. He was moving east from California, he said, and his old motorcycles were going with. I had no good reason to ride two aged European bikes from San Francisco to Tennessee with an old friend, so that's what I did. Mostly on rural two-lanes, treating corners like games in between taking long breaks to sit under trees and suck down bottles of water.

Smithology

I had never seen a Kansas yard sale. Certainly not on Highway 50, and by that point, we had been conveyor-belting down it for a day already. Fifty bee-lines across the state's southern third, pin-straight, changing heading or elevation once a county at most. The scenery is variable but not varied, mostly threshers and silos. On a motorcycle, alone in your helmet, time dilates. Fugue states blow in like weather, wipe any memory of breakfast that morning or what you did five minutes ago.

And so I found myself with the bike stopped, on a section of highway that sloped down into a shallow valley of still air, walking toward a house. White clapboard with a gable roof, next to a weathered pole barn and a stand of maples. There were no signs, nothing to advertise a sale, just a short driveway with a few tables and an older man in a folding chair.

Chaffee downshifted to a stop at the end of the driveway. He hung his helmet on a mirror but stayed on the bike, lighting a cigarette and waving me on in disinterest. A few feet away, under a carport, a chocolate lab raised his head from the concrete, half asleep, then laid it back down, as if he had read all the books where country dogs do that sort of thing and didn't want to disappoint.

The man at the table looked late 60s, or maybe far older, in that fuzzy way farm country can age people. Loose jeans and a plaid shirt. The tables held random household bits. VHS tapes, a few collectible drinking glasses, a dusty blender that could have known Eisenhower.

He smiled. "Hello."

"Hi. All this for sale?"

A chuckle. "Either that or my wife is going to be real unhappy I gave it away for no money."

"Mind if I look around?"

"Sure. Nice motorcycle. Seventies?"

"Yes, sir. Friend's." I gestured to the road. "Just helping move it."

"Where you headed?"

"Tennessee."

"Long way."

"Been fun, though."

"Bet it is."

The dog did the head thing again. I chalked my mood up to long miles in the saddle. The next few minutes were spent in that universal yard-sale sketch, where you poke through someone's cast-offs as they watch, each of you pretending to not be drawing conclusions about the other. A milk crate held a small collection of crooner records, half of them duplicates. Several books on photography sat atop a short stack of fashion magazines, covers faded thin from hours in the sun.

I leafed through the top photo book, then set it back down. The stack shifted a little, and a flash of blue peeked out from the bottom. More washed ink, a sliver of familiar font, letters once yellow but now almost white. I carefully lifted the magazines and slid the blue cover out from underneath.

"An old Haynes manual? For Weber carburetors?"

The man cocked his head. "You like old cars?"

"All my life. You own something with Webers?"

"A street rod with a small-block and IDFs, long time ago. Never ran right. Book helped, though. Idle circuit does more than you think."

"Right. Have a DCOE on a bookshelf at home, as reminder. Or maybe reason to forget."

Another chuckle. "They make good noise."

I flipped through the Haynes. The vintage jet tables in the back had been crossed out with thick black marker. Figures. Modern fuels are more oxygenated.

The wind picked up, ruffling the magazines on the table.

"You in a hurry to get back on the road? Got some stuff in the barn, might be up your alley. Cars, parts. Some pretty good, just need a new home."

I looked back at the bikes. Chaffee was lighting a second cigarette.

"Got some time," I said. "And re-homing is my ... weak point."

"I know the feeling."

He stood up slowly, fishing into a pocket for a set of keys. They jangled as he shuffled down the drive to the barn. The door handle stuck some, needing a wiggle to release the lock. When it gave, he turned, cracking the door before walking through.

"Wife calls this my other family. Says I treat them better than her."

The door opened to the unmistakable smell of fresh construction, new paint and treated wood, but also a whiff of oil and rubber. He reached for a switch, and banks of fluorescents winked to life beneath wooden rafters. The space was simple but large, its coated concrete floors bordered by tidy drywall. The sheetrock, a warm cream, had been painted to match the house.

The barn seemed larger inside than out. Two rows of cars, maybe a dozen in all, covered loosely and parked side by side, stretched to the rear wall, around a wide center aisle.

I took a few tentative steps inside. The shape closest to the door looked familiar, but I couldn't place it. He walked over, gently pulling the cover up and onto the car's roof.

"Aztec Gold. Originally black seats and dash, but it was converted to saddle from new, factory parts. Sat at the dealer down the road for three months before it sold, nobody wanted the color. My son spotted it driving by one day, talked about it for weeks.

"Bought it after a year's work at the meatpacking plant in Garden City, then went off and enlisted, deployed, never came back. Four thousand miles. He put the Daytons on it. Always did like wire wheels."

A late-1990s Mustang. An SN95, shiny and straight and with that tell-tale hint of factory orange peel, never resprayed. I looked in the window: and an automatic. Taut and unwrinkled leather. A hideous package, impeccably preserved.

I didn't know what to say, so I smiled and said what my Southern mother always had in moments of lost words.

"That's, uh . . . very nice."

He beamed. "V-6. Has the tall diff, so it's quiet on the highway."

"The V-6," I repeated, slowly. My eyebrows quietly made for the ceiling.

"Always thought that was the engine you wanted, with a Mustang."

"You might say that."

"Great shape. Tank drained. Probably start right up with fresh gas."

He lifted the cover from the roof and set it neatly on the trunk. An expectant look.

"Pretty good, right?"

I fibbed. "Oh, uh, yes. Very much."

The tour continued. Over the next short while, he proudly removed cover after cover, half the cars in the room. Seen whole, the collection carried no theme but mediocre surprise, no thread but the widely unloved. Fifteen feet away, over a small puddle of gear oil, lay an AMC Pacer. Limited trim, not even the sport pack, one more automatic in a room full of them, beige paint on the original wavy panels and indifferent gaps, just under 10,000 miles on the clock. A 95-point car, frozen as if in amber, exactly as Kenosha had built it.

Ten feet over was a late-1980s Camry, silver, the anemic base model, its park-bench bumpers seemingly right off the showroom floor. We walked by three identical covered blobs that looked suspiciously like early Ford Tempos, then the slumping form of a 1990s Chrysler Sebring. A Gremlin was parked in the back, almost an afterthought, an impeccable period respray in flake bronze, just as perfect as the rest. Filigreed pinstripes on the flanks.

I had the odd sense of having stumbled into someone else's dream.

"How did all this stuff find you?"

"I went looking for it."

"Really?"

"Well, mostly. After a fashion."

We talked as we walked. He inquired on our trip, where we'd been and what we'd seen. Then I asked more on the fleet, and the stories came out. Every car in the barn had been carefully chosen, and nothing was there by accident. Each machine had a story, some reason why the original owner had walked into a dealer somewhere and driven off in that particular make and model.

The first check written by a cancer survivor after her doctor declared remission. The first person from a small-town family to go to college, who had then bought his mother her first new car. The new convertible a janitor drove home after investing wisely and earning enough to buy the company. Each story ended with the change that had prompted a sale. A death, a birth, old age; never a want, always a need.

All of this was logged. He showed me the journal in each trunk, a mix of hand-written notes, receipts, copies of photos, all gifted or scanned or recorded at time of purchase. A library of human experience, how one unique person came to love one car for reasons beyond the machine, then moved on.

The chat was uplifting, but after a while, I sensed the old man was working toward something.

He looked at the ground for a moment. "You know," he said softly, "I could make you a deal. It all runs. Have a container of spare parts behind the house. I can't be caretaker anymore, but it all needs looking after. By someone who cares about history and stories. I'd take whatever you could pay."

The building suddenly felt hollow. I put my hands in my pockets and bit a lip.

What came out next was truth, polite as I could manage. "I'm sorry," I said, haltingly. "The stories are worth saving, and what you've done here is wonderful, but I think you've got the wrong impression. I don't have a lot of money or space to begin with, but more than that, these just... aren't for me."

His face fell. Then he smiled a little warmer. He moved toward the Gremlin, where he began to slowly replace the cover. I fumbled for a consolation.

"I wish I were the one here. I'm just not. I can't be."

When he finally looked back, he seemed distracted. "No harm, I suppose. I understand."

"I'm sorry. I really am."

A moment passed. He paused with the cover, thoughtful. "You have one more minute? Maybe I could show you the back room?"

It was getting late. My mind ran through ways to beg off, then caved.

"Alright. But then we really have to get back on the road. Cross off another few counties before bed. You know how it is."

"I do." Another warm smile.

He walked to the building's rear, moving quicker now. On the back wall, a thick metal panel hung loosely from a narrow rail, castered to slide left and right. I hadn't noticed it when we walked in, would have sworn it wasn't there. He lifted a padlock from the latch.

"The stuff in here isn't much for me, but I haven't been able to pull the trigger and get rid of it. Just not the selling type, I guess."

He paused, as if considering something.

"Give me a hand? Door's heavy."

The steel groaned as we leaned on the handle, but it moved. The room behind was small and densely packed, a tidy mirror of the one up front and lit from the same switch. The cars were closer together, though, mirrors inches apart.

More covers, but lines here, I knew better: a late-1990s Acura Integra, with its low cowl and arcing roof; a boxy Lancia Delta; a Fox Mustang's argument of creases.

In the back, crouched behind the rest, lived something smaller and more curving. After a moment, he walked over and pulled that cover. My throat went dry.

"Figured this would push your button," he said. "Only a few people know it's here."

"I mean . . . It looks . . . Is it real?"

"Probably needs everything, but it's all real. Even has a few rare accessories. Hasn't run in years. Bought it for $5000 in the early Seventies. Lot of money, but we had inherited some, and I'd always wanted one. Turns out I don't like it, probably the only person on earth to say so. Don't fit. Friend gave me a ride once. Fastest car I've ever been in. Sure is pretty."

Whoever looked at a real 1960s Shelby Cobra without going weak in the knees? It was an unrestored 289, leaf springs, a slab-side, early and pure, before Carroll's guys put that 427 under the hood with a whip and a chair. The odometer showed real miles, but far less than it would take to wear a car like that out. The paint was flat and oxidized, and the plating had dulled, but the rest was as it had left the line. That tiny shop in Marina del Rey.

I knelt next to a fender, watching light pool on thin lacquer. English roadster by way of a bunch of hot-rodders on the west coast.

These cars were never cheap, even 50 years ago. But what's a survivor 289 now? A million dollars?

My host sighed. "I know what it's worth. But if I'm honest, I don't need the money. We've got enough, and the other cars can go to charity when I'm gone. Would rather this one just find somebody who loves it but can't afford it, might give it what it needs."

I wrung my hands a little, then knelt at the grille. Every slat in the egg crate was flat and straight. "Sir, I can't imagine it needs much, even in this shape. I love it. But I can't be your man. Even that steering wheel is worth more than I've got."

"I don't think you understand."

"I'm not sure I . . ."

"There's no deal here. Made my mind up a while back. You took time to listen to the stories about all that stuff out front. Didn't laugh. Didn't ask if I'm crazy. Couple people have made offers for the lot, but nobody treats it with dignity, and that's worth something. Not many people remember to be kind anymore."

My face felt numb. He bent over the cockpit, opened the glovebox, retrieved an official-looking slip of paper.

"Hell with it," he said, holding the paper out. "Yours now. Glad to find a good home."

I gaped, hesitant, then willed myself to move. My hand reached out, unsteady.

A familiar voice echoed from behind.

"You ready? Storm on the way. We should get moving."

I turned, startled.

Chaffee was standing in the doorway. The room was now much darker. The wide dirt floor held nothing but scraps of lumber and a few crushed beer cans. That big metal door was off its hinges, quietly rusting up against a wall. A small gash in the roof, left long ago by a fallen tree, let in the only light. No one but Chaffee and I had been there in years.

"Everything okay? You look a little weird."

A blink or two. My head began to clear. In the distance, a truck went by.

"Sorry. Got distracted. Been a long day."

"We probably have a few minutes, if you want to poke around a little more."

I glanced around the barn. "Nah, that's alright. We should get going. No reason to get stuck in weather."

We walked outside, boots crunching over gravel. There was no yard sale, no tables, and weeds filled the drive. The handmade plastic sign nailed to the front door was cracked and dulled with age, but its yellow letters still wore enough paint to spell out FOR SALE BY OWNER. A weathered dog dish sat under the carport, full of old rain.

The bikes waited patiently on the shoulder. I put on my gear, taking only a bit longer than usual, fussing with the helmet strap. As I went to hit the starter, Chaffee leaned over, bike already running. He flipped up his visor.

"Just seemed like an old pole barn—I miss something?"

I shook my head. "Nah. Not really."

We pulled back onto the highway, eastbound, away from the storm. More towns slipped by in the dark. Houses hunched near the road, passing in shadow, and while many were empty, most were not. I rode on, feeling lucky, and thought mostly of dreams in the night.

The Le Mans All-Nighter

Fords, Toyotas, and brain-warping sleep-dep in what will forever be known as the year you had to go.

Some things are worth doing simply because no one will ever be able to take them away from you. Others, because you'll never remember them. Staying up all night at your first Le Mans while hammering gibberish into a keyboard? Both.

ROAD & TRACK, SEPTEMBER 2016

This was the year. The year that Ford went back to the great endurance race, absent since a string of wins in the 1960s. The year Porsche defended its first overall win in more than a decade. The year Toyota took the fight to the Germans, came within inches of victory—after years of trying at that race, years of heartbreaking defeat—and coasted to a halt with three minutes left. What has been called the most gutting Le Mans finish in ages.

This story is not about any of that.

You can, and should, read the news reports on what happened during the 2016 24 Hours of Le Mans. This is something fuzzier. A bright-eyed look at a 93-year-old spectacle. Notes on the ground from a 35-year-old writer who had wanted to see the place since fourth grade.

And maybe a hint, as racing struggles to stay relevant, at why a long day in France remains one of the best things on earth.

PARIS | CHARLES DE GAULLE AIRPORT
Thursday, 8:00 A.M. My plane lands from the West Coast. Didn't sleep in the air. Wandering Charles de Gaulle, I decide to stay awake for the entire race. In the fog of jet lag, having never been to Le Mans, it seems like the only reasonable option.

In the annals of sport, Le Mans stands alone. Privateers and factory-backed professionals, in some of the fastest cars on earth, for 24 hours. An 8.5-mile, nine-decade-old course made partially of closed public roads. The track has been updated over the years for safety, but the race still pours a quarter-million spectators into a small city two hours from Paris. An event that once boasted virtually stock street cars now features million-dollar prototypes and purpose-built, production-derived sports cars.

The top class, Le Mans Prototype 1 (LMP1), offers experimental, 900-plus-hp hybrids like the V-4 Porsche 919 and the V-6 Audi R18. Those cars are spaceships, packed with secret tech and short enough to trip over. They run alongside amateur drivers and factory pros in a range of entries that includes slower, lesser prototypes but also Ford GTs, Porsche 911s, and Corvettes.

2:00 P.M. I catch a TGV, France's high-speed train, to Le Mans. It's common to hate how the French run motorsport. Too many rules, an ironic lack of joie de vivre. For one reason or another, a country with few world-beating race teams now controls both European motorsport, through the FIA, and Le Mans specifically, through the Automobile Club de l'Ouest (ACO).

TGVs can cruise at 200 mph. Somewhere outside Chartres, in a reclined, overstuffed chair in a silent cabin, I'm lulled into a daze by the *whufwhuf* of overpasses. It occurs to me that the French are not wrong about everything.

LE MANS | GARE DU MANS STATION
5:00 P.M. Funky, changeable weather. Blue sky, then clouds, then blue again. Spitting rain, as if the weather wants to be polite but also just wants you to go home.

The crowd at the train station is a cartoon. Stray dogs that manage to look both extremely French and like ordinary stray dogs. A troupe of primary-school girls jabbering dramatically through stinky cigarettes. A hundred Brits, walking quickly. As in Paris, every other woman wears heart-stopping pants. Unlike in Paris, most of them smile. Outside, under a wooden shed, a man sells brown eggs and soft cheese.

My taxi leaves the station and immediately comes to a halt in a line of cars. Le Mans traffic on race weekend is a Manhattan tunnel on a Friday. Many roads are closed because they're part of the track or they intersect with it. Every third corner holds a billboard advertising Porsche or the Ford GT. Then you crest a rise and almost fall into the town airfield, next to  that famous front straight. The Dunlop bridge sits in the distance. The scale of the place means you rarely see more than two corners at once.

I have been up for over 24 hours and Le Mans is already the only place in France.

LE MANS | CATHÉDRALE SAINT-JULIEN
Friday, 6:00 P.M. The drivers parade through town in convertibles. I mill around near a massive Gothic cathedral while parade guest and team owner Jackie Chan waves at crowds from the back of an Excalibur. The French are very excited about Jackie Chan. (Parade announcer: "*ZhhhackieChan!*")

Le Zhhhackie.

At dinner that night with Ford people, we listen to driver Andy Priaulx. "You're doing 180 mph, and then you're back in the motor home, putting the kettle on," he says. "At 2:00 in the morning, someone shakes you and says, your stint, 15 minutes. And you're back on the Mulsanne, thinking, Why am I doing this?

"Long straights, lot of time to think, to lose concentration. It's like Chip [Ganassi, Ford's team chief] says—you've got to drive everyone else's car, too."

The race starts Saturday, at 3:00 in the afternoon. I sleep only four hours that night and can't explain why.

LE MANS | CIRCUIT DE LA SARTHE
Saturday, 10:30 A.M. Hitch a ride to the track with Aaron Robinson and Mike Duff of *Car and Driver*. The motorway is a parking lot. Sleep-deprived, I ask Mike, an Englishman, about French drivers. He drops into a tour of English insults. (Collective favorite: "feckin' twunt melon farmer.") We discuss European cultural differences vis-à-vis a German woman attempting to illegally pass our car on the shoulder. ("Aaron, they can't just take what they want anymore! Don't let her have your Sudetenland!")

2:00 P.M. The teams are lined up on the grid, flag girls and pomp. French paratroopers skydive in to deliver a flag. On the front straight, Brad Pitt will drop the flag to start the race.

A Jumbotron shows Pitt, Jason Statham, Patrick Dempsey, and Jackie Chan gathered with officials. After a parade lap, the skies open. Raining so hard it hurts. Teams scramble to change to full-wet tires on the grid. Brad Pitt scrambles not at all, because Brad Pitt don't scramble.

3:00 P.M. The rain gets worse. For the first time in history, due to standing water on the track and atrocious visibility, Le Mans starts under a safety car. Pitt stands in the middle of the straight and waves a French tricolor. The passing cars shoot up waves of spray, soaking his clothes. This is oddly satisfying.

3:53 P.M. The race finally has some sense of speed. It's still raining, so you hear the pace instead of see it, cars cracking into the chicanes and barking around off-line.

I wander the grandstands in a stupor. There are more obvious fans of American cars here than you see in most of America. Blue Ford Chip Ganassi shirts line the fences. Japanese tour groups wander the grounds in yellow Corvette shirts.

My friend Josh Welton, a tradesman welder from Detroit, is here as a tourist. He meets me at the Ford chicane.

"I'm actually excited for tonight. For it to be 2:00 in the morning. For no one to be here."

6:00 P.M. I get lost in the track's fan village. Among thousands of people:

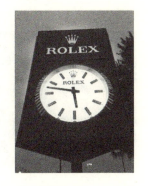

- A Jumbotron showing the race broadcast, no sound. A large crowd sits in front, utterly silent.

- A visibly drunk Frenchman actually yelling the words, "*Vive la France!*"

- A middle-aged Englishman whose shirt reads, in capital letters, "WILL I ALWAYS RIDE FAST MOTORCYCLES?" A few inches below that, "DOES A SPIDER CRAB HAVE A WATERTIGHT ARSE?" (Not being an expert in crab anatomy, I can only assume the answer is "yes," or perhaps "maybe, but he'll reconsider when he has children.")

7:10 P.M. Private jets climb out from the nearby airport, banking over the stands. Because of course you would go home from Le Mans for the evening if you had a jet—Paris, London, wherever.

The main straight is surprisingly narrow. It sits at the bottom of a man-made canyon, the pit garages on one side and steep grandstands on the other. I try but can't make my eyes reconcile history with that view: Porsche's 917 and 956, Ford's GT40, longtail McLaren F1s, the magnesium-bodied Mercedes that catapulted into the crowd and killed 83 spectators in 1955.

Almost on cue, a Ford GT goes snarling past. F-O-R-D on the windshield, that thin 1960s font. The white in its livery is gray with dirt.

Edsel Ford II is here with his sons. A recent picture of him in the garages, looking pensive, went out on the wire earlier, from Ford. Edsel last visited Le Mans in 1966, with his father, Henry II. The first year that Ford won, after spending half the money in Detroit to do it.

It's hard to look at that picture, or a modern GT, without feeling simultaneously giddy and a little manipulated. So you focus on the giddy, because you're not nuts, and sometimes manipulation is okay, and sweet 40-inch-high Christ, *those are Ford GTs at Le Mans.*

8:30 P.M. The paddock is a maze of trucks and quick-fab buildings, each team hiding its logistics and spare-parts operations behind a liveried, two-story partition. Walking past the Risi Ferrari installment, I hear Radio Le Mans over the PA: ". . . one of the best Le Mans 24s in recent memory."

Not unbelievable. The race appears astonishingly even, or at least managed into evenness by the ACO. The French equalize lap speeds through artificial, in-season regulation of curb weights and engine output, according to a team's success.

The process, called Balance of Performance, is widely loathed but brutally effective. Still, great racing is great racing, so it's hard to gripe. Lap times of the Audi, Porsche, and Toyota prototypes are separated by tenths. The slower GT cars fight and screw with each other constantly, all while being passed by prototypes. It is something like what would happen if the World Cup were played on only one field, and all of its games were played at once, and all the fans sat there and watched until everything was over.

Dan Gurney once told me that, 50 years ago, you either conserved a Le Mans car by driving under its limits, or you broke before the end. Gurney won overall in 1967, co-driving a GT40, then one of the most unburstable cars ever built. Great leaps in durability mean the race is now essentially 24 hours of qualifying—every lap a blitz.

9:00 P.M. In the Porsche hospitality center, I watch live in-car video from the marque's prototypes on two large TVs. Every minute or so, a 919 will get caught in the setting sun, washing out the camera. You see bugs and oil on the windshield, a blaze of opacity, and you know that the sunset lasts for hours here, and you also know that the drivers must drive into the sun without slowing even when they cannot see a thing. On a two-lane road, running so fast the TV helicopters can't keep up.

Every hour, a camera shows a pro somehow avoiding an amateur driver who is doing something stupid, usually trying to get out of the way. It always looks like magic. And is just another illustration of how the race is a giant dice roll.

The old line holds that you don't win Le Mans, the track lets you win. You can't spend your way to the podium here because you can't outspend chance. There's just too much to go wrong, for too long.

9:45 P.M. As if to emphasize the point, Scottish driver and Le Mans vet Marino Franchitti plows the No. 67 Ford GT into a wall at the end of the tree-lined, four-mile Mulsanne straight. It's hard to watch—people call the Fords steamrollers, despite the fact that they're a new and unproven car run by a new, unproven team. Steamrollers aren't supposed to hump the pea gravel.

The Mulsanne has two safety chicanes, installed for the 1990 race. For the 67 years prior, the straight, normally a narrow highway leading to the town of Mulsanne, was the ballsiest road-racing asphalt on earth. Cars ran a sustained 200 mph there in the 1960s and topped 250 in the 1980s. Last year, Mark Webber hit 211.4 mph in a Porsche 919. Which could be seen as slow.

If you're insane.

10:05 P.M. I head to the track's media center to do some research. A chair, out of the elements. Relaxing.

10:06 P.M. An Italian journalist from the newspaper *La Gazzetta dello Sport* approaches the next desk on the right. He gestures indignantly and spits rapid-fire Italian, which I do not speak. After a few moments of confusion, his message becomes clear: I have apparently stolen his chair.

I did not steal his chair. I stay put, firm but polite, on principle. More gestures. He shrugs every time I say something in English—doesn't speak the language. He moves a cup of water onto my desk dramatically—up, over, down. This is supposed to tell me something.

Tired, I relent. Receiving the chair, he gives a little bow and returns to his laptop. A few moments later, after sourcing another chair, I sit down. I glance at his screen, at the story he is writing.

It is in English.

11:00 P.M. There is something so immensely professional about racing at night. No headlights can keep up with 200 mph; no spotter can erase the speed differential between a purpose-built prototype and a Porsche 911; no group of people is predictable when they've been up for most of a day. None of it seems natural. Which, paradoxically, is why Le Mans feels normal at night, its own little world.

The cars become neon: fluffy exhaust flames. Brake rotors glowing orange. Traces on your eyelids when you blink.

11:15 P.M. Exhaustion has begun changing my brain. A kind of dyslexia sets in—the sign across the Ford chicane reads AUTOMOBILE CLUB D'LOUDEST. The cars are somehow louder and faster in the dark. Even the people seem lit and shiny. There is an entire team of German drinkers wearing plastic Viking helmets. They yell unintelligibly and ride around the infield on small, noisy go-karts. Fifteen feet away, a few Frenchmen stand quietly at a trailer, selling crepes.

World War II suddenly makes a lot more sense.

11:30 P.M. Everyone and their brother is in the garages. Audi, Porsche, Aston. Cars are coming apart, breakage or crash damage. Another journalist calls the pits a "simultaneous f***fest." I briefly try to picture a nonconcurrent f***fest. The pits are organized panic—zip-tied bodywork, running, mechanics working against the clock and occasionally glaring at TV cameras when they get too close.

In the Radio Le Mans trackside broadcast booth with host John Hindaugh, right, and R&T correspondent Marshall Pruett.

Sunday, 1:00 A.M. The stands are nearly empty. Toyota and Porsche are engaged in a titanic battle for the lead, racing as if it were noon—sliding around, air over curbs, nose-to-tail at 200 mph.

The atmosphere improves with context, knowledge of the stories at play. But even without, the place carries a rare air. A circus crossed with a royal wedding and the Olympics. The feeling of being on some kind of forced exhausting holiday with a quarter-million of your closest friends.

It's amazing that we haven't ruined it. Not through ill intent, but because humans are so rarely able to see when our progress has screwed something up. Well-meaning changes that diminish the spectacle. Chicanes in the Mulsanne. Adding slow corners near the Dunlop bridge, where it used to take balls and trust to go fast.

And yet the glory persists. Maybe the well is just too deep to drain.

2:00 A.M. Le Mans has a midway with carnival games and a Ferris wheel. You can see at least 25 percent of the track from atop the wheel. I go up in the thing because it's there, and because I'm falling asleep on my feet and want to stare at race cars on the ground. It turns out I have a significant and previously undiscovered fear of heights.

4:15 A.M. I meet up with Matt Tierney, *R&T*'s art director. We drive his rental car to the Mulsanne, which takes about 15 minutes, and traipse through the woods. This process may or may not include mild trespassing, jumping a small creek, and armed police. Then, boom: Armco at the edge of a dark office park. A flash of yellow whomps down a nearby road.  Huge, booming noise. No one in sight save a few race marshals in a cherry picker.

My brain does a quick kind of early-morning math: Race car plus yellow plus boom plus Le Mans: Pratt & Miller Corvette. The Chevy's headlights form a flickering tunnel in the trees. I walk through tall grass to the fence. One of the Audi prototypes whistles by, the Vette still audible in the distance.

I think two things: *This is impossible* and *I want to stay here forever.*

4:30 A.M. Someone following my Twitter account asks which car outshouts the rest. I find the words in my notes: "Corvettes are still the chicken dinner."

5:04 A.M. For the record: The Chevrolets are rolling, crackling weather fronts. The Astons are nasally Corvettes, more tea. The Fords are tenors, snarly and ugly under closed throttle. The hybrid P1 cars sound like grumbling. The 911s echo off the grandstands in this funky, atmospheric whoop, like the forest speeders in *Return of the Jedi*.

5:09 A.M. Still dark out, but a glow builds on the horizon. I visit a crepe trailer. You get a choice between plain, Nutella, fruit jam, and Grand Marnier.

The Grand Marnier is a Le Mans cliché, but I order it anyway: boozy suede breakfast candy. The Nutella one tastes like Nutella, which is to say that, if you are human, you want to smear it on your face and fall over happy and dead.

To borrow a line from the film Ghostbusters II, *once, I turned into a dog, and this nice lady helped me.*

5:30 A.M. People trickle back into the circuit. The sidewalks grow crowded again. Colors go pastel in the sunrise. For 15 minutes, the landscape is a Monet.

7:21 A.M. The Toyota mechanics do group calisthenics in their garage —metronomic, in sync, fully suited in safety gear. They look ported in from a 1960s B-movie about robot space invaders and the physically gifted women who love them. The dawn produces a second wind. I could go forever.

7:22 A.M. Legs weak. Race doesn't end for seven and a half hours. Body is shutting down.

7:30 A.M. Find the espresso machine in the media center. Drink two and pour a third into a small bag of Haribo gummy candy. (The media center hands out bags of Haribo.) Eat the bag.

7:31 A.M. Arms are made of cotton. I type notes on my laptop. After five minutes of staring at the keyboard, I realize my fingers are indexed one key off—S instead of A, semicolon instead of L.

7:45 A.M. In the media center, a stern-looking woman in a Porsche Motorsport jacket walks around distributing press releases. They're filled with finely detailed updates of race happenings: One of the factory 911 RSRs got a new steering assembly in five minutes, etc. No other team makes a rep go desk-by-desk to journalists, but then, no other team has won here 17 times. I'm reminded how Porsche has this odd ability to be both underdog and indomitable titan.

Also, seriously: Five minutes to change a power-steering system? What did they do, jack up the horn button and drive a new car underneath?

9:21 A.M. I sit down on a curb. My eyeballs register the lack of forward motion and give up. They detach from my optic nerves and walk across the room.

1:00 P.M. The back half of the field has been a Yakety Sax crashfest since morning. Cars in the gravel. Cars in other cars. Cars spinning off behind cars that are themselves spinning off. Men out of their damn minds on fatigue toxins. I would be homicidal on a bicycle right now, and they're being told to push.

In America, at this exact moment, Fox Sports—the country's only Le Mans TV broadcast—switches to golf.

1:48 P.M. Toyota leads LMP1 with Porsche 32 seconds back. Ford is ahead of Ferrari by about a minute, but that gap seems highly fluid. Failure details are trickling out of the garages: Over the last 22 hours, the Audi pit has dealt with failing brake rotors, a broken turbocharger, a door falling off a prototype. One of the 919s lost a water pump around midnight. Toyota has seen contact damage but little else.

Toyota's prototype is new this year; the Porsches and Audis are older. Porsche won overall in 2015. Audi has won overall 13 of the past 16 years.

After 22 hours, no one will put money on the finish. I run into Aaron from *Car and Driver*: "It's like that guy in *The Matrix*," he says. "I know this is all fake, but it tastes great and I love it."

2:00 P.M. Porsche gives a few journalists a quick garage tour. They brought 30 engineers—three oh!—to the race. The two prototype garages are each only slightly larger than a family sedan. Small hand tools are magnetized to overhead scaffolding. When a car comes down pit road, the sound echoes into your pockets.

We visit Porsche's 919 composites tent, across the paddock. Three sets of bodywork, flight cases everywhere, a pile of skid plates. A spare chassis, four engines, four front gearboxes (919s are all-wheel drive), four rear gearboxes, 60 wheels.

Porsche and Audi are part of the same company. The first year that the two battled each other at Le Mans, the combined effort was said to cost $500 million.

Half a billion dollars so a single corporation could take a pair of armies to France and fight itself. All funneled through a space half the size of a McDonald's.

3:00 P.M. It is impossible to avoid the ending of the race. Ford wins the GTE Pro class, but not without drama: Their pace was much quicker than in practice, and everyone whines that the GTs sandbagged, then were "allowed" to be too fast. By contrast, the factory 911s, in the same class, were uncompetitively, almost comically slow, likely due to the Balance of Performance. (Porsche motorsport head Frank-Steffen Walliser broke into tears at the pre-race press conference. Months of stress and frustration, a guy pushed to the bounds of tolerance.)

A lone Toyota leads LMP1—and overall—in the closing hour, having spent most of the night drawing blood to stay ahead of the second-place 919. In the penultimate lap, the Toyota loses a turbocharger connection. The Japanese car goes into limp mode on the back half of the course, the Porsche close enough to smell blood.

The lead Porsche after the race, nearly invisible in the scrum.

The Toyota dies in front of the start/finish stands, one lap to go. The air pressure seems to change, as if a quarter-million people had instantly deflated their lungs.

Smithology

The Toyota's driver, Kaz Nakajima, sits in the car, powerless. (Radio Le Mans announcer John Hindhaugh: "Oh no . . . It couldn't have happened on the Mulsanne, where he could have cried his little head off by himself.") His team members are either draped on the wall or in the garage, ashen.

Porsche is gifted a win. The marque's 18th, and a last-minute surprise. Because their cars kept going, because they were in the right place at the right time, because they fought like dogs for 24 hours. The team had boxes of T-shirts reading "Finally 18!" but those boxes were put away when Toyota appeared to have the race locked. The pits erupt.

After the race, a few members of the Toyota team quietly enter Porsche hospitality. Eyes low.

The Germans notice. There is a standing ovation.

I woke up the next day, in a hotel near the Paris airport, and stood in the shower for 45 minutes. I had been walking or standing for nearly 37 hours. I let the soap run into my eyes because there seemed to be dirt there.

Real life seemed a slower, cleaner place than Le Mans. A good, long race that cannot be predicted or shaped to fit a narrative or even fully understood by the people who love it. And who love the irresponsible, wasteful, happy jazz of it all. Standing in the Mulsanne grass in the middle of the night, watching men try to prove something at 180 mph. When the whole world comes down to a moment that couldn't be anywhere else, just dark and noise and staggering light, between quiet office parks and stands of trees.

Coventry Wake

A 400-mile journey from disbelief with the only Jaguar we all remember.

> *A happy little awakening with one of America's most celebrated roads and one of the most beautiful vehicles in creation. Conventional wisdom can be dangerous when you believe it, even more dangerous when you don't.*

HAGERTY DRIVER'S CLUB, JULY 2021

A car, almost a myth. Launched in 1961. Body like liquid expletive. Six cylinders, a four-speed manual, inboard rear discs. Independent rear suspension at a time when most Ferraris still snorted around with a solid axle.

The Jaguar E-type was known for hitting a cool 150 mph in a period when most family sedans would clear 100 mph only if shot into space. The E-type was built much like the D-type, a 1950s race car that had taken Jaguar to three overall wins at the 24 Hours of Le Mans. Books said a drive would weaken your knees.

I read those books as a kid. Before I thought they were all hooey.

Opinions are always dangerous when rooted in reality. I grew up around a restoration shop. After college, I worked on European cars for a living, then sold Jaguar parts at a dealer in Chicago. By the age of 25, I had watched multiple men restore E-types from bits. In school one summer, I helped a tech replace a clutch in an E-type roadster, one of the late V-12 models, a two-day job iced with profanity. At the dealer, I burned lunch hours poring through factory manuals and fiche, marveling at ship-in-a-bottle subassemblies; here was a machine of byzantine service notes, sustained only by frequent care and feeding. The rear suspension looked like a medieval torture device.

Logic said effort had to equal return. Why else would anyone put up with it?

Then, in my 20s, I met the hero. A friend bought an early 4.2-liter roadster. I climbed behind the wheel and we tore off down some tree-lined road. Ten minutes later, I sat at a stop sign for a second and quietly wondered if I was having a stroke.

The owner elbowed me in the ribs. "You love it, right?"

I lied and changed the subject.

Jobs at car magazines followed, as did other cars. There was the 100-point Series I coupe that seemed glass-fragile and slow as tectonic plate; the survivor 2+2 that stopped and turned like a 1970s Lincoln; the hot-rodded 4.2 roadster with some British tuner's "fast comfort" suspension, neither fast nor comfy.

These were all quality cars, well-kept and heartbreakingly pretty. The best offered about as much of the fabled glory as an old refrigerator. Later, I track-tested a D-type for work, yelling four-letter words at 100 mph, floored that the books could be so right with one piece of the rock and so wrong with another.

D-types are seven-figure investments. Wouldn't it be great, I thought, if you could have that vibe without spending millions?

Lord, I was a doofus.

Not all icons earn celebration in old age. Drive one of these things, people talk to you at stops. Generally along one of two themes:

ONE: *Pretty car. What is it?*

TWO: *Oof wow the legend in the flesh, how fast have you had it, my mother's sister's dog once dated a guy whose boyfriend ripped one from Alaska to Texas in a single day England forever amen.*

One week last summer, I met those conversations again. In Tennessee, at our trip's beginning; in Virginia, at its end; and everywhere in between. People moth-flamed to our car at stops and overlooks, drawn wordlessly, staring for a second before offering a belated hello, as if they had briefly forgotten how to talk.

Most of those meetings took place on or near a 469-mile scenic parkway commissioned by the American government. They happened while standing next to a 1964 Jaguar E-type Series I coupe, black, 3.8 liters, an aged but well-kept restoration. When I planned this drive, the parallel made me happy: The E-type is a design icon, and the Blue Ridge Parkway was famously constructed as a public-works project under Franklin Roosevelt's New Deal. One of these landmarks is a travel tool of staggering beauty and the other is a road bridging North Carolina and Virginia via more than 200 overlooks and countless mountains. Beauty underpins the lore of each.

Imagine the Jaguar factory in Coventry in 1961; picture its squat, nondescript buildings. At 7:00 on a winter evening, a freshly rebuilt E-type coupe left, bound for Switzerland. The man at the wheel, a former racing driver and contemporary Jaguar PR man named Bob Berry, aimed for Dover, nearly 200 miles away, and the midnight ferry across the English Channel. Landing in a dark, rainy France in an age before blanket speed limits, he tore south. He became disoriented by fog in Reims, then increased his pace, making up for lost time—triple digits between corners, as fast as the car would go. At 11:40 the next morning, he pulled into the service drive of Geneva's small Jaguar dealer.

Attendants began cleaning the car before he had even climbed out. Minutes later, Berry was back on the road, headed to a nearby park, where Jaguar's founder, Sir William Lyons, stood waiting to make an announcement. Some 200 journalists were gathered. "Good God, Berry," Lyons said. "I thought you weren't going to get here."

The car was revealed. The crowd gasped.

The numbers have long carried outsize weight. In the weeks before that trip, Berry's mount hit 150 mph during testing. If you wanted a 150-mph road car in 1961 England, you could buy something like a Ferrari 250 GT—nearly £6000—or the £4700 Mercedes-Benz 300 SL. The Jaguar cost £2100 and made speed like the Ferrari but was less fussy in traffic. The Mercedes was virtually faultless, but the bank draft for one 300 SL would buy two E-types and leave money in your pocket.

On top of this, the Jaguar looked like an E-type: half airplane and half submarine, plus a healthy dose of lady bathing suit.

We left my house in Knoxville in early morning. The air was sticky and hot and the hills were fuming—trees shrouded by narrow towers of fog, the Smoky Mountains living up to the name. The Blue Ridge Parkway starts around 80 miles southeast of Knox, past a national park and thousands of acres of back roads. Sun bent through the fog, underlighting the forest.

I had figured the trip for a dawdle. The Parkway is mostly fourth-gear corners, sweeping and manicured, the posted limit never topping 45 mph. My friend Mark Hoyer drove the first stint, because the car was his. Mark is a volunteer firefighter from Southern California and the editor-in-chief of *Cycle World*. He is the sort of wry 50-year-old who says "rad" often and wears Adidas Sambas with shorts; he occasionally tours California on his 1954 Velocette MSS motorcycle; he once described a computer-controlled suspension as "Super Glidetron 7000."

Mark is also a walking encyclopedia on matters E-type. On the road, I would ask him something simple, like how much choke one might offer an XK six-cylinder on cold start, and 45 minutes later, he would be wrapping up a detailed history of the Skinner's Union carburetor, having briefly digressed into the recitation of a lightly profane rhyming couplet referencing how certain British cars look remarkably like a specific anatomical component of the human sexual experience.

You own a finicky old Jaguar with the wrong attitude, Mark once told me, you come dangerously close to having a bad time. An hour in, after a long rip over coiled highway, we reached the Parkway gate. As the sun rose over the mountains, the land went purple, this graduated stair-step of tone. At a photo stop, Mark offered me the wheel, and I took it.

The cockpit was tasteful and quiet, a drawing room of stretched animal, everything organic. Even the headliner was wool. The car seemed to move in long strides, the sort of sharp but yielding highway comfort that once sold people on European cars, before those cars all grew too stiff. Machines long of footwell and gearing, happiest in big corners. Familiar stuff.

The dampers, though. And the cohesive whole, how the car felt in time with itself. Something was different.

I brushed it off. *An E-type, right? They're all the same.*

The engine hummed the quiet and busy little thrum of a machine with connecting rods long as your forearm. Torque was everywhere, no lugging, just utterly flexible pull and a sense of telegraphing down to a distant boiler room when you wanted more. When you cracked the throttle, the car simply gathered itself and waterfalled thrust, no waiting. We climbed farther into the hills.

The E-type was created by multiple people, but its shape sprang almost entirely from the mind of Malcolm Sayer. Jaguar's chief engineer in that period, Bill Heynes, once called Sayer "the most charming man you could ever meet."

Sayer was also, as the saying goes, south of normal. He left university in 1938 with a degree in automotive engineering, then spent the war working on airplanes for Bristol. As an adult, he made furniture for his children from trash. He also drew odd cartoons, played the piano, built artificial plants, wrote silly poems, taught himself languages in days. He was married twice, having met his second wife atop a double-decker bus while still married to his first. One year after that second wedding, he moved his family to Baghdad to work for a university, then disappeared for six months.

When Sayer joined Jaguar in 1950, his first project was the body of Jaguar's next Le Mans project, the C-type. The following year, that car won the French classic overall. The D-type that followed was an aerodynamic masterwork and visual ripsnort hailed by factory testers as one-hand stable at 190 mph. In an era when most designers focused on minimizing drag, in service of pure straight-line speed, the man cared most about aerodynamic lift and crosswind stability, because those qualities impacted how a car felt.

You read all that and think, Great, okay, makes sense: This bright and complex spark simply sketched up one of humanity's slinkier thunderclaps through testicle and testament. Nope. The man styled cars through a sort of analog spreadsheet, a huge grid of calculated figures he called "body coordinates." He would start with a rough drawing at full scale—the C-type was laid out on a floor in chalk—then spend months on formulas and logarithms.

The results helped shape a body buck, and boom, a Le Mans winner or a production prototype to curl your toes.

I always liked the bit about trash furniture.

North Carolina was a land of gifts. The first was a view to the horizon, the road diving gracefully into a small and tree-lined valley, no traffic. So I chose to hold that toothpick-rimmed wooden wheel with fingertips and flex my foot until that long throttle met its stop.

On a curvy, lumpy piece of pavement, from around 1400 rpm in second gear, the engine snarled up to six grand. The sound began as a rushy and multifaceted kind of grumble, then mutated into a thick, back-throat snort, as if the muffler were packed with blankets. At the bottom of the valley, as the road bent softly to the right, the car hit a large midcorner bump at full compression and did exactly nothing. No upset, just some impossibly velvet damping, and then we tore up another hill.

I looked down; somewhere in the whole exercise, I had grabbed third without thinking. We were gliding along in a deeply illegal form of extended-legs prowl. The wheel wiggled lightly in my hands.

"Mark?" I said, cautiously.

"Yeah?"

"This car is not like . . . the others? You know?"

"Yeah?" He watched the trees for a moment. "Well, cool."

He told me about the rear shocks later. New-old-stock Girlings, older than me, four at the rear axle, as an E-type had from the factory. They were part of the equation but not the whole—and more important, Mark quietly admitted, not cheap, perhaps more than most sane folks would pay for mummified car parts.

This was, as I learned, indicative of Mark's obsessively chill approach to maintenance—things as they were, plus long thought on the details. His car had been restored years prior by a California man named Ray, at a shop called "Dr. Jaguar." Mark had handled the 30,000 miles since, and much of the service required in that period, himself. There was apparently much learning and tweaking and question-asking of metal-cat physicians.

"You know," he said, somewhere in upper North Carolina, "you develop a support network, owning one of these. People who know how the cars are supposed to be, because you can't just screw them together and expect them to automatically feel right.

"Hell, some of them didn't drive right from the factory, subframes cross-threaded and tweaked, that sort of thing. There are good ones and bad ones, and it has nothing to do with money."

"No money," I said. "Check."

"My support network is Ray. I was talking to him when I bought my Jaguar Mark II"—picture a four-door, live-axle E-type—"saying, you know, it's nice, the car has this adjustable steering column. And he was like, 'Well.'

"It turns out there's this thin piece of cardboard in there, like a greeting card, the insulator between hot and ground. And so you move the column a bunch, it wears through, and one day, you have smoke coming out of your steering column and don't know why."

I was reminded of the older man, in his 70s, who came into my Jaguar dealer almost 20 years ago. His XJ sedan was in the shop for something nearly every month. Once, a technician and I politely asked him: Why not find another car? Or even a Jag that didn't need work every four weeks?

"Well," he said. "I love this one. You've been in love, right?"

A wink. Then he wandered off to wait in the customer lounge while his dashboard was reassembled for the third time that year.

Clouds drifted across the road. It began to rain, fitfully, and then the Parkway rose above the weather, over valleys carpeted with clouds, past spotty patches of wildflowers.

"I did 130 mph in this car once," Mark said, unprompted, chuckling. "There was more. But I lost . . . interest."

As a kid, I spent a long time thinking that great inventions are only ever created or appreciated by people with a sense of humor. Turns out that isn't how the world works, except when it does.

The rain picked up. There was no traffic, so we did not slow. I looked in the mirror and saw the mountains forming a bowl behind us, maybe 50 miles wide.

They did airflow tests with tufts of wool. Little four-inch bits of sheep taped onto the bodywork. Sayer would ride in a car alongside, watching the wool move. He also rented a wind tunnel, mostly at night, when nearby villages were asleep and the tunnel could draw enough electricity off the grid to run at max pressure. But he preferred the road for research.

Shortly before Geneva, Jaguar invited English magazines *The Autocar* and *The Motor* out to drive a prototype E-type at 150 mph. Top-speed testing had begun months before, on a proving ground, then shifted to public highways.

Much of this work was handled by Jaguar's chief test driver of the time, Norman Dewis. "Very often we would be doing 150," he once said, "and other [test] cars were there as well . . . high speeds, Aston Martin and other firms."

Years later, in England, Dewis told me that he would drive one-handed at 150 and wave at other factory drivers. He found this funny, but then, when we spoke, he was holding a glass of gin.

Smithology

"If [drag] were the only problem," Sayer once said, "it would be very easy. But . . . stable . . . this is much more difficult."

The E-type is one of just nine cars to have entered the permanent collection at New York's Museum of Modern Art. Under "artists," the exhibition lists three men: Sir William Lyons, Malcolm Sayer, and William M. Heynes.

The road continued. Hours, days, that magnificent scenery becoming almost rote until we reached a part of Virginia lower and less spectacular. Honeysuckle dotted the shoulder for miles. Traffic remained oddly absent.

Sayer laid out the roadster, but the E-type coupe—arguably a more resolved shape—was someone else. A Jaguar stylist named Bob Blake tacked 3/16-inch steel rods onto a roadster one day, playing with form. Then Lyons walked in.

"He put his hand to his mouth," Blake said, "the way he did . . . just walked 'round and 'round . . . said to me, 'Did you do this, Blake?'"

Yes, Blake told him.

"He said, 'It's good. We'll make that.'"

In person, the shape resembles frozen ballet. Possibly a self-fulfilling perception, because the car feels balletic at speed, its reactions suggesting measured choice. Like anything with soft springs and thin tires, an E-type wants slow hands; you can almost feel the wheels compress as the car ramps into load. The steering is similar at 25 mph and 100, never too talkative, just a subtle nudge for attention. And little wiggles of kickback on bumps, so you know.

Twenty-five-hundred rpm in fourth was 65 mph.

Warmed, the engine started on half a crank every time.

We reached the end of the road. Not the real end, but a detour. A construction zone had closed the road maybe 100 miles early. We took the highway north, attempted to re-enter near Charlottesville and finish the road backward. Only the entrance there was socked through with fog, visibility down to a few feet. So we headed home.

355

The Parkway by then felt like anachronism, this fluid thing apart from the world, where driving works as it does in your dreams. Which was odd, because the car itself had somehow mutated, when I wasn't looking, into a machine entirely free of excuses and every bit the lore, both separate from normal life and wholly capable of dropping into modern traffic without complaint.

On a nearby interstate, I briefly allowed the Jaguar to cruise natural. In the meat of the tach in fourth gear, there was so little wind noise, you could hear the window cranks turn. I became lightly aware of a quietly blooming desire to never drive anything else.

The last E-type was built in 1975. Few that remain see regular sunshine or public eyes, and fewer still spend their days crossing France at a buck-forty. Which means that our faith in the legend has to do most of the legwork of keeping the thing alive.

A tall order. You love an object from afar for long enough, the gap between story and reality can sting. Or maybe, after countless tries, you get lucky. The stars align, a familiar tale gets retold in a familiar place, and you remember that faith often goes a long way. As does the realization that you were once too young, and possessed of too many facts, to believe in something so happy and perfect as the truth.

The Art of Bracing for the Rain
Beneath the clouds, learning to look up.

The Pacific Northwest wasn't always an easy place to live, but I liked it. It just took me a while to figure that out.

HAGERTY, OCTOBER 2020

We lived in Seattle for five years, all of them happy. The plan was always to stay, and then, last year, skyrocketing living cost drove us out. Bemoaning a change like that can make you feel better for a while but is ultimately unproductive. Housing markets and their knock-on effects are generally unpredictable and about as tunable as the weather. One of those signs that some parts of life will simply remain out of reach, even if they seem already in hand.

So it goes, as Taylor Swift sang. Or maybe it was Billy Joel. Or Kurt Vonnegut, the genius humorist, except he didn't sing. He just ran a Saab dealership in West Barnstable, Massachusetts, in the late 1950s, then wrote fiction that dented how we see the ineffable ridiculousness of the human condition.

I was drawn to Vonnegut's work for the same reason I was drawn to Seattle—the notion that life is a series of trade-offs. That city being a place of mild weather and unspoiled nature, where the only trade-offs are high cost of living and a staggering amount of rain.

That last bit broke me like you break a horse. Not for the worse.

Stereotype says the Northwest sees buckets of precipitation. In truth, the region's annual volume of sky water is less than what falls on Nashville or Houston. The frequency is what gets you. In one winter of our five-year stint, the Seattle office of the National Weather Service reported something like three full days of sunshine between November and March. Most of those days held at least a little rain, usually a spitty drizzle that came and went.

When we moved to town in 2015, in the warmth of an unusually early spring, I had marveled at the sunlit tulips and firs. By October, the city had remembered itself, gray and depressing, and I almost lost my mind. Blue sky seemed to hide behind a blanket until the Fourth of July.

I never minded rain driving, in the same way that, as a kid, I had never minded my mother's gray, overcooked pot roast. Not the end of the world, but not worth seeking out, either. In Seattle, I'd find myself caught on some back road in a sudden storm and just think, Oh, okay, fine, fun over. Then resigned waiting for the next, better thing.

The shift in my thinking began on Sunday afternoons. I had started taking long drives born of boredom, of missing the road and waiting for nicer days. I'd head east from the city and Puget Sound, climbing through the Cascades, looking for sun. A zigzag up to foggy elevation followed by a long coasting back down, a loop of one or two hundred miles, not home until well after dark.

It was just one Sunday, at first. Then two, and three, and more. The skies varied from light clouds and that same spitting rain to true mountain weather, the sideways toad-drowners you only get up high. After a bit—several weekends or a few months, I don't remember—the trips became less a hunt for sun than a search for something else.

You can probably see where this is going. I was just thick enough that the reason wasn't immediately obvious.

The lessons have filled books: the stuff that wet pavement forces you to remember, how smoothness and slow hands can take advantage of available grip, loading the nose and rear tires gently. How a slick surface forces you to think more about what you're doing, lean less on muscle memory. Modern tires will take heaps of lateral load in the wet, but you have to build to that point; surprise the carcass, the rubber will lose traction and break loose well below its actual limit.

So much learning. Especially given my occupation, a job that has you driving stacks of new cars every year, meeting different engineering philosophies and blueprints. If you're even halfway awake, you get object lessons in how tire compound and tread design matter, how that impact differs on standing water versus mere moisture-slicked pavement, how different types of asphalt feel when drenched and undrained. How a tire can slide progressively, smooth as greased velvet, or grip only in fitty snatches. You come to respect and love the rubber and cars that treat traction like a rheostat, to roll your eyes at the ones that slip loose suddenly, their talents harder to balance.

Not to mention good software. Years ago, when a vehicle's computers did little more than manage its engine, who would have thought that blind spots in code could as much as they do? That carmakers would eventually throw silicon at differentials and steering columns and vehicle stability but occasionally miss a few steps in the programming?

Those missed steps don't always kill the whole dance. My wife's 2019 Volkswagen GTI, for example, is a relatively fun and resolved little thing, with relatively nice steering feel. Its electrically assisted rack is thoroughly alright everywhere save wet pavement, over which the wheel becomes a dead fish. As it turns out, the mass and function of every modern electric power-steering system inherently serves to dampen feedback at the wheel, no matter how a system's components are laid out or engineered, a byproduct of the tech's design goals. Wheel feel with those systems hangs on which tire forces that a team of engineers have told a piece of software to allow through to your hands. As a wet road gives lower tire forces and more nuanced suspension response, a system calibrated mostly on dry pavement will rarely feel as dialed in the rain.

Information is always important when controlling a machine; the human brain runs on pattern recognition, the identification of predictable cause-and-effect. The steering problem is mirrored in electronic stability control, a government-mandated safety feature found on every new passenger vehicle, which uses digitally managed chassis hardware to keep a car on the road when a driver's inputs appear to be leading elsewhere. The hitch being that those systems aren't perfect, either, can often be tripped into incorrect intervention by blunt driver inputs.

Smoothness still matters, in other words. Hands and feet capable of gently ramping tires into load without an excess of feedback, slinging a car into a corner quickly but without abrupt spikes in force. Lose those qualities, you're less driver, more point-and-shoot monkey.

So many voices in the rain. Seattle tilted my ear. People who like driving but hate rain say they miss the aggression of dry inputs and forces. In that first winter in Washington, that idea began to seem like missing a sandwich when all you have is a slice of pizza. What is pizza, if not also a hell of a lunch?

You carry bits of your past everywhere you go, as Vonnegut said. And he really did run a Saab dealer in his, in an era when the brand's cars were seen by many as quirky torture for quirk's sake. There's a whiff of that occupation in his writing, this acceptance that sustainable existence often means pulling what positives you can from the unexpected or absurd. Alongside the suggestion that most of life is unavoidably unexpected or absurd.

One of my favorite Vonnegut lines lives in his novel *Slaughterhouse-Five*. The main character, Billy Pilgrim, is discussing his fate with an individual gifted a wider perspective on the notion:

> *"That is a very Earthling question to ask, Mr. Pilgrim. Why you? Why us, for that matter? Why anything? Because this moment simply is. Have you ever seen bugs trapped in amber?"*
>
> *"Yes."*
>
> *Billy, in fact, had a paperweight in his office which was a blob of polished amber with three ladybugs embedded in it.*
>
> *"Well, here we are, Mr. Pilgrim, trapped in the amber of this moment. There is no why."*

The amber of the moment. What a piece of language.

Smithology

You can read that section a few ways. I always saw it as hint at optimism, the idea that up is as natural as down. Bad days exist to balance the good. You either revel in both or miss the point.

I know a handful of ways to do the former. And if that particular angle on the world is the one free and lasting thing gifted to me by that wet and lovely old city on the coast, well, so be it.

We weren't able to keep a house there, but in the long run, that doesn't matter. We moved from one amber moment to the next, and our spirits, like the rooftops of Seattle, were no more dampened than the national average, no matter how it felt at the time.

Greens of Summer
In the Moment with a life, a wife, and a film.

Another In the Moment—*the Hagerty column format I invented as an excuse to geek over historic images. This one is different, however. An experiment in sharing the personal.*

For reasons that will become apparent, this story was built around my own photos, a few of which are reprinted here. Those shots were taken more than a decade ago, many on Kodak's Kodachrome 64 color slide film, a hallmark of 20th-century photography.

The images here had to be printed in black and white, but they work better in color, as you'd expect. As with the Stirling Moss In the Moment *on page 49, the original story can still be viewed, as-run and with color intact, on Hagerty's website.*

The photo of Adrienne at Utah's Bonneville Salt Flats was taken on the way to our wedding in 2009. We drove from San Francisco to Chicago in my 1990 BMW M3, a car I later sold and still miss. Note the look on Adrienne's face: When I hit the shutter, we had been fighting about some trivial thing I can't recall. One of those instances where something small and unimportant can seem so large and weighty when fresh and new.

Hagerty, November 2022

Morning, everyone! We're going to change things up this week. Unlike previous installments of *In the Moment*, this story's main image didn't come from the Getty Images wire archive. It has never been published.

This photo is quite personal, so this edition of *ITM* will be a little different. I'm going to share a story from my life. It will begin with cars but not stay there.

Let's get started.

This is a scan of a 35-millimeter frame of slide film. It was taken with a 1970s Canon Canonet QL17 rangefinder.

The camera and photographer exposed this image in Northern California, near the city of Monterey, in a natural bowl in the mountains, in the pits of a track then known as Mazda Raceway Laguna Seca.

The image depicts a moment on the afternoon of Saturday, October 18, 2008. It shows a pit stop by the Audi factory team during an American Le Mans Series (ALMS) professional road race. The car is one of just two Audi R10 TDIs—diesel Le Mans prototypes—campaigned in that race. This R10 finished first overall, but there was contact.

The team is doing a quick repair on the engine cover. A 29-year-old German driver named Lucas Luhr sits in the cockpit, waiting. His face is obscured by a mirror. His helmet livery contains multiple small Ls.

Those carbon panels are dirty. See the scrapes on the number board and Michelin logo, the fraying vinyl wrap?

I happen to know a bit about this photographer. I know he wasn't happy with this image. It's a compromise, exposed for shadow and sun and spot on for neither. I also know that, on the day of this photo, the shooter had a tri-tip sandwich for lunch.

Spoiler: The shooter was me.

This is Kodachrome. The word from that 1970s Paul Simon song! The most famous film in history. Again, I took this in October of 2008. I was living in Michigan but visiting Monterey for work. The slide was, for various reasons, not developed or scanned until 2010. At which point I lived in Northern California.

Those details may seem irrelevant. At the core, however, racing resembles photography: a series of decisions compassed by time and your own previous choices.

I began writing about this image as if it were any other *In the Moment*. Then I realized it was different.

Let's back up.

The author, age 27, Ann Arbor, Michigan, 2008.
Canon QL17, Kodak Ektachrome 100.

Smithology

Fourteen years can feel longer than it is. Ten years and 48 months ago, in the fall of 2008, my girlfriend and I lived in Michigan, in the college town of Ann Arbor. We had met two years prior while working at a now-defunct car magazine called *Automobile*. Adrienne was a copy editor. On January 15, 2006, my first day, I popped by her office and introduced myself. She had a master's in journalism and a penchant for skirts. I was the newly minted assistant editor, 25 years old, a former Jaguar parts guy and one-time contender for the mantle of world's slowest professional mechanic. Ten months later, we were dating.

To this day, I have no idea what she saw in me. All I knew was that she was smart and funny and looked great in those skirts. Plus, she laughed at my stupid jokes when I swung by to drop off page proofs. (Her, years later: "They weren't that stupid. Mostly.")

A monitor at the Automobile *office, 2008. It was a serious place. Canon QL17, Kodak BW400CN.*

Salad days are always on a clock. In late '08, Adrienne and I loaded a moving truck and left Michigan for the Bay Area. Mostly for me, so I could take another job. I told friends it was simply time for a change, and it was. At the core of that was an older truth—I had wanted to live in Northern California since childhood.

Wanting can seem as a good a reason as any, when you're young.

In a way, the change was practical. Writing about and testing new cars for a living had me in California half the year anyway. The state is thick with carmakers and race shops , not to mention killer roads. If I was purposely minimizing anything, it was how the combined salaries of two journalists without family money would only go so far in the long run. But the long run seemed a long way off, as it always does.

Maybe I just assumed we'd find a way to climb. The copy editor had just landed a remote job with a firm in Chicago; she could live anywhere. My writing was beginning to get noticed and had won a few small awards. We had minimal expenses, few possessions, and zero debt. Optimistic, I went job hunting. After a few months, I accepted an editorial position at a small publishing house half an hour north of the Golden Gate Bridge.

That operation produced a few car magazines, including a fairly prominent Porsche title called *Excellence*. I was so dead set on the end result that I took a significant pay cut for all this, having caved immediately when the hiring manager balked at matching my old salary. (Not that stupid. Mostly.)

By Christmas, we were established. A tiny apartment, with an attached and 0.75-car garage, near the city of San Rafael. The copy editor had agreed to marry me. I was a few months from turning 28. I could ride my old Honda CB400F to work on deserted back roads every day of the year and hike in the redwoods on weekends. The burritos were incredible, the outdoors even better. On top of that, my work-life balance was noticeably improved, job travel basically absent.

I remember when I realized it was all falling apart.

The Canonet, that film camera from the Audi shot, had come from eBay a year before. It cost 60 bucks shipped but arrived cleaned and adjusted, a bargain. A photography blog I enjoyed called the QL17 "the poor man's Leica," which is nice but also like calling a Volkswagen Beetle a poor man's Porsche 911.

Still, people like Beetles. The QL17 was a 1970s rangefinder, this fun little clock of parallax. Rangefinders were obsolete 50 years ago, but the format's unique focus mechanism allows the camera to carry its lens uncommonly close to the surface of the film. For a number of reasons, that fact means a rangefinder lens can be designed relatively free of compromise; the good ones approach or nail mathematically perfect optics in a remarkably small amount of space. As for the shooting of film itself, I shot digital regularly for work but was drawn to chemical photography by the abundance of cheap, high-quality used hardware. (Then as now, everyone wanted digital.) I stayed for the dynamic range and creamy shadows, where silicon had yet to catch up.

You get to pick how you drop your blood pressure. If only we could choose what lifts it.

Stress is insidious. It's also quiet and patient. My selfish choices for a life in California meant, of course, that our money was tight. But we signed up for that, knew it going in. I had never met anyone as kind and thoughtful as Adrienne, and she was, to her credit, game for anything. The greater hurdle, one I feel uncomfortable sharing even now, is how the copy editor and I were perpetual strangers in a strange land.

The copy editor and the Bonneville Salt Flats, 2009.
Borrowed Leica M3, Summicron 50 f/2, Ilford HP5 400.

It sounds silly and small but was one piece of a puzzle. We had dated for two years before moving to California and moving in together. Neither of us had previously lived with a significant other. We were each dumb and territorial about our space, as kids can be. Our families were thousands of miles away. We had a couple of friends locally, fellow transplants from back east, but they tended to socialize in ways that took money we didn't have.

Californians don't like to admit it, but the state's social language is too often a closed door. We tried and repeatedly failed to meet new people, to break out of the box of that apartment. Seasons passed. The firmware of our lives shifted. I began to loathe my work and couldn't say why. Paradoxically, I also began to worry I wasn't doing enough there. I started staying late to get more done, though that choice only made other problems worse.

I worked in a small office with four supervisors as my only coworkers. My desk sat solo in a converted lobby, as if on display. Each morning, I would leave the house, where I felt alone, and go to work, where I felt even more alone.

Sister drinking, Kentucky, 2008. Borrowed Leica M3, Summicron 50 f/2, Ilford HP5 400.

Wanting to fix things but not knowing how, I aimed for the closest target. I churned more and more, gave longer hours at the job, felt the sanity behind that churn slipping away. When the fighting began at home, I tried for patience and failed. When the arguments grew more regular, I simply made sure the house had enough cheap tequila. And when those fights began arriving twice a day—before work, after work, sometimes a fight about a fight about a fight . . .

Well, I had to decide between giving myself a drinking problem and finding other ways to cope. So I shot more film.

Adrienne, San Francisco, Canon QL17, Ilford HP5 400, 2009.

Those fights were asinine and potent, powered by stress. I was an expert at picking molehills to die on. I insisted on wrestling every single issue down to the ground, as if things like *who drank all the juice* actually mattered. When our cumulative blood pressure reached a peak, fights seven days a week, we discussed axing the wedding.

We were still undecided when, in the early fall of 2009, I lost my job.

The reason why is immaterial. I felt better, years later, when my former manager told me he was sorry, that they had been wrong to let me go. Regardless, we were adrift. When I was a child, my parents had drilled into me the importance of looking difficult moments and your own missteps in the eye. Adrienne and I each took a deep breath, and then we went triage. We hadn't been in California long enough to save enough to move back east. If we axed our health insurance and every discretionary spend over five bucks, we figured, her meager salary would buy us a few months of rent and cheap noodles. A ticking clock while I looked for work.

So that was what we did. I hustled. In the background, a remarkable thing happened. The arguments stopped. We somehow remembered that we liked each other. Stability had gone out the window, but something else had come back in.

It seemed frivolous, but I kept taking pictures.

Oskar Justice Barnack Chaffee Dog, San Francisco. Borrowed Leica M3, Summicron 35 f/2, Ilford HP5 400, 2009.

We could afford it, barely, but that doesn't mean we could *afford* it. The months that followed were a heavy squeeze, even as I found work writing. But we did have those two local friends from back east. One was a former coworker at *Automobile*, Jason Cammisa, who now works for this company. (You may know him from his millions of views on YouTube; he stood up in my wedding.) The other friend, my pal Michael Chaffee, lived across the Golden Gate, in San Francisco.

Each helped whenever they could. Chaf in particular was like a brother to me. We had met, years before, through track days and old-BMW ownership, back when things like E30 M3s were cheap. Just as important, he had in his apartment a scanner and the chemicals to develop black-and-white film.

"There's Ilford HP5 in the freezer," he said, one day. "Yours if you want." Because he bought the film in bulk, he passed it to me at cost or free, three bucks a roll at most. After I'd run a few through the Canonet, I'd shove the canisters into my jacket pocket, fire up the Honda, and bop over the bridge to Chaf's apartment.

I was making something. It helped.

No photographer who has made their living with film will romanticize the hours lost to the medium's logistics. My friend Regis Lefebure has long shot motorsport professionally. "Sure, get romantic and artsy," he once told me. "You didn't have to fight the stuff on the road, praying you got the shot. Just take a RAW file, crank up the grain, you're close enough."

I'm not a professional photographer. Nor am I a pro mechanic or musician. And yet I take photographs, I rebuild cars, I play instruments. We all have reasons for doing what we do when we're not getting paid.

That second year in California, I made a choice. I consciously changed how I looked at relationships, my wants, and, most important, other people. I built a freelance career that eventually saw me working regularly for places like *Wired, The New York Times, Esquire,* and *Car and Driver.* Adrienne and I got married. We acknowledged that we couldn't afford to live and raise a family anywhere in California that made sense for my job, and we began to pave a road out.

That freelancing eventually led to a position as executive editor at *Road & Track*, where the team I helped lead was nominated for a National Magazine Award, a car-magazine first. That job led to this one, at Hagerty. I am now lucky enough to work with some of the smartest and kindest people I've known.

Which brings us to now. And Kodachrome.

That name fades in meaning with every passing year. It is a brand but also a patented chemical process and a delicate brickwork of saturated dye layers. It was first sold as a color slide film in 1936. Maybe you know that Paul Simon song?

Nice bright colors, he sings. Sometimes. The film's exposures always seemed to sparkle and glow consistently only in the hands of professionals, people who shot it every day, who knew intimately its strengths and limitations. What the film gave amateurs was in my eyes much better, a more subdued and old-world palette, almost cinematic. Plus the kind of crackly, projectable detail—3.5 centimeters of virtually unbelievable resolution—that was, with slide film, once the reason for the season.

Production lasted 74 years. The formula saw changes, but Kodachrome in 1936 was basically Kodachrome in 2009. By the time that last year rolled around, Kodak had narrowed its offerings to just one speed, ISO 64, and one size, 35-millimeter. There was also in all the world just one lab certified for processing, a small industrial building in the town of Parsons, Kansas, a photography supplier and developer called Dwayne's Photo.

1972 Porsche 917/10 Spyder Can-Am car, Laguna Seca. Canon QL17, Kodachrome 64, 2008.

Even by the wacky standards of color-positive film, Kodachrome development is odd and expensive. The process was designed to produce a perennially stable image of high clarity, and it succeeded. Most color film fades after a few decades, but evidence suggests a Kodachrome can hold fast for at least a century when kept away from moisture. The tradeoff was a painfully narrow exposure window and a recipe so brutally unforgiving that Dwayne's famously kept a degreed chemist on staff solely to analyze film solutions.

Smithology

The late Alice Smith, in a rare moment absent laughter. Canon QL17, Kodachrome 64, 2007.

Get the light and cook right, though? Colors that hit like a warm blanket. Or a Monterey summer.

Kodak stopped making this stuff in 2009. The people at Dwayne's, however, those heroes, they knew it was still out there. They vowed to keep the line going as long as they could, as long as Kodak kept shipping out the required chemicals. Over the next year, thousands of rolls arrived in Parsons, shades and tones from all over the world.

My Laguna shot was in there.

In early 2010, a few months after our life in California had changed, I found in my desk a few forgotten canisters of K64, exposed but undeveloped. They were unlabeled, no dates or subject notes on the cans.

Kodak had already killed the film. Dwayne's would continue

accepting exposures until the end of the year, but I didn't know that then. I looked up the processing cost online. Three rolls was roughly equivalent to a nice dinner for two, even before shipping to Kansas.

We were still broke. I had no idea what was on that film and absolutely no business paying for costly and tiny plastic pictures round-tripped from some Midwest chemistry mecca. I grew determined anyway. A door was about to close, and once it did, whatever was in those film cans would be locked in there forever.

We scrimped further. From the cheap noodles to the nearly free noodles. Weeks later, when I had saved enough, I sent the chromes off. More weeks went by. When the film returned, I rode down to Chaf's place. In the end, the Laguna photo was the last to hit the scanner. A decent shot, but nothing special. With that old Kodachrome trick, though: Colors as I remember them, if not as they really were.

In late 2008, I had flown to Northern California for work. I took a weekend off to walk around that idyllic track, shooting the race for fun. A few days after I flew home, we loaded a moving truck and aimed west.

Adrienne and I now live in Tennessee. We have two fun and quirky little girls in elementary school and an old house where the stairs creak at night and I occasionally have to tell those girls to not draw ponies in toothpaste on the bathroom mirror. When we left San Rafael in 2011, it was the responsible choice, heading east to stay with relatives for a bit, to recover financially. In the nine years after, we lived in Detroit, Chicago, Ann Arbor again, Seattle, and, finally, Knoxville.

Each of those moves was driven by family and work and nothing like childish want. I could tell you I don't miss the West Coast, but I'd be lying. Still, that was then and this is now, and we are, to my only occasional surprise, happy.

This image is then, too. It makes me think of the guy behind the camera and what he wanted. A life that was so close to, but also so very far from, the one he came to need.

Section Five
The White Rat
(Our Hero Finds a Smelly Friend)

Hagerty
August 2020 – May 2021

IT CAN TAKE SO LONG to figure out who you are. Not that you don't know much of the landscape by, say, your mid-twenties. Just that some dots take a bit longer to connect.

I am, I have come to realize, a BMW person.

That feels weird to admit.

Nurture can outshout nature. When I was young, my father ran a restoration shop for British cars. MGs mostly, roadsters and coupes built in the south of England from 1930 to 1980. Dad had loved that breed since high school, but he's a curious person, and so other marques came and went from his driveway over the years—BMWs, an Alfa Romeo, a handful of GM trucks and Jeeps, a funky old Mercedes or five, you get the gist.

In retrospect, I met so much wheeled variety growing up, I could have fixated on anything. Add in the standard-issue exposure of a strange career, driving hundreds of new and vintage cars, year after year, for years on end, and the result is essentially a giant dice roll.

Maybe, in some alternate timeline, there is a Sam Smith in every way identical to this one, except he has owned and loved not several dozen high-mile old Bavarian sport sedans, but the same number of . . . I don't know, Toyota Deliboys?

Probably not. But maybe. (The Deliboy is pretty spectacular.)

This is what happens when you're smitten with an idea. When a person falls head over heels not just for a particular carmaker or model, but for the machine and driving in general.

My friend Colin Comer restores vintage cars for a living. He is also a born and raised Wisconsinite, so he has a knack for getting to the point. Several years ago, the two of us were standing in his shop next to a 1960s Jaguar E-type. A good E-type is almost heartbreakingly pretty; people often get caught in the shape's gravity while walking past and stop to stare for a bit. Which is what we were doing.

For one reason or another, Colin and I got to talking about how a person can come to love not just a machine individually, but the collective peaks of Car as a whole. At one point, I opened the Jag's door and took a whiff of the leather and wool inside. Then I made some comment about the thing's appeal—the almost boundless list of intangibles, the history and humanity in styling and feel, that an E-type represents.

Colin was quiet for a second. Then he nodded.

"The good shit."

I watched light fall on the Jag's fenders, silent myself. Sometimes, I thought, four-letter words are the only ones that work.

Colin didn't stop to break down the idea, but I knew what he meant. A kind of automotive Venn overlap: Genius engineering and a knee-weakening sensory package mated to a 100-proof background, the car's origin story a dense little neutron star of detail that highlights all the perseverance and creative fizz that makes humanity unique.

If that combination sounds like little more than a way to balloon up the phrase "great car," well, that's the point. And it's why I am, like Colin, a drooling fool for so much on wheels. For the great MGs as much as for the great Jaguars and Shelbys, but also for the killer Bugattis and Alfas and McLarens and Renaults and Citroëns and even some of the hopelessly crappy ones, the list goes on, we do not have time for the whole list, and, lest we forget, there are those three letters, the Bavarian Motor Works, Bey Em Vey, as the Germans say, BMW is on it.

Some folks are content to let a passion start and stop in one place. I have met more than a few individuals who own literal warehouses of old Porsches. A friend once built himself a private Honda museum. Nicola Bulgari, the Italian jewelry magnate, famously owns roomfuls of Buicks. The one-answer path was never my vibe. And certainly not with BMWs —too much of what the Bavarians have built in the modern era has simply left me cold for too long.

The film critic Roger Ebert once wrote that his job was not, as most people thought, to crown films as "good" or "bad." Those words, he said, were lazy and vague; moreover, he added, they're usually just shorthand for personal taste. Instead, Ebert believed that the critic's job was to help unpack why we love or loathe something. To set preference aside and pull apart how a piece of art hits or misses its goal. (Ebert died in 2013, but in 46 years of writing about movies, he more than once gave four stars to a film he didn't much like.)

Cars are a form of industrial art. I've written things that could pass for criticism but am not a critic. Still, if I put on my Ebert hat, I could say that, for more than half a century, BMWs did a version of the automotive job better than most. As these words go to press, the marque's cars too feel too often unrelated to that past, too gaudy, heavy, and numb. They have been like that for years, falling further and further behind in crucial intangibles as other carmakers continued to push forward on those same fronts.

Imagine if an old friend who had never let you down began to change the part of their personality that had drawn you to them in the first place . . . and then they began to let you down.

An odd quirk of being a car person: As silly as it sounds, a faceless company in a far-off land can come mean a lot to you.

And yet. Nearly three decades of buying and fixing funky old German iron . . . years of track days and road racing . . . friends and projects made and traveled with and lost . . . years of life-changing moments . . .

Well, I am apparently . . . inarguably . . . you know.

The past is no place for breathing folks to live, but this isn't about old or new. Merely the kind of spark you'd noticing if you cared enough to look. The stuff that can make a person remember why they came to the party in the first place.

A person who loves driving. Who maybe can't afford or justify a sports car, but who hangs an almost embarrassing priority on balance and feedback, a sense of function over form.

I was drawn in by a century-old engineering tradition both satisfying and practical. Cars that could, in the right hands, take a remarkable amount of use and abuse, often for millions of miles. Those machines might have needed repair with age, sure, but that just kept used prices sane. Moreover, those repairs could usually be done in a driveway without much trouble, so they never felt like a big deal.

There was, if you can believe it, a sense of the underdog.

Which brings me to the final section of this book.

The seven short stories that follow were published by Hagerty between 2020 and 2021. In a certain light, they show little more than a middle-aged man and some silly choices. In another sense, they're a look back at a few ideas that once mattered a great deal to somebody. At a relief valve turned to less and less over the years, and ironically as it was needed more and more, pulled as this person was by demands of job and family, and often by the stories in this very book.

Smithology

These stories don't show a critic. They show a hopelessly rusty old car, the cockeyed blend of romance and humor that saved it, and some terrible weld bead between friends. Plus a curious man rediscovering, after years away, a large part of who he is and has always been.

Part One
A 2002 for 1800, and Why

The author, age one, clearly out of his mind.

I have a billion memories. Maybe, one day, I'll remember all of them.

J.D. Power would call this a problem of initial quality. If the human brain were a car, your narrator's hippocampus would have left the factory with rats chewing the wires.

Things have been like this for as long as I can recall. (Don't think too hard about that last sentence.) Vivid images among fuzz—that time I did that thing, for example! With that person! Or was it that other person? Where were we, again?

I got married, once; I remember that. The books on my office shelf have been read, to the best of my recollection. All else is suspect. Except, of course, the BMW 2002, a machine I will never forget.

The first one is memorable mostly for how we parted. I was 17, in Louisville, Kentucky, in 1998. The car had been in my life only a few seasons. A 1974 2002tii, the last year for factory fuel-injection. Thick Earl Scheib paint, a flies-in-the-soup redo of the original metallic blue.

Mom and Dad had always told good stories about the 2002 they had owned when I was little, so the classified ad hit a nerve. The $3500 asking price consumed both every penny I had saved and a small loan from my parents. Less than a year later, that BMW and I were sitting at a light when a Ford LTD walloped over from the oncoming lane. Fat Detroit bumper met small German headlight at 40 mph, and physics did the rest.

I was fine, physically unhurt. In the moments that followed, I limped the BMW to a side street, deflated, and started estimating repair costs in my head. The nose had been punched in more than a foot, the hood was now jammed against the windshield and doors, and the front fenders were cutting the tires.

When you are 17, a material object can mean too much. When the police arrived 30 minutes later, I was sitting on a curb, watching coolant run into the gutter and thinking up sad little limericks around the word "totaled." The officer who wrote the accident report saw the look on my face and patted me on the shoulder.

"You didn't get hurt, kid, be thankful. It's just an old car."

The report he wrote misspelled the model: *2002tit*.

The second example, a '76, popped up a few months after. Zero rust, relatively low miles, and mostly original paint, a bright shade of orange the factory called Inka. A friend and I were driving past the University of Louisville when I spotted a familiar roofline in a staff parking lot. We were teenagers with nothing else to do, so we stopped.

I walked around the car slowly, then lay down next to it, eyeballing floors and frame rails, smearing dirt on the pants that my mother had said to keep clean. Not an ounce of rust or undercoating; the dash was uncracked; the headliner was perfect. It looked almost new, nicer than half the cars in the lot.

Butterflies in the stomach. Then blind, unfounded hope. I grabbed my backpack, tore a scrap of paper from a notebook, and left a note under a wiper. A few days later, I was fishing a Pop-Tart from the toaster when the orange car's owner, a clarinet professor at the university, called my parents' house line. When Mom handed over the phone, the professor threw out a number so close to the insurance settlement on the blue tii that I dropped the Pop-Tart. I walked on air for days, as you do when impossible things happen before breakfast.

The insurance company hadn't paid much for the '74, even in 1990s money. But then, 2002s weren't then seen as much. Car collectors of the time generally thought the cars too pedestrian, less desirable than an Alfa Romeo or a Porsche of the same era. As a useful machine, however, the BMW was fun and practical and durable, and so die-hards had grown attached, keeping the model alive in pockets, especially in dry climates.

*Dad being useful, late 1970s, with a useful car.
And a white Triumph TR250.*

My parents weren't die-hards, but I liked to pretend they were. Mom and Dad had bought their 1976 2002 new, from a tiny dealer in Louisville, not much more than a gas station, shortly after getting married. They sold that car before I left diapers, but in the summer of 1994, they took me and my sister on a vacation to San Francisco to visit family. What I saw there dented my skull.

Before the Bay Area became a tech-fueled Monaco, the region was a gold mine of daily-driven classics. At 13, dorked for cars and sauntering off a Kentucky plane with a Sony Walkman on my belt, I had no idea what was coming.

Our relatives lived north of the city, across the Golden Gate. On the 40-minute drive to the bridge, my mouth gaped so much, my tongue went to sandpaper. It started in the airport parking garage, where a 1960s Mercedes *Heckflosse* waited patiently for its owner in a corner spot. When we pulled outside, 1970s Fords and Chevys dotted airport service roads, common as pigeons. Porsche 356? Have two before you lose sight of the runway. At this gas station, a hydraulic Citroën; there in Arrivals, a sliding-window Mini.

The tally bloomed as we hit the freeway, a nonstop feed of improbable that kicked off run-on streams of thought like, *Is that a Ferrari Dino in traffic why is there a Dino in traffic is this Oz this must be Oz.*

Dad was the reason I knew those names, why I saw them as something worth seeing. I had been reading car books since I was little. My father simply kept them around en masse, on half the shelves in the house and filed seemingly at random. (Danielle Steele novel, Danielle Steele novel, book on prewar Jaguars. Mom, Mom, Dad.) But I had never seen so much vintage sheetmetal on the road in one place, and certainly not without any ceremony or pomp.

Five minutes up the highway, the kicker: A 2002 barged past in the left lane with a blinker on. A minute later, another dashed by on the right, bending into an off-ramp with a puff of smoke out the pipe. (Valve-guide wear. Common problem, though I didn't know it then.)

Huh, I thought—more than one. Neat.

It was the drop before a deluge. A blink later, I spotted a third. Then a fifth, a seventh, a ninth, the count rising constantly, the cars seemingly everywhere I looked, too many to believe. The little BMWs zipped down side streets visible from the freeway, ran below as we crossed overpasses, sat no-big-deal at city meters.

Most were far from perfect, dirty and dented here and there, wearing a quilt of bumper stickers or mismatched paint. The honest wear and character that real cars acquire in honest use, from real people going about everyday life.

My face smeared against the window. I began to count aloud, rattling off the numbers. Twenty-five. Thirty? *Forty-five?* I told Dad and he smiled and Mom humored me and my sister didn't care and nobody in the car seemed to understand why this mattered. Even me.

We hit downtown, sat in congestion for a while near the financial district, then continued heading north. On the approach to the Golden Gate Bridge, an early 1600, the 2002's virtually identical predecessor, zipped up the ramp next to us, six-volt headlights dim as candles.

Forty-six?!?

Bay Area roads have changed some over the last three decades, but not enough to skew napkin math. If you ask Google Maps, the shortest-time path from San Francisco International Airport to the Golden Gate now covers nearly 19 miles of pavement.

Father and son, early 1980s. The BMW is not a 2002, but nevermind that. All that matters is that you witness my father's magnificent hair and pose and, should the two of you chance to meet, ask why he no longer styles himself in this fashion and if it is simply because he no longer wishes to be seen as an enviable sex beast.

Forty-six cars in 40 minutes. More than one 2002 per minute. Take that Google estimate, smudge down a little for good measure, call it two cars per mile. One model of BMW, then more than 20 years old, going on for what might as well have been forever.

We crossed the bridge, heading north. I stopped counting and collapsed back into the seat, exhausted.

In retrospect, there was no cosmic reason for all this. It was just happy circumstance, the right place and right California time. In the state that rust forgot, old cars fun and durable often miss the chance to die. And in a dense, quirky little city that had yet to excise its middle class or its quirk, in a region long a hotbed of imported automobiles, in a town without extremes of temperature or snow, why wouldn't people gravitate to a practical and cheeky little German sedan? Especially if it was great to drive and cost next to nothing?

One of the truisms of the car business is that quality doesn't always appreciate. The 2002 was costly when new, especially in America, a small four-cylinder sedan priced hundreds of dollars above a V-8 Mustang. It sold anyway. Between 1966 and 1976, over ten years of production, BMW moved more than 800,000 examples of its '02-series cars globally. In 1968, the editor-in-chief of *Car and Driver*, David E. Davis, Jr., famously called the 2002 "one of modern civilization's all-time best ways to get somewhere sitting down."

That magazine has since touted the model as the blueprint for the modern sport sedan. The 2002's success helped re-establish BMW, struggling since the 1950s, as a going concern; it gave the company a foothold in the crucial American market; and it established the brand as an industry benchmark in feedback—that intangible alchemy of driver feel—a position only recently lost.

I knew none of that at the time. But that day, I made a decision, sudden and final, as kids do: The 2002 had to be wonderful. It looked that way, all taut and purposeful. Wasn't that enough?

Brain damage rarely cures itself. After we flew home from California, I dove into a nascent internet. While poring through the archive of a vintage-BMW mailing list, I found where some innocent had asked the difference between the 2002 and its Italian contemporary, the Alfa Romeo Giulia coupe.

"BMWs are like Alfas," some wag had replied, if sturdier. I can't recall the exact language, but the post said something like, "If an '02 wants to get up every day and go to work, Italian cars just want to lie around and sex you."

Being a certain age, I stood up from the computer, walked to one of my father's shelves, and pulled down a book on Alfas.

Dad had once owned a Giulia GTV. I went into the kitchen, found him making a sandwich.

"You probably shouldn't live with an Alfa until you're older," he said, between bites. Those words made no sense then but make all the sense now. Spectacular cars. I would no sooner have steered teenaged me toward one than given teenaged me a flamethrower.

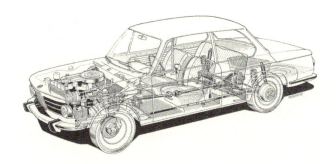

I remember my friend Seth Teel buying a clean '68 2002 our senior year of high school. He paid for the car by selling what he called "recreational plants." Two weeks in, he jumped behind its wheel and nearly killed us both. We had been listening to *The Who's Greatest Hits*, tearing around town in circles after school, and I had been wondering what it meant to *substitute / me for you*. Then we flew into a downhill right-hander 10 mph too fast and my face nearly substituted for the hood ornament of an oncoming Buick. We were in high school, so we got a slice of pizza after and laughed about it.

I remember the happy way an '02 bats into a corner, the quick but soft settling as that simple suspension geometry does awful things to a tire. The ability wouldn't matter if that nerdy little form didn't seem to egg you on: *Here, I have this much, take all of it.* The recipe was bolstered by a generous trunk, a decent back seat, and a seemingly unburstable 2.0-liter four. In the 1980s, BMW took the 2002's engine-block geometry into Formula 1, landed more than 1000 hp in turbocharged qualifying trim, and won a title. The first BMW M3, developed a few years later, used a 7200-rpm twin-cam built on a virtually identical casting.

In college, while studying in St. Louis, I stumbled onto a BMW Car Club of America track-driving school at a nearby road course. I had never done anything like that, but the program looked rad, so I signed up. The $250 entry fee smoked my savings account and the orange car's brake pads burned down to their backing plates in an afternoon, but I was sunk. That '76 went up on plane in a corner, skimming along on skinny tires, forgiving in a slide and almost comically free of vice.

Years later, I would go club racing, lap supercars and pro-racing machines as an editor at *Road & Track*, enter exactly one professional road race (long story), and drive a factory-supported 2002ti and BMW 3.0 CSL in the prestigious Monterey historic races. Looking back, none of it seems possible, until I remember where it started.

Good cars hint at where they can take you. The great ones stick in memory long after they're gone, a reminder to stop thinking so much and just go already.

A few years later, when Seth decided to sell his '68, Dad and I pooled funds and bought it. Then we stripped the car down and went road racing with the Sports Car Club of America. We got a few unspectacular but fun seasons before I ran out of money and sold my couch to pay for a set of race tires. Shortly after, I ran out of furniture and had to stop racing. Dad still owns Seth's car; I don't miss the couch.

I remember the championship I won. A borrowed car in a modest little California amateur road-racing series a few years ago, but a title nonetheless. A crew of 2002-owning friends from San Diego had asked for advice on suspension setup, and that somehow evolved into a ride for few years. Hanging out at the track with those folks quickly became so much goofy fun, the driving was fringe benefit; I would have showed up just to sweep out the trailer.

There were so many more '02s and people. Engineless shells and track rats towed from A to B. Running projects driven back from the West Coast for friends. That orange '76 daily driven across four seasons.

To say nothing of the cars and motorcycles that have entered my life because they shared parts with a 2002 or reminded me of one, rabbit holes all their own. Machines that did nothing perfectly but everything well, and with gusto.

The volume slowed only as the world wised up. As I grew older, the cars grew too expensive. Or maybe they weren't too expensive, just once again priced right for what they deliver. Either way, they were no longer affordable enough to be viewed as punky little social cast-offs. For me, the disconnect between the 2002's personal meaning and its market value grew too great, and my writer's salary remained too modest to keep up. I moved on to other things.

It's both comforting and not when a cherished cult object becomes an Instagram-famous oligarch commodity. Fifteen years ago, a friend connected me with a clean 1974 2002 Turbo for sale—the rare, 170-hp factory hot rod, one of the first turbocharged production cars built. The seller wanted $15,000, around five times the cost of an ordinary '02 in good shape. I had always loved Turbos, but I passed. If you want one of those cars now, add a zero. Fifteen grand these days will get you a scruffy tii, rough around the edges.

2002s no longer dot the streets of San Francisco or anywhere else. They are now widely treasured and coddled, tucked away in garages, aired out mostly for Sunday drives. A little German box that begged to be used every day, that was best in daily use, essentially retired from service, the cheap ones gone.

Except when they aren't.

This one found me. We'll discuss how another time. For now, just know that the $1800 stack of oxide in my shop is a very early 1972 2002tii, white with a black interior, another factory-fuel-injection car, the 70th in the breed built for the American market.

If that price sounds like a knockout, know that I nearly passed out when I first looked under the car. The rear subframe mounts are vapor, rusted out of existence. The rockers are gutted, the shock towers split open. From floors to roof, not a single panel is free of rust holes or undamaged by rot, every corrosion trap the cars are known for. The whole mess moves under its own power, but real mileage would be suicidal. No humane individual would leave this collection of hurt alone with small children, or a lady, or even a politician.

I couldn't say no.

Piles like this present a few options. The sensible path would be to part the car out. Alternately, you could restore it, grinding and welding the body whole and glossy, rebuilding every ounce while keeping the good bits, years of labor to save little more than a transmission tunnel, a firewall, and a serial number. Barring all that, you could shell-swap it, transplanting mechanicals and trim to an uncorroded tub.

For various personal reasons, those options now seem, in order of appearance, cruel, financially insane, and boring as toast.

The tii's previous owner, an elderly gentleman named Earle, had driven it for decades. Safety concerns prompted him to take it off the road around 10 years ago. Our agreed price was less than half the car's value in parts. An obvious kindness.

As I loaded the BMW on a trailer, he smiled softly, eyes distant.

"I hope you fix it," he said, "and drive it."

The look on his face reminded me of someone I knew a long time ago. This kid on a curb.

So I came up with a plan.

Part Two
Stay of Execution

Hagerty, September 2020

The first decision had the car as too awful to die and too good to kill. The second call involved rollers. Old Borranis seemed necessary. Borranis are Italian, the caviar of vintage steel wheels. The car was too scruffy for alloys, but you have to aim high somehow. And regardless, decisions move you forward.

I finished strapping the 2002 onto the trailer and shut the trunk. A piece of brown oxide the size of my palm came off in . . . well, my palm.

Smithology

The tii had mounted the trailer under its own power, on tires at least a decade old. The engine sounded remarkably healthy, idling with the quiet dignity of a machine whose grace exceeds that of the surroundings. Imagine an espresso machine at the bottom of a well.

I turned off the key and watched the open hood wobble in the breeze. Bits of it fluttered separately from other bits, tied to the whole but not of it. Like a wave crashing on the beach, as Tom Petty said.

Should fix that, I thought.

When you pay good money for a Dumpster fire, advice finds you. Part it out, they told me, cut up the tub. "They" being virtually everyone who saw the 2002 as I was towing it home, from gas-station bystanders to friends who texted clever jokes like "Nice Cthulhu, what year?" and "Did you lose a bet?"

The tii had been for sale in Baltimore, 500 miles from my house in Tennessee. My friend Paul Wegweiser, a BMW mechanic who lives in Pennsylvania, has Baltimore roots and knew Earle, the owner. Paul acted as intermediary, and he met me in Maryland to help retrieve the car. A week before, he had told me by phone that the tii was rusty but solid. I believed him, because Mama Smith didn't raise no fools, except that one guy who became a journalist.

Paul, a barn-find junkie, told me to buy it. I was initially resistant, begged off, no time or money. Paul kept calling and texting, adamant. After a few days of this, the insistence began to come from a voice in my head. The one that tells you to buy 10 pounds of ice cream and marshmallow fluff whenever you visit the grocery.

Earle had told Paul his asking price. The specific number is immaterial; all that matters is the fact that it made me recall a few prime lessons of adulthood. Namely how Ice Cream Voice is rarely wrong but simultaneously almost never right.

One morning, after staring into an unusually strong cup of coffee for a little too long, I texted Paul with a heinous lowball.

"See if he'll take $1800."

Why that exact figure? Simple: It was both every penny I had spare and a blessed exit, an almost guaranteed no. After all, I thought, who sells a running, fuel-injected 2002 for 1800 bucks?

Earle, apparently.

A week later, I was standing in a Maryland driveway, buzzed off the relentless absurdity of life and gazing dreamily into a hole where a left rear subframe mount had once lived. Each rear shock tower held a foot-long gash tall enough to let various suspension bits peer into the trunk. Rust holes zitted out over the roof and quarter panels. One frame rail was half dust. More than a foot of the trunk lid's rear lip was simply absent, and the rockers and floors were engaged in an epic struggle to confirm their own existence. The whole car appeared one large pothole away from splitting clean in half.

Paul had not seen the BMW in person before. Standing there, clearly ashamed, he actually hung his head.

"I am . . . sorry. I thought it had . . . subframe . . . yeah . . ."

He trailed off. I ran a finger along the left windshield pillar, inexplicably chipper. My finger accidentally poked a hole in the steel.

"Don't be!" I said. "Lost causes are neat."

"I thought you didn't buy cars sight-unseen," my wife said, a week later. "You broke your own rule?"

"It was more of a bend," I said. ("The subframe is still mounted to the car," Earle had offered, over the phone. I should have asked *how*.)

Ice Cream Voice was relentless: *Hooray! A running tii for 1800 bucks!* I was torn between wanting to reward the voice with a triple-decker waffle cone and figuring out how to feed it horse tranquilizer until the grown-ups could sort things out.

That afternoon, I texted photos of the car to my father, who once ran a restoration shop.

"I am truly amazed," he texted back.

"Really?" I said.

"Yes. By what's not there."

At home in Knoxville, divorced from the twin drugs of travel and novelty, one fact became clear: The 2002 could not stay as it was for long. If nothing else, entropy would see to that. Me, I had no plan whatsoever, which was somehow comforting. I just knew that the heart wants what it wants, even when said want stinks of hantavirus.

Smithology

In his day job, Paul is a consultant at a BMW parts house. After putting the car on jack stands and poking at it for a bit, I picked up the phone and called him, firing out questions of availability and cost.

"It's not like 10 years ago," he said. "Now that '02s are actually worth something, people are spending $600 on factory euro turn signals, $900 for the fancy Italian-market ones. Front control arms used to be 70 bucks or whatever, now they're more than $200. BMW is less interested, and its Classic division has been cut to a skeleton crew.

"You can't get tii cold-start or pressure-maintenance valves, injectors, standard service bits. Don't get me started on the rare period stuff, like factory Recaros or Alpina bits; they're through the roof. The cars are Sunday runners now, garage queens, not driven like they used to be. Too many people being too precious."

Perhaps you see where this is going.

A subframe mount, once.

As I hung up, truths coalesced. After years of screwing around with old cars, I couldn't bring myself to put this one in the ground. It had somehow managed to beat the odds, a gnarly little survivor dodging the crusher for years, too rusty to keep driving and too insignificant to save.

Restoration was patently insane; I lacked the time and space to do the work myself, and any good shop would bill six figures at least. A shell swap made no sense; rust-free '02 tubs are still out there, but the tii's underbits weren't nice enough for the trouble. And even if they had been, a rebody represented a kind of throwing away in itself.

I squatted by the BMW's nose, picking at rust on the bumper. The original headlight grilles, valuable and fragile, had been painted black but were otherwise straight and clean. The core of a 2002's face, solid.

I stood up, full of questions. Why are we so locked into certain ways of doing things? Who says a car can only die or be restored, anyway? What if you wanted an old crapcan hulk to drive like hell simply because it reminded you of the days when you were younger and even more stupid, when most of the things you loved and drove like hell were crappy to begin with, because that was all you could afford?

Could you stave off an execution, I wondered, by going all rapid-fire kludge-zombie, welding in structural tubing quick and dirty, tapping in friends for help? Keep the whole mess alive and driving in spite of itself? Do none of the work traditionally "right" but all of it . . . enough?

Not too long ago, racehorses got shot for a broken leg. This would be . . . crutches. Maybe a visible exoskeleton?

The more I stood there huffing headliner mold, the more the idea made sense. Rebuild a car in that fashion, you'd have an icon in the garage but nothing to lose. Any abusive environment normally off-limits—snow, dirt, Baja—you could just lean in.

The cosmetics could stay untouched, because anything else would cost real money and lose the rampant sense of dead-rod indifference. Maybe I could set aside some cash for vintage aftermarket speed parts, neat old bits more desirable than the car itself, because their presence would be funny, next to the uggo.

Not a new idea, but a good one. A stab at yelling into the void. And proof that you don't need money to have fun with old cars that everyone wants, just a complete lack of shame and a willingness to burn MIG wire like fireworks in July.

Any project attracts monikers. A friend dubbed the car Shitii, for obvious reasons. I needed a hashtag to keep photos together on Instagram, so I came up with #weissrat, from *weiss*, the German word for white, and "rat," which is English for "rat." (You know, experiments, for science.) My friend Ben Thongsai, a BMW wrench from Chicago, named the tii Suzanne, after a James Taylor song.

The connection wasn't random; Earle had given me a small paper trail that suggested the musician had actually bought the car new.

"I got ahold of his people, years ago," Earle had said. "Guy came back and said yeah, he had owned a BMW in 1972, couldn't remember what it was. I think he bought it for a lady. Carly Simon?"

Last week, during a quiet lunch hour, I called my friend John Krewson, another former 2002 owner. We shot the breeze for a bit, and then he asked about my purchase. I mentioned the tii's 1971 build date and the possible Sweet Baby James connection—not my musical bag, but hey, fun trivia.

Smoke wisping from beneath the car later, near a series of rusty doomholes in the left rear fender.

"Huh," John said. "*Two-Lane Blacktop* came out in '71. That movie, that whole period—wasn't that guy on a lot of heroin?"

"Yeah," I said. "Spooky stuff. Why?"

"Nothing, really," he laughed. "It's just . . . man. Taylor's decisions around then . . . I mean, they were just *awful*."

Part Three
I've Seen Tired, and I've Seen Pain

Hagerty, September 2020

Paul was crouched in the back seat, face coated with grinding dust, aiming a $9 Harbor Freight heat gun at a sheet of floor insulation. Acrid smoke wafted up, wisping around his glasses.

He sighed. "Why did you buy this piece of crap, again?"

Like a lot of parts guys, Paul has both a warped sense of humor and the ability to look legitimately grumpy on command. His face does this thing best described as I Am Deeply Unimpressed With Both Life and

Your Particular Views on It, at which point you are gifted the sense that he is about to either turn and walk away or take a deep breath, pull a Zippo from a pocket, and calmly set your shirt on fire.

I grinned, leaning through one of the car's windows. "You literally called me and told me to buy it."

Raised eyebrows. "I don't remember that happening."

A second later, someone in the trunk unloaded on the car with a hammer. Big smacks. *Whamwhamwham.*

"Not like that," a voice said. That was Tim. "Lemme see it." Then a louder banging, more determined: *WHAM WHAM WHAM.*

Owen's voice bubbled up, cheery. "Oh! Okay!"

WHAMWHAMWHAM.

I popped my head out of the car. The two stood at the rear bumper. "See?" Tim said, grinning at Owen. "Don't be nice to it."

I have always depended on the kindness of people who enjoy smacking the crap out of trash with a hammer.

Forty-eight years ago, this car bore no trash. Some diligent individual drove a Riviera Blue 1972 BMW 2002tii off a West German assembly line and into a shipping lot, and shortly after, the car rode a boat to America's northeast coast, where it lived for years. After some time, an owner paid for a light restoration, including rust repair and a repaint to white.

Miles were added. The rust reappeared; miles kept coming. Then, last summer, Paul called me. I woke up one morning, not at all interested in rusty old piles of BMW, and by bedtime, I owned one.

Mark my words, I will drive it to both oceans at least. Maybe Alaska. I have, in the past, done dumber things.

But first, welding and sheet-metal piracy.

The project had snowballed, as projects do. I counseled in Ben, the Chicago mechanic friend, for advice—was my rehab idea even possible, I asked, without getting in too deep? Ben considered the details and allowed as how he thought it was. Then he offered space and help at his shop, so I towed the car to Illinois for a weekend of investigation.

Word of mouth saw other friends show up to help. They were drawn partly by a large refrigerator of beer and partly by the appeal of working on an old car so far gone that wrong answers were impossible.

Tim Skwiot drove in from Minnesota; an electrical engineer by training, he owns multiple old BMWs and a turbocharged Lotus Exige and writes fuel-injection software as a hobby. Owen Nelson, a Chicago software engineer just out of college, grew up in his father's business, which just happens to be a BMW service and restoration mecca in Southern California. Paul drove his favorite barn-rat 2002—he has several—in from Pittsburgh at the last minute while listening to loud punk rock in his head and somehow managing to not get arrested, despite averaging a million miles per hour through Ohio in a stickered-up German snotrocket.

Normal people, in other words. I have never known anything but.

Evening parking-lot beer nonsense; Owen and Veronica.

Other area friends filtered in that first weekend—varied in age and background, from early 20s to newly retired. Most had either restored or rebuilt some flavor of vintage car. Experience helped but was less than necessary, given the rule-free nature of the job at hand.

That quality also made even pessimistic timeline predictions sound wildly optimistic. Early on, Ben guessed it would take three or four weekends of work to make the car safe and drivable, so long as the labor erred toward slam-fabrication and high-spirits triage. After a day of poking at the thing, everyone present seemed to agree.

Half of that first day was simple damage inventory. Panels were pulled and rust ground away to facilitate survey of the remaining metal. The car's body was so rotten as to be comically uplifting: holes big and small, holes hidden and obvious, even holes that had somehow managed to grow and nurture their own private little collections of smaller and lower-ranked orbiting holes. (Late that first night, high on sleep deprivation and gin drinks, I named a few of them: Holey! Holeface McGee! Holevis Presley!)

At least four feet of the outer floors on each side of the car were attached by nothing more than the factory seat mounts, thin steel bridges tying floor to sill. Two of the four rear spring perches were so rust-gnarled as to be relocatable by hand. On top of all this lay countless typical barn-find service items: brake and suspension rebuilds, driveshaft repair, a new windshield to replace the cracked original, and so on.

Friday night, Ben walked to the back of the shop and gathered the steel he had ordered. A length of round tubing appeared first, 1.5 inches in diameter, 0.120-wall. Then a length of rectangular tube, 0.083-wall and three inches wide.

"Alright," he said, "Let's drink some beer and design this shit."

Paul with heat gun and floor holes, scraping off factory sound-deadening pads. Note long rust hole just outboard of his elbow, running the length of the car's sill.

I knelt down, eyeing the new metal. "Why these tubes?"

"Six feet is the longest UPS will ship—over that, the rate goes way up. I didn't get you DOM"—Drawn Over Mandrel—"though. Way more expensive. This thing isn't nice enough for that."

"No, I mean, where are they going on the car?"

He shrugged. "I have plans."

I stood up. Having nothing else to do, I absentmindedly allowed my leg to kick one of the holes in the right rocker. My shoe disappeared to the ankle.

"Tough," I said, "but fair."

Ben, another trained engineer, laid out the changes with casual indifference; I served mostly as half-intelligent metal-prep and welding labor, plus a sort of compass, setting project heading and cost but otherwise trusting everyone to do half-sensible work.

Grinders were plugged in and cutoff discs screwed down; by early afternoon, the car was a swarm of humanity, three or four jobs going at once. Requests for direction were rare, save a few obvious knee-jerks as questions arose. (Sample exchange: "You want me to clean this?" Me: "Make this car less visually upsetting and I will end you with a knife.")

Budget was both true north on the project and the whole point. We don't talk much about ownership cost around here, but classic cars are a luxury; they take significant money to own and feed. That fact can make the hobby seem desperately out of reach for ordinary people, and the effect compounds if you want a model even half wanted by everyone else. Nor does satisfaction necessarily track with spend. Intensely valuable cars best appreciated in regular use often mutate into stationary garage art, stagnant for months at a time.

Logical in one sense, a wastey bunch of hooey in another. I can't afford a nice 2002tii. Complaining about that would be like moaning about the tide. Instead, as sparks flew in Chicago, I decided the project would be a rejection of precious thinking, along a specific and personal arc:

1. **Lack of money can be a roadblock,** unless you lower your standards so far as to leave the road being blocked

2. **Traditional standards of quality** are generally important

3. **Except when they're not**

4. **Anything is possible** with a welder

5. Literally anyone can weld, if you don't mind welding badly

6. If the front door to a dream is locked, try a side window

7. Cars should be a means to an end, not a silent museum to your own taste

8. Wabi-sabi

9. Safety first.

As a unibody car, lacking a traditional separate frame, a 2002 draws torsional rigidity from its bodywork. The thin pillars and bulkheads ensure that most of the tub's load is carried by the relatively simple rocker- and suspension-mount structures. Let a 2002 corrode enough, the car will literally collapse in on itself, a rusty black hole. Best case, some suspension component falls off while parking or the doors no longer shut. At worst, maybe the whole megillah breaks apart on the freeway and everybody dies a little.

Left: Subframe mount that isn't, prepped for reconstruction. Right: Same part of the car from above, with a fraction of the new steel that would be used to rebuild it.

The white car wasn't quite at singularity status, but it wasn't far off. Rust and at least one saltwater flood had reduced the factory mounting points for the rear subframe, normally box-section steel, to mere bolts hanging from a decimated floor.

On a healthy 2002, those box sections are strong and disperse load; on my car, road use would have quickly torn out that now-weak section of floor, leaving the rear suspension attached by only the differential. Which, naturally, would then be very much surprised and insulted by its new responsibility, taking the opportunity to seek out greener pastures, like the nearest ditch.

To fix this, Ben and I landed on something like an exoskeleton. ("Load path," Ben said, eyeing a door frame. I nodded, sagely, like a person who knows things.) The remains of the car's rockers would be cut away, Ben decided, and the spaces they had occupied would each be filled, from beneath, with a steel-tube sandwich, round tube above rectangular. Each of these tubewiches would then be plug-welded into the car from above, through holes drilled in the door sills.

At the front of the car, just behind the front wheels, each tubewich would be fish-mouthed onto a vertically oriented tube that had been welded in parallel to the A-pillar. ("Oh," I said to Ben as he test-fit the steel, "Load path!" His face did a fairly accurate impression of Paul doing an impression of a person who has just seen an idiot.)

The rest of the fixes were relatively simple. Just forward of each rear wheel, each rocker-tube assemblywich would tie into a new structure built to mimic one of the original subframe boxes. The rear spring perches, the rotten left-front frame rail, and the rear shock towers would see "blanket" patches—not proper repairs, but sheet steel hammered and welded over rust holes, to hold things together.

Chiefly, much of the rust would be left intact, mummified underneath those steel blankets, because $1800 car. And because, as Ben put it, "You don't have $80,000 or years to do it right."

"How long," I asked him, "until this thing is structurally dorked again, if I actually drive it?"

"Who knows? Unless you go chasing salt and rain . . . 20 years?"

"Am I a bad person if I leave the big floor holes? They're fun."

That shrug again. "This reminds me of the 1980s. A bunch of shops stopped working on 2002s when the cars were just coming apart from daily use. I always worked on them; I didn't care. But you did have to find ways to make the, uh... discount repair happen."

"That 'one more winter' thing."

A shock tower, he said, had failed on one of his dad's cars, once. Punched through on a family trip. They had to get home, so they used a block of wood to jam the tower back in place.

Paul, working on something across the room, yelled a response: "I bought a car with some wood in it once!"

The whole affair reminded me of those times in grade school when I would slam together a plastic model airplane in a single afternoon, all glue mess and no paint, just to have something to play with.

"It should all be reversible," Ben said later, as we poked at the sills, "just in case anyone ever actually loses their mind and tries to properly restore this thing."

"No one should ever do that," Paul yelled, from the back of the shop.

"Down, boy!" I hollered. "Back!"

"Arf!" he barked.

Paradoxically, the more we patched up the car, the larger the rust holes became. In idle moments, I would take a screwdriver or even just a fingernail to pick away at a fender or a floor, turning latticed metal into air. Forced entropy. Everything we were doing mattered, except it didn't. We were building a small protest, a drivable parts car, a quiet middle finger to... well, I wasn't quite sure. But it certainly felt like something.

Next to real restorations or the average YouTube build—"I bought the cheapest Ferrari in the world, and now we're going to turn it into a working replica of the Large Hadron Collider!"—the project was both meek and unambitious, but I couldn't stop thinking of places I wanted to drive it. Or of all the attainable cars and motorcycles I had wanted to try as a kid. Those years where you sit at home, reading and watching movies and videos, building a list, patiently waiting for a job and funding. Only by the time I got those things, everything on my list had appreciated out of reach.

Miles seemed like a good goal. A lot of miles. Maybe aim for more in a year than most internet builds see in a lifetime.

Start at the bottom, nowhere to go but up.

I mentioned this fact in our last installment, but the BMW's paper file holds evidence that the car was purchased new by James Taylor. The Massachusetts songwriter.

As the BMW shed metal, I began singing songs. Little tunes aimed at no one while working, over a grinder or behind a welding mask, hummed or bellowed as mood required. The contentment of a mind down a rabbit hole:

> *Just yesterday morning*
> *I saw your floors, they were gone*
> *Shitbox, the miles they made put an end to youuuu*
> *Flushed the throne this morning*
> *And I wrote down this song*
> *Then I huffed some floor-tar melt and felt better nowwwww*

I made three more trips to Chicago. It got much better. At the same time—this should come as no surprise—it got so very much worse.

Part Four
This Thing Cannot Get Any Worse

Hagerty, October 2020

"You're going to have to excavate the rocker panel and pull the tube up into it."

Paul, crouched next to the car, flicked a piece of rocker steel with his finger. "So this will need to be cut, then."

Ben shrugged. "I don't even think you need the cutter. Just bend it back and forth a few times."

Paul made a face. "What am I, a savage?"

He lay down on the floor and began poking at the rocker. Ben walked off. Seconds later, a barely audible muttering under the car: "Alright. Maybe I *am* a savage."

This was late Saturday. The Weissrat's second weekend in Chicago was going well. Or maybe it was going poorly. I couldn't really tell, and it didn't seem to matter. The BMW was in pieces. Most of us smelled funny, and I smelled the worst. I had slept in Ben's shop the night before, but not without reason: The shop fridge was chock-full of beer, and a hotel room was expensive anyway, and we had needed to make space in the fridge for the rest of the beer Ben had bought, so we stuck around the shop at the end of the day emptying the fridge of cold beer, you know, as you do, and then I was in no condition to drive, as can happen, so I just crashed on an air mattress in the back of Ben's office and woke up stinking of yesterday.

I would tell you that this money-saving choice was part of the plan from the beginning, but that would be a lie. That would imply I was in Chicago primarily for the car.

I mean, the car was important.

It's just that the beer and the lunatics were more important.

Paul and his '02. This was before he worked on my car in his very own—I am not making this up—full-body unicorn costume.

Paul[1] drove in from Pennsylvania again. For some reason, he felt compelled to bring a die grinder with him from home—this little air tool the size of a small flashlight. He was protective of it in a way that made me laugh. Late one night, hopped up on a combination of cold brew and Three Floyds Zombie Dust, I named the grinder WenDie, after Paul's girlfriend, Wendy. Paul scowled when I told him this, but Paul scowls at everything, so it seemed like a good move.

Saturday morning, we were test-fitting a long steel tube inside the remains of the car's right rocker. Athletic support, I called it, when no one was looking.

"You realize what WenDie is helping make, here," I said.

Paul raised an eyebrow. "Oh?"

"A body-on-frame 2002."

Ben, nearby, chimed in: "Well . . . yes."

"Ah ha!" I said, pleased to be right about something.

"The car has pretty much lost most of its unibody," Ben said. "The main point of the rocker is to connect the A-pillar to the rear subframe."

"Like a truck," I said, "blunt force or happy stupid tool or something."

"A-pillar, subframe," Ben said. "It doesn't matter much what happens in between."

In the beginning, Ben and I had planned four weekends. Twelve days to take a 1972 BMW 2002tii from parked refuse to functional hoopty that wouldn't disintegrate under use. Friends heard about this and wanted in. Most were not from Chicago, so those weekends saw a host of people flying or driving, parachuting into town each Friday and then hammering on the car until Sunday afternoon, at which point everyone would fly or drive back home. Saturday nights usually held a barbecue in the parking lot, drinking and watching the sunset. Which, in Chicago, a place bookended by flat plains and a large body of water, can be pretty great.

Twelve days seemed like more than enough time. At least, so long as nobody got carried away and tried to execute any of the body repair . . . properly.

Structurally useful and safe not being the same as right, you see.

Rusty cars tend to hide their damage under carpets and trim panels, so you learn things as you blast one apart. Work methods on the white car thus evolved based on what Ben had on hand in weldable raw steel (a lot) and how much metal the car retained in critical repair areas (generally microscopic). Cheap aftermarket body patch panels, surface-rusted from shelf rot, were slammed over the shock towers and spring perches and welded down. (Ben: "I have had these on the shelf for years." Me: "I can't see why." Ben: "Yep.") In the interest of ROI on time and cost, the rear-subframe boxes, body reinforcements critical for safety, were built up in near-factory fashion, from quality aftermarket parts.

Ben, who does not enjoy being photographed.

If all this sounds happily stupid and slapdash, that's because it was. Call it the bodywork equivalent of Spanx. The outer structure holds things together and smooths it all over, jiggly bits carry on inside, wholesome exercise remains unaccomplished.

All the while, people kept stopping by. Mostly locals, often car-club connections I had made almost 20 years ago, when I moved to Chicago after college. But also friends of friends who had heard about the 2002's sickness and simply wanted to witness the horror in person.

My favorite line came from Joe August. Joe is an engineer by trade; like a lot of engineers, he happens to be joyfully direct. He owns several old vehicles seems always moderately amused by their flaws, which is good, because humans are flawed and so none of the things we make are ever perfect, and that's how you should be.

When Joe saw the car for the first time, he stood at the rear bumper and blinked repeatedly.

"Sam," he said, without an ounce of emotion, "this car is awful."

"Funny," I said, "how everyone uses that exact word."

He pointed to the rear floors, the in-progress subframe mounts.

"This is a car you have to weld stuff onto . . . in order to weld stuff onto it."

I was reminded of that scene in the first *Lord of the Rings* movie, where Sean Bean discusses the difficulty of entering Mordor.

"One does not . . . simply . . . weld . . . into shitbox?"

"Huh?"

Clearly not a Tolkien guy.

"Never mind," I said. "The way things are going, when this is over, I might have a few grand in the car. Early tii! Round taillights! I think the point here is a zero-stakes version of the money-heavy classic I always wanted. Just with, uh, less investment ennui, or whatever."

Joe blinked in a way that suggested but did not actually express surprise. "You think? You don't know?"

"What do you mean?"

"Aren't you leading this project?" He sounded unconvinced.

"I'm not really sure?" I waved a hand at the three people nearby who were busily kicking or beating or welding something. "This all just sort of took on its own momentum."

A funny look. Then he shrugged and grabbed a hammer and started hitting something constructively, because that's how engineers work.

Perhaps you have noticed the large quantity of shrugging.

The outer rockers came off by hand, as Ben had said. Paul took a Sharpie and scrawled LEFT on one and RIGHT on the other, and then we set them aside. (I would later discover those labels to be purposely incorrect. Ben, Owen, and Paul found this very funny.)

The extent of the rocker damage was amusing; in one of the car's past lives, some enterprising body man had opened up the sills to repair rust and found the box-shaped factory reinforcement structure corroded to nothing. Rather than replace the box properly, he simply cut out its remains, welded new exterior steel over the empty hole, painted the area with a broom, and charged for the work. A house all drywall, no frame.

If you ever get to thinking that working on cars is hard, if you're ever afraid to start, just remember that an awful lot of people out there think this stuff is easy. And most of them are worse at it than you.

Saturday afternoon, in a moment of contemplation, I mentioned that idea to Paul. In a past life, he was a restoration tech on high-end classic cars, Mercedes Gullwings and the like. When I said something to him, he was in the middle of taking a grinder to the 2002's floor. He stopped and thought for a second.

"Sometimes," he said, "one man's trash is just . . . another man's trash."

I felt a pang of guilt at the idea of having him work on my garbage and said so.

"Are you kidding? This is a pleasure. Professionally? Taking the rear end out of an E-type that hasn't moved in 30 years, mouse skeletons falling on my face, or putting a 300 SL frame back under the body—there are consequences. Not here. This is lovely. This thing cannot get any worse."

His hair was caked with a fine layer of flaked rust. A few feet away, Tim and the MIG welder briefly set some undercoating on fire. The

Smithology

smoke was inky and black. I chucked a carbide bit into WenDie and began to make a rusty hole less rusty and larger.

I love this stuff. Maybe I'm broken.

Not that better instincts didn't tempt. Muscle memory for process kept ghosting up, born from the years I've spent working on cars as both amateur and professional, and from watching talented people do good work properly, all the way back to hanging out at Dad's restoration shop as a kid. I kept thinking about how I have never really been satisfied with the results of my work, always aiming for better.

Toward the end of the weekend, I found Ben with a beer and raised the subject.

"Do you have that slippery-slope voice in your head?" I said. "The one that just keeps telling you to do all this right? Instead of whatever it is that we're doing here?"

"Well, yeah," he said. "But not here. Have you looked at this thing?"

Naturally, some parts of the car were simply beyond my ability to improve. I am a mediocre welder on my best day. Early on, while stitching together a shock-tower patch, I fell down a rabbit hole. The patch metal was thin and cheap and didn't enjoy the abuse. I burned a hole in the steel almost immediately, moving the puddle too slow, then ground down the bead I had just made and attempted a fix. Then I ground down that ugly repair and tried to fix it again.

As that last weld was cooling, I flipped the mask up. Owen had been watching my little circus and was chuckling.

"It's awful," I said, flipping the mask back down, striking another arc. "I'd laugh, too."

He smiled. "It's not like I weld any better."

In his later years, the astronomer Carl Sagan wrote about science and existence. One of his books holds this nice little passage about our efforts to understand the universe, and the balance between futility and necessity therein. I read those words in college and was enthralled, fascinated by the notion that some complex situations are worth making sense of, while others not so much. And by the idea that much of life is simply the struggle to develop the ability to see the difference.

I looked at the weld again.

"I know I should lean in here," I told Owen. "I mean, it's not like pretty welding makes the car less of a pile. We're putting a kludgey patch over rusty towers and then a kludgey patch under them and the rocker tubes are the basically like gluing crutches to someone's arms after they've broken a leg. So why does it bug me that this weld looks so bad?"

Ben, walking by, overheard. "What would Carl say?"

Owen didn't miss a beat. "He'd say cut it up."

Not Sagan. Carl Nelson, Owen's dad. He runs a BMW service and restoration shop in La Jolla, California, where Owen grew up. Carl is a wonderful human with a PhD in geology who wears shorts every day of the year and works within sight of a beach. A friend once described him as "an optimistic Disney character." He seems to enjoy lost causes, which is convenient, because we hang out.

The strangeness of California, where a rusty hole in a floor can mean Junk the Thing. Or at least, it once did for 2002s, when the cars were everywhere there, generally in good shape, and worth almost nothing.

I stood up and headed to the office to grab a bottle of water. As I stepped out the door, I overheard Owen talking to his girlfriend, Veronica, who sat nearby.

"You know," he said to her, "I bet this actually turns out to be a really good car. I bet it's great."

Smithology

When I returned from the office, a repetitive thumping was echoing from the far side of the car. I walked over to find Ben hitting the right rear quarter panel with a fist, strong raps, near a rocker tube he had just tack-welded in place. The steel rang cleanly, no buzzing or rattling, each hit producing an airy boom.

"Man," I said. "It did not sound that good yesterday. Solid now?"

"Solid."

He wasn't wrong.

But, you know, he wasn't *right*, either.

---

1. Re: Wegweiser zoology and greasy knees, see page 461.

Part Five
Your Trailing Arms Are Too Short to Box With Carl

HAGERTY, OCTOBER 2020

By this point, we had spent two nonconsecutive weekends at Ben's shop. The project would end up consuming six weekends in total, the work spread across summer and fall. The timing of our trips to Chicago was dictated by family and work commitments for all parties involved and thus hugely irregular. Things mostly just happened when they happened, whenever the Crapcan Avengers could assemble.

Smithology

On the third weekend, around noon on Saturday, I saw Carl walk outside with two trailing arms—large steel parts, the heart of the independent suspension at the 2002's rear axle. In the parking lot, he knelt on the pavement and began wire-brushing them clean. Clearing off paint and rust by hand.

The act struck me as odd. I walked over and watched for a moment.

"There was this thing," I said, as Carl brushed, "where, several weekends ago, in this very shop, I kept trying to make bits of this car nicer. Ben made fun of me for it. Because the rest of the car is so bad."

"He was right," Carl said, flatly. Still brushing.

"But you are making those arms nicer."

He did not look up. "I am."

My brow furrowed. "I don't understand."

Warm smile. "You probably shouldn't."

Know the rear suspension of a 2002, you know half the car, much of its character in a corner, and a good deal of BMW history. The firm now known as Bavarian Motor Works was born in the second decade of the 20th century and from a baffling arrangement of German companies. The players included an aircraft manufacturer, a builder of aircraft engines, Germany's third-ever carmaker, and the amusing particulars of German business logic.

The Bayerische Motoren Werke name was first attached to one of those firms in 1917. The famous black-white-blue "roundel" logo first appeared that year; 1917 was also the first year the letters "BMW" were used on a product, a six-cylinder aviation powerplant. BMW historians, however, now mark the marque's founding annum as 1916, because the 1917 BMW later sold its name and engine-making operation to the aforementioned aircraft manufacturer, which was—you guessed it—founded in 1916.

Confusingly, that sale took place in 1922, a fact that is neither here nor there and included in this narrative mostly as amusing reminder that you should never ask a German to tell you a story about anything without first ensuring reliable access to strong drinks.

Regardless, BMW spent the years until World War II making neat stuff. There were stout motorcycles and practical slow cars and impractical fast cars, and important races were won. In the second World War, the marque built aircraft engines, including some of the first workable turbojets. By the 1950s, Germany's decimated economy had left the company struggling. As the firm flirted with insolvency, its factories kept the lights on by cranking out affordable, bare-bones transportation.

The first of those low-cost machines was the Isetta 250—a two-seat, 12-hp steel pimple designed by an Italian refrigerator manufacturer and built by BMW under license. (In perhaps the Madison Avenue overstatement of the century, one ad called it "7.5 Feet of Thrill-Packed Driving!") In 1957, the Bavarians released a 9.5-foot-long derivative, a four-seat, 20-hp "limousine" called the Isetta 600.

The 250 was made of simple parts; its rear wheels were supported by a single pivoting suspension member, or swing arm. Being a big boy of supreme power and comfort, the 600 needed sturdier hardware, so company engineers hit the drawing board. The rear suspension that resulted comprised two triangular control arms, one per wheel, the twin pivots of each arm canted toward the outside of the car. Drive came from a Volkswagenish transaxle and two half shafts with flexible joints.

A rear suspension, allegedly.

Suspension of this type is commonly referred to as "semi-trailing arm"—the "semi" representing the arms' cant, or sweep angle. (In engineering terms, a true trailing arm of this type is unswept, the axis of its pivot points perpendicular to the car's fore-aft centerline.) The setup was far from novel but cheap and effective. Moreover, the basic idea carried on under new BMWs for decades, from the company-saving 1500 four-door of 1962—an all-new Hail Mary that could have killed the brand if it flopped—to the last Z3 sports cars built in 2001. Every

3-series sedan and coupe before 1992 wore semi-trailing arms, as did every 5-series prior to 1996, every 7-series to 1994, the first two BMW M5s, the first M6, and the first M3.

The design evolved along the way. Geometry was updated to improve wheel control. Subframes and bearing carriers were enlarged to benefit masters like torsional rigidity and the ever-rising grip of consumer road tires. In the end, the concept worked well enough with the 1500's 80 hp and pencil-thin 165-section rubber, and it remained adequate for the 315 horses and 245 rear meats of a 2001 Z3 M Coupe.

Plus, it was fun on a bun.

There were drawbacks. A semi-trailing arm can show a tire a relative heap of suffering. The design generally allows a wheel's vertical tilt, or camber, to change drastically with suspension compression or droop, altering cornering and braking ability on the fly. On top of that, bushing compliance under braking or a sudden throttle lift can cause the rear wheels to abruptly steer a little to the outside.

In normal driving, that brake/lift steering effect can help a car point into a corner. As forces rise, however, the effect blooms. Given the right load and conditions, the "steering" of the rear wheels can briefly outshout that of the fronts.

Loose, as they say in NASCAR. *Dorifto*, in Japan. Or in the U.S., "Martha, Timmy wrapped the M5 around a telephone pole again."

Naturally, there are better answers. Semi-trailing arms were once used by a host of carmakers, but the layout was long ago eclipsed by other suspension arrangements, nearly all of which can be tuned for greater grip, comfort, and stability.

Still, for years, that funky, vibrant feel meant something to the faithful. When you fired an old BMW into a corner, you felt the thing all vivid in your hands, fizzy and alive.

Which brings us back to my half-dead pile of crap.

When Saturday morning rolled around, Carl and Mark Francis were still on West Coast time. They had flown in from San Diego on Friday night, landing at O'Hare. From there, they cannoned into Ben's shop, where they met the small gathered crowd, disappeared an industrial quantity of beer, and eventually caught a ride to a hotel. The two men returned around noon the next day.

Mark said he was not hung over. Then he walked over to the 2002 and used a large mallet to hit a floor panel repeatedly while cackling. At that point, I believed that he was not hung over, but I was not exactly not hung over, so I mostly just stood there and breathed slowly while trying to figure why a sixtysomething professional TIG welder from California was intent on hollering directly into the gaping maw of my all-consuming headache.

It was probably because he is my friend.

Side note: I go road racing with these people. Ben (engineer for our little team), Carl (crew chief, excels at paddock parties), Mark (owns the car, specializes in metal fabrication and sundry hooting). Along with a rotating cast of around 10 other lovely folk, we campaign a 1972 2002 in a West Coast club-racing series. When the car does not do well, it is generally because I have failed as a driver, or because the previous evening contained obscene quantities of beer.

Paradoxically, beer is also why we have won races, and if you do not understand that sentence, then you have never been sucked into the money-eating whirlpool of illogical joy that is zero-stakes amateur racing.

Mark (left) and Carl, twin champions of the realm.

Carl strolled into the shop and dropped a large duffel on the floor. It hit the concrete with a clang. "TSA looked at me funny," he said.

Carl and Mark are roughly the same age. Each has lived in San Diego for decades; they met several years back after Mark bought a 2002 on something like a lark and realized that one of America's preeminent vintage-BMW authorities was just down the street. Apart, the two men are relatively sedate; together, they catalyze into good-natured trouble, like fissionable Muppets. When Carl is really busy or simply having a great time, his hair points straight out, like the patterns in a Tesla coil.

"I got the secondary inspection at the airport," he said. "For the meat backpack."

I glanced at the tii's rear subframe, on the ground a few feet away. "They didn't ask about the, uh, large steel suspension parts?"

"Oh no," he said. "Those were in a checked bag."

From the depths of that checked duffel then arose two unrusty and ex-California 2002 trailing arms, to replace my car's terminally rotten versions of same. Carl's backpack, unloaded into the shop fridge the night before, had carried across the country 40 pounds of raw tri-tip steak, planned for the shop grill on Saturday night. (A 40-pound raw pig also sat in the building, also aimed at that grill, but that's a story for another time.)

The welding began early. More floor and subframe-mount repair. Mark fired up Ben's TIG machine. Matt McGinn, in from Connecticut, grabbed the MIG gun. Matt is ex-Army in both resume and profanity; like Carl, he runs a BMW-centric restoration shop. Over the course of the weekend, welding almost nonstop, he and Mark formed a strange bond. The two would lie under or in or on the 2002 for hours on end, pouring MIG wire and TIG stick into it simultaneously. In the process, each developed a habit of yelling increasingly creative four-letter words on something like the hour, or if the weather shifted, or whenever the twin welding machines pulled enough current to trip one of the building's electrical breakers. When anything happened at all, really. Maybe overdosing on the smell of electrically melted steel sets your synapses to "bellow."

That afternoon, Matt was in the car, walloping the rear floor with a hammer while merrily shouting obscenities. It seemed like a good time to thank him for coming to town.

He paused. "Are you kidding? I love this. I mean, where else would I be—at my daughter's soccer game? Which is great, but like, I'm not getting self-actualized. Where am I on the f***in' pyramid?"

Francis and McGinn, twin champions of the ... weld-yelling.

Walloping recommenced. As if on cue, Carl walked up with a newly cleaned trailing arm. Mark set down his TIG gun, stood up, and took the arm in hand, focused. He then produced a large piece of allthread, running it through both of the arm's bushing holes and securing it at each end with a nut. Satisfied, he grabbed a small piece of bent steel—a patch—and started test-fitting it into the crook of the arm.

"Wait," I said. "What's going on?"

Carl hung out nearby, looking content. "The allthread keeps it from warping under weld heat," he said.

"No, I mean the patch?"

A standard 2002 trailing arm has two legs. Each is C-shaped in cross-section, with the C's open side to the inside of the arm. The 2002tii was a performance model, so the factory reinforced those arms by closing off

Smithology

the C with steel. Most people now see this reinforcement as nice but unnecessary, a classic piece of overengineering. Fresh off the line, a 1972 2002 featured 4.5-inch wheels and 113 hp. The tii of that year stepped up to 5.0-inchers and 130. The delta wasn't exactly a Hemi swap and drag slicks, but that's old-world Germans for you. Some parts of a 2002 were made cheaply; others were comically overdone and last forever.

By this point, Mark had his welding mask down and was poking at the MIG machine. He flipped the mask up, eyes wide for effect. "It's a tii!" Then he slapped the mask down again and began welding, a shower of sparks. "Needs the box," he muttered.

Carl gave the straightest of all possible faces. "He made patches."

"It's a tii!" Mark yelled, still welding. Same inflection, like a broken record.

I gawped. "It's not a museum piece. Are you joking?"

"No," Carl said. "We never joke."

On a race car wearing factory arms, the tii reinforcement genuinely aids arm stability—but then, Mark's '72 2002, given Hoosier R7 race tires, can pull around 1.5 g in a corner. My car was about as likely to meet a full g as it was to meet the Dalai Lama.

I considered opposing themes for a second, then went on to something else. Past a certain point, when one of your companions is busily grilling a combined 80 pounds of meat, you don't ask questions.

Once Mark had boxed both arms, Carl handed them to Paul. He painted them with a spray can, then installed new brake lines and set the whole thing aside.

Pretty. Not unsatisfying. In the end, though, Paul's face wrinkled, concerned.

Kneeling next to an arm, he carefully turned its wheel bearing with a finger. Then he looked up at me.

"I don't like the way this feels."

I reached down and rolled the bearing with a finger. The inner race felt lumpy.

Bearings aren't supposed to lump. I called Carl over, asked if he had brought new bearings. He was unperturbed.

"Oh, that? That's fine. I looked at them—this car, it won't matter."

The two men each had a lifetime of experience with old BMWs. Paul cocked his head. Carl noticed.

"Don't worry about it."

Ben walked over, glanced at the arm. On that day, his shop held enough 2002s for a parade. "That?" he said. "It's fine. Those bearings are huge."

Carl said something about having seen maybe a handful of worn-out 2002 rear wheel bearings in his entire career. I briefly contemplated the thousands of cars that might pass through a California BMW shop in more than three decades.

"It'll smooth out with load," he said. "They rarely even get noisy. Way too big for the job."

"What about the race car?" I asked. "Surely they wear, with R7s?"

"Oh, hell no. Not the rears, at least. Start with new ones, they don't budge. Last forever."

Ben chuckled. Carl stepped outside to answer his phone. Paul hung the brake assemblies on each trailing arm, then installed the stub axles.

When he was done, an hour or so later, he showed me an axle, rolled it in the bearing.

"Feel that."

I did. Still lumpy.

"See?"

"I dunno, man," I said. "I would normally think twice, but these guys have done this a billion times more than you and me put together."

He poked at the arm for a second, then ambled off to smoke a cigarette. I stood in that corner of the shop for a minute, watching sparks cascade out from the 2002.

"Build quality," I heard my voice say, to no one in particular.

What a loaded phrase. And how remarkable, our obsession with measurable value. You work on the car, as a fine man once wrote, and the car works on you. In a fluid world, overbuilt objects are a sort of testament. That testament grows only more interesting when you consider the whys of compromise and of making anything. How a company can design a product for a certain kind of person, the choices during that process so ideal for a given point in history that their appeal outlasts the object itself.

For better or worse, BMW now is not the BMW of old. Same for German cars in general. Mercedes-Benz ads toot about The Best or Nothing, and if you drive a 1950s Gullwing, that line seems to flirt with reality. Then you learn about the chronic rust of an early 2000s S-class or the repair costs of a late-model C63, and the idea backs up a little.

Quality becomes fungible, negotiable for the day, but the appeal of never shrinks. After all, it says something when an individual decides to do good work. Even more when a person makes that choice with little in the way of resources. A few pieces of steel, say, a tired old car where a few parts really matter, and a problem, however simple, to be solved.

Sam Smith

Project Weissrat:
Work Accomplished — Weekend Four

- Trailing-arm bushings replaced
- Trailing arms cleaned/painted
- Doors removed
- Right rocker reinforcement-tube welding completed
- Right-floor rust repair (mostly) completed
- Right subframe-mount repair completed
- Left rocker reinforcement tube installed, plug welded to sill
- Left floor repair (mostly) completed
- A-pillar vertical reinforcement tube welding begun
- Brake master cylinder replaced
- Front brake rotors and right front brake caliper replaced
- Subframe mounts replaced (2X)
- New hard brake lines bent/installed, rear suspension
- New flexible brake lines installed
- New hard front brake lines bent/installed, front struts
- Windshield removed
- Rust hole under windshield seal cleaned, welded shut
- Windshield reinstalled (hasty, five minutes, not permanent)
- Doors reinstalled
- Brake drums painted hi-viz yellow by Paul for the sole purpose of irritating Sam
- Open ends of rocker reinforcement tubes capped with steel, welded shut

- **Forty-pound pig** (right) cooked on Weber grill (1X)
- **Car floor hit with hammer,** by Mark, for no reason, while laughing (10X)
- **Body weight in beer** drank, by Mark, for, as he claimed, "welding reasons" (1X)
- **Car slowly pushed back into shop storage** (1X).

Part Six
When You're On the Way to Fix a 2002 and Your 2002 Breaks

HAGERTY, FEBRUARY 2021

It began with Paul's head gasket. Somewhere in Ohio, on the freeway from Pittsburgh to Chicago.

Paul likes dragging ass-faced old cars from barns and then driving them around as if they were normal vehicles, neither ass-faced nor redolent of barn, which is partly why I enjoy Paul. On this particular Friday, he was caning one of those barn funkos across a Buckeye interstate at some speed north of sanity. In a 2002, that means fourth gear, the highest one available, and 4000 rpm or more, the whole thing cooking along in seemingly unstoppable momentum, like a pot of water on rolling boil.

Except: Water needs heat to boil, is far from unstoppable. And so, it turns out, was Paul's crapwagon '02. Somewhere in the great upper Midwest, the decades-old head gasket under that hood took one last look at its surroundings, grabbed its coat and hat, and said, after hours of endless whippery, *No*.

When Paul told me this story hours later, he was laughing. And so I thought, well, that's nice. As a lady who used to cut my hair once said, who doesn't love a good bang?

The crapwagon in question.

Our fourth weekend in Chicago. Four weekends with a grand experiment, each Friday bringing a slightly different collection of out-of-towners to Ben's shop, mostly without plan. Parts were shipped to Ben's door by methods various and sundry. Welding wire was consumed by the crateload. All because a certain individual had decided to save a car far worse than Paul's from the crusher.

It had made sense to me, once, in a way. That was months ago. After a point, some projects simply carry their own inertia, like a chain reaction. Or maybe just that feeling you get when you start eating pizza and don't stop until your stomach dwarfs Cleveland.

Smithology

So much was unplanned. The day Paul's engine took a breather, I was on crutches. We could discuss exactly how I managed to snap clean in half the outermost metatarsal in my right foot, but all you really need to know is that margaritas were involved, plus some friends and a party, and it was one of those evenings where you're wheeling around the kitchen having a grand old time like a big fat Muppet, and then, suddenly, you are not.

That was weeks before, in Connecticut. The hospital to which I was taken was near Lime Rock Park, which is a neat memory, because I had been at that track that day for a TV shoot. No Lime Rock visit is ever not a neat memory, even if you later in that same day end up breaking some crucial part of yourself.

"Oh my," the X-ray technician had said. Like a parent to a toddler. A suppressed giggle.

Across the room, lying beneath a large radiation gun, I sighed, dejected. "I am going to get nothing done."

"Well, not for a while, anyway."

"Are you sure?"

She paused, careful with words. "Well . . . that's for the doctor to say, but you did a number here."

I thought for a moment. "A fun number? Tap-dancing, singing?"

The tech, no longer amused, turned back to her monitor. "No."

Crutches.

My brain performed a version of the award-winning act where it hears something it doesn't like and immediately looks out the window and starts composing fun little songs about puppies.

"You're not really useful anyway," Ben said, a few weeks later, when I wobbled into his office. "This isn't much of a change."

"Har," I replied. It sounded like challenge. Then I tried to carry my laptop bag across the room and nearly face-planted into a shelf.

Ben is a man of subtle gestures. He grew up in Chicago and has the kind of droll personality you get from living through more than 40 Illinois winters while fixing people's salt-eaten daily drivers. He has seen most things Car before and thus trades generally in eyebrow raises.

"Sit down," he said. "You're going to break something."

"I already did. Me."

"Something valuable."

I couldn't sit, though. The car wasn't done. Why I went to Chicago in the first place.

Which is partly, if not entirely, why this story is about other people.

Have you ever witnessed a storm building on the horizon, watched the clouds grow, then been delightfully humbled as the whole thing rumbles and rolls into town?

Some people view properly executed improv as the highest form of art. Paul is a resourceful sort. He is also lucky. When that head gasket failed on a dark fall afternoon and almost immediately began throwing heaps of cylinder pressure into wind and engine coolant passage, he pulled off at the next exit. Through the remarkable grace of God or the clockwork of the universe or whatever deity you subscribe to, that exit happened to hold a parts store, a Harbor Freight, a U-Haul franchise, and a pizza joint. All within a mile of each other.

"I had what I needed," Paul said later, proud.

Ben cocked his head. "Except a head gasket, at that parts store."

"Touché." He pointed a finger in Ben's direction, as if that proved something.

Naturally, when Paul swung into Chicago that weekend, it was with an empty U-Haul box truck and a nearly dead 2002 on a rented trailer. That night, as on every other weekend when folks had come together to throw tools and steel at my car, beer bottles were opened. Someone cracked a handle of gin. And the next morning, as I rode a wave of prescription-grade goofballs for the pain, everyone but me got to work.

A head-gasket replacement is straightforward work on most old cars, which makes it a fun job to watch. Once you strip an engine of its intake and accessories and disconnect the valvetrain from the engine's bottom end—the exact steps vary from car to car—you are free to unbolt the cylinder head and replace the large composite gasket sealing head to engine block. A 2002's head is cast aluminum, and while that casting is not small, one person can lift it out of the car without much trouble.

Pull a cylinder head, you can stare down at piston tops. I've always found open cylinders soothing, enjoyed imagining the pressure and traveling flame they can contain. I had not, however, previously stared into a headless block while having neat little hallucinations about the strange and magnificent nature of generous friends.

Maybe it was the painkillers. (Munitions-grade. Talked to my toes as they kicked in.) It might have been the rampant sleep deprivation caused every night by my screaming foot. It might have simply been the fact that, four weekends into this silly endeavor, people just kept showing up at Ben's place, without being asked, to work on my hurt little dirtbomb.

The meds were pretty good, though.

I lost count of the bodies working in the shop. Six? Fifteen? Ben's service bays were occupied by other projects, so Paul and Carl began decapitating Paul's car in the parking lot. Larry, who lives near Tim in Minnesota, showed up, his first weekend in the mix, and immediately set about sifting through spare sheetmetal. Owen took to cleaning something.

Two seconds with a straight-edge showed that Paul's cylinder head had warped in the wake and heat of the failed gasket, so it needed to be decked, shaved flat at a machine shop. Carl plopped the head on the ground and proceeded to relieve it of its plumbing.

I took a few pictures and then crutched carefully into the shop and over to my car. Long-term projects can play tricks on perception; timelines can seem to compress and drag out beyond the space they eat on a calendar. When I trailered the BMW to Chicago, months prior, it had been almost existentially rusty. The car was now noticeably more stout but even less existentially sound; the tub held something like rockers, floors, and subframe mounts, just not in the traditional sense. The machine that had left Bavaria 50 years ago in spot-welded precision was now perhaps 50 or 60 percent less precise, held together by a garter belt of mild-steel pipe and sheet-metal sarcophagi.

In short, it was coming back around to resembling a car. Probably. From 20 feet away.

The swarm of activity continued as on previous weekends. For the first time, however, I was a fixed point, idle, apart from the swirl. Larry lay down under the tii's front floor and began busily excavating one of the rotten frame rails, yanking out dirt and rotten metal. Tim was poking at the right rear quarter, measuring something. Ben walked up to the right rear window and squinted suspiciously at a rust hole. Then he and Tim conferred on something, a brief closed-shoulder huddle, two engineering degrees murmuring near the rear fender. One of them said, "can you do linear approximation of that pipe?" In the background, an angle grinder lit off.

Having a Jewish mother and also a conscience, I felt immediately guilty. I had worked on this car with these people. The project wasn't theirs or mine, it just was. Stillness seemed wrong.

Smithology

There were early attempts at protest. I teetered around, stumbling through the close quarters of Ben's shop and knocking my crutches into things, trying to keep people from doing work. Giving earnest sentiments like *stop it, I can't help, this is silly, Paul's car has real needs, we'll deal with my pile in the next trip, why don't we all just grill some food for lunch and drink a morning beer and not worry about it.*

Lather, rinse, repeat at anyone with a tool in their hand. No takers.

Owen finally shut me up. He overheard the tail of one of those pleadings while walking across the shop, then caught my eye. He gave an impish grin and a little palms-up shrug, like Alfred E. Neuman. "What fun is that?"

New steel at the left front wheel: vertical A-pillar tube meets horizontal rocker tube.

You ever get the feeling that literally every single one of your friends is smarter than you?

A switch tripped in my noggin. I decided to roll with it.

Paul's cylinder head went out for repair shortly after lunch. It was a Saturday, and Ben's machine shop was closed, but Ben hopped in his car and drove there anyway. Ninety minutes later, he was back, and the head had a fresh cut.

Ben made it clear to Paul that he had called in a favor. Being a clever man, he did so in a fashion that both hinted at mild annoyance and made everyone laugh.

"I hope you know," he said, "I don't do this for everyone."

Paul squinted at Ben in what was obviously gratitude but would not be announced as such. "Oh, I know." Then he took a drag off his cigarette and eyed his car as you might eye a dog that has just taken a dump on the carpet.

The hurricane of activity resumed. While Paul's engine went back together outside, Carl bent new brake lines for my rear subframe. Owen readied a steel tube to mate what remained of the 2002's rear wheel arches with the tubes that now passed for rocker panels. Larry got to welding on the floor. (Once, football-size holes. Now, something less.) I tried to busy myself with small jobs and bench work, but everyone else moved faster and wasn't tied to a pair of derpy aluminum sticks. In a cramped space, I mostly just got in the way.

Around 3:00 that afternoon, I crutched over to Larry, who had moved on to stitching a steel coat around the withered left frame rail. Larry is what he calls "a recovering corporate engineer"—several years ago, he quit his job with a large company in order to open a restoration shop. He is exceedingly polite and executes the kind of stellar bodywork that all but guarantees you a long customer waiting list, which his shop has. I hobbled up just in time to see him kick a footlong piece of rusty steel out from where he was lying under the car.

"Just curious," I said, leaning down. "How much of a pain is this rail for you?"

He slid out and stood up, brushing off his coverall legs. "It's not bad. Just time. You have to get through the rust and dirt and the paint and the tar and . . . it just blows up, lights the whole thing up. So you kind of do one pass of weld to clean it out, and then another to actually weld it. You have to sort of make it up as you go along."

Larry versus A-pillar remains.

"There isn't an ounce of this project that hasn't followed some version of that pattern."

He laughed. "You knew this going in, of course."

"All I knew was, it seemed really dumb to do anything but junk this thing, so that seemed like good reason to not junk it. Honestly, I'm still just shocked that everyone's working on it. Instead of doing literally anything else."

More drive-by zingers: Paul happened to be walking by, carrying a piece of steel. As he walked, he pointed at the car, then at me, then his chest, over and over, with a smarmy grin.

"I mean, what can I say? People like *animals!*"

I had been sipping on a bottle of water. I hucked it at his head without stopping to cap it. Paul ducked and the bottle missed, but it arced a geyser over the shop floor as it flew. Ben scowled and told me to clean it up.

Everyone's a comic.

A few feet away, Carl piped up gently, in the tone of a person who has seen almost everything. "Don't be silly. It's not about the car."

That happy little your-friends-are-smarter-than-you thing again.

Sunday morning, his 2002 once again whole, Paul turned back to my tii. He hung a new center bearing and flex disc on the driveshaft, then finished rebuilding the brake hydraulics while Carl and Owen bolted down the diff. All straightforward work, but it would have gone faster with another pair of hands. Mine just sat there on my right leg, as they had the day before. In a folding chair on the shop floor, the leg propped up on a bucket to stem the swelling.

The pills had worn off, but my foot didn't feel that bad. Humility is solid anesthetic.

I write these words months later, out of the cast and walking again. My right foot is still a little sore, and one toe has a habit of going numb at odd times, but that's trivial. You deal with the remnants of injury as you deal with bad weather, and weather rolls through your life in the same manner as people. Sometimes, as with a broken foot, you don't see it coming. Then the sky is clear again or the bone has healed, everything back to normal, and the memory is all that's left.

Along with, in this case, a rusty old pile of rat-car disaster. One that was beginning to seem like it might soon be mobile.

Maybe.

Still much to do.

Fingers crossed.

Part Seven
Until You One Day Wake Up and Have Actually Gone Someplace

HAGERTY, MAY 2021

At 11:52 a.m. Chicago time, on Sunday, October 11, year of our trash car 2020, structural metalwork was declared complete.

A lot of people did a lot of things to get through that year. For my part, some friends and I went all goober-weld obsessive and gave life to a dead old BMW for virtually no reason.

What do you do with a machine that almost certainly lived through a saltwater flood and is missing some 80 percent of its body structure below the seat mounts and should by all rights be thrown away?

Follow-up question: What if you bought said machine on a whim, because you're a softie and the seller was a nice guy and the car was cheap as old socks?

Follow-up to the follow-up: If you're not a softie for lost causes and old loves, are you even a car person to begin with? Wouldn't your money be better off in the bank?

So much on the 2002 was gone. We didn't bring all of it back; that would have been a stupid bridge too far, and just as important, I didn't have the money. So we went somewhere else entirely.

I bought the BMW last summer. Last winter, after leaving Chicago, I replaced, serviced, cleaned, adjusted, or rebuilt nearly everything consumable and/or untouched at Ben's, from every wear part in the suspension to the door panels, the internal door-latch grommets, a driveline list a mile long.

That labor consumed most of my spare time in the cold-weather months, hours and hours on evenings and weekends, but that stuff was easy, meditative, nothing special. The real work went down last fall, a truly massive amount of slapdash welding and exoskeleton installation and bracing, over those six weekends in Chicago. At the end of each day, we'd all sit outside in the parking lot and eat grilled dinner, watching the sun set over one of my favorite cities and trying not to think about the rest of the world.

This tale has been published on this website in installments. Early in this project, someone jumped into the comment section of one of these stories and expressed concern for my liability. Nonfactory "restoration" done as a larf, they noted, can leave the "restorer" open to lawsuits in the wake of a traffic accident. People have been sued for their involvement in nonstandard vehicular body repair before, and for far less deviation from factory methods than our work represents.

I meant to reply to that comment and didn't, but it's irrelevant. I long ago decided that this car will either leave my hands as scrap steel, cut up in a Dumpster, or not leave them at all.

Sam Smith

A quick summary of what went down in Illinois:

SILLS: Rotten factory rocker structure excavated and replaced with rectangular tubing the length of the car, plug-welded into the cabin sill from beneath.

A-PILLAR AND REAR-SUBFRAME REINFORCEMENT: Round tubing was built into an L-shape and used to reinforce the weakened A-pillar structure, creating something like a load path for the rocker tubes. A similar idea was used at the rear subframe.

REAR-SUBFRAME MOUNTING STRUCTURES: The factory ones were gone, vanished. New box sections were built and welded to the floors, using aftermarket repair panels, in factory style.

SHOCK-TOWER PATCHING: A sarcophagus of steel patchwork was created around the original shock towers, which had split and torn from rust. The bad is still in there, but now it won't come out for a bit.

FLOORS: Holes of varying size (from "football" to "golf ball") were patched, sloppily, to be less holey. There may still be a hole or two and some weld drips left, but who's counting?

COMPONENTS REPLACED, SOURCED, OR REPAIRED: Windshield, driveshaft flex coupling, driveshaft center bearing, gearbox mount, motor mounts, trailing arms, rear subframe, rear subframe rubber mounts, main (high-pressure) fuel feed line, front bumper, strut bearings, front wheel bearings, wheel cylinders, calipers, rotors, brake flex lines, most of the rigid brake lines, brake master cylinder, and this is not even the complete list, I forget the complete list. You get the picture.

And then, on November 16, 2020, at 10:44 in the morning Central Standard Time, I drove the thing onto a trailer and dragged it 550 miles south, to my house in Tennessee.

You do not get to see our awful work in detail. Not unless you spot it on the road in the months ahead, or at some car show I have entered for laughs. If that happens and you are impressed, find me. I will buy you a drink and a hamburger and ask why you insisted on eating paint chips when you were little.

I have driven it! On real roads! In traffic, and at real speed over mountains and back roads! It acts like a half-decent vehicle of appropriate motion and ability! An achievement that shouldn't be surprising but manages the trick anyway. I first drove this 2002 on the day I bought it, from the seller's driveway to a U-Haul trailer down the street. The subframe creaked in protest; wind blew through the carpet from beneath, poofing it up. Days later, in Tennessee, the subframe mounts crumbled when I poked them with a screwdriver.

It's good now. A strange word to use in this context, but what else do you call a vehicle that tracks straight at 80 mph, hands off the wheel?

My wife, when I shared with her that last fact: "Are you sure you want to do 80 mph in . . . that?"

Me: "It's a real car!"

Her: "Don't put the kids in it."

Me: "You're just saying that because they're healthy."

When the BMW hit Illinois, the A-pillars lacked undergarment; the sills were made of hate; the body was a bendy straw in general. The doors now latch on a finger. That last bit is one of those delightful little details that can, at the tail of a complex project, be far more satisfying than you expect. (For the record, back in Knoxville, I had to shim and tweak-hammer-twist-bludgeon the right door to get it to close without the striker hanging, because the B-pillar was, as they say in spy novels, dislocated.)

(The left door, though: Shut like butter.)

You know that feeling you get after eating a satisfying but unhealthy meal that took hours to prepare? That point where the table is finally empty, and the dishes are the only job left?

You ever just take a minute right then and there to lie on the floor and moan at the ceiling?

With most life-altering decisions, the end result matters less than the doing. Which is why I want to take a moment to tell you about the seats. I bought them online late one night, after much thought, fueled by a dangerous mix of dark-roast coffee and Sour Patch Kids.

In the late 1960s, German aftermarket company Recaro rose to prominence through the development and sale of sports and racing seats. The company's early offerings made novel use of foam padding—most seating companies then built cushions from horsehair—but also large bolsters, to help a body stay in place.

Recaro became so known for quality that some carmakers began offering the company's seats as factory fitment. Porsche famously used a particular Recaro *sportsitze* in the 911 S of the 1960s and early 1970s; the same model was offered in early 2002s. Original versions of those seats in good condition now bring more than $10,000 per pair.

My 2002 did not come with good seats. It entered my life with an absolutely roached set of Flofits, aftermarket buckets maybe 40 years old. The fabric was torn and mildewed, the foam half dust.

I spent a lot of time thinking about those seats. A margarita helped, at one point. A savings account was eyed. Budget retconning occurred on grand scale.

Did you know that there is an Italian seating firm called BF Torino, and that this company will ship you a set of brand-new early Recaro clones, straight from Italy, in mere weeks? Like the rare Borrani steel wheels that the tii now wears, those seats represented the target: period DGAF rat, plus a few nice touches.

It's remarkable, what you can convince yourself is necessary, when absolutely nothing is necessary. Moreover, I figured, if you're actually going to drive a thing and use it to go places, why skimp on the skeleton holster?

What I didn't realize was how the car was mutating into a different kind of project. It started off as a way to kill time and salute a period when machines like it were cheap and disposable. Except you don't put $2000 worth of seats in a junkyard AWOL-er you built for a laugh.

Or maybe you do?

That final weekend in Chicago amounted mostly to cleaning and reassembly of the interior. In a fit of optimism, someone announced the metalwork complete, the shell safe to drive. That afternoon, everyone sat down and had a beer in Ben's lot. Paul, ever industrious, rolled under the car to tackle some last-minute detail on the driveshaft. The flex disc there wore new hardware, bright and shiny, its nuts and bolts twinkling against a backdrop of lightly undone rot.

Once, years ago, I wanted to keep vehicles forever. I have since and over the course of many purchases learned that I am not this person, save the odd exception. There is for example the Mercedes-Benz W108 that my grandmother bought new, that my parents left their wedding in, that I left my wedding in; that car is in my father's garage and will eventually come live with me. There is also an old German motorcycle that has seen many miles at my hands and will move into the house, pickled in the living room, when I have grown too old and frail to ride it. Every other vehicle I've owned has left the building, as they said of Elvis, sold on, to make funds or room for some other interest.

An old friend helped make the white car happen. It was his shop and his gifted time and knowledge that helped the car come back to life; it was he who told me the idea wasn't stupid. Or, more accurately, that it was just stupid enough.

Just before I took the BMW home, we were talking in his office. For some reason, I flashed back to watching him weld a reinforcement over one of the rear spring perches.

"I've been thinking about that spring perch," I said. "How long it'll last, you know?"

Another of those shrugs. "I don't know," Ben said. "If it breaks, we just fix it again."

If a project is worth doing, it begins on one feeling and ends on another. You take stock and you get to work, and that work can take months or years. Small jobs become big jobs, the demands of real life cause simple tasks to stretch out unbelievably—it can take three weeks to find the 90 minutes needed to install the front suspension—but you keep moving anyway.

Then, of course, there is that surreal moment when you release the clutch. When the whole stack of hours moves again, after so long, surprisingly light on its feet. You lose track of time and just glide along, your body filled with air, and you are not thinking about when the grocery closes today or whether the kids need picked up from school or if the laundry is backing up for the fourth time this week, nothing like that at all, and the whole thing feels like a gift, it is a gift, there is no asking why or how or whether it was all worth it, of course it was worth it, how could it not be, not with a feeling like this, unique and so rare and brewing, buoyant as helium, all the way down in your deepest of bones.

At which point you stop and realize you're much further from home than you thought.

There are miles to go. Mostly nearby, for now. Then more venturing, farther and farther, as you do. Until you one day wake up and have actually gone someplace, gone there in this once-hulk dragged back to life, this improbable little pile of work and memory that you didn't know you needed until the day it showed up.

Until it invited itself in and you thought, *I mean, we weren't expecting guests, but.*

Time passes. You may wonder about letting go, about selling. Then something shifts. Who kicks family out of the house?

The first part of the job is over. Time to get to work on the rest.

Sam Smith

And What Since, Huh, Smith? (A Rat Epilogue)

A lot, actually. I took the car apart again. That first winter after bringing the 2002 home was a storm of sorting—rebuilding or replacing almost everything mechanical untouched in Chicago. Then, in August of 2021, I drove the BMW to California and back, 5000 miles in all, to enter it in a fancy car show, during the prestigious Monterey Car Week, as a joke.

The trip went off without hitch. I mean, I had to reattach the driveshaft center bearing in the parking lot of an Arizona Penney's, and a rusty brake line burst open in L.A. freeway traffic, but who's counting?

Time since has been dull by comparison. I pulled the engine last winter to fix a few leaks and install a light flywheel. The rusty hood skin has come loose and inflated like a balloon on the highway a few times, but that's a ten-second fix with pop rivets. These days, the BMW is used mostly for long trips and back-road snorts in the mountains near home. My kids have nicknamed the car Holey.

The engine is strong, but the pistons clatter on a cold start and the valve guides are tired, so a rebuild might be in the cards. Or maybe I'll simply keep driving the wheels off it, think about that later.

— December 2023

Afterword

When I began production on this book, I consulted a few friends with time in self-publishing. One, a former coworker, was a font of encouragement. Her most resonant piece of advice had to do with looking back on the work.

"Say something," she said, "about what it all meant."

What did it all mean? Good question. Months later, I still don't have an answer. I'm not sure I ever will. What I do have is a few smaller observations from all this that have come to mean a lot to me. Maybe they'll mean something to you.

I know that speed makes a car no more than shoelaces make a shoe, and that a horsepower rating is merely an address on a map, not the place itself. I know that the automobile has changed us as we have changed it, and that cars are a way for many people to be what they could not be otherwise, a key to places they can't or simply don't feel capable of going on their own.

I know that writing for a living has taught me a great deal about things that are not writing. That how we tell stories about ourselves can unintentionally reflect how we think the world should work; that clarity isn't always romantic; that rules exist for a reason; that some rules exist to be broken. And I know that, when you're learning, you tend to break the wrong rules first.

Afterword

I know that I probably made my job a lot harder by believing all of the above to matter in an industry built on numbers. But then, we are each stubborn in our own unique ways, and we often make our lives harder for reasons that matter only to us.

Two decades of doing anything can fool a person into thinking they know what comes next. In reality, we're all just mercury on a skillet, never tracing the same path twice. That's partly why driving can be so compelling, I think, why it can, on the best days, feel like a sketch of something larger. Every mile is a little different, even when road and car are the same.

Twenty years ago, I had no clue what I was doing in this job, but I loved discovering how much I didn't know. I hope to never reach the end of that path. I'm beyond lucky to have found the beginning.

Acknowledgments

This book was a labor of love, a happy and grateful survey of the first 20 years of a dream job. Like the body of work from which it draws, it exists because I have been helped, over the years, more times than I can count.

What follows is an attempt to thank the major players on that field. It is space-limited and by no means complete—for those I have had to leave out, please forgive me.

FIRST, TO YOU: Anyone who has spent their valuable time with something I have had the privilege to make or help make, whether that means reading, watching on TV or YouTube, or listening to a podcast. Your subscriptions, viewing hours, site visits, downloads, letters to the editor, and comments have made it all possible. What's more, you have reached out constantly over email and direct message, even found me at shows and races, to share what my work has meant to you. This book exists because you literally asked for it, and that fact is beyond humbling.

TO ADRIENNE, for her endless patience, kindness, editing, and support. And for all the sacrifice and solo parenting while I traveled for work, especially during our half-decade in Seattle, 2015 to 2020, when I was gone every other week for five years straight. You give your family and friends more than you know. And all I had to do to join that club was walk into your office at 120 East Liberty and put my feet on your desk like a pig.

To Marion and Vivien, the brightest of lights. Being your dad is one of my greatest joys. May you have the courage to dream big and laugh and fall and then dream all over again.

To John Krewson, who consulted on the production of this book and wrote the introduction. You have been an invaluable and deeply funny sounding board, collaborator, and friend for much of my life. If that weren't enough, you are an all-time, top-five, desert-island uncle to M. and V. I remain your biggest fan.

To the wonderful folks at Hagerty Media and Hearst Autos, who graciously consented to the republication of select stories from my work for Hagerty and *Road & Track*, respectively. Special thanks are due to Eddie Alterman, the Hearst Autos chief brand officer, and to Larry Webster, Hagerty's vice president of content and the editor-in-chief at *R&T* during much of my time there. As with so many moments in my career, this book would not have been possible without your generous support.

To Justin Page and Dave Burnett, the talented artists whose work graces the covers of this collection. It's an honor.

To Michael Chaffee, for all the film I swiped from your fridge and everything else. You are a Thing That Is Good.

To Peter Egan, for the compass.

To Sam Posey, for the reminder that spark and enthusiasm only stop flowing if you let them. And for making us feel, while dining in your kitchen, as if we belonged in the long line of greats who have had the privilege of your company there.

To Denise McCluggage. Words fail. You made a dent, ma'am.

To Dan Gurney, for being exactly who so many of us needed. And for the "make something beautiful" line, which I'll carry with me to the end of my days.

To Travis Okulski, for the brave year that was, and for always believing in your people. Which is the best kind of bravery.

To Carter Hendricks, for the phone calls that are always a shot in the arm, and for giving me a lifelong home at Quattroroute, regardless of how rarely I get back to St. Louis.

To Ross Bentley, for all the coaching that didn't have a thing to do with driving.

To Stanley and Malcolm Ross, for the trust. And for knowing, above all, that the stories are greater than any of us.

To everyone who made *Proving Grounds* on NBC Sports possible. But especially Michael Kane, J.F. "01001010 01000110" Musial, Matt "Hidden Temple" Hardigree, Leh Keen, Parker Kligerman, Will Barber, Armin Balg, Will Schultz, Ryan Symancek, and last but not least, a man who insists we are not friends, Zack Klapman. To paraphrase Rick Moranis in *Ghostbusters II*, once, I turned into a giant cup of coffee, and you guys helped me. Our silly little show was an improbable joy—I would have liked to have seen fourth-season Montana.

To Satch Carlson, the longtime editor-in-chief of *Roundel*, for giving a byline and patience to a young man who thought the written word best applied with a fire hose. And for mentioning my name to someone at *Automobile* in 2005. That first job interview didn't pan out, and I went back to working in parts at that Jaguar dealer. The second interview, though, months later—that changed my life. Write hard, die free, Bill Spear pins forever.

To Jean Jennings, who took a chance on a kid who wanted to work at her magazine so badly that he literally offered to clean the toilets. Thank you for the lessons and guidance, for not making me clean those toilets, and for keeping me around all those times I deserved to be kicked out.

To *Esquire*'s David Granger, whose work and perspective are an inspiration, and who welcomed me onto the masthead of an institution beloved by generations of writers. I never really believed I was good enough, but you never suggested otherwise.

To Barb Adams, Dave Farnsworth, Larry Schettel, Chris Simon, and everyone else in the Windy City chapter of the BMWCCA from 2003 to 2012. None of you knew me from Adam when I showed up, but from day one, you made a group of people and a newsletter feel like a second home, arms open.

To Marc Noordeloos, for the example, and for being kind that day with that Ford GT. Both echoed longer than you know.

To the late Gary Bossert, a fan in the best way. I would have signed this one, Gary. Hell, I would have stolen Dad's Seven and hand-carried a copy to Jersey in winter. We are never given enough time.

To Pete Cage of Maryland and Dan Hise of Mississippi, for the uplifting conversations and correspondence, which always seemed to come at the right time. I don't know what prompted either of you to first write to me, but I'm awfully glad you did.

To Bill Caswell, who taught me to go when I thought I knew how.

To Drew Doukas. I still can't believe you drove to Grattan with a Spec Miata and donuts. Amazing, bub.

To Jeff Lane, who is forgiving. And who knows, as much as anyone, that they weren't built to be parked.

To Chuck Squatriglia, for the pens and positivity.

To Ben Thongsai, for the forms of encouragement and help that only you can provide, and for being a part of more light-bulb moments than one man deserves. Prime in that last category being the time when you threw an E30 M3 into a Chicago on-ramp with me in the passenger seat. A formative experience, a Skippy in your debt.

To Mark "Kackle" Francis, the wonderfully ridiculous older brother I never had, and Carl "Have a Beer" Nelson, the world's kindest and most dangerous enabler. I don't know why the two of you and Ben decided I was worth warming a race seat in that 2002, but falling into the MFR family of lunatics was a once-a-lifetime gift. We made the red sled heaps faster, but that was never the point. It's a spiny fish.

To Joe August, Josie Babin, Veronica Ellis, Wendy Francis, Bruce Harris, J.P. Hermes, Matt McGinn, Owen Nelson, Sara Nelson, Larry Schmidt, Tim Skwiot, Kaelin Thompson, Paul Wegweiser, Dr. Amy Weinheimer, Chef Andy "Katering" Wong, and everyone else who made the red race car, the terrible tii—or the cruise-ship-buffet/conga-line parties that always sprung up around those projects—happen in any way whatsoever. It all helped renew something in me, and I will never meet a better group of people.

(Except Wegweiser. In that case, I will never meet a better rodent.)

Finally, to the Talahi four: Seth Teel, my oldest friend, who believes. ABS, because fish is fish; we miss you more than we can say. SAS, who never gives up. And DMS, who opened the door.

For all the friends and heroes, here and gone, who have kept the faith. The machine is only ever the beginning. I owe you all so much.

—Knoxville, Tennessee
December 2023

A Brief Ask of the Reader

Hi!

Did you enjoy this book?

Please let me know—visit Amazon and leave a review!

This is me, Sam, producing these words. Actually, with the exception of this title's marvelous foreword and introduction—Jay and John were quite kind—I produced everything here.

Self-publishing takes a great deal of work. In this case, months of nights and weekends while working a day job and helping raise a family. I gathered my old writing and wrote this book's new components, of course. But there was so much more: I pored through my entire catalog of published work, millions of words across dozens of outlets, paring it to a printable selection of variety and balance. I pursued reprint rights for those stories and select images; I line-edited for continuity, copy fit, and style; I commissioned and workshopped the cover; I designed this book's interior and personally laid out each page. Finally, I promoted the end result as best I could, given my virtually nonexistent marketing budget.

To be frank, I have no idea if the results will find an audience. This was all a passion project, commenced out of love for the written word and immense gratitude for the help I have received from others. And because, when I was young, a book much like this set me on the path to being a writer.

For these reasons and more, I would love to hear what you think.

If you have a minute, please leave a review on Amazon. Every review matters, and I will read them all. On top of that, reviews impact how Amazon promotes a work of this nature, and thus how it sells. If I break even on this book, I might be able to do another. That would be a gift.

I hope to hear from you. Above all, thanks for reading. I hope you liked it.

About the Author

SAM SMITH is a writer, an amateur racing driver, and a former mechanic who once spent an entire lunch hour annoying colleagues by walking around the shop and making a pair of safety-wire pliers appear to talk in a high and squeaky voice. In a mark of the unearned good fortune that has highlighted his travels, Sam's coworkers refrained from violence, and he somehow took that as encouragement to create things for a living.

An automotive journalist for 20 years, Sam has written for a wide variety of publications, including *The New York Times*, *Esquire*, *Wired*, *Car and Driver*, and *Popular Mechanics*. As a television and video presenter, his hosting and writing talents have been tapped by clients as diverse as NBC Sports and classic-car insurance provider Hagerty.

From 2012 to 2020, Sam was executive editor and then editor-at-large at *Road & Track*. In that period, he managed to both purchase a Renault Le Car from an Indiana Chrysler dealer and win awards for his work in media. Much to his chagrin, those events were not connected.

Sam lives in Knoxville, Tennessee, with his family, two scruffy old European motorcycles, the BMW 2002 from these pages, and a vintage Swiss typewriter that functions only in the presence of cocktails. This is his first book.

Updates, links, funky merch:

ThatSamSmith.com

Booking, general inquiries[1], requests for sundry gibberish:

SmithologyBook@gmail.com

@thatsamsmith

---

1. Questions? Want my help making something rad? Just want to say hi? Drop a line.

The Last Page

Paul Wegweiser in Chicago, all dolled up for crapcan prom, with his date.

Did he work on my car in that full-body nightmare?

Was this act a sad, fluffy cry for attention?

Was it also marvelous?

Clearly.

America: *Be like this man.*

Made in the USA
Las Vegas, NV
21 December 2024